HUMAN DIGNITY
AND THE FUTURE OF
GLOBAL INSTITUTIONS

HUMAN DIGNITY AND THE FUTURE OF GLOBAL INSTITUTIONS

Mark P. Lagon and
Anthony Clark Arend, Editors

Georgetown University Press
Washington, DC

Library of Congress Cataloging-in-Publication Data

Human dignity and the future of global institutions / Mark P. Lagon and Anthony Clark Arend, editors.
     pages cm
Summary: The 21st century has witnessed a proliferation of international institutions, including traditional intergovernmental organizations, non-governmental organizations, private sector entities, and other partnerships. The premise of this anthology is that these institutions need a common, animating principle in the service of the person, which is the ultimate end of global politics. The concept of human dignity, the editors claim, serves this purpose and transcends the seemingly intractable conflicts in human rights debates: political rights v. social and economic rights. Conceptually, human dignity rests on two principles: exercising agency to realize one's potential, and recognition by society of one's worth. In light of this formulation of human dignity, the anthology has two purposes: First, contributors will examine the degree to which traditional and emerging institutions are already advancing human dignity as a central mission. Second, in the spirit of developing best practices and prescriptive recommendations, contributors will identify strategies, methods, and modalities to make human dignity more central to the work of global institutions.
     Includes bibliographical references and index.
     ISBN 978-1-62616-119-1 (hardcover : alk. paper) — ISBN 978-1-62616-120-7 (pbk. : alk. paper) — ISBN 978-1-62616-121-4 (ebook)
     1. Dignity.   2. Human rights.   3. Respect for persons—Law and legislation. I. DeGioia, John J. writer of preface.   II. Lagon, Mark P. editor.   III. Arend, Anthony C. editor.
     JC571.H76265 2014
     341.2—dc23   2014011284

Cover image: Henry Moore, "Draped Seated Woman: Figure on Steps" 1956. © The Henry Moore Foundation. All Rights Reserved, DACS 2014/www.henry-moore.org

∞ This book is printed on acid-free paper meeting the requirements of the American National Standard for Permanence in Paper for Printed Library Materials.

15 14 13   9 8 7 6 5 4 3 2 First printing

Printed in the United States of America

This book is dedicated to MSFS students—
past, present, and future—
as they work to set the world on fire.

Ad Majorem Dei Glorium inque Hominum Salutem

CONTENTS

ACKNOWLEDGMENTS

Human Dignity and the Future of Global Institutions is a collaborative project of members of a true community: the faculty, alumni, students, and friends of the Georgetown University Master of Science in Foreign Service Program (MSFS). Its evolution and insights flow from dialogue in that community, a microcosm of the dialogue we propose in our concluding chapter. As part of this dialogue, the contributors have been intellectual collaborators in an ongoing conversation that transcends their individual contributions.

Institutional support for this project has come from both Georgetown University and the Council on Foreign Relations. We want to thank the Edmund A. Walsh School of Foreign Service at Georgetown, including Dean Carol Lancaster and Senior Associate Dean James Reardon-Anderson, who provided their enthusiasm and help with the production of this volume. We wish to thank Kathleen McNamara and Moira Todd of the Mortara Center for International Studies and Thomas Banchoff and Erin Coleman of the Berkley Center for Religion, Peace and World Affairs at Georgetown University for their partnership with MSFS and their support respectively during the June 7, 2012, and March 19, 2013, conferences that reviewed draft chapters. Thanks to Gina Hart at the MSFS Program for administrative leadership in support of the book's contributors. And we would offer a very special thanks to Georgetown's President John J. DeGioia for his support and his willingness to write the preface.

We want to thank the Council on Foreign Relations (CFR), where Mark P. Lagon is Adjunct Senior Fellow for Human Rights, for helping germinate some of the ideas, notably at the first conference on contributors and friends we convened on November 16, 2011. Chapter 6 by Mark P. Lagon and Ryan

Kaminski was adapted from the Issue Brief, "The Global Human Rights Regime," published by the Council on Foreign Relations (CFR) in February 2012. The brief is part of CFR's Global Governance Monitor from the International Institutions and Global Governance program, generously funded by the Robina Foundation.

There are a number of colleagues who offered advice, notional formulations, feedback on chapters, and presentations and comments at conferences we held at CFR and at Georgetown University to whom we want to express our appreciation. They include: Evelyn Aswad, Mathew Carnes, Samantha Custer, Mark Dybul, Stein-Ivar Eide, Lee Feinstein, Felice Gaer, Dylan Groves, Ross Harrison, Ryan Kaminski, Peter Katzenstein, Carol Lancaster, James Lindsay, Katherine Marshall, Kathleen McNamara, Sarah Moran, Alberto Mora, Michael Morfit, Kate Potterfield, Pierre-Richard Prosper, Andrew Reddie, George Shambaugh, Kristen Silverberg, Anne-Marie Slaughter, Karen Stauss, Fred Tipson, Michael Walzer, Matthew Waxman, David Watkins, Jennifer Windsor, and Diane Yeager.

We would also be remiss if we did not signal out two MSFSers. Benjamin Boudreaux, a onetime student and now alumnus who offered welcome and canny research help earlier in the project. And in a special category is Mathew R. Caldwell who as an MSFS student and William V. O'Brien Fellow in International Law played a substantial role in the revision and integration of the volume and helped organize a March 19, 2013, conference. His indefatigable energy, judgment, passion, and spectacular good humor were essential to this book coming to fruition.

We have been blessed working with Richard Brown and Deborah Weiner at Georgetown University Press. Their enthusiasm for and insights on improving this project are deeply valued.

Mark P. Lagon enormously appreciates the enthusiasm, support, and love of Elena Lagon and Zofia Lagon. Above all, he cherishes his wife, Susan Sullivan Lagon, for love and emotional backing to the hilt and sage advice to a fellow teacher.

Anthony Clark Arend would like to thank Jaclyn Halpern Bates, Spencer Bates, David Gutschmit, Doug Shaw, and Kevin O'Brien for their support throughout this project.

Finally, we want to thank all our students at Georgetown for challenging us and helping us develop our thinking on human dignity. It is to them that we have dedicated this book.

PREFACE

JOHN J. DEGIOIA

Emerging out of the darkest years of the modern era—following a Holocaust, two world wars, and a one-hundred-year period when more than 260 million people died at the hands of their own governments (Rummel 1994)—the greatest contribution of the twentieth century was the introduction and implementation of a regime of human rights. Launched with the adoption of the Universal Declaration of Human Rights in 1948 by the member states of the United Nations, this was the first international agreement to use the words "human rights."

In the sixty-plus years following its adoption, over forty agreements were created through the United Nations that deepened and broadened the regime, addressing issues ranging from the right to organize to the rights of the child.

A thorny question for the drafters was the matter of justification. What was the basis for making the claims that the rights identified in the Declaration's thirty articles were, in fact, universal? Even though the drafting committee invited one of the most distinguished philosophers of the age, Jacques Maritain, to assist in articulating the justification, ultimately the document was silent on the topic. The committee's chair, Eleanor Roosevelt, determined it was more important to entrench these rights immediately following the war than it was to offer a justification for them.

In her wonderful history of the drafting of the Universal Declaration, Mary Ann Glendon provides an important insight into the document's underlying logic: "Maritain liked to tell the story of how a visitor at one meeting expressed astonishment that champions of violently opposed ideologies had been able to agree on a list of fundamental rights. The man was told: 'Yes, we agree about the rights but on condition no one asks us why'" (Glendon 2001, 77).

In place of a justification, the Universal Declaration posits a collection of rights, each flowing from the first words of the first article: "All human beings are born free and equal in dignity." It is our inherent human dignity that is to be protected and respected by the concrete rights described in the articles that follow. In turn, these rights, grounded in a respect for human dignity, became the starting point for constructing the postwar international system whose aim was to ensure that the delineated rights did not remain abstractions. Rather, they would be realized via institutions that, while international in scope, were national in focus.

Thus, the second half of the twentieth century saw the development of the World Health Organization (WHO); Food and Agriculture Organization (FAO); United Nations Education, Science, and Culture Organization (UNESCO); World Bank; International Finance Corporation (IFC); International Monetary Fund (IMF); and more recently, the Millennium Development Corporation and the Global Fund. These—and many more—represent concrete structures whose efforts aim to realize our commitment to human rights, making it come alive through their ongoing work. As Robert Bellah and his colleagues noted, "we live in and through institutions" (1992, 256). Through these international institutions we ideally celebrate human dignity.

But are the institutions that emerged in the mid-to-late twentieth century adequate to respond to the challenges of the early twenty-first? Issues like climate change, human trafficking, water security, and weapons of mass destruction, to name a very few, are in fact borderless in origin and impact and are not easily addressed within a logic that gives primacy to national sovereignty. Yet at the same time, the twenty-first century offers us digitized tools and the onrush of social media—plus powerful currents unleashed by a "globalized" economy. These represent potentially *connecting* forces whose effective harnessing depends on revisiting questions about what it means for us to protect and respect the human dignity of all of our peoples.

- How best can we ensure we are building institutions that enable us to live this commitment to foster and protect human rights in light of "connecting" opportunities?
- What values will guide us as we imagine and re-imagine such building?
- Can we ensure that among these values is an ever-deeper commitment to human dignity?
- Are the social practices embedded in existing institutions sufficient to provide the framework for new types of structures? Are they, in fact, sufficient for current institutions to ensure a respect for our shared dignity, manifested in a commitment to human rights?

A respect for human dignity has origins in religious practices throughout the world and has been the source of deep philosophical engagement, notably by Immanuel Kant. There is an abstract quality appropriate to theological and philosophical reflection, and every generation lives with the questions thereby. But there are practical issues as well. It is now our time to examine the nature of the international order for which we share responsibility and ask whether our global institutions enable us to respond to the challenges of our time.

References

Bellah, Robert N., Richard Madsen, William M. Sullivan, Ann Swidler, and Steven M. Tipton. 1992. *The Good Society*. New York: Vintage.

Glendon, Mary Ann. 2001. *A World Made New: Eleanor Roosevelt and the Universal Declaration of Human Rights*. New York: Random House.

Rummel, R. J. 1994. "Important Note." In *Death by Government*. New Brunswick, NJ: Transaction Publishers. Accessed February 20, 2013. http://www.hawaii.edu/powerkills /NOTE1.HTM.

Introduction

Human Dignity in a Neomedieval World

MARK P. LAGON AND ANTHONY CLARK AREND

What is human dignity? Over the centuries, philosophers, theologians, pundits, and even public officials have attempted to employ the term as an idea that unites humanity. More recently, persons as diverse as Melinda Gates, Jack Welch, Aung San Suu Kyi, former Archbishop of Canterbury Rowan Williams, the Dalai Lama, George W. Bush, and Barack Obama have referred to the notion.[1] For example, in his first inaugural address as president of South Africa, Nelson Mandela said, "We enter into a covenant that we shall build a society in which all South Africans, both black and white, will be able to walk tall, without any fear in their hearts, assured of their inalienable right to human dignity" (Mandela 1994). Similarly, the Aga Khan IV, the hereditary iman of Ismaili Muslims and major philanthropist, said in an address in 2006 in Evora, Portugal: "The search for justice and security, the struggle for equality of opportunity, the quest for tolerance and harmony, the pursuit of human dignity—these are moral imperatives which we must work towards and think about on a daily basis" (Aga Khan IV 2006). Here are two prominent thinkers who recognize the centrality and vitality of human dignity as a touchstone for action. Yet what does human dignity *mean*? And what role should it play in guiding the mission of international institutions? Despite spanning cultures and continents and providing great potential for building a consensus, human dignity lacks a common definition. This book will offer just such a working definition designed to animate the work of increasingly complex, heterogeneous international institutions. In this introduction, we will, first, explore the context of those heterogeneous institutions in a changing international system. Second, we will lay out a picture of the near paralysis of human rights discourse today. Third, in light of several major

1

historical understandings, we will offer our conceptual formulation of human dignity, situating it in concepts of the agency and recognition of the individual person. Fourth, we will offer a roadmap of how this book will employ that formulation to explore both how international institutions have increasingly served this concept and how they might better order their work based on this central norm.

Institutions in a Neomedieval World

Students of international relations have typically claimed that the birth of the modern international system took place with the conclusion of the Peace of Westphalia of 1648. Westphalia was seen as enshrining the recognition that the territorial state was the primary actor in the international system and the principle that these states enjoyed "sovereignty." Sovereignty meant, in a nutshell, that states were autonomous; they were the legitimate governing authorities over what took place in their territories. States were juridically equal and could thus not be subject to any higher authority or bound by any higher law without their consent. What this principle meant was that for any international institution to possess political and legal legitimacy, it needed to be created by states. Accordingly, as states began to perceive the need for international organizations—first specific-purpose organizations, like the Central Commission for the Navigation of the Rhine, and later more general-purpose organizations, like the League of Nations—they created intergovernmental organizations through treaties requiring the consent of each member state.

But new developments in international politics have raised questions about these assumptions. As early as 1977 in his classic work, *The Anarchical Society*, the late Oxford Professor Hedley Bull speculated that one possible future for international systems was what he called a "neomedieval" structure. Under such an arrangement, Bull explained, states would still exist as important actors in the international system, but alongside those states, there would be a variety of other dissimilar actors that would also play critical roles in international affairs. As Bull notes, the central element of such a neomedieval system would be "overlapping authority and multiple loyalties" (Bull 2002, 245). In other words, states would "come to share their authority over their citizens, and their ability to command their loyalties" with other actors (246). And as such, states would not be sovereign in the Westphalian sense of the term.

In *The Anarchical Society*, Bull suggested five trends that point to the possible emergence of a neomedieval system: (1) the Regional Integration of States, (2) the Disintegration of States, (3) the Restoration of Private International Violence, (4) Transnational Organizations, and (5) the Technological Unification of the World. Today, over a third of a century since Bull's publication, these trends have continued and seem to strongly suggest a movement toward a neomedieval world (Arend 1999, 171–85). First, it is commonplace to point to Europe as the primary example of regional integration. In the years since 1977, the European Economic Community has become the European Union (EU), more states have joined, and the depth of integration has increased. Whereas the recent economic crisis in the Eurozone has caused some observers to speculate about the progress of European integration, it could certainly be argued that the transformative effect on the concept of state sovereignty has continued. Bull suggested a critical juncture would exist when there would "be real doubt in theory and in reality as to whether sovereignty lay with national governments or the organs of the 'community'" (Bull 2002, 256). In the world of the twenty-first century, the institutions of the EU clearly enjoy the ability to make decisions that are binding both upon the governments of the members and, in some cases, directly binding on individuals or corporations within member states. It may not be correct to say that the organs have "sovereignty," but it certainly seems accurate to say that in some cases the organs have independent authority that was traditionally held only by states. Moreover, there seems to have also been a transformation of the loyalty of individuals; persons still have loyalty to their state, but there also seems for most to be an undefined loyalty to Europe. It should, of course, be noted that while the European experience has not led—in any real sense—to other such tight integration in other regions of the world, the very existence of even one such powerful regionally integrated actor in the international system challenges the notion of Westphalia.

Second, there have been dramatic disintegrative tendencies. But, as Bull notes, for the state system to be fundamentally changed, it is not enough that there simply be new states emerging from larger ones, but that substate actors emerge with a level of autonomy that challenges the sovereignty of the larger state. Bull explains: "If these new units were to advance far enough towards sovereign statehood both in terms of accepted doctrine and in terms of their command of force and human loyalties, to cast doubt upon the sovereignty of existing states, and yet at the same time were to stop short of claiming that state sovereignty for themselves, the situation might arise in which the institution of sovereignty itself might go into decline" (Bull 2002, 257). Clearly, since the end of the Cold War, small states emerged from larger states— witness the breakup of the Soviet Union and Yugoslavia, and more recently Sudan. But at the same time, we are seeing a variety of substate groups that both exercise control over people and receive their loyalty. Hamas, Hezbollah, the Revolutionary Armed Forces of Colombia (FARC), and even criminal groups in parts of Latin America and elsewhere are increasingly providing service and social welfare assistance to individuals and are capturing a large measure of their loyalty.

Third, while one of the touchstones of sovereignty is the state's monopoly on the use of force, there has been a resurgence of private international violence in recent years. The most obvious manifestation of this nonstate use of force is by transstate political groups like al-Qaeda and its various progeny. The significance of the power of such groups can be seen in the days following September 11, 2001, when the United Nations (UN) Security Council acknowledged that these nonstate actors can be held accountable for engaging in an armed attack in violation of the UN Charter, and can be the subject of international sanctions, a penalty typically reserved for states. But what Bull notes as a particularly significant aspect of this increase in the use of violence by these nonstate actors "is the fact that their claim of the right to do so is accepted as legitimate by a substantial proportion of international society" (Bull 2002, 259). As far back as the mid-1970s, there were elements of the international community that accorded a certain legitimacy to liberation movements and other groups seeking to fight so-called colonial, racist, and alien regimes. Indeed, the Definition of Aggression Resolution adopted by the United Nations General Assembly in 1974 specifically mentioned "peoples under colonial and racist regimes [and] other forms of alien domination" and acknowledged "the right of these people to struggle to that end [self-determination] and to seek and receive support, in accordance with the principles of the [UN] Charter and in conformity with the above-mentioned Declaration." Even though this right is couched in terms of the UN Charter, it seems clear that this resolution was seeking to lend great international legitimacy to substate actors using violence. Of course, the Soviet Union and its allies were well-known for supporting the use of force by substate groups fighting "wars of national liberation" (Arend and Beck 1993, 41). Indeed, under the so-called Reagan Doctrine, even the United States recognized the legitimacy of violent antistate actors in the 1980s, such as those in Angola, Nicaragua, Afghanistan, and Cambodia (Lagon 1994).

Since the 1970s, a wide variety of groups have continued to gain international support, but more importantly, domestic populations have often accorded such nonstate actors with legitimacy. As noted earlier, groups like Hezbollah, the FARC, and others have been providing goods and services to individuals in circumstances where states have been unable to do so, thereby empowering these actors to gain loyalty traditionally reserved for the state.

Fourth, there has also been a proliferation of transstate organizations, what Bull calls "transnational organizations." For Bull, these organizations run the gamut from transnational corporations (TNCs) to transnational political movements (including those that use violence) to professional associations to religious organizations to nongovernmental organizations (NGOs) to traditional intergovernmental institutions (IGOs). In recent years, the number and diversity of these organizations have grown and they have increasingly gained real power in the international system. The effects of some of the transnational political movements have already been noted above, but other organizations have also been playing critical roles. Despite the Westphalian turn away from a secular role for the church, religious organizations have increasingly commanded the loyalty of people. And even transnational corporations have gained inroads on states. As the late Susan Strange wrote in her 1996 book, *The Retreat of the State: The Diffusion of Power in the World Economy,* "we can conclude that while TNCs do not take over from the governments of states, they have certainly encroached on their domains of power." "They are," she notes, "increasingly exercising a parallel authority alongside governments in matters of economic management affecting the location of industry and investment, the direction of technological innovation, the management of labour relations, and the fiscal extraction of surplus value" (Strange 1996, 65).

Finally, even in the late 1970s, Bull could write of the "technological unification of the world." In medieval Europe, Christianity served as a unifying force for people. In a secular neomedievalism, Bull opines, perhaps technology could serve to provide a similar unifying role. He observes that "[i]t is sometimes contended that the demise of the states system is taking place as a consequence of the technological unification of the world . . . which is bound to lead to the politics of 'spaceship earth' or of the 'global village' in which the states system is only a part" (Bull 2002, 236). Without doubt, the internet and social media tools such as Twitter, Facebook, and YouTube have been able to link people in disparate parts of the world. They also have been able to allow people to gain access to information in ways that the state can regulate only with great difficulty and at the risk of international condemnation. While it cannot yet be claimed that technology has brought about a "global village," it seems certain at the very least that the technological revolution has challenged the ability of states to maintain control in the same ways they had in the past. And undoubtedly, the information gained by citizens has in some cases contributed to the delegitimization of some of the traditional instruments of state power.

If we accept the proposition that the international system is becoming something akin to what Bull called neomedieval, what does this mean for human dignity? At some level, it means that the traditional system of accountability is being loosed from its moorings. In a system where states have legal and moral legitimacy because they are accountable to their citizens, intergovernmental organizations have legitimacy because they are creations of states. In other words, the legitimacy of IGOs is derivative of that of states. But when we suddenly fast-forward to a world where states are losing some of their monopoly of legitimacy through the presence of powerful nonstate or nonstate-created actors, it becomes a challenge to find such accountability. Perhaps it lies somehow in the concept of "human rights"?

Human Rights Discourse and Beyond

In the world of 1648, sovereignty meant that states had complete authority over their citizens. As such, under international law, states could treat their citizens essentially as they chose. There were no international legal obligations on the part of states to behave in a particular fashion toward their own citizens; there was no international human rights law as the term is used today.

This state of affairs did not really begin to change until the post–World War II period. With the revelations of the Holocaust and other cases of inhumanity that took place during the war, the founders of the UN resolved to make human rights a critical goal of this new global intergovernmental organization. And so, the preamble of the UN Charter boldly declares the determination of its members "to reaffirm faith in fundamental human rights, in the dignity and worth of the human person, in the equal rights of men and women." This was the first time in history that a general purpose, global intergovernmental organization declared the promotion of human rights as one of its goals.

Not surprisingly, over the course of the next several decades, the UN supported the development of multilateral agreements that sought to establish legal obligations on the part of states to uphold the rights of their citizens. These agreements included such noteworthy treaties as the Covenant on Civil and Political Rights; the Covenant on Economic, Social, and Cultural Rights; the Genocide Convention; the Torture Convention; and the Convention on the Elimination of All Forms of Discrimination Against Women. Taken as a whole, this panoply of international agreements, together with emerging customary international law, gave rise to a human rights regime and the accompanying "international human rights discourse" that have predominated in the post–World War II era.

This human rights discourse has greatly advanced the idea of state responsibility to citizens and has transcended older notions of sovereignty. It has helped empower intergovernmental organizations to break through the veil of state sovereignty to support individuals. But while the existing human rights regime has established an essential foundation to help people to flourish, it does not seem adequate to fully address the challenges to the human person in the contemporary international system. This seems to be true for several reasons.

First, there is far too often an impasse in human rights discourse due to the sterile debate between political and civil rights on the one hand and economic and social rights on the other. Even as the creation of a new postwar human rights regime was proceeding, the Cold War and the rise of the developing world were challenging the ability of states to achieve a consensus on human rights. While some common human rights treaties were produced, the negotiations that produced those instruments were often fraught with disagreement. It was not uncommon for Western states to reject the notion that economic and social rights were truly "rights." And at the same time, it was typical of states from the Soviet sphere to claim that the granting of economic and social rights was necessary before the states needed to advance civil and political rights. While the intensity of this debate may have moderated since the end of the Cold War, there continues to remain divisions about efficacy of these different types of rights.

Yet these divisions may represent a false dichotomy. For example, American NGO leaders Gary Haugen and Victor Boutros on the one hand and Amnesty International's former global chief Irene Khan on the other argue that there is a link between political and economic rights. In particular, they both stress that guaranteeing access to justice—a political right—is vital to economic empowerment (Haugen and Boutros 2010; Khan 2009). Moreover, confounding expectations it would dismiss economic and social rights, the presidential administration of George W. Bush—whatever its failings—embraced major efforts to globally combat HIV/AIDS and human trafficking, both dilemmas in which marginalized groups' access to economic opportunity, basic social protections, civil rights, and justice were inextricably intermingled. Focusing solely on traditional human rights discourse could prevent a movement beyond this conundrum.

Second, frequently the rights discourse stops with the assertion of the "equality of persons" and misses the importance of acknowledging and recognizing "difference." In the initial phases of rights movements—whether it is women's rights movements, civil rights movements, gay and lesbian rights movements, and so on—there is a tendency to make a claim for equal treatment. A woman should be treated just like a man. The claim was for equal political rights under the law. Clearly, these rights claims were critical to put disenfranchised groups under the protection of the law. Yet, as many of these movements developed, they began to adopt a "postrights" discourse. That is, they began to argue that while certain basic rights were fundamental, and equality under the law was a critical starting point, different people are in fact different. And a legal system, while recognizing the primary imperative of the equal value of each person, must also properly acknowledge difference and accord the correct respect due this difference. An example from feminist literature may serve to illustrate. Women bear children. Of course, women should have equal political rights to men, and they should receive equal pay for equal work, but the legal system must also acknowledge that only women bear children, and it must give them the appropriate treatment in light of that fact. In other words, they must, in some cases, be treated *differently* than men, precisely *because* of this difference. It is not clear that the current human rights regime adequately addresses the problem of difference.

Third, another challenge of contemporary human rights discourse is that because of the need for human rights agreements to spell out precise rights, legal discussions can frequently fall into technical discussions of definitions and miss the big picture. Following the attacks of 9/11, for example, government officials in the United States and elsewhere engaged in lengthy debates about the precise meaning of "torture" and other potential legal terms. While these discussions are not insignificant, it was interesting to note that the deeper philosophic question of how persons should be treated—irrespective of whether the treatment is torture or not—was often ignored. Otherwise, one could make the mistake, in that case, of parsing a case for applying cruelty short of torture as being justified.

These challenges—and others that could also be noted—suggest that existing human rights discourse might need an augmentation. As noted earlier, while the contemporary human rights regime has moved the international system in important, positive directions, another concept may be needed to both strengthen and better equip the existing state of human rights in its effort to affirm the value of individual persons. We propose to build on the essential foundations of the human rights discourse in a way that frees it from some of its paralysis.

The Concept of Human Dignity

To advance human dignity as the guiding principle for contemporary international institutions, a working definition is crucial. If this concept is to transcend an arguably exhausting, if not exhausted, debate about human rights, it must be built upon the human rights tradition rather than casting it aside. One way to successfully win consensus on a definition of human dignity as the touchstone for global collective action is to weave together critical threads of related thought through the ages: (1) the Ancients, (2) the Judeo-Christian tradition, (3) Kantian liberalism, (4) secular universalism of mid-twentieth century human rights norms, (5) jurisprudential social science, (6) thought on capabilities and development in the last quarter century, and (7) a rich post–Cold War vision of identity that ties Ancient and German modern thought. Needless to say, there are innumerable historical approaches from other world faiths and traditions that are centered on human dignity (Yadollahpour 2011; Lo 2009). This nonexhaustive exploration, however, reveals the essence of human dignity applicable to international institutions today.

The Ancients

Among the ancient philosophers, self-worth is a crucial notion. Plato observed in *The Republic* that a person only lived well when the three parts of his soul were properly in balance—the rational, appetitive, and spirited. Spiritedness, or *thymos*, is associated with feeling valuable, not just insularly but relationally—valuable in the eyes of others in society (Bloom 1991). We will return to the importance of this element of dignity.

In addition to self-worth, "potential" plays a key role in the thinking of the Ancients. Aristotle believed the ultimate goal that is unique to human beings is the realization of human potential in the form of what he called *eudaimonia*—human flourishing. Foreshadowing a modern notion of responsibility necessarily accompanying freedom, this value is not a state of mind or thinking but is developed and exercised in ongoing activity. It involves developing character traits that fuse reason to virtue (Bartlett and Collins 2012). This lofty conception of human potentiality is to be distinguished from that of Epicurus, who associated achievement of eudaimonia with maximizing hedonistic pleasures.

Judeo-Christian Thinking

The dignity and worth of humankind is a primary focus of the Judeo-Christian faith traditions. In these traditions, every human is made in the image of God. Genesis 1:26 holds, "And God said, Let us make man in our image." This opening text from the Hebrew scriptures goes on to say human beings were given dominion over all other creatures and resources—fish, fowl, cattle, and the Earth. Genesis 2:19–20 suggests, no less, that the Creator brought all beasts and fowl "unto Adam to see what he would call them" and he named them. An animal rights or environmental activist today might resist these notions at a literal level, but the implication that human beings all have a special status and role is central. George Kateb's quite secular 2011 study, *Human Dignity*, adopts this "breed apart" formulation about human beings, based on their level of consciousness. Moreover, beyond naming other creatures, that each human has a distinct name implies value in each. This idea echoes Aristotle's view of the unique function and value of human beings.

The innate value of human life is, of course, embodied in one of the great Ten Commandments given to Moses: Thou shall not kill. Or to provide a more literal translation of the Hebrew: You shall not murder. In the Torah, this commandment is established as a law: No human being has the standing to kill unjustifiably.

Within the Jewish tradition, human dignity is also affirmed in the injunctions to provide special care for those possessing special needs: the poor, the widow, the orphan, and the stranger (e.g., Deut. 26:12; Zech. 7:10, Jer 7:6). Isaiah, for example, issues a strong condemnation to those who do not tend to the disenfranchised:

> Woe to those who decree iniquitous decrees,
> and the writers who keep writing oppression,
> to turn aside the needy from justice
> and to rob the poor of my people of their right,
> that widows may be their spoil,
> and that they may make the fatherless their prey! (Isaiah 10:1–2)

The Christian scriptures continue to affirm the belief in the innate value of the human person, perhaps best encapsulated in the Golden Rule. And much like the words of Isaiah, the Gospel affirms a vision of human dignity that requires active service to each individual, including those with special needs. In the parable of the Great Judgment, for example:

> the King will say to those at his right hand, "Come, O blessed of my Father,
> inherit the kingdom prepared for you from the foundation of the world;
> for I was hungry and you gave me food, I was thirsty and you gave me
> drink, I was a stranger and you welcomed me,
> I was naked and you clothed me, I was sick and you visited me, I was in
> prison and you came to me" (Matt. 25:34–36).

Such thinking has reemerged often over the centuries and in contemporary religious guidance, such as Pope John Paul II's 1993 encyclical on human dignity.

Kantian Idealism

A slightly different tradition, that of modern German idealism, also places special emphasis on human worth. Immanuel Kant justifies the claim that humans have intrinsic dignity by pointing to the fact that humans are agents: They must choose their own actions and give themselves goals. Humans, therefore, are not just beings with value but also the sort of beings that create or construct value to begin with. It is their capacity to give things value that implies they are, more precisely, "above all value." Kant's admonition to never treat another human being as a mere means is based on the equal value of all human beings. Kant argues that humans only act freely (and actually live a life of dignity) when they act on a law that requires that they give of themselves. The law that persons must give of themselves to be free must take a form such that it applies to everyone, no matter who the person is or what the person desires. This categorical imperative of acting as if an action could be generalized into a universal principle implies that other people and their worth must be treated with consistency rather than capriciously. No one can make an exception of themselves, including autocrats.

Postwar Secular Universalism

Kant's *Perpetual Peace* called for universal law and a "league of nations." It inspired the establishment of the League of Nations in 1919, although it foundered. After World War II, the world took another run at forming a global organization to sustain peace. The UN Charter invokes "the dignity and worth of the human person" within its first forty-five words. Peace could not be detached from respect for dignity. When in its infancy the UN set about elaborating norms on human rights in the Universal Declaration on Human Rights (UDHR) of 1948, extensive soundings were taken by the UN to establish a common basis for the document. Harvard Law School scholar Mary Ann Glendon notes in her treatment of Eleanor Roosevelt's role in shaping the UDHR, *A World Made New*, that

> where basic human values are concerned, cultural diversity has been exaggerated. The group [of United Nations Educational, Scientific and Cultural Organization philosophers] found, after consulting Confucian, Hindu, Muslim,

and European thinkers, that a core of fundamental principles was widely shared in countries that had not yet adopted rights instruments and in cultures that had not embraced the language of rights. . . . The philosophers concluded that even people who seem to be far apart in theory can agree that certain things are so terrible in practice that no one will publicly approve them and that certain things are so good in practice that no one will publicly oppose them (Glendon 2001, 222).

Dignity was not the *result* of rights but an a priori imperative undergirding rights. Following some objections about the language of dignity, Glendon observes: "Mrs. Roosevelt, when her turn came, said that the word 'dignity' had been considered carefully by the Human Rights Commission, which had included it in order to emphasize that every human being is worthy of respect. In the scheme of the Declaration, Article 1 did not refer to specific rights because it was meant to explain why human beings have rights to begin with" (Glendon 2001, 146).

Glendon observes that the UDHR "was far more influenced by the modern dignitarian rights tradition of continental Europe and Latin America than by the more individualistic documents of Anglo-American lineage" (Glendon 2001, 227). Hence, Eleanor Roosevelt forged a meeting of the minds with other delegates by implanting into the UDHR all of the Four Freedoms her husband had hailed (*of* expression and worship, and *from* want and fear), thereby bridging political and economic rights.

The New Haven School

Soon thereafter, one sees the concept of dignity emerge in a rich—if now underappreciated—intersection of the law and social science. Yale University's Myres McDougal and his intellectual partner Harold Lasswell shaped a jurisprudential framework, sometimes referred to as "the New Haven School" (see Reisman et al. 2007). It offered analytical tools drawn from the social sciences aimed at strengthening a world order rooted in human dignity. McDougal and Lasswell identify a transcendent consensus as the justification for dignity's centrality: "All systems proclaim the dignity of the human individual and the ideal of a worldwide public order in which this ideal is authoritatively pursued and effectively approximated" (McDougal and Lasswell 1959, 24).

They define human dignity as: "a social process in which values are widely and not narrowly shared, and in which private choice, rather than coercion, is emphasized as the predominant modality of power" (McDougal and Lasswell 1959, 19). While some serious thinkers and practitioners claim otherwise

(Tipson 1973; Reisman et al. 2007), this definition may not be tangible enough to individual human beings' needs to be of great operational use to contemporary institutions and this project. However, regarding the values to which it refers—harking back to the Ancients' view of facilitating people's potential—the school identifies eight value categories human beings seek: power, enlightenment, wealth, well-being, skill, affection, respect, and rectitude. A world order favoring human dignity facilitates people pursuing these values through choice. (Later we will see a special role of respect among these values, though it is not central to the school's own vision of world order.) The school's real significance is as a major post–World War II jurisprudential approach for international governance and institutions explicitly fashioned to normatively advance dignity. As a result, this school made the intellectual move to find the ultimate touchstone of international law not in the claims of states enjoying sovereignty but rather of the individual person.

Capabilities-Based Development

Contemporary thinkers about human development have picked up on the ancients' concept of tapped potential and thriving and echoed the New Haven School's focus on catalyzing people's ability to freely pursue values of choice. As the United Nations Development Programme (UNDP) administrator Helen Clark of New Zealand observed on March 9, 2010:

> [T]he human development paradigm championed by UNDP for two decades [is]very much inspired by India's Nobel Laureate, Professor Amartya Sen. Human development is about placing people at the centre of development, enlarging their capabilities, and expanding their opportunities and freedom to lead lives which they value.

Sen helped fashion the Human Development Index for UNDP's first *Human Development Report* in 1990 with the late economist Mahbub ul Haq, the series founder. He and American scholar Martha Nussbaum have elaborated on an approach to development based on enabling the capabilities of individual human beings. Nussbaum identifies ten crucial capabilities: life, bodily health, bodily integrity, senses (imagination, thought), emotions, practical reason, affiliation (community, association, social basis of self-respect), other species, play, and control over one's environment (political participation, personal property). In *Women and Human Development,* she argues that each of these capabilities is needed in order for a human life to be "not so impoverished that it is not worthy of the dignity of a human being" (Nussbaum 2001, 72).

The Fukuyaman Synthesis

One of the more provocative broad-gauged social science thinkers in the United States, Francis Fukuyama, offers some crucial insights on dignity applicable to institutions—himself a political theorist reaching back to the Ancients. He is known for having broken with neoconservatives over the invasion of Iraq, contradicting their own professed skepticism about social engineering, and especially for his earlier exploration of whether the passing of the Cold War presaged an "end of history." On the latter claim, more people have fixed upon his 1989 *National Interest* article than his 1992 book, *The End of History and the Last Man*. Thymos is the engine of his vision of history steadily driving toward the elaboration of human freedom and democracy. Recall that Plato in *The Republic* argued that a person only lived well when there was a proper balance among the three elements of the soul—Reason, the Appetites, and Thymos. This third element, thymos, is sometimes translated as "spirit" and encompasses a sense of honor and self-worth. Fukuyama writes: "Thymos is something like an innate human sense of justice: people believe that they have a certain worth, and when other people act as though they are worthless—when they do not recognize their worth at its correct value—then they become angry" (Fukuyama 1992, 165).

Yet even more than the Ancients, he draws from the thinking of another German idealist, Hegel, for whom "the primary motor of human history is not modern natural science or the ever expanding horizon of desire that powers it, but rather a totally non-economic drive, the *struggle for recognition*" (Fukuyama 1992, 135). Fukuyama applies this idealist–vice materialist–view of dignity to explain twentieth-century struggles from that of Vaclav Havel against Communist repression, to that of Americans for racial equality.

> The indignity of racism in modern America lies only partly in the physical deprivation brought on by poverty among blacks: a black is (in Ralph Ellison's phrase) an "invisible man," not actively hated but unseen as a fellow human being. . . . Virtually the entire civil liberties and civil rights agendas, while having certain economic components, are essentially thymotic contests over recognition of competing understandings of justice and human dignity (Fukuyama 1992, 176).

In short, Fukuyama observes, "[t]he 'struggle for recognition' is evident everywhere around us" (145).

His interpretation of Hegel pinpoints a human being's "own sense of self-worth is intimately connected with the value that other people place on him" (Fukuyama 1992, 146). Dignity is hence something necessarily established within a community or a social context. While Fukuyama has an uncommon interpretation of Hegel drawn from Alexander Kojeve, this socially grounded basis for human thriving represents a tradition running from ancient thought to the birth of modern international law. Grotius writes, for instance, "among the traits characteristic of man is an impelling desire for society, that is, for the social life—not of any and every sort, but peaceful, and organized according to the measure of his intelligence, with those who are of his own kind; this social trend the Stoics called 'sociableness'" (Grotius, in Beck, et al., 1996, 40).

A Working Definition of Dignity

Drawing from many traditions and of course on Hegel's view of synthesis driving history, the Fukuyaman synthesis helps form a working definition of dignity operationally applicable to international institutions. This definition best rests upon the concept of *agency*. From the Ancient Greek and Judeo-Christian view to Kant, human beings are set apart as special. From Kant to the rich perspective on enabling capabilities of Sen and Nussbaum, the modern view of what is special is their role as agents. Dignity lies not only in preventing denials of agency but in unleashing humans' agency to achieve their potential and thrive. This contemporary version of eudaimonia—human flourishing—requires that people as agents exercise their muscles of responsibility. Yet Fukuyama's socially based notion of *recognition* adds a missing piece to a useful, applied definition of dignity. The worth of all human beings does not exist in isolation. In his recent volume, *Dignity: Its History and Meaning*, Harvard political theorist Michael Rosen observes the import of the recognition of others' dignity: "Our duty to respect the dignity of humanity is—on this I agree with Kant—fundamentally a duty to ourselves. . . . In failing to respect the humanity of others we actually undermine humanity in ourselves" (Rosen 2012, 157). More broadly, people must be recognized, by society and in working governance structures, as equally worthy—human beings in full. Here one of the eight values McDougal and Lasswell identify but do not singularly emphasize—*respect*—is of special importance. The quest for recognition or respect can of course take pernicious pathological forms (e.g., dictators or groups asserting dominance over or committing violence against other groups—what Fukuyama calls "megalothymia"). Yet in its positive form, the claim to recognition offers a secondary pillar to a definition of dignity.

A definition based on the pillars of agency and recognition can be illustrated in positive empowerment and negative denial. Girls who are given an opportunity to get an education to equip them to have more choices about their future are an archetypical example of dignity catalyzed. So too would freedom of assembly and association for factory workers in China.

In the obverse, mass murder, displacement, or sexual violence against a particular class or category of people—whether sponsored by or merely left unchecked by authorities—is an obvious case of dignity vitiated. Human trafficking as acute sexual or labor exploitation to the point that categories of people (children, women, minorities, migrants) are turned into mere commodities is another example.

And so, we offer the following working definition: *Human dignity is the fundamental agency of human beings to apply their gifts to thrive. As such, it requires social recognition of each person's inherent value and claim to equal access to opportunity. To be meaningful, human dignity must be institutionalized in practice and governance.*

The purpose of this book is not to settle for the ages on this definition as the touchstone of the work of international institutions, as even its contributors will offer varied elaborations and applications. Its purpose is to launch a normative agenda to deepen and refine this notion, always with an eye to applicability to actual institutions, and all the more to the actual human beings they are ostensibly devoted to help.

Overview of the Book

Purposes and Challenges

This book has two purposes. First, it will seek to examine the degree to which several prominent traditional and emerging institutions are already advancing human dignity as a central mission. For example, Tod Lindberg's chapter 2 on the International Criminal Court (ICC), a traditional institution, explores the role of the ICC in providing restitution to atrocity victims and thus affirming their dignity. Rosalía Rodriguez-García's chapter 8 examines a hybrid institution, the Global Fund to Fight AIDS, Tuberculosis, and Malaria, and discusses how it advances dignity by helping HIV-positive populations transcend social stigma.

Second, in the spirit of developing best practices and prescriptive recommendations, the book examines how to make human dignity a greater focus of international institutions' work. It seeks to identify the strategies, methods, and modalities to make them all the more, as it were, agencies for agency.

These aims entail several challenges. One challenge is to develop a method to build on the achievements of the human rights tradition while detaching a dignitarian agenda from stale and stalled debates, such as those between political-civil rights and socioeconomic rights. One must take care that breaking *through* stalled debates and stalled implementation is not a rupture. The answer lies in viewing human dignity not as a newer successor concept to human rights but as an older foundational concept upon which the rights tradition was erected. In order that *norm-creation* more often becomes *norm-implementation*, we propose this "back to basics" approach.

Another challenge is to take full advantage of the great potential for consensus across countries, regions, cultures, and faiths human dignity offers. McDougal and Lasswell saw that potential fully six decades ago. How can it be realized in practice?

There are clearly numerous paths to establishing human dignity's centrality. Drawing inspiration from the historic 1945 San Francisco Conference on International Organization where the UN Charter was adopted, some might suggest that it is time for a new "San Francisco moment." Yet, in a neomedieval world or what one might call a state of "mosaic multilateralism," there could not be an actual new San Francisco Conference to redirect institutions or create new ones. A conference or summit would not be a feasible vehicle to realize consensus in a neomedieval context precisely because of the multiplicity and dissimilarity of the actors. Moreover, the process of establishing the centrality of human dignity cannot be reduced to a "moment." Instead, it should be an ongoing dialogue. The dialogue this book offers is meant to hasten the social construction of consensus (Wendt 1992).

A final challenge remains: Once consensus is built, *who* will organize the mosaic multilateralism of today to privilege dignity above other goals? Needless to say, there will be numerous actors who will play an organizing role. But, we believe the United States ought not to be coy. While it does not have the hegemonic power it enjoyed seventy or even twenty years ago, it has a special role to play as catalyst. Like no other longstanding or rising power, the United States will remain a leading player to most of the institutions and partnerships in question. Its role will not be hegemonic norm-setter and guarantor. Nor will it solely be that of convener in formal organizations. Not least because of the way in which ideals are intermingled with interests in US statecraft, the United States has a special role to play in making a consensus on dignity an implemented reality. To succeed, the US approach must not be "our way or the highway," but it can fruitfully enable this agenda in varying roles as thought-leader, coach, quasi-pastor, co-opter, hub of networks, and partner to other actors. Without the United States, it is less likely to become implemented in reality.

A Roadmap for the Book

In addressing how institutions already serve to promote human dignity and how their role might be increased, this book explores two types of institutions that exist in a neomedieval world. Part I explores the first type: traditional IGOs, which, however imperfect, remain crucial vehicles for promoting dignity. In this part, three essays look chiefly at institutions within the UN—the heart of traditional IGOs. Based in part on her experience as a diplomat at the UN Security Council focusing on Africa, Nancy Soderberg explores how the UN Security Council has grappled with the most critical and violent human rights problems since the 1990s. She examines evolving Council practice regarding the Responsibility to Protect doctrine and the need for the Council to reform to enlarge its legitimacy for action on behalf of people's dignity. Tod Lindberg's unique contribution on the International Criminal Court suggests that its little-appreciated mechanisms for victim assistance and restitution have a potential impact on restoring the respect and recognition victims are due and are as vital as the perpetrators' prosecution. Former UN Secretariat official Abiodun Williams offers a rich appraisal of the UN secretary-general as a norm entrepreneur advancing human dignity, examining in vivid detail Kofi Annan's self-conscious effort to link security, development, and human rights holistically through new norms and institutional arrangements.

Three further chapters in part I address traditional institutions beyond the UN proper. In chapter 4, former assistant secretary of state for African Affairs Chester Crocker examines the considerable role of regional organizations in managing violent conflict as the highest-order threat to people's dignity. He demonstrates that the impact in practice that respective organizations can have on people's dignity on the ground depends on how each resolves tensions between their member states' perceived national security interests and that organization's increased focus on human security. The director of the International Monetary Fund's (IMF) Asia and Pacific Department, Anoop Singh, illustrates the dignity-enhancing role the IMF plays by helping national governments build stronger rules of law and governance, reducing the size of informal economies, and enlarging social inclusion in the fruits of economic growth. Mark P. Lagon and United Nations Association fellow Ryan Kaminski comprehensively assess the efficacy of global, regional, and national architecture devoted to human rights. They identify best practices and innovations to advance dignity by shifting from norm promulgation to implementation and by holistically bridging civil-political and socioeconomic rights. Finally, Anthony Clark Arend addresses how terrorism by its very nature violates innocents' dignity. He argues that counterterrorism measures must not violate the dignity of those who are alleged to have committed terrorist acts. He makes several recommendations for institutional action to address the challenges of counterterrorism and the root causes of terrorism.

Part II of the book treats another type of institution—emerging hybrids and partnerships. Having worked for the Global Fund to Fight AIDS, Tuberculosis and Malaria (Global Fund); the World Bank; and the International Labor Organization assessing impacts on communities of HIV/AIDS investments, Rosalía Rodriguez-García examines the need to transcend social stigma against groups vulnerable to HIV/AIDS. She compares how UNAIDS and the Global Fund developed policies to surmount social stigma as a barrier to their interventions' effectiveness. Raj Desai's and Homi Kharas's essay looks at new partnerships and actors promoting poverty alleviation and economic development, notably private sector actors who use social media to mobilize micro-lending to developing countries. They highlight institutional arrangements that not only advance the agency of loan recipients in developing countries but also harness the sense of agency of private sector actors moved by a dignity-based rationale to invest in them. Benjamin Boudreaux explores how and why stateless people lack standing with or support from public institutions and offers conceptual and institutional reforms so they are no longer rendered less than human. Based on leadership roles in government, NGOs, and corporate coalition realms, Mark P. Lagon examines in another essay when and why multistakeholder institutional partnerships succeed in enlarging the dignity of actual or potential human trafficking victims. Chapter 12, by Georgetown University vice president for global engagement and Professor Thomas Banchoff, focuses on the Catholic and other faith traditions as nonstate forces engaged in advancing human dignity. Board member of two leading faith-based NGOs, Nicole Bibbins Sedaca treats why and how various faith-based institutions have emerged as major actors that advance peace, pluralism, and prosperity and have a surprising potential not only to partner with secular institutions but to operate in countries with majority populations of a different faith. Founder of the Business and Human Rights Program at Yahoo! Inc., Michael Samway offers a practice-oriented treatment of information technology companies' legal and ethical obligations on human rights and provides methods for assessing how their operations and relationships with suppliers and governments impinge on human dignity.

Part III of the book consists of our closing chapter, which offers a path for a constructivist dialogue on human dignity as the principle to guide the work of global institutions. A dialogue on dignity as the central ordering idea in an increasingly fissiparous neomedieval world would address: (1) the extent of consensus on first principles, (2) how to operationalize dignity in practice, and (3) the priorities and trade-offs in implementation by global institutions. Norm entrepreneurs could spur an authentic discourse in traditional IGOs, hybrid institutions, the digital realm, and elsewhere that is designed to welcome challenges and incorporate refinements to the concept of human dignity based on agency and recognition of each human being. To avoid being either too didactic or too aloof, the United States should and can help cultivate the dialogue in a post-unipolar era. Based on a robust consensus with an even broader reach than similar liberal and human rights norms, traditional and hybrid global institutions could go beyond serving as fora for this dialogue. These institutions could be leading implementers—agencies of agency and recognition, as it were. The future of global institutions would be to help empower not states but people to realize the fullest fruits of their potential.

Notes

1. Melinda Gates: "For far too many women with HIV: they take the blame for this disease, even when they're blameless. We can't cure these women, but we can help them live with dignity." The World Economic Forum, Davos, January 25, 2007.

Jack Welch: "Dignity is not only 'the right thing to do' from a moral perspective, it invariably makes companies more competitive." With Suzy Welch, "The Difference Dignity Makes," *Business Week*, June 2009.

Aung San Suu Kyi: "A most insidious form of fear is that which masquerades as common sense or even wisdom, condemning as foolish, reckless, insignificant or futile the small, daily acts of courage which help to preserve man's self-respect and inherent human dignity." Accepting the Sakharov Prize for Freedom of Thought, July 10, 1991.

Former Archbishop of Canterbury Rowan Williams: "Shared dignity is the condition for what you could call 'civic warmth'—the sense of being able to trust not only immediate neighbours but the wider social fabric. If government is visibly working for dignity in citizenship, trust will follow." Sermon for the New Parliament, Westminster Abbey, June 8, 2010.

The Dalai Lama: "Buddhism too recognises that human beings are entitled to dignity, that all members of the human family have an equal and inalienable right to liberty, not just in terms of political freedom, but also at the fundamental level of freedom from fear and want." Buddhism and Democracy, Washington DC, April 1993.

George W. Bush: "No nation owns these aspirations, and no nation is exempt from them. We have no intention of imposing our culture, but America will always stand firm for the non-negotiable demands of human dignity." State of the Union Address, January 29, 2002.

President Barack Obama, accepting the Nobel Peace Prize: "Only a just peace based upon the inherent rights and dignity of every individual can truly be lasting." Oslo, Norway, December 10, 2009.

References

Aga Khan IV. 2006. "Cosmopolitan Society, Human Safety and Rights in Plural and Peaceful Societies." Remarks by His Highness the Aga Khan IV at Evory University Symposium. February 12. Evora, Portugal.

Arend, Anthony Clark. 1999. *Legal Rules and International Society.* New York: Oxford University Press.

Arend, Anthony Clark, and Robert J. Beck. 1993. *International Law and the Use of Force: Beyond the United Nations Charter Paradigm.* London: Routledge Press.

Bartlett, Robert C., and Susan D. Collins, trans. 2012. *Aristotle's Nicomachean Ethics.* Chicago: University of Chicago Press.

Bloom, Allan David, trans. 1991. *The Republic of Plato.* New York: Basic Books.

Bull, Hedley. 2002. *The Anarchical Society.* New York: Columbia University Press. First Published 1977.

Fukuyama, Francis. 1992. *The End of History and the Last Man.* New York: Free Press.

Glendon, Mary Ann. 2001. *A World Made New: Eleanor Roosevelt and the Universal Declaration of Human Rights.* New York: Random House.

Grotius, Hugo. 1925. "Prologomena" of *De Jure Belli Ac Pacis.* In Robert J. Beck, Anthony Clark Arend, and Robert D. Vander Lugt. 1996. *International Rules: Approaches from International Law and International Relations.* New York: Oxford University Press.

Haugen, Gary, and Victor Boutros. 2010. "And Justice for All: Enforcing Human Rights for the World's Poor." *Foreign Affairs* 89 (3): 51–62.

Kateb, George. 2011. *Human Dignity.* Cambridge, MA: Belknap Press.

Khan, Irene. 2009. *The Unheard Truth: Poverty and Human Rights.* New York: W. W. Norton and Company.

Lagon, Mark P. 1994. *The Reagan Doctrine: Sources of American Conduct in the Cold War's Last Chapter.* Westport, CT: Praeger.

Lo, Pilgrim W. K. 2009. "Human Dignity—A Theological and Confucian Discussion." *Dialog: A Journal of Theology* 48 (2): 168–78.

Mandela, Nelson. 1994. "Inaugural Address as President of South Africa."

McDougal, Myres S., and Harold D. Lasswell. 1959. "The Identification and Appraisal of Diverse Systems of Public Order." *American Journal of International Law* 53 (1): 1–29.

Nussbaum, Martha. 2001. *Women and Human Development.* Cambridge, UK: Cambridge University Press.

Pope John Paul II. 1993. "Encyclical Letter: *Veritatis splendor.*" Origins 23 (18): 298–334.

Reisman, W. Michael, Siegfried Wiessner, and Andrew R. Willard. 2007. "The New Haven School: A Brief Introduction." *Yale Journal of International Law* 32: 575–82.

Rosen, Michael. 2012. *Dignity: Its History and Meaning.* Cambridge: Harvard University Press.

Strange, Susan. 1996. *The Retreat of the State: The Diffusion of Power in the World Economy*. Cambridge: Cambridge University Press.

Tipson, Frederick S. 1973. "The Lasswell-McDougal Enterprise: Toward a World Public Order of Human Dignity." *Virginia Journal of International Law* 14: 535.

Wendt, Alexander. 1992. "Anarchy Is What States Make of It: The Social Construction of Power Politics." *International Organization* 46 (2): 391–425.

Yadollahpour, Behrouz. 2011. "Human Dignity and Its Consequences in the Holy Qur'an." *International Proceedings of Economics Development & Research* 10: 551–55.

TRADITIONAL INSTITUTIONS

When one reflects upon institutions poised to promote human dignity, the work of traditional institutions comes most readily to mind. As the term is used in this book, "traditional institutions" refers to intergovernmental institutions—international organizations that states join in their official capacity. Part I of this book explores several such institutions, including the United Nations Security Council, the United Nations Secretary-General, the International Criminal Court (ICC), regional organizations, and international financial institutions.

Not surprisingly, one of the main roles these institutions play in promoting human dignity is norm creation. In chapter 1, Nancy Soderberg discusses the role of the Security Council in promoting and developing the norm relating to the "responsibility to protect." Similarly, in chapter 3, Abiodun Williams explores how Secretary-General Kofi Annan acted to advance both that norm and others in service of human dignity. In a slightly different direction, Tod Lindberg, in chapter 2, explores the unique role of the ICC in developing what he calls the "responsibility to respect" the victims of atrocities by providing them with restitution. Likewise, in chapter 6, Mark P. Lagon and Ryan Kaminski examine a broad range of norms developed by a variety of global institutions that form the "human rights architecture." And, finally, in chapter 7 Anthony Clark Arend discusses the need for clearer norms relating to the treatment of terrorism suspects.

But these chapters also explore another critical role of traditional institutions: norm implementation. Not only is it necessary to develop norms, human dignity demands that norms be made real in practice. Lagon and Kaminski stress the gap between rights norms and implementation. Soderberg,

Williams, Lagon and Kaminski, and Lindberg explore in detail the implementation of several norms aimed at advancing dignity. Chester Crocker in chapter 4 pays special attention to the role of regional organizations as norm implementers in the area of conflict resolution. And in chapter 5, Anoop Singh examines the vital role of international financial institutions—including the International Monetary Fund—in promoting strong domestic institutions needed to realize the economic opportunity that is critical to human dignity.

CHAPTER 1

The United Nations Security Council

NANCY E. SODERBERG

In August 2000, I sat in the informal Security Council room at UN head-quarters in Turtle Bay pressing my colleagues for broader language in a draft UN resolution establishing a war criminals tribunal for Sierra Leone. Serving as the Alternate US Representative, I wanted to make sure that the war crimes tribunal we were authorizing could target the Liberian dictator Charles Taylor. Since 1991, through the sale of blood diamonds, Taylor had supported a ruthless rebel force fighting the democratic government. These rebels were responsible for tens of thousands of random killings, mutilations, rapes, and recruitment of child soldiers. Chopping off hands and eventually limbs had become a particularly sadistic practice, initially designed to scare people from voting as their fingers were dipped in indelible ink. The war had killed an estimated 50,000 out of a population of six million.

Talking back and forth by phone with then assistant secretary of state for African Affairs Susan Rice, we agreed to keep pressing Russia and China to accept language that would go beyond citizens of Sierra Leone. They and others had concerns over sovereignty and legitimacy for prosecuting foreign war criminals. The resolution formally requested the creation of an independent special court to bring to justice those responsible for the horrific war crimes committed during the civil war. With strong support from Britain, the former colonial power in Sierra Leone, I secured language that included "crimes under relevant Sierra Leonean law committed within the territory of Sierra Leone." That would include Charles Taylor. The United Nations Security Council (UNSC) Resolution 1315 passed 15–0 on August 14, 2000 (UNSC 2000).

This was personal to me. The summer before, I had traveled to Sierra Leone and visited a shelter for victims of the war. One of the most searing moments in my nearly thirty years in conflict prevention was holding a two-year-old girl—wide grin, sparkly eyes, a pretty flowered dress—missing both her arms. What kind of human barbarity could propel another human to chop off both a little girls' arms? I vowed then to do all I could to bring the perpetrator to justice. I had regretted not acting more forcefully to stop the 1994 genocide in Rwanda while serving as the third-ranked official on the National Security Council. The scene I visited in December 1994 in the western village of Nyarbuye in Rwanda still haunts me. Entering a church, there were still bodies everywhere of men, women, and children strewn over the floor. Little girls in dresses, men in suits, still lying where the killers had struck them down with machetes. An estimated 800,000 men, women, and children had died from April to July 1994.

Thus, it was particularly gratifying when in April 2012 former Liberian president Charles Taylor was finally brought to justice for his role in the Sierra Leone civil war—the first former head of state since Nuremberg to face such justice. The Special Court for Sierra Leone found Taylor guilty of eleven counts of war crimes and crimes against humanity, including murder, rape, and conscripting child soldiers. Expressing no remorse for his role in the atrocities, Taylor was sentenced on May 30, 2012, to fifty years in prison—essentially a life sentence for the sixty-four-year-old former dictator.

Others, too, have been brought to justice through courts set up by the UNSC. Have these prosecutions saved lives? No. They all occurred after the killings. Are they a deterrent to future killers? Probably not, yet. In fact, in the short term, the indictments might push leaders to cling to power longer, as may well be the case today in Syria. But in eventually bringing justice, they have helped support reconciliation and the peace processes that follow the violence. This represents real progress for the UNSC in standing up for human rights and dignity around the world. Its words do matter.

While the process of justice is important, so is actual intervention to stop the killing. But the UNSC has failed to prevent the slaughter in Syria, the killings in the Democratic Republic of the Congo and in Somalia, the crisis in Mali, and other conflicts around the world. What more should and can the UNSC do to protect lives and maintain human dignity in the twenty-first century?

The UN was set up in 1945 to maintain international peace and security and is based on the principle of the sovereign equality of all its Members. The Security Council's purpose is to determine the existence of any threat to the peace and to make recommendations to maintain or restore international peace and security. The protection of human dignity does not appear in the Charter as a function of the Security Council. And yet today, we look increasingly to the UN—and especially to the Security Council—to do just that.

This chapter explores the state of play in the role of the UNSC in promoting human dignity and offers recommendations on how to improve its capacity and performance in that important realm.

The Security Council

After two world wars that witnessed the greatest human tragedies the world has seen, the global powers met in 1945 to establish an institutional structure to prevent another such war. Previous attempts to institutionalize global peace and security after the First World War, such as the League of Nations and the Kellogg-Briand pact, proved to be failures when World War II broke out in 1939. The UN was founded to replace these efforts with a lasting structure to prevent another world war.

The UN Charter—created in 1945 and amended in 1965—established a fifteen-member Security Council, the principal organ of the UN charged with maintaining peace and security.[1] This body is charged as the premier international watchdog and guarantor of global peace with the authority to impose binding decisions on all UN member states. The great powers that were the victors of the Second World War received the most coveted positions as permanent members on the Security Council, with the all-powerful veto. The Charter designates five permanent members, the P-5—China, France, the Soviet Union (with Russia as its successor), the United Kingdom, and the United States—which were seen as the primary guardians of global security.

In addition to the permanent members, ten additional members are elected for two-year terms based on their contributions to peace and security and regional representation. While the Charter does not designate seats on a geographical basis, in practice the nonpermanent seats have been divvied up among regional blocs (McDonald and Patrick 2010). The regional groups include Asian, African, Latin American and Caribbean, Eastern European, Western European, and Others (which includes the United States and Israel).

Once established, the Security Council quickly got wrapped up in the great power politics of the Cold War and often became a showcase for the US-Soviet rivalry. Today, however, the debate is more diffuse, often focusing more on the question of sovereignty than on some ideological debate. The P-5 largely have the power to block any issue of their choosing. Thus, today when the P-5 disagree, the UNSC is hamstrung and largely ineffective. That means Russia will block interference in the crisis in Chechnya, China will do the same regarding human rights in Taiwan and Tibet, and both will water down any efforts to sanction their allies, such as Sudan, Syria, and Iran. The United States uses the veto to protect Israel from unbalanced resolutions, and disagreements continue on the issue of terrorism, where some members continue to defend the use of terrorism by Hezbollah and Hamas against Israel.

The principle of sovereignty on which the UN is based has come under increasing challenge, however, through the development of a new norm in 2001 called the Responsibility to Protect (dubbed R2P or RtoP). Led by then UN secretary-general Kofi Annan, it was a response to the genocides of the late twentieth century, which resulted from internal conflicts not interstate conflict. There was a growing recognition that the world had a responsibility to intervene to save lives if a state failed to do so, and a groundbreaking report by the International Commission on Intervention and State Sovereignty (ICISS) argued that "the principle of non-intervention yields to the international responsibility to protect" (International Commission on Intervention and State Sovereignty 2001). In 2005, due in large part to the persistence of one of the ICISS co-chairs, Gareth Evans, the UN General Assembly finally agreed to the principle, although in a watered-down version, pledging to take collective action to help a population at risk (UN General Assembly 2005). In the end, many member states accepted the language only grudgingly. But, in some ways, this proposed new norm can be considered a neomedieval revival of a world in which borders are no longer sacrosanct.

Putting it into practice, however, demonstrates that we are still very much in the Westphalian phase of international norms in which the protection of sovereignty is placed above all other interests. The Responsibility to Protect has yet to be institutionalized or systematized at the UN or even within member states. For instance, it failed to overcome objections by Sudan to stop the genocide in Darfur. Thousands continue to die each month in the Democratic Republic of the Congo. It failed to intervene to stop the crisis in Mali, which erupted in the spring of 2012. The UNSC authorized the protection of civilians in Libya but has largely stood by while over 100,000 have died in the crisis in Syria since 2011.

How can we address this inconsistency and better institutionalize the protection of human life and dignity by the UNSC? First, it is important to understand the challenges of legitimacy, legality, and sovereignty in protecting human dignity.

Legitimacy of the UNSC

One key challenge for the members of the UN is the increasing lack of legitimacy of the UNSC. How is it today that the P-5 retain a privileged role among nations, both with permanent seats and a veto? How is it that France and the United Kingdom (UK)—which contribute far less to the global institutions than do Japan and Germany—retain their permanent privilege? How can Africa, Latin America, and the Arab states remain on the sidelines? When the current system was established six decades ago, 142 of today's 193 member states did not yet exist and were either under colonial control or considered part of another state. Today's Security Council's decisions increasingly lack legitimacy in the eyes of many of those member states that are denied a voice in the process. Certainly, the UNSC remains the most authoritative international institution on international peace and security issues, although states often defy the sanctions against rogue regimes (McDonald and Patrick 2010). The lack of a more representative Security Council offers an excuse to those seeking to avoid implementing fully the Security Council's decisions. A better balance would help get other nations invested in tackling today's global challenges.

The institution has failed to adapt to changes to the postwar global order that occurred either concurrently with or following the Cold War, such as decolonization, the rise of the BRICS (Brazil, Russia, India, China, and South Africa), and globalization. As such, the Security Council today represents an outdated structure that is not responsive enough to the concerns of peace and security in the twenty-first century. As the role and mission of the Security Council have grown more important in meeting today's challenges, modernizing its structure will be an essential part of improving its ability to protect and defend human dignity through increased legitimacy.

It is well past time to bring the Security Council into the twenty-first century and recommendations on how to do so are offered below. But even with such institutional changes, the challenge of deciding whether and when to intervene to protect civilians will remain.

Peacekeeping—When to Intervene against a State's Will to Protect Civilians

For the UNSC's first four decades, state-to-state relations dominated the Security Council agenda. The Council's defining actions included the authorization for and conduct of the Korean War—a conflict between the United States with allied forces under UN auspices and North Korea with Chinese support—and the coalition forces against Saddam Hussein in 1991 following his invasion of Kuwait. The UNSC authorized just under twenty peacekeeping missions between 1948 and 1989, largely between states; a peacekeeping observer force has been in Kashmir since 1949 and a truce supervisory force in Israel since 1948. But the rise of intrastate conflict following the collapse of the Berlin wall in 1989 posed new challenges for the Security Council, which has authorized nearly fifty peacekeeping operations since 1989. Each has struggled with the challenges of threats to human dignity not just from states but also from nonstate actors. The UN has gotten better at combatting nonstate actors—more, better trained forces, security sector reform, better policing, and better intelligence on the ground. But the UNSC remains reluctant to challenge the sovereignty of a state abusing its population. The issue remains one of the most divisive issues in the UN today.

Therein lies the major dilemma faced today by the UNSC: how, when, and whether to intervene in the internal affairs of a state to protect civilians. In the two decades since the end of the Cold War, the UNSC has done so rarely and largely poorly. The UN Charter authorizes the use of force in only two instances: Article 51 for self-defense and Article 42 to address threats to international peace and security, both under Chapter VII. Since the end of the Cold War, preventing atrocities has been of increasing concern to the Security Council, but the Charter is silent on the issue. As threats to civilian lives came increasingly to the attention of the Council after the Cold War, the P-5 nations have often disagreed on the appropriate course of action. Differences in the willingness to intervene in the affairs of other states have driven the UNSC to make inconsistent decisions in its interventions to protect life and human dignity.

From Kosovo to East Timor, atrocity prevention has become one of the primary functions of the Council. Recent developments in Libya and Syria have brought this role to the forefront. A short review of some of these interventions can illuminate lessons for improving the response of the UNSC to threats to civilians and for addressing the challenges of legitimacy, legality, and sovereignty.

The case of Côte d'Ivoire offers key lessons on how to conduct an intervention in a civil war.

Kosovo: UNSC Legitimacy versus Legality; the Role of Regional Organizations

In early 1998, Serbian president Slobodan Milosevic accelerated a policy of repression and intimidation of Kosovo-Albanians in Kosovo, a province that had enjoyed large autonomy until the end of the Cold War. During the 1990s, Belgrade's violent measures in the small province fueled aspirations for independence and fostered the emergence of the Kosovo Liberation Army, a small insurgency group. Serb forces drove some 300,000 Kosovar Albanians from their homes, and refugees began pouring over the borders as Serb forces ethnically cleansed the province. As the Serb obstruction continued, one Serb diplomat even joked, "a village a day keeps NATO away." On January 15, 1999, following three days of artillery shelling, Serb forces entered a village in southern Kosovo, Racak, and executed forty-five people.

In September 1998, as a response to the violence in Kosovo, the Security Council passed Resolution 1199, which recognized that the situation constituted a threat to regional peace and security. It demanded a ceasefire, a withdrawal of Serb forces attacking civilians, and a negotiated solution to Kosovo. The vote was 14–0, with China abstaining, fearing a precedent that might lead to international interference in its own affairs. Russia was wary but voted yes. The resolution contained the Chapter VII reference and defined the situation as a "threat to peace and security in the region." However, in an example of how detailed the negotiations in the UN can get, Russia had refused a reference to "international" threat and blocked the inclusion of an authorization of "all necessary means," to counter the threat, UN-speak for the authorization of the use of force (UNSC 1998).

Having dithered in stopping the violence in Bosnia, President Bill Clinton took the lead in the fall of 1998 in threatening Milosevic with NATO air strikes against Serbia proper if he did not halt the atrocities in Kosovo. NATO announced on January 1999 its intention to use force to compel compliance should either the Serbs or the Kosovars reject the proposals. Despite the strong opposition of China and Russia, UN Secretary-General Kofi Annan urged NATO to endorse the approach, declaring that the wars of the 1990s had not "left us with any illusions about the need to use force, when all other means have failed. We may be reaching that limit, once again, in the former Yugoslavia" (Annan 1999).

Russia had endorsed the political strategy but strongly opposed the use of force and indicated that it would veto any Security Council resolution authorizing the use of force. Hence, to avoid a situation in which the Security Council explicitly rejected an authorization to use force, NATO members in the Council did not seek authorization for its use of force. Instead, it used NATO to provide authorization to its action, circumventing the Council in an action that would save lives—but undermine the UN's authority as the sole arbiter in international law of the authorization of the use of force.

Although the United States and its NATO allies anticipated that a short, intense bombing campaign would quickly coerce Milosevic to the negotiation table, Belgrade instead hastened its ethnic cleansing of Kosovo, expelling most of the Kosovar Albanian population from their homes. In all, nearly three-fourths of the prewar population of 1.8 million ethnic Albanians were driven from their homes. Eight hundred thousand were forced out of the country; another 500,000 were internally displaced.

By late May, NATO launched Operation Allied Force, which included as many as 300 strike sorties a day against the Serbs' air defense network, infrastructure, command centers, airfields, main army units and heavy weapons. While NATO expected a short campaign, it instead lasted for seventy-eight days. NATO conducted 38,400 air sorties, including nearly 10,500 air strikes against Serb targets. Not one NATO fatality occurred.

While the campaign initially failed to deter Milosevic's ethnic cleansing of Kosovo, in the end it succeeded in reversing the ethnic cleansing when the Serb troops withdrew. On June 12, peace-enforcing troops from NATO and non-NATO countries entered Kosovo. Within five days, 20,000 troops had been deployed as part of the force that would eventually reach 46,000 from 39 countries, including the 12,000 European Rapid Reaction Force troops and 25,000 US troops.

Thus, NATO's war in Kosovo was initiated without explicit UNSC authorization, although the military action was endorsed by NATO, the UN secretary-general, and a large part of the international community. In addition, the campaign's political goals were supported by a series of previous UNSC resolutions and by all the key leaders in Europe, thus guaranteeing strong international support for the policy's implementation once the military campaign ended. Today, 760 US troops continue to serve as part of the NATO force of 5,600 in Kosovo.

Unlike the 2003 Iraq War, also undertaken without an explicit UNSC resolution, the operation in Kosovo is viewed as largely legitimate because it saved lives and had regional European buy-in, as well as authorization by NATO. Therein lie three key lessons going forward. First, in cases where any one of the P-5 is prepared to veto an operation, the UNSC is powerless to act. Russia and China successfully blocked the UNSC from supporting the intervention in Kosovo and, later, any forceful intervention to stop the Darfur genocide throughout the first decade of the twenty-first century. The UNSC, in fact, let the government of Sudan dictate the UN's efforts to stop the very genocide the government was orchestrating in Darfur—a dismal failure. The UNSC has never intervened in Chechnya, despite the immense toll of the war on civilians there over the last two decades. That means the veto power of the P-5 can undermine the positive development of international norms on atrocity prevention that has occurred over the last two decades. Essentially all that a human rights-violating regime has to do for self-preservation is to become allies with one veto-wielding member of the Security Council—most often that will be Russia or China.

Second, the key validator in the absence of any UNSC action is a regional organization. While still considered "illegal," regionally authorized missions can serve as key validators to an operation designed to save lives. Norms have shifted in recent decades, from the public and policymakers alike both in the United States and abroad, towards less tolerance of human rights violations (Council on Foreign Relations 2011). With it must shift the legitimacy of operations to protect lives that do not have UNSC authorization. In addition, regional organizations will be key to securing the postconflict reconstruction investment essential to maintaining peace as neighboring nations have the most at stake in ensuring peace.

Third, one of the P-5 nations must be prepared to act and usually that means the United States. Had the United States not been willing to lead in the decision to use force, even with NATO authorization, more lives would have been lost.

In the case of Libya, the UNSC did authorize intervention, but the divisions remained throughout and the escalation to a regime-change mission will haunt future efforts to secure UNSC authorization.

Libya: Intervening against a State's Will to Protect Lives—the Exception or an Evolution?

The operation in Libya represents the importance of regional support as well as UNSC authorization. The UNSC was divided over the initial authorization and even more so after it became an effort to overthrow the regime. Whether it sets a new bar in the willingness of the UNSC to intervene in the internal affairs of a nation remains to be seen. Early indications are that it will not (Kumbaro 2001).

In late 2010 and early 2011, an entire region was inspired by the actions of one man. A street vendor named Mohamed Bouazizi set himself on fire in Tunisia in protest of being hassled over bureaucratic violations as he sought to sell his wares. The regime in Tunisia quickly fell and was soon followed by dramatic street protests in Egypt, leading to the ouster of President Hosni Mubarak. International attention soon turned to Libya and the protests against then president Muammar Qaddafi. However, the Qaddafi regime proved to be tougher and more violent than what the world had anxiously watched in Tunisia and Egypt. Attacks on civilians worsened, and the man once known as the "mad dog of the Middle East" was making public threats to slaughter his own citizens "like rats" in the opposition stronghold of Benghazi.

On March 17, 2011, the UNSC took action. The body approved Resolution 1973, imposing a ban on all flights in the country's airspace—a no-fly zone—and tightened sanctions on the Qaddafi regime and its supporters. The demand was to end the attacks against civilians, which it said might constitute "crimes against humanity." The 10–0 vote with five abstentions authorized the NATO-led Operation Odyssey Dawn for civilian protection. Those abstaining included Brazil, India, Germany, Russia, and China.

This was a significant move in the development of the Security Council's role in atrocity prevention. Resolution 1973 marked the first time the Council had authorized the use of force for human protection purposes against the will of a functioning state (Bellamy and Williams 2011). There are a number of factors particular to Libya that led to the international decision to use force. First, there was a widespread regional consensus for intervention. This support came from the Arab League, Organization of the Islamic Conference, and Gulf Cooperation Council. Another significant factor was the poor international standing of the Qaddafi regime. Qaddafi had no advocates on the Security Council, the way that Serbia did with Russia in the Kosovo case. There was a clear and immediate threat to civilians. Qaddafi had publicly announced his intention to slaughter civilians in Benghazi. Finally, of course, was the fact that Libya has oil. Rarely is the international community faced with such a combination of factors in favor of intervention.

But UNSC agreement quickly fell apart as the NATO-led operation rapidly escalated into a regime-change operation. Rather than only use air strikes to protect the citizens of Benghazi, NATO began to attack the regimes' forces around the country, eventually targeting Qaddafi's troops. NATO forces even contributed in the hunt for Qaddafi as surveillance drones guided Libyan rebels to the former dictator's final location where he was captured and killed.

In the end, the operation halted the crimes against humanity. But its expansion beyond that, to overthrowing the regime, was not supported by Russia or China and had mixed support in the Arab world, clearly contributing to the later lack of enthusiasm for action to stop the bloodshed in Syria. And tragically, a misreading of support for the United States among the people of Benghazi led to lax security measures at the US Consulate there, resulting in the tragic death of US Ambassador J. Christopher Stevens and three other Americans in September 2012.

The Libya case, therefore, is not likely to set a low floor for interventions in the future. Rarely is the region going to come together to give the action legitimacy; rarely is NATO going to be willing to act. Rarely is a leader going to have so few defenders among the P-5 as did Qaddafi.

The Libya experience points to two additional lessons. First, the escalation from a civilian protection mission to regime change will raise the bar for future such UNSC authorizations. Even though none of the P-5 stood up for the Qaddafi regime, China and Russia strongly opposed the mission's escalation. While other factors are also at play, we are already seeing a backlash in

Russia's strong defense of Syria's sovereignty and opposition to UNSC authorization for intervention.

The second lesson is that Libya has further devolved the concept of sovereignty; it is clearly less and less an immutable shield of a recalcitrant state than it had been. That, in and of itself, is an important development in the evolution of the definition of sovereignty at the UN. The operation was designed clearly to defend civilians—although no such intervention in a state's affairs is authorized by the Charter. We do not yet know if the intervention will prove to be the exception or the evolution. Perhaps the legacy of Libya in the longer run is to set the bar a bit lower in the willingness of the UNSC to take on the issue of intervention over a state's objections in the effort to protect civilians.

But that is not the case in Syria.

Syria: Reluctant Region, Clear Failure to Protect Civilian Lives

In March 2011, nationwide protests demanded the resignation of Syrian president Bashar al-Assad and the end to the nearly half century of Ba'ath Party rule. Unlike the efforts in Egypt and Tunisia, the regime reacted brutally, unleashing a crackdown against both the rebels and civilians. In August 2011, President Obama called for President Assad to resign, and the United States imposed sanctions designed to undermine Assad's ability to finance his military operation. He later sent aid to the opposition, at first only nonlethal, but he eventually agreed to send arms as well. In mid-December 2012, he also joined other European powers in recognizing the Syrian Opposition Coalition as the legitimate representative of the Syrian people. The United States also designated the group Jabhat al-Nusrah as a terrorist group linked to al-Qaeda in Iraq.

But Assad dug in, and by early 2012 nearly 9,000 had been killed, and human rights groups were demanding action. The United States and Europeans had rallied behind a diplomatic push by the Arab League for a peace plan that would have involved Assad yielding at least some of his powers and paving the way for the creation of a government of national unity led by an individual with backing from the government and opposition. Yet, in February 2012, Russia and China vetoed a Western and Arab League-sponsored resolution condemning Syria's violent repression of the nearly year-old antigovernment demonstrators. This action threw the heft of Moscow and Beijing behind a beleaguered and repressive President Bashar al-Assad as he intensified a military operation aimed at crushing the uprising. At the time, Russia's envoy, Sergey Lavrov, underscored the impediment sovereignty represents, saying, "We are not friends or allies of President Assad. . . . We try to stick to our responsibilities as permanent members of the Security Council, and the Security Council by definition does not engage in domestic affairs of member states" (Khan 2012).

The UN-Arab League envoy, the distinguished former UN secretary-general Kofi Annan, resigned in August 2012 after only six months on the job. He bitterly blamed the lack of progress on Syrian government intransigence, increasing militancy by Syrian rebels, and the failure of a divided Security Council to rally forcefully behind his efforts. His replacement, former UN official Lakhdar Brahimi, has fared no better.

Over the course of the next year, Assad continued his assault on the population, including the use of chemical weapons, with over 100,000 estimated by the UN to have been killed by the fall of 2013, largely by the regime's forces. The game appeared to change significantly when Assad's regime unleashed a significant attack using chemical weapons on August 21, killing over 1,000 men, women, and children. Graphic pictures of the bodies of hundreds of children with obvious symptoms of a chemical attack—foaming at the mouth and ears, frozen stiff in death—flooded the airwaves. President Obama, having declared the use of chemical weapons a "red line," felt compelled to act. On September 1, he announced he had decided to take military action against Syrian regime targets to hold the Assad regime accountable, to deter future such acts, and to degrade the regime's capacity.

However, momentum for military action quickly stalled when Secretary of State John Kerry casually answered a press question on what, if anything, the Syrians could do to avoid a military strike: "Sure, he could turn over every single bit of his chemical weapons to the international community in the next week—turn it over, all of it without delay and allow the full and total accounting (of it), but he isn't about to do it and it can't be done" (Mohammed and Osborn 2013). The Russians quickly seized on the opportunity to secure a Syrian agreement to do just that, ending any talk of military intervention. The Organization for the Prohibition of Chemical Weapons, awarded the 2013 Nobel Peace Prize, moved quickly to secure and eventually destroy the weapons, ensuring the Assad regime would never again use them against the population. While denying the regime the ability to use chemical weapons to slaughter its people is certainly a good thing, it has done little to stop the broader killing or the civil war. Supported by Saudi Arabia and Qatar, radical groups, including al-Qaeda affiliates, are now infiltrated into the opposition, and the Assad regime appears entrenched with continued support from the Russians and Iranians. Neither the Free Syrian Army nor the government appears powerful enough to prevail on the battlefield. Few are optimistic that UN sponsored peace talks in Geneva will make significant progress.

Throughout the conflict, President Obama has remained at arm's length, keeping any US ground troops off-limits. His options had already been complicated by a vote in late August in the British Parliament against joining the United States in military action. Shortly afterwards, President Obama decided to first seek congressional approval of the use of force but awkwardly made the case in a nationwide address for military action after he had already decided to give the Russian initiative on chemical weapons a chance. The vacillation in the use of force and in seeking congressional approval sparked harsh criticism of the Obama team's foreign policy. By December 2013, 57 percent disagreed with the way the United States acted in Syria and only 34 percent agreed with his overall foreign policy (Pew 2013). By April 2014, 150,000 Syrians had been killed, with 2.5 million refugees and another 9.3 million in need of assistance (USAID 2014). Assad's control appears to be tightening.

The tragedy of Syria underscores a brutal lesson in the reality of protecting civilians and human dignity in the second decade of the twenty-first century. The UNSC cannot adopt a resolution authorizing the use of force with the objections of a permanent member of the Council (in this case two, China and Russia). Unlike NATO, the Arab League is wholly unprepared to intervene in the region. Despite the experiences of Côte d'Ivoire and Libya, the world is far from prepared to act in any consistent and principled way. The people of Syria are paying the price for this inaction.

Recommendations

These very different instances of UNSC intervention to protect human life and dignity demonstrate the difficulties of this challenge in the twenty-first century. Political will is the biggest hurdle, followed by the lack of regional capabilities. The P-5 play a key but uneven role in the decision to intervene—and thus interventions will be inconsistent and sporadic. From the discrepancy between legality and legitimacy to the conflict between sovereignty and the need to back up diplomatic efforts with a credible use of force, the challenges for action will likely remain for some time. In a neomedieval world, where an increasing number of actors are playing a critical role, the protection of civilians will require a varied and multifaceted approach that includes state actors, regional organizations, nongovernmental organizations, and global bodies.

Going forward, there are no easy solutions or quick fixes. Each avenue offers trade-offs between legality, legitimacy, sovereignty, and effectiveness.

The world may have adopted the principle of Responsibility to Protect, but it is far from creating any kind of standards for actually implementing it. Regrettably, that is likely to remain the case so long as half of the world is not democratic and wants to maintain its immunity from outside interference. And the democratic half often is unwilling to assume the responsibility to intervene.

The UNSC, which was founded to be the chief protector of global peace and security, must do better. The international community can take steps to increase the legitimacy of the UNSC actions, the capacity of the operations it authorizes, and the use of instruments to protect human dignity more boldly.

1. Pursue United Nations Security Council Expansion to Address Twenty-First Century Global Power Structure. To maintain its legitimacy and consequent support for its actions, the Security Council membership must reflect the current reality of twenty-first century global power. Authorizing interventions and peacekeeping missions must involve the regions affected; those providing significant financial resources to the UN must have a stronger say in its decisions. The challenges beyond human protection the United States and the world are likely to face in the future—climate change, terrorism, economic development, nonproliferation, water resources—will become increasingly global in nature, requiring global solutions that must include voices from all the world's regions.

It is important to recognize that an expanded Security Council will not necessarily work better, be more efficient, or produce bolder solutions to these challenges. But it will make the decisions more legitimate and achieve stronger regional buy-in—a key element to maintaining support for the Security Council's decisions and lasting stability. In other words, expansion is a vital, if imperfect, pursuit. Without it, the UNSC decisions will not have global buy-in.[2]

The most practical solution is to expand the Security Council's permanent membership from five to twelve, to include Brazil, Egypt, Germany, India, Japan, Nigeria, and South Africa. This step means adding an additional seat to the previously discussed two African/Arab slots. Specific criteria on contributions to the UN could be developed to determine (and justify) the selection of these new members. One could possibly split the Arab and Africa groups and initiate a review of the European membership on the Security Council—or even totally revise the current regional groupings.

There would be no immediate change in the veto, although the current P-5 would agree to limit even further their use of it. The issue of the veto would be reviewed every ten years, with the ultimate goal being its elimination. There would still be ten impermanent elected members, making the total Security Council membership twenty-two. Over time, the United Kingdom and French seats could be collapsed into one European Union (EU) seat, leaving twenty-one members.

This move would help balance the Security Council and give it more credibility in the global arena. Not only do the countries listed above contribute more financially to the UN than other members, but their admission would also bring a greater representation of the global population as well as the current global power structure. Most of these countries are regularly elected onto the Council for the rotating seats for the regional representation. It is important to note, however, that such agreement would be very difficult to achieve as strong divisions remain over the veto and the appropriate regional candidates.

2. Strengthen Regional Organizations for Atrocity Prevention. The world's capability to intervene to protect civilians or prevent and contain conflict varies greatly. While Asia, Europe, Latin America, and North America generally have the capacity to intervene in their region, Africa and the Arab nations will need continued international support to develop the capacities to do so. Particularly as the United States and its NATO partners tire of being the port of first call for military interventions, the international community must begin to strengthen the capabilities of regional organizations and regional peacekeeping forces. Nations in the neighborhood bear the brunt of the conflict, in terms of refugees, lack of trade, and a variety of negative consequences to war. They are the ones that will benefit most from conflict prevention and containment; they are the ones most willing to send troops into combat to defend their clear interests. As we saw in the case of Kosovo and Libya, regional organizations also can confer legitimacy on military operations.

The League of Arab States lacks the capacity—and the will—to intervene in defense of human dignity. The organization's charter maintains the primacy of state sovereignty, and its membership has mostly consisted of autocrats disinclined to intervene to protect civilian lives. However, as the Arab Spring began to sweep the Middle East in 2011, the Arab League played an increasingly highlighted role, even pushing for action on regional security issues. Its rapid, unified response to Muammar Qaddafi's brutal crackdown in Libya likely tipped the balance at the UN in favor of NATO's military intervention. Its suspension of Libyan and Syrian membership, the observer mission, and pursuit for a Security Council resolution are significant steps (Lynch 2012). These were all political steps, however, underscoring the utter lack of capacity to act militarily to support civilian lives in the conflict. That role fell to NATO.

The abysmal failure to intervene to stem the Syrian crisis demonstrates the divisions within Arab states on when, whether, and how to intervene. Saudi

Arabia, in fact, is sending support to the opposition forces in Syria, but in March 2011 they sent 2,000 troops to Bahrain to crush the uprising there. The Gulf Cooperation Council for the first time used collective military action—but it was to help prop up Bahrain's king, a Sunni ruler in a Shia-majority nation, and crush the Shi'ite uprising. So long as these Arab regimes commit significant human rights abuses at home, they will remain on the sidelines—or even on the wrong side—of the protection of human dignity.

The continent of Africa faces the biggest gaps in capacity to protect civilians, with vast deficiencies in civilian structures and military forces to maintain peace and stability. For instance, the UNSC resolution passed in December 2012 authorized an African force of 3,300 to help the weak armed forces of Mali oust rebel forces who were terrorizing the population in northern Mali. However, the resolution recognizes that there is not yet a realistic military plan to do so—a clear recognition that the African force is not up to the task.[3]

Since its inception in October 2008, the United States Africa Command and NATO have been critical partners in helping Africa address a range of challenges, including counterterrorism capacity-building, disaster management, peacekeeping capacity-building, humanitarian operations, demining, and other key activities, such as counterpiracy activities off the Somali coast. The United States has also conducted extensive bilateral efforts through its Global Peace Operations Initiative program initiated in 2004 to address major gaps in international peace operations support. These efforts should be broadened, with the ultimate goal of an international system of regional peacekeeping forces—and at times intervention forces—to be the port of first call to protect human rights. International peacekeeping training centers, such as the one in Jakarta, Indonesia, could help implement standard levels of capabilities worldwide. Regionally based centers of training, with standard training and equipping doctrines, could be useful in developing centers of first response in conflict areas, limiting conflict and perhaps even preventing it.

The State Department's Bureau of Conflict and Stabilization Operations must look at ways to strengthen support, especially when implementing its mandate to strengthen civil capacity. Extensive consultation with Congress will be necessary as the Bureau has yet to be adequately funded or staffed, and many in Congress attempted to eliminate funding in 2011. In addition, Congress should continue its financial support of the United States Institute of Peace, a vital partner in the conflict prevention and resolution realm that was created by an act of Congress in 1984. The International Crisis Group is also a critical partner in these efforts, which deserves robust US support.

Such a worldwide system of capable regional forces, however, can only come about with the strong support of and coordination by the UN.

3. Stronger Support for UN Peacekeeping—A Key Line of Defense of Human Dignity. A little-noted fact is that the UN has the second largest deployed security force in the world. With over 100,000 troops and police in the field on seventeen missions, the UN is second only to the United States. The world is turning increasingly to the UN to deploy peacekeeping missions to protect civilians, meaning these troops are often on the front lines of protecting human dignity. Considerable progress has been made since 1999 when the first mandate to protect civilians was included for the peacekeeping mission in Sierra Leone. Over the past twelve years, the secretary-general has put forward over one hundred recommendations on the protection of civilians to the Security Council, many of which the Council has acted upon, including country-specific decisions and in thematic resolutions to improve the protection of civilians. Countries have deployed troop and police personnel to difficult environments to fulfill protection of civilian mandates.

Many peacekeeping missions, however, have failed to provide systematic or consistent protection of civilians. The UN leadership recognized in 2009 that it needs "better planning for missions mandated to protect civilians, a more coherent approach to protecting civilians, and improvement of the guidance available to missions mandated with this task" (Holt and Taylor 2009). It has undertaken a systematic review to identify the gaps in policy and preparedness it faces and has sought to have better coordination from the Security Council, countries contributing troops and police, the UN Secretariat, and the field. But it is up to the member states to fill those gaps.

Not only is the increased demand for protection of civilians a challenge, the sheer magnitude of the peacekeeping missions is as well. There has been a five-fold increase in peacekeeping since 2000, from 20,000 peacekeepers in the field to a present capacity of 100,000. The complexity of peacekeeping has grown as well. Since 2003, UN peacekeepers have deployed to no less than eight complex operations, often operating simultaneously.

The United States now recognizes that effective UN peacekeeping operations are central to US national security interests. President Obama's 2010 National Security Strategy includes a commitment to "strengthen the UN's leadership and operational capacity in peacekeeping, humanitarian relief, post-disaster recovery, development assistance, and the promotion of human rights" (US National Security Council 2010). The Pentagon's 2010 Quadrennial Defense Review makes the Department of Defense's commitment to support and enhance the capacity of the UN quite explicit (US Department of Defense 2010). Since taking office, the Obama administration has paid off peacekeeping arrears accumulated over the previous four years, including approximately $2 billion for the UN's peacekeeping budget in 2009 and almost

$3 billion in humanitarian and development assistance for the eight countries that host multidimensional UN peacekeeping missions. In 2009, the United States also provided more than $600 million for training, equipment, and logistics assistance to fifty-five nations to help bolster their capacity to contribute troops and police for peacekeeping operations (Soderberg 2011).

These steps are partly in response to the UN's impressive progress in implementing reforms and managing the explosion of peacekeeping operations over the two decades. Twelve years after the 2000 Report of the Panel on UN peace operations, known as the Brahimi Report (United Nations 2000), the UN has implemented many of the suggested reforms to make peacekeeping faster, more capable, and more effective. Those reforms focused on improving five key areas: personnel, doctrine, partnerships, resources, and organization. The UN also set up a "Peacekeeping Best Practices Section," which has helped synchronize effective information management practices and strengthened the development of policy and doctrine, as well as institutionalized learning systems for peacekeeping. It has worked to establish predictable frameworks for cooperation with regional organizations, including common peacekeeping standards and modalities for cooperation and transition, and to conduct, where possible, joint training exercises (UN Secretary-General 2006; Soderberg 2011).

Yet, gaps in personnel and other civilian and military resources remain. Some of the Brahimi reforms have only been partially implemented, such as a global logistics strategy and effective integrated planning mechanisms. Given the extraordinary growth of UN peacekeeping, and with no reduction in need on the horizon, the ready stocks and funds to deploy missions have not been sufficiently adjusted to meet the needed, higher levels (UN Department of Peacekeeping Operations and Department of Field Support 2009). Civilian gaps include equipment and training, individual police officers, additional corrections staff/consultants to undertake corrections specialist projects, and experts on justice and corrections.[4] The military gaps include mobility (surface and aerial) capability, aviation assets, and basic training and equipment.

These basic gaps hinder the ability of the UN's missions to carry out their mandates from the UNSC, especially those relating to the protection of civilians. While the United States is not in a position to provide much of the UN's requests itself, a better and higher-level process is needed to ensure these civilian and military gaps are appropriately addressed and provided for—either by the United States when it is able to or by other nations with the necessary capabilities. High level direct requests by the United States—especially when made by senior Pentagon officials—can often galvanize other nations to meet the UN's needs (Soderberg 2007).

Despite the recognition by the United States of the importance of UN peacekeeping, today the United States provides only thirty-one troops to UN peacekeeping operations and another ninety police and military experts. One of the UN's priorities is to close the increasing supply and demand gap by enlarging the base of troop contributors beyond its current top five: Pakistan, Bangladesh, India, Nigeria, and Rwanda. One way to do that is to increase the commitment of the P-5 to participation in peacekeeping operations, which today is less than 4.5 percent of the 100,000 UN-deployed troops, police, and military experts. As the United States withdraws its troops from Afghanistan, it should consider providing additional troops to the UN. Such deployments would not only help galvanize others to contribute, it would also offer the United States important training opportunities for future US efforts. To help the UN peacekeeping missions to be better able to protect civilians, the United States should also deepen its support for the UN with regard to filling civilian and military gaps and provide more US personnel to UN headquarters and police. The UN's New Horizon plan encourages Western Countries (particularly in Europe) to return to more robust UN peacekeeping participation (UNDPKO and DFS 2009).

As the UN seeks to significantly enhance levels of interoperability among its peacekeeper-contributing countries within the decade, more efforts will be needed to achieve interoperability among and between military peacekeepers, police, and Formed Police Units. The United States could integrate the training of potential UN troop contributors into its training efforts, perhaps through the combatant commands. There is a clear need to establish a UN Clearing House to track capabilities and needs to better coordinate efforts by donors (Soderberg 2011).

Lastly, some form of a UN crisis response reserve force should be established. While it remains controversial, it is critical that the UN have a capacity to move quickly to stem a growing crisis. Over-the-horizon proposals are under discussion, but many countries do not want to pay for a standing force not in use. The UN continues to need this capacity and hopes to reopen the dialogue in the context of the global force posture. One option is something between a full reserve and training from scratch (Soderberg 2011).

4. Strengthen US Support for the International Criminal Court as a Tool for Human Dignity Protection. One of the tools for the protection of human dignity is utilizing the UNSC's power of referrals to the International Criminal Court (ICC). The earlier special tribunals for Rwanda, the former Yugoslavia, and Sierra Leone have brought us a long way in the development of international humanitarian and criminal law. And while the ICC is still developing and its role in international politics has yet to be fully fleshed out, it has grown significantly in importance. Furthermore, the willingness to support the ICC is growing among states, even those with traditionally absolutist views on sovereignty.

While Bill Clinton signed the Rome Statute establishing the ICC at the very end of his presidency in 2000, Congressional objections to jurisdiction over US soldiers and other concerns continue to prevent Senate ratification. The United States, along with Russia, China, India, Pakistan, Indonesia, and most of the Arab world, has still not joined. Although for much of George W. Bush's first term the United States was openly hostile to the court, there has been a great deal of progress in the US-ICC relationship in recent years. The Bush administration pushed through Congress the American Service-Members' Protection Act of 2002, which blocks some cooperation with the court and sanctions the invasion of the Netherlands to liberate any Americans detained for ICC trials. At the UN, it also insisted under the threat of a veto of all peacekeeping missions that any peacekeepers be exempt from the ICC. While the UNSC agreed to provide US personnel an exemption for a few years (UNSC 2002), the effort stalled by 2004.

Today, the United States is increasingly using the ICC to further its foreign policy goals. For instance, in 2005, despite the strong opposition of President Bush to the ICC, the United States abstained from the vote that referred Sudan's President Bashir to the ICC, thus allowing the indictment to occur. In 2011, the United States took a further step. Along with the United Kingdom, France, and non-ICC members China and Russia, the US supported UNSC Resolution 1970, which referred the situation in Libya to the prosecutor of the ICC and called on Libyan authorities to cooperate fully with the Court. In the spring of 2011, the Obama administration opposed deferring several cases relating to the 2007–2008 violence in Kenya. And in the fall of 2011, the Obama administration also sent one hundred military advisers to help Uganda apprehend the head of the Lord's Resistance Army, Joseph Kony, who was indicted by the ICC for the use of child soldiers and other war crimes. Another arrest warrant is out for the president of Sudan, Omar Hassan Ahmad Al Bashir, for war crimes in Darfur.

Since coming into effect on July 1, 2002, the ICC has indicted more than twenty leaders for their abuses in seven African nations. Three state parties have referred situations to the ICC—Uganda, the Democratic Republic of the Congo, and the Central African Republic. In all, 121 nations have joined the treaty, including all of Europe and South America, as well as most democracies.

The Obama administration has signaled its support for the ICC in a variety of ways beyond the support for referrals and indictments. It decided to take up the role of observer in ICC Assembly of States Parties meetings and the Kampala Review Conference. The United States has a program, Rewards for Justice, that makes payments to those who provide information leading to the arrest of indicted fugitives of the ICC. In 2012, President Barack Obama created the Atrocities Prevention Board to coordinate US government prevention activities, including US posture on the ICC's pursuit of atrocities indictments (Scheffer 2012). Its record to date is mixed, and many question whether the Atrocities Prevention Board will survive beyond the Obama administration. In addition, the administration is supporting the ICC in all cases where the ICC has issued an arrest warrant, providing assistance for ICC investigations and prosecutions, including information-sharing and help with witness protection and relocation, and providing diplomatic and political support for the arrest and transfer of ICC fugitives to The Hague (Coughlan 2011).

While ratification of the ICC is probably unrealistic in the near term, the United States should continue providing such prosecutorial, political, and diplomatic support to the Court absent ratification of the Rome Statute. In addition, the United States should increase its public statements in support of ICC investigations. As the new ICC prosecutor mentioned, such statements by high-level government officials can be helpful to the Court on the ground in places where there are ongoing investigations (Council on Foreign Relations 2012).

David Scheffer, the first ambassador for War Crimes Issues, argues that with increased support, the United States has become a de facto member of the ICC and that there is more the United States should do short of de jure participation. The United States could take the initiative in the UNSC to ensure the investigative and prosecutorial costs of the Security Council's referrals to the ICC are at least partially paid for with UN funds. He also suggests repealing the American Service-Members' Protection Act of 2002 (Scheffer 2012).

Others argue that the Council follows a double standard in its referrals—only two in its decade of operations, Sudan and Libya—calling into question its impartiality and independence. Human rights organizations have criticized the UNSC's failure to act in places such as Sri Lanka and Syria, and the fact that the United States, Russia, and China are permanent Security Council members but are not subject to the court's authority. As one human rights activist put it, "When it comes to ICC referrals, the United States, Russia, and China seem more concerned about prosecuting their enemies and protecting their friends" (Human Rights Watch 2012).

Surely, the ICC has shortcomings that must be addressed, including inconsistencies, inexcusably slow processes, and the failure to take action outside of Africa. But overall, in the development of international criminal justice, the growing willingness among states, even those with traditionally absolutist views on sovereignty, to deliver justice is notable. The more involved the United States is in its decisions, the more likely the decisions will do more to protect human dignity.

Conclusion

These recommendations are meant to provide a series of options to further human dignity in the new century. As outlined above, the global environment regarding human dignity is complex, but there is great promise. Increasingly, the world is seeing individuals around the globe standing up for their economic and political rights. At the same time, international institutions are increasing their role in international politics and thus have a growing responsibility in protecting these rights. The UNSC is the most powerful organization when it comes to matters of war and peace, and it must adapt to the changing nature of global politics in the twenty-first century.

Over a dozen years into the twenty-first century, international politics continues to develop at a dynamic and rapid pace. Democratic developments have pushed forward—unevenly across the Middle East but dramatically so with Aung San Suu Kyi being elected to parliament in Burma and South Sudan obtaining independence. These events offer tremendous opportunity for progress—but also risk descending into chaos. Also, the long festering conflicts in Somalia, Yemen, the Democratic Republic of the Congo, and Kashmir as well as the civil war in Mali and the crisis in Syria will demand greater attention. Surely, the instances of violations of human dignity will continue to pose challenges for decades to come.

Especially as awareness and capacity to act grow, calls to address violations of human dignity will grow too. Whether the UNSC will be up to the task will depend in large part on stronger US leadership in the decades ahead. We must meet that challenge to be, as President Obama has said, on the right side of history (Obama 2011).

Notes

1. In 1965, the UN Charter was amended to expand the UNSC from eleven to fifteen members, adding four impermanent members. Amending the Charter requires approval of two-thirds of the UN General Assembly and ratification of domestic implementing legislation by two-thirds of the member states, including all of the P-5.

2. Some disagree with this assertion. Ian Hurd has an interesting essay arguing that enlargement might not add to legitimacy. See Ian Hurd, "Myths of Membership: The Politics of Legitimization in UN Security Council Reform," in Paul F. Diehl and Brian Frederking,

The Politics of Global Governance: International Organizations in an Interdependent World,
4th ed. (Boulder, CO: Lynne Rienner, 2010), 91–110.

3. See UNSC Resolution 2085, UN.org.

4. Current Critical Rule of Law and Other Civilian Capability Gaps in United Nations
Peacekeeping Operations, June 2, 2010, 1. Note that the United States built barracks for the
Congolese armed forces battalion trained in the Democratic Republic of the Congo, African
Union: email exchange with DOD November 1, 2010.

References

Annan, Kofi. 1999. "In Statement to North Atlantic Treaty Organization." Brussels,
Belgium. January 28.

Bellamy, Alex J., and Paul D. Williams. 2011. "Côte d'Ivoire, Libya and the Responsibility to Protect." *International Affairs* 87: 825–50.

Coughlan, Geraldine. 2011. "Interview with U.S. Ambassador-at-large for War Crimes
Issues, Stephen Rapp." Radio Netherlands Worldwide. January 7.

Council on Foreign Relations. 2011."Public Opinion on Global Issues, Chapter 8: World
Opinion on Human Rights." Accessed April 18, 2014. http://www.cfr.org/thinktank
/iigg/pop/index.html.

———. 2012. "The International Criminal Court: A New Approach to International
Relations." Accessed September 21, 2012. http://www.cfr.org/courts-and-tribunals
/international-criminal-court-new-approach-international-relations/p29351.

Holt, Victoria, and Glyn Taylor. 2009. "Protecting Civilians in the Context of United
Nations Peacekeeping Operations: Successes, Setbacks, and Remaining Challenges."
New York: United Nations.

Human Rights Watch. 2012. "UN Security Council: Address Inconsistency in ICC Referrals." Accessed January 6, 2013. http://www.hrw.org/news/2012/10/16/un-security
-council-address-inconsistency-icc-referrals-0.

International Commission on Intervention and State Sovereignty (ICISS). 2001. "Responsibility to Protect." Ottawa: International Commission on Intervention and
State Sovereignty.

Khan, Azmat. 2012. "Violence Intensifies in Homs after U.N. Resolution on Syria Fails."
PBS. February 6. http://www.pbs.org/wgbh/pages/frontline/foreign-affairs-defense
/syria-undercover/violence-intensifies-in-homs-after-u-n-resolution-on-syria-fails/.

Kumbaro, Dajena. 2001. "The Kosovo Crisis in an International Law Perspective: Self Determination, Territorial Integrity and the NATO Intervention." Albania: North Atlantic
Treaty Organization.

Lynch, Marc. 2012. "Making the Arab League Work." *Foreign Policy,* April 8. http://
www.foreignpolicy.com/posts/2012/04/08/making_the_arab_league_matter#sthash
.40aiT9qJ.dpbs.

McDonald, Kara and Stewart Patrick. 2010. "UN Security Council Enlargement and
U.S. Interests." Council on Foreign Relations. Accessed August 1, 2013. http://www
.cfr.org/international-organizations-and-alliances/un-security-council-enlargement
-us-interests/p23363.

Mohammed, Arshad and Andrew Osborn. 2013. "Kerry: Syrian Surrender of Chemical Arms Could Stop U.S. Attack." *Reuters,* September 9. Accessed April 18, 2014.

http://www.reuters.com/article/2013/09/09/us-syria-crisis-kerry-idUSBRE9880
BV20130909.

Obama, Barack. 2011. "Remarks by the President on the Middle East and North Africa." May 19. Department of State, Washington, DC.

Pew Research Center for the People and the Press. 2013. "America's Place in the World 2013." Accessed December 3, 2013. http://www.people-press.org/2013/12/03/public
-sees-u-s-power-declining-as-support-for-global-engagement-slips/.

Scheffer, David. 2012. "America's Embrace of the International Criminal Court." *Jurist Forum*, July 2. http://jurist.org/forum/2012/07/dan-scheffer-us-icc.php.

Soderberg, Nancy E. 2007. "U.S. Support for UN Peacekeeping; Areas for Additional DOD Assistance." Center for Technology and National Security Policy. National Defense University Press.

———. 2011. "Enhancing U.S. Support for UN Peacekeeping." *Prism* 2 (2). National Defense University Press.

United Nations. 2000. "Report of the Panel on United Nations Peace Operations—Brahimi Report." *UN Document A/55/305-S/2000/809*. August 21.

United Nations Department of Peacekeeping Operations and Department of Field Support (UNDPKO and DFS). 2009. "A New Partnership Agenda Charting a New Horizon for UN Peacekeeping." New York: United Nations Department of Peacekeeping Operations and Department of Field Support.

United Nations General Assembly. 2005. "60/1 2005 World Summit Document." *UN Document A/RES/60/1*. October 24.

United Nations Secretary-General. 2006. "Peace Operations 2010 Reform Strategy." New York: United Nations.

United Nations Security Council. 1998. "Resolution 1199 (1998)." *UN Document S/RES/1199*. September 23.

———. 2000. "Resolution 1315 (2000)." *UN Document S/RES/1315*. August 14.

———. 2002. "Resolution 1422 (2002)." *UN Document S/RES/1422*. July 12.

US Agency for International Development (USAID). Accessed April 18, 2014. http://
www.usaid.gov/crisis/syria.

US Department of Defense. 2010. "Quadrennial Defense Review." Washington DC:
US Department of Defense.

US National Security Council. 2010. "National Security Strategy." White House.
Washington DC.

CHAPTER 2

The Responsibility to Respect

*Victims and Human Dignity at the
International Criminal Court*

TOD LINDBERG

The concept of "human dignity" or the "dignity of the person" has become increasingly important to the normative framework of national and international law, as well as to the broader discourse on human, political, and civil rights. Some have sought in the concept of equal dignity a ground for human rights as such. Though some have taken a very contrary view, wondering whether the concept of dignity adds anything at all to discourse on rights and duties, others have rejected what they consider to be excessive claims made in the name of dignity but have sought to retain the concept in some other capacity (M. Rosen 2012, 1–10). The editors of this book in chapter 1 have proposed a definition of dignity grounded in a classically liberal view of the autonomous individual in pursuit of her own vision of the good in the context of a Hegelian ethics of mutual recognition: Human dignity is the fundamental capacity of human beings to apply their gifts to thrive. As such, it requires social recognition of each person's inherent value and claim to equal access to opportunity. To be meaningful, human dignity must be institutionalized in practice and governance.

The question before authors of chapters in this book is how international institutions serve to advance human dignity according to the definition above and how they might better do so. The issue boils down to how well an international institution does foster or can foster the "social recognition of each person's inherent value and claim to equal access to opportunity"—which is the prerequisite of "the fundamental capacity of human beings to apply their gifts to thrive." How well an international institution serves to promote "social recognition" of this view of human beings is an eminently reasonable and answerable question. Promotion of "social recognition" is a matter, first, of embracing institutionally a principle of equal treatment of persons (and their right to equal access to opportunity) and second, of extending that view outward by the means at the disposal of the institution.

The International Criminal Court (ICC or Court) at the Hague, established by the Rome Statute of 1998, has as the subject matter of its jurisdiction some of the world's worst atrocity crimes: genocide, crimes against humanity, war crimes and, not yet in effect, the crime of aggression. As of this writing, the Court has 121 member states. The United States is not a member, but since the second term of the George W. Bush administration, has adopted evolving policies of increased cooperation with the Court. Its work in the promotion of human dignity is the subject of this essay. We will consider here especially the Court's novel work with victims of atrocity crimes. The Court has a treaty mandate not only to hold perpetrators of crimes to account but also to be cognizant of the plight of victims. This is not merely a matter of vindicating the rights of victims but includes as well a sense on the part of the Court throughout its operations of an institutional responsibility to show respect for the dignity of victims and their suffering.

Crime Victims and Their Rights

However one chooses to approach the substantive content of "human dignity," the term would be bereft of all meaning if we could not say with some confidence that those who have fallen prey to *genocidaires* and perpetrators of atrocities—including murder, forced relocation or ethnic cleansing, enslavement, child-soldier conscription, rape, and other such criminal acts specified in the Rome statute—have also suffered an affront to their dignity as human beings. The jurisdiction of the ICC begins with *crimes*. And crimes begin with harm suffered by *victims* at the hands of perpetrators.

Well-functioning modern national criminal justice systems exist to enforce the law, which they do by investigating harm suffered by victims, identifying suspected perpetrators, proving their guilt against the presumption of innocence of the accused (who also have specified rights, such as the ability to confront their accusers), and imposing punishment.[1] In addition to the criminal law, victims have recourse to civil courts and the law of torts to claim compensatory and sometimes punitive damages for losses they have suffered. These modern legal systems are backed by the sovereign power of states, which can compel individuals to participate in criminal and civil proceedings under threat of imprisonment for defiance; incarcerate individuals against their will upon and in some cases prior to conviction; exact fines upon conviction; in some jurisdictions, impose the death penalty upon conviction or other corporeal punishments; and order damages to be paid on findings of liability.

The role of the victim in these state proceedings varies from jurisdiction to jurisdiction and has evolved over time. At risk of oversimplification, modern criminal (though not civil) justice systems have traditionally tended to depersonalize crime and punishment; the offense is deemed to have been committed not merely against the person of the victim but also against the state itself (or "the people"). Such a view taken to an extreme essentially deals the victim out of the proceedings beyond the role of mere evidence-giver. No special solicitation is due for the suffering of the victim, whose opinions about the personal effect of the crime are irrelevant to the determination of guilt or innocence and perhaps even to sentencing (especially during the heyday of the view of imprisonment as correctional in character—that is, aimed at rehabilitating the convict).

In response to the perceived indifference of the legal system to victims, by the 1970s various movements promoting victim's rights began to gain strength in the United States, leading to widespread passage of so-called Victims' Bill of Rights legislation at the state level. The protections enumerated in such legislation typically include the right to be notified of and be present at proceedings, to make a statement to the court, and to receive restitution.

Rule 60 of the Federal Rules of Criminal Procedure is devoted to victims' rights, which include timely notice of proceedings, a qualified right to attend proceedings, and a "Right to Be Heard on Release, a Plea, or Sentencing." Advocacy organizations have also long promoted a federal constitutional amendment spelling out victims' rights. At a more philosophical level, the priorities of the justice system leaned away from its traditional emphasis on retributive justice (centered on criminals) and toward restorative justice (centered on victims) and the desire to promote healing, rehabilitation, empowerment, a sense of closure, and in the context of atrocities, reconciliation at the community or even the national level (SáCouto and Cleary 2008, 77–78).

The increased attention to victims' rights has not been without controversy (O'Hara 2005, 230–33). The biggest concern is that victims' rights will come at the expense of the accused, undermining the presumption of innocence and the legal norm dating to Blackstone: "better that ten guilty persons escape, than that one innocent suffer" (Mosteller 1997). O'Hara notes that notwithstanding swings of the pendulum from victims' to defendants' rights, the "trend in the direction of victim involvement will no doubt continue" (2005, 242).

For comparative purposes, the civil law systems prevalent in continental Europe make it "easier to accommodate the interests of victims at trial without disturbing the adversarial balance that is central to American criminal trials" (Pizzi and Perron 1996, 41). Pizzi and Perron describe the occasionally used German *Nebenklage* procedure, which allows for the participation of victims (or their lawyers) of such serious crimes as murder, assault, kidnapping, and rape as a secondary accuser during the trial. "A victim who chooses to participate as a secondary accuser becomes, in essence, a party at the criminal trial and receives treatment equal to that afforded the defendant in the courtroom" (60). T. Markus Funk notes, "In most civil law countries, victims ('injured persons') long possessed the right to participate at various stages of the criminal process, from the pre-trial phase to the appeal. Such participatory rights included the qualified right to cross-examine witnesses, introduce evidence, brief motions, and seek additional investigation" (2010, 30–31).

A turning point in the movement of victims' rights into the arena of international law came in 1985 with the adoption by the UN General Assembly of its Resolution 40/34, "Declaration of Basic Principles of Justice for Victims of Crime and Abuse of Power." Funk writes, "The Basic Principles . . . sought to internationalize victim-centric rights that by the mid-1980s had received broad acceptance in many domestic justice systems" (38). The 1985 Declaration focused on rights of individuals within national justice systems. Yet the establishment of victims' rights internationally proceeded swiftly in regional courts and culminated in the extensive protections for victims written into the Rome Statute of 1998. In 2006, the UN General Assembly revisited the subject of victims, this time explicitly in the context of international law, passing its Resolution 60/147, "Basic Principles and Guidelines on the Right to a Remedy and Reparation for Victims of Gross Violations of International Human Rights Law and Serious Violations of International Law."

The Workings of the Court

The primary purpose of the ICC is to prosecute the worst perpetrators of human rights violations, but another important purpose is to give victims recognition and a chance to reconcile. The Court has not only a punitive function but also a restorative function (ICC 2009a, ¶3). The ICC does this by granting broad participatory rights to victims during Court proceedings, protecting victims and witnesses that come to the Court, providing access to reparations, and through the workings of its trust fund for victims (Bassiouni 2006, 230). Through these processes, the Court hopes not only to charge human rights offenders and deter future atrocities but also to demonstrate respect for victims and their suffering.

The Rome statute, as well as the Rules of Procedure and Evidence (RPE), applied in 2002, established the Court's forward-leaning system of victims' rights. Rule 85 defines victims as "natural persons who have suffered harm as a result of the commission of any crime within the jurisdiction of the Court." The term also applies to "organizations or institutions that have sustained direct harm to any of their property which is dedicated to religion, education, art or science or charitable purposes, and to their historical monuments, hospitals and other places and objects for humanitarian purposes" (ICC 2002b, 85). The definition of "victim" set forth by the ICC is very inclusive: It incorporates people harmed directly or indirectly by human rights violations as well as by certain institutions. The breadth of the definition greatly increases the number of potential victims who have access to the Court.

To obtain rights as a victim, applicants must satisfy certain criteria, first of which is meeting the definition spelled out in Rule 85. Next, applicants must be able to prove that they were harmed (directly or indirectly) by the accused. Whereas the notion of "harm" is established on a case-by-case basis, it generally refers to physical pain, economic loss, or psychological trauma. Candidates must then fall within the complementarity jurisdiction of the Court. (In other words, national courts must be unavailing in their circumstances: "[T]he Court shall determine that a case is inadmissible where . . . the case is being investigated or prosecuted by a State which has jurisdiction over it, unless the State is unwilling or unable genuinely to carry out the investigation or prosecution" [ICC 2002a, 17.1{a}].) Finally, claimants must prove a causal link between the actions of the accused and the harm they suffered (Guhr 2008, 130). Potential victims fill out an application (typically with the assistance of nongovernmental organization [NGO] personnel locally) setting forth these facts and send it to the Victims Participation and Reparations Section (VPRS), which then passes the application on to the appropriate chamber of the Court—the Pre-Trial, Trial, or Appeals Chambers—to determine if the victim has participatory rights at that stage of the proceedings (ICC 2010e, 19–20).[2] Between 2005 and 2011, the VPRS received 4,773 applications for participation, declaring 2,259 as victims (ICC 2011a, 1).

An applicant granted the status of "victim" gains the right to participate in the trial in that capacity rather than merely as a witness. Whereas witnesses to crimes are evidence-givers in a particular circumstance, victims in the ICC have an enhanced status. They have the right to participation, information, legal representation, safety, and dignity throughout the proceedings (ICC 2010e, 12).

The scope of the role granted to victims during the course of a trial is somewhat ambiguous. The Rome statute uses the terms "party" as well as "participant" to refer to victims. Victims as participants do not have the right to present evidence or examine witnesses, but victims as parties may have these rights (Bassiouni 2006, 230). Notwithstanding the ambiguity of the Rome statute, the Court agrees that victims can participate by attending Court hearings, making opening and closing statements, giving observations to judges during the investigation stage, presenting their views during the pretrial phase, and examining and cross-examining witnesses (ICC 2010e, 13).

According to Article 68 of the Rome Statute, victims can present their views where their personal interests are affected. This ambiguous definition leaves the particulars of participation up to each chamber. Because the Court does not operate on the principle of stare decisis, victim contribution can vary greatly from case to case. Though the Rome statute explicitly designates the ability of victims to participate during the pretrial and reparations stages, participation rights during the rest of the proceedings are less clear (ICC 2002a, 57, 75). A decision in the *Lubanga* case, however, may signal an augmentation of participation. The *Lubanga* case granted victims the right to participate in the investigations stage of a situation in order "to clarify the facts, to punish the perpetrators of crimes and to request reparations of the harm suffered" (ICC 2006, 16).

When victims appear before the ICC, they almost always do so with legal representation. These representatives are important because victims themselves usually lack legal expertise and do not understand the complex workings of the Court. Victims are allowed to choose their own legal representation, or it can be provided to them through the Court's registrar. In cases with a large number of victims, the Court may compel them to choose a common legal representative (ICC 2002b, 90). Under the Court's Rules of Procedure and Evidence, the registrar, whose office performs the administrative functions of the Court, is responsible for "assisting [victims] in obtaining legal advice and organizing their legal representation, and providing their legal representatives with adequate support, assistance and information" (ICC 2002b, 16). Within the registrar's office, the VPRS is the "victims' first point of contact with the Court," according to the website of the Office of Public Counsel for Victims (OPCV). The VPRS ensures that all victims have some form of representation.

Although the principal function of the VPRS is procedural—ensuring that victims' paperwork is properly filed and confirming that victims understand their rights before the Court—the Registry also has a statutory responsibility to ensure that victims have adequate representation. To this end, the registrar established the independent OPCV in 2005. The OPCV provides research and aid to victims' legal representatives and can also offer experienced individuals to serve as victims' representatives. In the *Lubanga* case, the OPCV represented individual victims and helped the Court by "undertaking . . . a coordinating and amicus curiae role" (ICC 2010a, 5). The OPCV has an impressive track record: From its establishment through 2010, the relatively small office assisted over thirty legal representatives and 2,000 victims (ICC 2010a, 6–8).

Victims who appear before the ICC do so at a certain risk. Those appearing before the Court to answer its serious charges have all been powerful figures, at least formerly capable of exacting harm on victims who might speak out against them. The Court has a responsibility to ensure that its proceedings are fair to the accused. At the same time, the Court must prevent any further harm befalling the victims. Therefore, throughout a trial, victim security and protection receive special consideration (ICC 2002a, 57, 64; ICC 2002b, 87, 88).

The Court has a duty to protect the confidentiality of witnesses and victims. Article 87 in particular notes that a chamber, at the request of a victim, can hold a hearing in camera and can order "that the name of the victim . . . be expunged from the public records of the Chamber." The Chamber can also prevent the prosecutor and defense counsel from disclosing a victim's identity to a third party and use technology to disguise appearances during testimony (ICC 2002b, 87).

In addition to confidentiality, the Court also provides for victims' physical security during and after a trial. Article 43 of the Rome statute calls for the creation of a Victims and Witnesses Unit (VWU) within the Registry responsible for victim protection. The Unit provides short- and long-term security for victims, as well as counseling and medical assistance (ICC 2002b, 17, 18). The VWU faces a serious ongoing challenge given the large number of victims typically associated with the crimes charged at the ICC. For example, there were ninety-three victims represented in the *Lubanga* trial alone (ICC 2009b, 5). Thus, the Court's agents must constantly adapt to new territories and conditions, and continually reassess the threat of reprisal to current and former victims.

One way the VWU attempts to protect victims is through relocation. Here, state parties have assisted. A common method is for states to agree to "host protected persons and [to be] responsible for all expenses related to assistance needs" (ICC 2010c, 6). At this writing, the Court had signed ten such agreements with state parties. State parties can also choose to contribute to the Special Fund for Relocations. If a state party has the resources to support a victim but for some reason cannot protect him or her in its own territory, it can contribute money to the fund. A state party willing to host a protected person but perhaps unable to pay the cost of doing so can then obtain money from the fund to defray expenses. State parties can also pay to support victims abroad. Although the psychological shock of relocation may cause additional harm to a victim, sometimes in the interest of safety there is little choice but to opt for a fresh start in a new state. If relocation is necessary, the ICC tries to place victims in territories on the same continent (ICC 2010c, 7). The Court tries to be mindful of the particular needs of individual victims.

The Court also helps victims through its promise of reparations. Whereas monetary support cannot necessarily annul the trauma victims have experienced, oftentimes economic incentives allow victims to begin to move on with their lives. The payment of reparations is a significant element of the ICC's protections for victims, as the international community struggles collectively to make amends for gross misdeeds.

Article 75 provides for reparations to victims. After the ICC convicts a person, the Court can order reparations in the form of a fine or forfeited property. These payments can be made only to victims and their families who have been harmed by the crimes for which the defendant has been convicted. Reparations under international law traditionally take the form of restitution, compensation, rehabilitation, satisfaction, and guarantees of nonrepetition (IFHR 2010, 5). Under RPE 94, victims can submit a formal reparations request by submitting an application to the VPRS. The Court then determines whether there is a basis for an award. Reparations from convicted criminals can take the form of a direct payment to victims or a mandatory contribution to the Trust Fund for Victims (TFV).

The TFV was established under Rome Statute Article 79 and RPE 98. It is responsible for implementing reparation payments and offering rehabilitation to victims. Under RPE 98, the TFV is to receive reparation payments from ICC criminals, but as of this writing there has yet to be a sentencing hearing before the ICC, and no money has flowed into the TFV through this mechanism. Instead, the TFV has collected donations from states and individuals committed to supporting the reintegration of victims into their communities. The TFV gives material support to individual victims and funds on-site physical and mental rehabilitation centers for victims who could not appear before the ICC. Most of the TFV's efforts are dedicated to communal integration and rehabilitation (IFHR 2010, 5). Under the TFV's second mandate, it can disburse funds to help victims in any situation being investigated by the Court, whether or not the victims have suffered directly from the crimes specifically charged in Court (IFHR 2010, 4).

The TFV is something of a breakthrough in the pursuit of international justice: Since 2008, "the TFV has directly reached an estimated 70,000 victims of crimes under the jurisdiction of the ICC. The great majority of these are victims from affected communities who are being reached through the TFV's reconciliation projects" (ICC 2010b, 7). At this writing, the TFV has sixteen active programs in Uganda helping an estimated 29,300 people. Most programs in Uganda are dedicated to helping mutilation victims, providing education grants, and promoting communal savings. There are also thirteen active projects in the Democratic Republic of Congo reaching 40,600 victims (ICC 2010b, 12). In 2011, the TFV raised €3.2 million to fund its diverse programs (ICC 2012). The largest state party donor in 2011 was the United Kingdom, which contributed £500,000 (ICC 2011b).

TFV activities have won acclaim for their efforts to identify and meet individual needs of victims. The TFV runs a varied array of programs designed for distinct groups of victims. For example, the TFV's sixteen programs in Uganda target different sectors of the population. The Northeast Chili Producers Association has helped 2,700 victims in the agricultural district of Lira by giving "farming materials in order to jumpstart local farmers' production and counseling to strengthen the agricultural community." At the same time, programs in the Gulu and Amuru regions hold "healing of memory" sessions for torture victims to speak about their experiences. In northern Uganda, one NGO performed reconstructive surgery for 160 mutilation victims at a hospital in Gulu. There is also an education and protection program for girls at risk of sexual violence in the Oyam District (ICC 2010d). These initiatives are a small sample of the projects paid for by the TFV.

The TFV has had a measurable impact. One survivor of a brutal Lord's Resistance Army attack commented on how the TFV helped her transform her life, saying "my stay at the Trust Fund's center removed me from my daily experience." She detailed how after the TFV provided her with training, three liters of cooking oil, three packets of wheat flour, cups, and a dozen plates, she was able make a profit selling cassava chips enough to support her husband and family (ICC 2010b, 18). Beneficiaries of TFV programs in Uganda have praised its programs, saying "the implementation of the activities funded by the Trust Fund for victims of the ICC developed hope, trust, confidence and a sense of belonging by victims. This move as it stands has developed peace of mind and trust among the victims and the affected communities" (VRWG 2010, 19).

The success of the TFV and the Court's broader outreach effort to victims is at least partially dependent on the participation of various human rights groups and NGOs. Organizations such as the Association of Volunteers in International Service and Interplast Holland implement the projects funded by the TFV (ICC 2010b, 11). Other groups are responsible for using their access in certain countries to provide information to the Office of the Prosecutor during investigations. Institutions such as Redress submit amicus curiae briefs to the Court and act as a critical oversight mechanism. Furthermore, NGOs play a large role in the ICC's outreach method. The ICC, tucked away at The Hague, does not have access to remote villages where human rights violations take place. The NGOs, who are often able to gain entry into difficult locales, take responsibility for promoting the potential benefits of working with the ICC (as well as alerting them to the security dangers of doing so).

The expansion of victims' participation through the ICC represents an augmentation of victims' rights globally. NGOs in the Democratic Republic of Congo have praised the role of the Court, contending that the ICC "has had a positive impact as it [has] allowed victims to feel valued through their implication in the legal process" (VRWG 2010, 18).

A Critical Review

Although the ICC and various NGOs have created a unique framework for the protection of victims' rights and respect for their dignity, the ICC remains a mostly untested institution, and many problems remain. First, it is clear the ICC has a large outreach dilemma. Although NGOs have been useful in collecting information on cases and helping victims apply, many potential victims still see the ICC as "just a rumor, more or less" (Glassborrow 2007). The ICC must work on globalizing awareness of its operations so that victims of atrocity crimes will feel more comfortable stepping forward.

Far from The Hague, the operation of the Court is often misunderstood. People who have been victims of atrocity crimes often fail to understand why the Office of the Prosecutor chooses to investigate certain specific incidents and not others. Victims in regions of Ituri (Democratic Republic of the Congo) not covered by present charges, for example, do not understand why "victims who suffer from the same atrocities, by the same groups, were not taken into account by investigators" (VRGW 2010, 13). But of course the prosecutor cannot feasibly investigate every atrocity incident, nor is it the function of a Court to do so: The guilt of perpetrators needs to be decisively proven, not comprehensively so in the sense of each atrocity committed. Yet this process leaves some victims on the outside. The Court must do all it can to keep them informed and to attend to their needs as well. But this limitation points to a need for broader institutional support for victims of atrocity crimes internationally.

Furthermore, the ICC has been an institution that works slowly and is consistently backed up with paperwork. The Registry, for example, has often been unable to process victim applications in a timely fashion, resulting in the denial of participation to persons who should legitimately be classified as victims (VRWG 2011, 7). The ICC must work to streamline its operations if it wishes to maintain the standards it has set for itself.

Other institutional growing pains are also apparent. The Rome statute and RPE state that victims must be informed at various stages of the proceedings, but as of this writing, no clear understanding has emerged of what that entails (ICC 2002a, 53; ICC 2002b, 50, 59, 69). Also, the extent of victims' rights will continue to evolve as judges make different rulings concerning victim participation (Spiga 2010, 185). It is too soon to say with any precision where the Court will end up and therefore too soon to assess its ultimate adequacy in attending to the human needs of victims.

The slow pace of trials and the paucity of convictions have contributed to a feeling of lassitude for some victims directly participating in the ICC. For victims, justice delayed can indeed look like justice denied. The boost to the credibility of the Court from the generally cautious manner in which it has operated is one side of the coin; the other is a loss of credibility that comes from moving slowly.

Observers report that off-site victims often fail to understand the Court's practical successes. The Court's own self-assessment notes that victims in Ituri feel they are "shadows, without a face, without a voice, without light, wondering when the truth on . . . the crimes will be revealed" (VRWG 2010, 16).

Some have expressed concern that the Court's concern for the rights of victims goes too far, impinging on the rights of the accused. One critic cites the lack of clarity as to the type of fact-finding the Court employs with regard to victim participation: a judge-driven inquisitorial method or a party-driven accusatorial method (Zappalà 2010, 139). Some commentators have expressed concern that the decision in the *Lubanga* case represents a "systemic encroachment on the rights of the accused" (Guhr 2008, 127).

A stocktaking session devoted to the Court's treatment of victims at its Assembly of States Parties review conference in Kampala in 2010 frankly acknowledged a number of challenges the Court faces, especially in outreach. The Court has now made a priority of outreach to women and children (ICC 2010a, 80). The review conference also acknowledged the potential problem of development of unrealistic expectations among victims: "[I]t is inherently impossible to repair the losses and fully alleviate the suffering caused by heinous international crimes" (ICC 2010a, 97). Awareness of the existence of the TFV may itself create undue expectations for relief; the TFV will never have sufficient assets to meet the needs of all claimants and will accordingly have to target its efforts (Keller 2007).

As the Court matures, it must build on its symbolic and substantive successes in the expansion of victims' rights and respect for the dignity of victims to include concrete improvements in the lives of victims. The ICC currently offers the most forward-leaning example of victim advocacy in the international system. Gioia Greco calls its work "a glaring achievement in the international field" (2007, 531). But there is much work still to do to fully operationalize its commitment to victims (Bachvarova 2011). And as noted, the court by the nature of its mandate will never reach all victims of atrocities, only those harmed by the specific crimes charged in each case. This leaves a substantial gap that other institutions and national governments must fill.

Rights and Dignity

The Court mainly uses the language of "rights" with regard to its obligations toward victims. What specific and different obligations the Court perceives with regard to the *dignity* of victims is a topic that has received little attention.

This primary focus on rights is hardly unique to the Court. Courtrooms, at the national or international level, are in the business of adjudicating the law, and the law confers rights as well as obligations. Rights lie at the core of our understanding of the modern political world, at both the national level (for example, the US Bill of Rights) and increasingly, internationally (for example, the Universal Declaration of Human Rights, adopted by the UN General Assembly in Paris in 1948). In addition, lawyers—no less international lawyers—are accustomed to thinking in terms of the rights of individuals: what they are, how to enforce them, how to reconcile them when they come into conflict.

And it is possible, of course, to identify or create new rights where they are perceived to be wanting, as in the case of victims' rights. I would like to suggest, however, that as the operation of the ICC has shown, precisely which rights victims can properly claim does not exhaust the subject of how to treat victims.

Consider the case of the woman mentioned above who received TFV start-up supplies for a business through which she was able to support her family. It is difficult to understand how a claim of right underlays the TFV's action—but perfectly easy to understand the TFV's action in terms of its perceived responsibility to respect the dignity of the woman. So the Court itself, in its solicitude for victims, seems to be venturing into a territory that goes beyond the rights individuals may have.

One fully respects the rights of others simply by refraining from violating those rights. A government respects people's rights by first refraining from violating them and second by maintaining court systems that intervene to annul B's reaction to A's action when A has the right to act as A did (Kojève 2000, 40). If A has the right to walk peaceably down the street and B assaults her and steals her purse, the criminal justice system will seek to hold B to account. The court is limited in what it can do to annul what B has done. Upon a finding of guilt, it can order B to pay damages or penalties and sentence B to prison. In the context of atrocities, the affected people have a right to their lives, and where a perpetrator of atrocities tramples on it, the perpetrator must be held to account. The ICC as a "court of last resort" performs this function with respect to perpetrators of some of the world's worst atrocities. But no court can ever simply *undo* what such a perpetrator has done. A rights-vindicating justice system, even on an international scale, can go only so far. The question, then, is whether it can go further in the promotion of "the fundamental capacity of human beings to apply their gifts to thrive" by some means other than the acknowledgment and vindication of rights. The operation of the ICC suggests that it can.

There is a distinction to be drawn between respecting the rights of others and respecting others. Clearly, when a person tramples on another's rights, for example, by perpetrating horrendous crimes of the kind within the jurisdiction of the ICC, that culpable individual is also failing to respect other persons. But when one refrains from violating another's rights, one has not necessarily shown respect for the other. One can be in conformity with respect for the rights of another while at the same time conducting oneself in a fashion that shows no respect for another beyond those rights. If I have a right to walk peaceably down the street, you—a person or a government—have a duty to allow me to do so. If you are the government, and therefore the guarantor of rights and the rule of law, you also have an obligation to take action to annul a mugger's unwillingness to let me walk peaceably down the street. But that does not exhaust the question of our relations. And as we have seen, annulling the wrongful action of the perpetrator is a necessary step with real consequences for the criminal once convicted but never sufficient to undo the mugging. If anything, this is even easier to see contemplating the horror of the Tutsi victims in Rwanda or the Syrians shelled by their own government.

I would suggest that outside the circle representing your rights as an individual lies an encompassing circle, coextensive with your person, representing your dignity as a human being. It is not enough for me to refrain from violating the inner circle of your rights. Under certain circumstances, neither must I trespass on the encompassing circle of your dignity. I have a responsibility to respect you—a responsibility not to breach that circle and, indeed, when others have breached it, to do what I can to help you repair it and restore its integrity.

Under what circumstances? Clearly, not all. A stand-up comic typically punctures the dignity of self and others. A world in which all persons show respect for all other persons at all times—whether the others are present or not—would be a dull and humorless dystopia. But certainly a person acting under color of authority, whether of a government or an international court, owes respect to those who come before her. And the institution in question, in the performance of its functions, ought also seek to institutionalize the responsibility to respect, not only in the negative sense of refraining from actions that trespass on dignity, but also in buttressing the dignity of individuals when others have trespassed. It seems that the ICC has sought to do this; even if it has been only partially successful, the Court itself deserves an according measure of respect from those who believe that a concept of dignity contributes something to human thriving that rights alone do not account for.

I note the variability of the content of dignity, at least as I understand it (M. Rosen 2012, 63–77). It is easy to see that an atrocity crime also constitutes an affront to the dignity of its victim. Likewise, it is hard to imagine how hurling vile insults into the face of another could be construed as anything other than an affront to dignity. Yet one's sense of dignity, or the respect one might like to receive, also has a substantial social and cultural component. Exposing oneself to the gaze of others while wearing merely a two-piece swimsuit is for one woman a day at the beach but for another an unthinkable display of immodesty.

There is no easy resolution to this problem. Claims to respect for dignity cannot be deemed legitimate solely on the basis of their assertion; indeed, dignity considered apart from right (that is, the outer, doughnut-shaped area of the encompassing circle) would not, per se, seem to generate rights claims at all. You do not have a *right* not to be offended or affronted.[3] But at the same time, any regard for the dignity of others must entail inquiry at some level into the matter of what others might consider an affront.

This inquiry is especially important with regard to those who have suffered in some of the worst circumstances known to humankind. As Judith Herman notes: "Traumatic events call into question basic human relationships. They breach the attachments of family, friendship, love, and community. They shatter the construction of the self that is formed and sustained in relation to others. They undermine the belief systems that give meaning to human experience. They violate the victim's faith in a natural or divine order and cast the victim into a state of existential crisis" (1997, 51).

Victims have in common the perpetration of crimes against them, but their responses are their own. Martha Minow writes: "Survivors of violence often ache for retribution against identifiable perpetrators, and for public acknowledgement of what happened. Some want financial redress; psychological or spiritual healing seems crucial to others. Some survivors, and their fellow citizens, place higher priorities on moving ahead with life, building or rebuilding trust across previously divided groups, and establishing or strengthening democratic institutions. Many believe that the entire society needs to stand behind efforts to punish the wrongdoers, and to deter any such conduct in the future. People understandably may have great trouble sorting out priorities among these possibilities" (1998, 4).

In responding, one size does not fit all. Determining an appropriate response on an individual basis is an essential element of the respect one must pay. Albeit imperfectly, in the ICC's nevertheless unprecedented regard for victims, the Court and its officers are working to fulfill this responsibility to respect.

Your dignity begins where you are, one might say: The first place one desires appropriate recognition and respect is where one finds oneself right now—within one's family, in one's community, walking peaceably alongside strangers on the street. It is not merely human rights that are violated in the case of atrocities, it is also this sense of dignity. I believe that when people say they feel violated, as crime victims often do, it is not merely the physical, material aspect of the crime to which they are reacting. Indeed, one may feel violated in the same way in the absence of the commission of any crime—perhaps as a result of an unwanted gaze that breaches one's sense of privacy (J. Rosen 2000, 18–20).

This sense of violation marks an affront to one's dignity. A court may take action to annul a violation of one's rights. But no court can ever annul such an affront to a person's dignity. All it or any institution or anyone can do—locally, nationally, or internationally—is accord such a person the respect all persons feel is their due, including respect for the affront suffered. That is the responsibility to respect in its broadest sense.

Notes

Thanks to Carly Hafner for research assistance.

1. I leave aside consideration of so-called victimless crimes.

2. A copy of this form can be found at "Application Form," http://www.icc-cpi.int/NR/rdonlyres/48A75CF0-E38E-48A7-A9E0-026ADD32553D/0/SAFIndividualEng.pdf.

3. Some, of course, do think they have a right not to be offended or affronted. It is the responsibility of liberal political and juridical order to address the requirements of their dignity without granting this right. The International Criminal Court has been accused of an imperialist propensity, namely the imposition on others of a narrowly Western set of values. I reject this characterization but agree that the Court is a classically liberal institution.

References

Bachvarova, Tatiana. 2011. "Victims' Eligibility before the International Criminal Court in Historical and Comparative Context." *International Criminal Law Review* 11 (4): 665–706.

Bassiouni, M. Cherif. 2006. "International Recognition of Victims' Rights." *Human Rights Law Review* 6 (2): 203–79. doi: 10.1093/hrlr/ngl009.

Funk, T. Markus. 2010. *Victims' Rights and Advocacy at the International Criminal Court.* New York: Oxford University.

Glassborrow, Katie. 2007. "ICC Struggles to Reach Out to Darfuris." *Institute for War and Peace Reporting.* October 26. Accessed August 1, 2013. http://iwpr.net/report -news/icc-struggles-reach-out-darfuris.

Greco, Gioia. 2007. "Victims' Rights Overview under the ICC Legal Framework: A Jurisprudential Analysis." *International Criminal Law Review* 7 (2–3): 531–47.

Guhr, A. H. 2008. "Victim Participation during the Pre-Trial Stage at the International Criminal Court." *International Criminal Law Review* 8 (1–2): 109–40. doi: 10.1163/156753608X265259.

Herman, Judith. 1997. *Trauma and Recovery.* New York: Basic Books.

ICC (International Criminal Court). 2002a. *Rome Statute of the International Criminal Court.* Available at http://www.icc-cpi.int/en_menus/icc/legal%20texts%20and %20tools/official%20journal/Pages/rome%20statute.aspx.

———. 2002b. *Rules of Procedure and Evidence.* Available at http://www.icc-cpi.int/en _menus/icc/legal%20texts%20and%20tools/official%20journal/Pages/rules%20of %20procedure%20and%20evidence.aspx.

———. 2006. Situation in the Democratic Republic of Congo, Case No. ICC-01/04-101: *Decision on the Applications for Participation in the Proceedings.* Accessed August 1, 2013. http://www.vrwg.org/VRWG_DOC/2010_Apr_VRWG_Impact _of_ICC_on_victims.pdf.

———. 2009a. Assembly of States Parties. "Report of the Court on the Strategy in Relation to Victims." Accessed August 1, 2013. http://www.icc-cpi.int/iccdocs/asp _docs/ASP8/ICC-ASP-8-45-ENG.pdf.

———. 2009b. "Summary Report" (paper presented at The Round Table on the Protection of Victims and Witnesses, The Hague, January 29–30, 2009). Accessed August 1, 2013. http://www.icc-cpi.int/NR/rdonlyres/19869519-923D-4F67-A61F -35F78E424C68/280579/Report_ENG.pdf.

———. 2010a. Assembly of States Parties. "The Impact of the Rome Statute System on Victims and Affected Communities." Annex V(a) to *Official Records.* Review Conference of the International Criminal Court. Kampala. May 31–June 11: 77–101.

————. 2010b. Office of Public Counsel for Victims. *Helping Victims Make Their Voice Heard: The Office of Public Counsel for Victims.* Accessed August 1, 2013. http://www .icc-cpi.int/NR/rdonlyres/01A26724-F32B-4BE4-8B02-A65D6151E4AD/282846 /LRBookletEng.pdf.

————. 2010c. "Summary Report on the Seminar on Protection of Victims and Witnesses Appearing before the International Criminal Court." Accessed August 1, 2013. http://www.icc-cpi.int/NR/rdonlyres/08767415-4F1D-46BA-B408-5B447B3AFC8D /0/ProtectionseminarSUMMARY.pdf.s.

————. 2010d. Trust Fund for Victims. *Learning from the TFV's Second Mandate: From Implementing Rehabilitation Assistance to Reparations.* Accessed August 1, 2013. http://www.trustfundforvictims.org/sites/default/files/imce/TFV%20Programme %20Report%20Fall%202010.pdf.

————. 2010e. *Victims before the International Criminal Court: A Guide for the Participation of Victims in the Procedure of the Court.* Accessed August 1, 2013. http://www .icc-cpi.int/NR/rdonlyres/8FF91A2C-5274-4DCB-9CCE-37273C5E9AB4/282477 /160910VPRSBookletEnglish.pdf.

————. 2011a. "Registry and Trust Fund for Victims Fact Sheet." http://www.iccnow .org/documents/Victims_Factsheet_March_2011.18apr1832.pdf.

————. 2011b. Trust Fund for Victims. "United Kingdom Contributes GBP 500,000 to the Trust Fund for Victims." Accessed August 1, 2013. http://www.trustfundfor victims.org/news/united-kingdom-contributes-gbp-500000-trust-fund-victims.

————. 2012. Trust Fund for Victims. "ICC Trust Fund for Victims Assists over 80,000 Victims, Raises Reparations Reserve." Accessed August 1, 2013. http://www.trustfund forvictims.org/news/press-release-23-march-icc-trust-fund-victims-assists-over -80000-victims-raises-reparations-res.

IFHR (International Federation for Human Rights). 2010. "Reparations and the Trust Fund for Victims," in *Victims' Rights before the ICC.* Accessed August 1, 2013. http:// www.fidh.org/IMG/pdf/10-CH-VII_Reparations.pdf.

Keller, Linda M. 2007. "Seeking Justice at the International Criminal Court." *Thomas Jefferson Law Review* 29 (2): 189–217.

Kojève, Alexandre. 2000. *Outline of a Phenomenology of Right.* Translated by Bryan-Paul Frost and Robert Howse. Lanham, MD: Rowman and Littlefield.

Minow, Martha. 1998. *Between Vengeance and Forgiveness.* Boston: Beacon Press.

Mosteller, Robert P. 1997. "Victims' Rights and the United States Constitution: An Effort to Recast the Battle in Criminal Litigation." *Georgetown Law Journal* 85: 1691–715.

O'Hara, Erin Ann. 2005. "Victim Participation in the Criminal Process." *Journal of Law and Policy* 13 (1): 229–47.

Pizzi, William T. and Walter Perron. 1996. "Crime Victims in German Courtrooms: A Comparative Perspective on American Problems." *Stanford Journal of International Law* 32 (1): 37–64.

Rosen, Jeffrey. 2000. *The Unwanted Gaze.* New York: Random House.

Rosen, Michael. 2012. *Dignity: Its History and Meaning.* Cambridge, MA: Harvard University Press.

SáCouto, Susanna, and Katherine Cleary. 2008. "Victims' Participation in the Investigations of the International Criminal Court." *Transnational Law and Comparative Problems* 17: 73–105.

Spiga, Valentina. 2010. "Indirect Victims' Participation in the *Lubanga* Trial." *Journal of International Criminal Justice* 8 (1): 183–98. doi: 10.1093/jicj/mqq007.

VRWG (Victims' Rights Working Group). 2010. *The Impact of the Rome Statute System on Victims and Affected Communities.* London: VRGW.

———. 2011. *The Implementation of Victims' Rights before the ICC.* London: VRGW.

Zappalà, Salvatore. 2010. "The Rights of the Victims and the Rights of the Accused." *Journal of International Criminal Justice* 8 (1): 137–64.

CHAPTER 3

The UN Secretary-General and Human Dignity

The Case of Kofi Annan

ABIODUN WILLIAMS

> The protection and promotion of the universal values of the rule of law, human rights and democracy are ends in themselves. They are also essential for a world of justice, opportunity and stability. No security agenda and no drive for development will be successful unless they are based on the sure foundation of respect for human dignity.
>
> (Annan 2005)

Of all the secretaries-general of the UN, Kofi Annan was the most impassioned advocate for human dignity. He viewed the role of the UN and that of the secretary-general as central in the promotion of human dignity around the world. He regarded the promotion and protection of universal human rights as one of the most important and effective ways for the secretary-general to advance human dignity. Annan believed that lasting peace and development could not be achieved without respect for human dignity, and throughout his decade-long tenure, he stressed the inextricable link between human rights, development, and security. In his address to the inaugural session of the Human Rights Council in Geneva on June 19, 2006, he said: "Lack of respect for human rights and dignity is the fundamental reason why the peace of the world today is so precarious, and why prosperity is so unequally shared." He added: "[T]he strongest states are those that most resolutely defend the human rights of all their citizens" (Annan 2006).

The secretary-general has an important role to play in shaping the values that guide UN action, a role that particular secretaries-general found implicit in the Charter. Equally important, however, have been the distinctive leadership styles—determined by personal characteristics—exhibited by occupants of the post (Killie 2006). This is a subject on which the Charter is silent. This chapter treats the secretary-general's office as an institution, but one that depends to a much greater degree on both the talents and inclinations of an individual, as well as on external circumstances. In short, whereas the office of the secretary-general creates the environment for the exercise of moral authority, the realization of the normative potential of the role has depended in large part on the individual officeholders.

Annan sought to advance human dignity in three ways: First, he worked through norms, particularly by promoting human rights standards and the Responsibility to Protect (R2P). Second, he worked through institutions, primarily by reforming the human rights machinery within the framework of a broader process of UN reform, specifically by establishing the Human Rights Council. Third, he worked through the UN's operational efforts in the field, especially in zones of conflict. In promoting human dignity in all three ways, Annan capitalized on his lengthy institutional experience at the UN (which spanned more than three decades), the unique geopolitical moment at the end of the Cold War, the growth of a global interest in human rights concerns, and increasing institutional capacity of nongovernmental organizations (NGOs) to address them.

The Role of Secretary-General and a Changing International Context

The secretary-general's role and responsibilities are broadly defined in Articles 97 to 101 of the UN Charter. Article 97 designates him as the "chief administrative officer of the Organization." Article 98 requires that he submit an annual report to the General Assembly on the work of the Organization, and Article 101 gives him the responsibility of appointing the staff in the Secretariat, one of the principal organs of the UN, according to regulations established by the General Assembly. The secretary-general's political role is based on Article 98, which also provides that the secretary-general "shall perform such other functions as are entrusted to him" by the General Assembly, Security Council, the Economic and Social Council, the Trusteeship Council, and Article 99, which empowers him to "bring to the attention of the Security Council any matter which in his opinion may threaten the maintenance of international peace and security." Although the powers granted by the Charter have appeared to many as limited in scope, they belie the influence that the secretary-general can wield. Although secretaries-general rarely invoke Article 99 directly, for example, the Security Council can look to the secretary-general for advice and sometimes even for leadership. Ian Johnstone explains that "the [s]ecretary-[g]eneral's normative role can be inferred from his position as head of one of the principal organs of the United Nations," with equal responsibility to other principal organs for promoting the purposes and principles of the organization (2007, 131).

Comparative scholarship on the secretaries-general has identified the importance that personal traits can have in navigating the seemingly rigid strictures of the Charter. Annan emerges from such analyses as a particularly strategic secretary-general, characterized by "responsivity" to external surroundings and an ability to capitalize on opportunities, a "belief in his ability to influence" and, in contrast, a lack of concern with personal "recognition," stemming from an emphasis on the organizational mission above his own ego (Killie 2006, 31). Annan's personal tendencies—an instinctive empathy with those in distress and a determination to represent the voiceless (Smith 2007, 306)—complemented this professional approach. The result was that in Annan, the world found a committed and effective advocate for human dignity.

Kofi Annan was the first UN secretary-general to be appointed from the ranks of the UN staff and had greater knowledge of the workings of the institution than any of his predecessors. He understood the UN's bureaucratic structure, its organizational pathologies, its limits, and its possibilities. Annan began his career in the UN system as an administrative and budget officer at the World Health Organization (WHO) in Geneva in 1962. He later served with the UN Economic Commission for Africa (ECA) in Addis Ababa and the Office of the UN High Commissioner for Refugees. In 1987 he became assistant secretary-general for Human Resources and Management at the UN Secretariat in New York, and in 1990 he was appointed assistant secretary-general for Program Planning, Budget and Finance, and Controller and security coordinator for the UN system. In 1993, Annan was appointed undersecretary-general for Peacekeeping Operations. His UN career was interrupted only by a sabbatical in 1971 to study at the Sloan School of Management at the Massachusetts Institute of Technology and a subsequent two-year position in the tourism office of his native Ghana beginning in November 1974. He thus climbed the UN's bureaucratic ladder—from its lowest administrative rank to its highest position—in thirty-five years.

Annan became secretary-general in the aftermath of the Cold War, which created the normative and political space for him to advocate for human rights. The collapse of the Soviet Union and the end of the Cold War allowed the UN to focus on activities that would have been impossible during the previous ideologically charged decades. Whereas human rights-related actions and policies had frequently been relegated to the margins of UN activity during the Cold War, without the fear of a Soviet veto in the Security Council, the UN could now pursue a range of human rights-related missions. In this changed international context, Annan had the freedom to speak from a human rights perspective without the systemic limitations faced by his predecessors. As James Traub notes: "The end of the Cold War transformed the moral promise of the role of the secretary-general. It allowed him [Annan] to place the UN at the service of the universal values of the Charter, without the constraints of ideology or particular interests" (2006).

Although challenges remained, as Annan was acutely aware, he nonetheless saw the potential for a "quiet revolution," one in which the principles of good governance, cooperation, and a dedication to human rights allowed the international community to work together to achieve broad-ranging goals (Annan 1998c, 123).

The 1990s also saw a rise in the influence and visibility of an international human rights movement and a heightened focus on individual rights as well as collective rights. The end of apartheid in South Africa was a striking example of the marshaling of international pressure to promote human dignity. In accepting the Nobel Peace Prize in 1993, Nelson Mandela linked the South African experience to a new awareness of human rights across the globe: "We live with the hope that as she battles to remake herself, South Africa will be like a microcosm of the new world that is striving to be born. This must be a world of democracy and respect for human rights, a world freed from the horrors of poverty, hunger, deprivation and ignorance, relieved of the threat and the scourge of civil wars and external aggression and unburdened of the great tragedy of millions forced to become refugees" (Mandela 1993).

Mandela's views were emblematic of a human rights community that was finding its voice and of the trends toward greater realization of individual rights in the many states freed from the political paralysis of the Cold War. The demands of this movement and of citizens with new freedom to express their yearning for enjoyment of rights were a spur for new attention to human dignity at the UN. Annan's experience and inclinations allowed him to take advantage of the moment and the opportunity.

Advancing Norms

Although the provisions of the Charter do not imbue the office of the UN secretary-general with explicit political power, the role provides great opportunities for exercising influence (Urquhart and Childers 1990, 22). Upon assuming the leadership of the UN in 1997, Annan sought to capitalize on the normative trends in the international community toward taking humanitarian interventions and human rights more seriously. In the early 1990s, the UN went through a crisis of expectations when peacekeeping forces were deployed in zones of conflict (Somalia, Bosnia, and Rwanda) without sufficient resources or a clear mandate to confront local forces engaged in genocide or mass atrocities. The resulting "blame game" led to a crisis between the UN Secretariat and the Clinton administration, and ultimately to the United States' vetoing Boutros Boutros-Ghali's bid for a second term as secretary-general. Yet Annan, the new secretary-general, was himself compromised in the eyes of at least a part of world public opinion by his role as undersecretary-general for peacekeeping operations for the very failures for which the Secretariat was blamed.

It was against this backdrop that Annan felt driven, both as a result of his personal implication in the crises of the 1990s and for the sake of the long-term credibility of the organization which he now headed, to consolidate the transformed normative environment that the conclusion of the Cold War augured. Arguably, it is the realm of norm entrepreneurship, which provides the greatest political space available to any secretary-general. Norm entrepreneurs are invariably well-placed individuals whose prominence enhances their ability to promote norms and prompt change in the international system. Their promotion of change is also generally grounded in strong notions about the standards of behavior to which actors in the international system ought to adhere. They "spot gaps in the existing normative architecture of world order and engage in moral proselytism in order to fill those gaps" (Thakur 2006, 13).

These highly motivated actors use their platforms or bully pulpits, in Annan's case the office of the secretary-general, to "launch their crusades" and to convince state governments of the import of a norm (Thakur 2006, 13). As a norm entrepreneur, Annan utilized the platform he possessed to raise the visibility of human rights challenges in the international system. Annan's normative impact can be seen primarily in two areas: first, advocating the belief that human rights are universal and indivisible, and second, promoting the principle of the R2P.

When Annan became secretary-general in 1997, human rights were not necessarily assumed to be universal. Some UN member states argued that human rights were geographically delimited—the product of Eurocentric Enlightenment assumptions—or the concern only of states that had reached a certain level of development. In his role as a norm entrepreneur, Annan challenged both these conceptions of human rights and argued that fundamental human rights were an innate demand of the human condition and not alien to any country, culture, race or religion. In his first speech to the Organization of African Unity in Harare, Zimbabwe in June 1997, Annan said: "The success of Africa's third wave [of democratization] depends equally on respect for fundamental human rights. The conflicts which have disfigured our continent have, all too often, been accompanied by massive human rights violations. I am aware of the fact that some view this concern as a luxury of the rich countries for which Africa is not ready. I know that others treat it as an imposition, if not a plot, by the industrialized West. I find these thoughts truly demeaning, demeaning of the yearning for human dignity that resides in every African heart" (Annan 1997a).

Six months later in an address at the University of Tehran on Human Rights Day, Annan declared: "Human rights are the foundation of human existence and co-existence. . . . Human rights are universal, indivisible and interdependent. . . . Human rights are what make us human. They are the principles by which we create the sacred home for human dignity" (Annan 1997b).

By the end of his first year as secretary-general, Annan had placed himself firmly on the side of universalism over relativism in human rights, signaled his intent to make human rights the touchstone of his work, and became an international spokesman for human dignity. This marked a break with previous occupants of the position, who tended to assume that their responsibility for peace and security took precedence over an outspoken position on human rights (Forsythe 1993). Annan's novel approach was recognized by the Norwegian Nobel Committee, which when announcing its intention to award Annan and the UN the 2001 Nobel Peace Prize observed that, "[Kofi Annan] has been pre-eminent in bringing new life to the organization. While clearly underlining the UN's traditional responsibility for peace and security, [Kofi Annan] has also emphasized its obligations with regard to human rights" (Norwegian Nobel Committee 2001).

In the late 1990s, Annan urged UN member states to resolve the tension between the principles of state sovereignty and the international community's responsibility to respond to massive human rights violations, such as ethnic cleansing. He believed that sovereignty implied responsibilities as well as powers.[1] And a critical duty was to protect people from violence and war, which were grave assaults on human dignity. In his view, national sovereignty was not to be used as a shield for those who wantonly violated human dignity. In his Ditchley Foundation Lecture in June 1998, Annan emphasized that if a regime was abusing its own citizens, the international community had a responsibility to prevent and end the abuse. As he put it: "The Charter was issued in the name of 'the peoples,' not the governments, of the UN. Its aim is not only to preserve international peace—vitally important though that is—but also 'to reaffirm faith in fundamental human rights, in the dignity and worth of the human person.' The Charter protects the sovereignty of peoples. It was never meant as a license for governments to trample on human rights and human dignity. Sovereignty implies responsibility, not just power" (Annan 1998b).

The remark was emblematic of Annan's instinctive emphasis on the dignity of individuals rather than on the prerogatives of states, and it came to define his approach to the role of the international community in the face of the commission of atrocities.

A year later Annan chose "humanitarian intervention" as the theme of his speech at the opening of the General Assembly in September 1999. The tragic failures of the UN in Srebrenica and Rwanda and the Kosovo crisis provided the context for the speech. Indeed, the Security Council had failed to act in the Kosovo crisis because of profound competing national interests and differences among its permanent members regarding state sovereignty and whether a moral imperative exists to take action in response to gross violations of human dignity. Annan underlined that the Security Council's paralysis threatened the credibility of the UN: "If the collective conscience of humanity—a conscience which abhors cruelty, renounces injustice and seeks peace for all peoples—cannot find in the United Nations its greatest tribune, there is a grave danger that it will look elsewhere for peace and for justice" (Annan 1999b). Indeed, when during and since Annan's tenure divisions in the Security Council have appeared irresolvable, the resulting temptation for member states to take unilateral action has threatened to erode the very foundation of the UN's effectiveness.[2]

Annan's General Assembly speech sparked a fierce and wide-ranging debate on how the international community could better protect the dignity and sanctity of human life. The speech was delivered in a climate where member states were staking their own claims on the issue, typified by British Prime Minister Tony Blair's so-called Chicago Speech in which he enunciated a "doctrine of the international community" (Blair 1999). In the wake of such declarations, Annan challenged member states to find a consensus on the vital issue of the international community's responsibility in the face of massive violations of human dignity. However, Annan acknowledged in his 2000 Annual Report on the UN: "It is, of course, relatively easy for the international community to assert that the tragedies of Rwanda and Srebrenica should never be allowed to happen again. But if the reaction to my address last year to the General Assembly is any guide, I fear we may still prove unable to give a credible answer to the question of what happens next time we are faced with a comparable crime against humanity" (Annan 2000b).

"The dilemma of intervention" was a main theme of the Secretary-General's 2000 *Millennium Report*. In it, Annan recognized "both the force and importance" of the arguments of member states who were concerned about the dangers of the concept of humanitarian intervention. But he added: "We confront a real dilemma. Few would disagree that both the defense of humanity and the defense of sovereignty are principles that must be supported. Alas, that does not tell us which principle should prevail when they are in conflict" (Annan 2000a).

The International Commission on Intervention and State Sovereignty (ICISS), a Canadian-led initiative that Annan facilitated as part of his norm entrepreneurship, restated the core issue at the heart of the debate on intervention—shifting from debate about a "right to intervene" towards the assertion of a "responsibility to protect." Its 2001 report, *The Responsibility to Protect*, was a comprehensive response to Annan's speech on intervention in the General Assembly. It correctly interpreted the secretary-general's idea of two notions of sovereignty—one for states, one for individuals—and underlined that the state exists for the benefit of its individual citizens, not the other way around (ICISS 2001). The aim reflected both Annan's normative ambitions as well as his awareness that, if it were to retain legitimacy in a new century, the UN could not open itself to further charges of "complicity with evil" (*Report of the Panel on United Nations Peace Operations* 2000, xi).

Of course, the international community already had a long-standing commitment to prevent and punish the crime of genocide under the Genocide Convention. The Security Council has also exercised the right to authorize military action to redress gross violations of human rights, such as ethnic cleansing, that it deems as threats to international peace and security. In April 2004, in a speech in Geneva commemorating the tenth anniversary of the genocide in Rwanda, Kofi Annan outlined a five-point action plan for preventing genocide: preventing armed conflict, which usually provides the context for genocide; protecting civilians in armed conflict by UN peacekeepers and other means; ending impunity through judicial action in both national and international courts; gathering information and early warning of crises; and taking swift and decisive action, including military action. In the speech, he also announced the appointment of a special adviser on the prevention of genocide, which was tasked with three functions: to collect information on potential or existing situations or threats of genocide; to act as an early-warning mechanism to the Security Council and other parts of the UN system; and to make recommendations to the Security Council on actions to prevent or halt genocide (Annan 2004).

In March 2005, drawing on the findings of a high-level panel—a collaborative means of working that was characteristic of Annan's inclinations as a convener of expertise—Annan issued a report, *In Larger Freedom: Towards Development, Security and Human Rights for All*, which contained a number of policy proposals to be taken up by heads of state and governments at the UN World Summit in September of that year. The central theme of the report was that the world must advance the causes of security, development, and human rights together; otherwise, none will succeed. Annan urged world leaders to embrace the principle of the Responsibility to Protect both the potential or the actual victims of mass atrocities. He recognized that many states were concerned that this principle would violate sovereignty. However, he believed that no legal principle should be allowed to shield genocide, crimes against humanity, and gross human rights abuses and that the R2P doctrine would not provide an open door to humanitarian intervention.

Annan's recommendation that member states endorse the "emerging norm of the responsibility to protect" was vigorously debated during the General Assembly consultations on his report in April. Whereas the European Union, the GUUAM group (Georgia, Ukraine, Uzbekistan, Azerbaijan, and Moldova), and several African states endorsed the principle, others, including the Non-Aligned Movement, rejected it as a reformulation of humanitarian intervention without any basis in the UN Charter or international law. However, the Non-Aligned Movement expressed its willingness to further discuss the issue ahead of the 2005 UN World Summit.

After intense intergovernmental debate, the World Summit, held in September 2005, produced a historic breakthrough on the R2P. In the Summit Outcome Document, all governments accepted clearly and unambiguously their collective responsibility to protect populations from genocide, war crimes, ethnic cleansing and crimes against humanity. While stressing the continued primacy of the UN Charter, member states also agreed to take timely and decisive collective action for this purpose through the Security Council when peaceful means proved inadequate and national authorities were manifestly failing to protect their populations.

The Summit's endorsement of R2P was a major advance in international norm setting that Annan had been advocating for several years. In its encapsulation of the universality, indivisibility, and interrelatedness of all human rights, R2P reflected the "Annan doctrine": that state sovereignty cannot be used as an excuse to shield human rights abuses. Emblematic of his norm entrepreneurship, Annan had helped to shift the narrative from the rights of states to the rights of individuals. He used the office of the secretary-general to put the emphasis where it belonged—on the people who needed protection because their human dignity was threatened with massacre or ethnic cleansing rather than on relations between states.

Reforming Institutions to Promote Human Dignity

The UN Commission on Human Rights (CHR), established in 1946 under the aegis of the Economic and Social Council (ECOSOC), played an important role in producing major international human rights standards. It drafted the Universal Declaration of Human Rights in 1948 as well as two covenants in 1966, one on Economic, Social, and Cultural Rights and the other on Civil and Political Rights. The Commission established several working groups on thematic issues and the Sub-Commission on the Promotion and Protection of Human Rights. It also designated special rapporteurs, experts, and representatives to investigate and report on specific human rights situations and violations (Terlingen 2007).[3]

Over the years, however, the international credibility of the fifty-three-member Commission had seriously declined. Notwithstanding the difficulty of determining which human rights standards are objective priorities, the Commission had been particularly characterized by politicization, selectivity, and double standards. Annan said: "We have reached a point at which the Commission's declining credibility has cast a shadow on the reputation of the United Nations system. Unless we remake our human rights machinery, we may be unable to renew public confidence in the United Nations itself" (Annan 2005).

To that end, in his *In Larger Freedom* report, Annan wrote: "If the United Nations is to meet the expectations of men and women everywhere—and indeed, if the Organization is to take the cause of human rights as seriously as those of security and development—then member states should agree to replace the Commission on Human Rights with a smaller standing Human Rights Council" (Annan 2005, 45). He also stated: "The creation of the Council would accord human rights a more authoritative position, corresponding to the primacy of human rights in the Charter of the United Nations" (Annan 2005, 64). Such a structure would provide architectural and conceptual clarity, as the UN already had councils that dealt with two other main purposes, security (the Security Council) and development (ECOSOC). He believed that a new council would help to overcome some growing problems, of perception and in substance, associated with the commission, allowing for a thorough reassessment of the effectiveness of the UN's intergovernmental machinery in addressing human rights concerns.

Annan had additional reasons for proposing the establishment of a full-fledged Human Rights Council. As a standing body, the Human Rights Council would be able to deal with imminent crises and allow for timely and in-depth consideration of human rights issues. Moving human rights discussions beyond the politically charged six-week session of the commission, it would also allow more time for substantive discussions regarding the implementation of decisions and resolutions. Furthermore, if it was no longer possible, as in the CHR, for regional groups to set slates of member states the General Assembly had to approve, it would make members more accountable and the body more representative. And the Council would have more credibility with authority derived directly from the General Assembly.

The World Summit mandated the creation of a new Human Rights Council as part of broader UN reform. In March 2006, a new Human Rights Council was established as a subsidiary organ of the General Assembly (subject to further review of its status after five years). Annan had hoped that this Council would have the status of a "principal organ" of the UN, on par with the Security Council and ECOSOC, but that plan was scuttled by influential developing nations that feared the new council would have the authority to make binding decisions, despite reassurance that such prerogatives would require an amendment to the UN Charter (Terlingen 2007). This highlights one of the main constraints on any secretary-general in promoting human dignity: In an intergovernmental institution such as the UN, the secretary-general can propose, but it is the member states that dispose.

The Human Rights Council, consisting of forty-seven member states, represents some structural improvements over the previous Commission. Elected by a majority of General Assembly members, it can suspend violators of human rights abuses from membership on the Council through a two-thirds General Assembly majority vote. The Council also has the authority to make recommendations of action or intervention directly to the General Assembly in the case of violations of human rights. Through the Universal Periodic Review process it assesses the human rights practices of all UN member states. The Council also meets more regularly each year for a minimum of ten weeks in three sessions, in contrast to the Commission, which met once annually for six weeks. Additionally, the Council retains specific rapporteurs and working groups through the UN's Special Procedures for nonstate-specific issues, including arbitrary detentions, enforced or involuntary disappearances, and the use of mercenaries.

Annan's *In Larger Freedom* report also recommended the strengthening of the Office of the High Commissioner for Human Rights (OHCHR) as part of a renewal of the UN human rights machinery. It observed that the Office was "woefully ill equipped to respond to the broad range of human rights challenges facing the international community" (Annan 2005, 51). In addition, Annan urged a more active role by the high commissioner in the deliberations of the Security Council and a new Peacebuilding Commission, also established in the wake of the 2005 UN World Summit. An Action Plan from the High Commissioner for Human Rights, Louise Arbour, for which *In Larger Freedom* called, identified poverty, discrimination, conflict, impunity, democratic deficits, and institutional weaknesses as priority areas. The plan recommended increasing the size and number of OHCHR's field offices, developing its capacity to deploy rapid response teams in human rights crisis situations, engaging with UN peace operations in conflict areas, and enhancing monitoring of human rights situations in countries. The UN World Summit backed the action plan and agreed to double the budget of OHCHR. During Annan's tenure as secretary-general, countries with OHCHR presence increased from fourteen in 1996 to more than forty in 2006, with the majority of the expansion in country offices occurring in the wake of the World Summit.

The Operational Dimension

As secretary-general, Kofi Annan measured the success of UN programs and activities not only in terms of the satisfaction of member states, but also how they affected the lives of people. As the former head of UN peacekeeping, Annan was conscious of the role of peacekeeping in facilitating political processes in countries emerging from conflict and in helping to create the political, economic, legal, and social conditions in which human dignity can be respected and enjoyed. He tells us in his memoirs: "From the Department of Peacekeeping Operations to the office of the secretary-general, I took with me, above all, the lessons of Bosnia and Rwanda. Evil in civil war zones occurs due to the will of the conflict protagonists, which must be rounded upon, confronted, and stopped—and through force if necessary" (Annan 2012, 78–79).

During Annan's ten years in office, UN peacekeeping grew both in terms of scale and efficacy, from fewer than 13,000 troops to 75,000 troops in eighteen operations worldwide. A burgeoning legitimacy in the eyes of member states, founded on Annan's convictions about human dignity and operationalized through his strategic diplomacy, enabled an increase in the annual budget for UN peacekeeping from approximately $1 billion in 1997 to approximately $5 billion in 2006.

Annan spearheaded the publication of key reports, which dealt with the operational responsibilities of peacekeepers, human rights workers, and humanitarian actors. Back in 1998, he introduced the "protection of civilians" concept in his report on "The Causes of Conflict and the Promotion of Durable Peace and Sustainable Development in Africa" (Annan 1998a). The Security Council responded by adopting three resolutions in 1999, 2000, and 2006 as well as a number of presidential statements relating to protection of civilians. Ian Johnstone writes: "The combined effect of these instruments is to set out standards of behavior expected of host governments, other parties to a conflict, other states, and international organizations, including the Security Council itself when it adopts peacekeeping mandates" (Johnstone 2007, 134).

The "protection of civilians" mandate is critically important, but often member states' will and the UN's capacity to fulfill it is lacking. Armed peacekeepers have not necessarily fared better. In addition, since 9/11 there is the perception by many host-country governments as well as local populations that international workers and peacekeepers operating in particular conflict zones are serving the wider aims of a Western or Northern agenda. As the terrorist attack on UN headquarters in Baghdad in August 2003 painfully illustrated, the UN is sometimes seen as neither independent nor impartial. Humanitarians and international peacekeepers can be perceived as a threat to one of the parties to the conflict, a point that is made more complex with the added involvement of the International Criminal Court. Moreover, although the integration of different components of the UN presence in a host country has gathered speed, as a result of the *Delivering as One* report, which Annan commissioned in 2005, concerns remain within the humanitarian community about the effects this will have on the impartiality of humanitarian assistance. Although Annan grappled with these issues, often in highly politicized contexts such as the postintervention situations in Afghanistan and Iraq, the challenge was largely one bequeathed to his successors.

In light of the growing complexities of UN peacekeeping, Annan appointed a panel of experts led by former foreign minister of Algeria Lakhdar Brahimi to review peace operations and suggest how they could be strengthened. The 2000 Brahimi Report stressed the importance of integrating human rights in peace operations: "[T]he human rights component of a peace operation is indeed critical to effective peace building. UN human rights personnel can play a leading role, for example, in helping to implement a comprehensive program for national reconciliation. The human rights components within peace operations have not always received the political and administrative support that they require however, nor are their functions always clearly understood by other components. Thus, the Panel stresses the importance of training military, police and other civilian personnel on human rights issues and on the relevant provisions of international humanitarian law" (*Report of the Panel on United Nations Peace Operations* 2000, 7).

When Annan assumed office, it was unusual for the Security Council to include human rights in peacekeeping mandates. Yet during his tenure human rights became a regular component of peacekeeping mandates. This doctrinal shift is reflected in the UN's peacekeeping manual:

The abuse and violation of human rights is at the heart of most modern conflicts and is also a consequence of them. Many of the worst human rights abuses occur during armed conflict and the protection of human rights must be at the core of action taken to address it. All United Nations entities have a responsibility to ensure that human rights are promoted and protected by and within their field operations. Most United Nations multi-dimensional peacekeeping operations are therefore mandated to promote and protect human rights by monitoring and helping to investigate human rights violations and/or developing the capacity of national actors and institutions to do so on their own. The integration of human rights and the sustainability of human rights programs should always be a key factor in the planning of multi-dimensional United Nations peacekeeping operations. (*UN Peacekeeping Operations* 2008, 27)

The evolution in peacekeeping doctrine that the 2008 manual reflects rests in large part on Annan's drive to operationalize his understanding of the relationship between human rights, development, and security. Annan recognized that safeguarding rights was a crucial component of achieving sustainable peace and fostering a rule-of-law culture in fragile environments. In the postconflict contexts in which peacekeeping forces are often deployed, both concrete action to protect human rights and a widespread perception that the mission is occupied with this task is essential for forestalling the recurrence of conflict.

Although the doctrinal shift in peacekeeping represented a significant change to the way the UN approached its own mission, Annan also recognized the importance of more effective collaboration with actors outside the UN system. This would not only enhance the effectiveness of global initiatives but would also co-opt actors in the international system that the UN had traditionally conceived as rivals or otherwise outside the scope of its activities. Annan championed development of the emerging hybrid institutional partnerships upon which this book focuses.

An important example in this regard was the creation in 2000 of the UN Global Compact, which reflected Annan's understanding that the private sector could be a crucial partner in furthering the cause of human rights and in supporting other UN aims, such as environmental protection and a reduction of corruption. Rather than viewing the private sector as an adversary, as many in the UN were accustomed to doing, Annan's inclusive inclinations and commitment to the ultimate aim of promoting human dignity drove him to form unusual partnerships. The Global Compact also underlined Annan's appreciation that progress could be made towards human rights through means other than the traditional intergovernmental process. In his speech to the World Economic Forum, which announced the formation of the Compact, Annan reminded businesses of the extraordinary influence that they themselves wielded: "Don't wait for every country to introduce laws protecting freedom of association and the right to collective bargaining. You can at least make sure your own employees, and those of your subcontractors, enjoy those rights. You can at least make sure that you yourselves are not employing underage children or forced labour, either directly or indirectly. And you can make sure that, in your own hiring and firing policies, you do not discriminate on grounds of race, creed, gender or ethnic origin" (Annan 1999a).

The Global Compact was an important example of the kind of networks that Annan formed to pursue his aims, which had all too often been stalled in familiar negotiations between member states. Annan's instinctive desire to convene all relevant actors to address issues concerning human dignity recognized the power of innovative partnerships, which as other mechanisms such as the Global Fund demonstrated, increasingly characterized his approach to international challenges as his tenure progressed.

Conclusion

It is clear that there are limitations on the role of the secretary-general both politically and in terms of his mandate defined in the Charter. The most significant is that the secretary-general is not a head of state or government but the chief administrative officer of an intergovernmental organization. The secretary-general takes instructions from the political bodies of the UN, particularly the General Assembly and the Security Council. The secretary-general can stake out the moral high ground—and Kofi Annan was adept at choosing occasions on which to do so—but he cannot get too far ahead of the member states. Given that the influence of the secretary-general is in large part dependent on the exercise of moral authority, when the basis of this influence is damaged—as many deemed it to be during the oil-for-food scandal and when the UN appeared impotent during the US-led invasion of Iraq— the pursuit of UN goals can be severely impeded. This reality reflects the delicate relationship between the Security Council and the secretary-general, which requires nimble diplomacy—both overt and behind the scenes. The secretary-general's personal qualities are critical in creating a productive and even harmonious relationship with the Council. As Marrack Goulding, former undersecretary-general for Political Affairs, noted, the relationship works best if the Security Council understands that the secretary-general is more than a chief administrative officer and the secretary-general understands that the Security Council has primary responsibility for maintaining international peace and security (Goulding 2004, 267–280).

Kofi Annan's contributions underline the fact that the promotion of human dignity by the secretary-general requires effective intellectual, moral, and political leadership. The ability of the secretary-general to provide leadership is the result of various factors including personal conviction, strategic planning, perseverance, patience, in-depth knowledge of the UN system, compelling communication skills, and charisma.

Annan's role in promoting human dignity is central to the meaning of his secretary-generalship. Annan stressed that lasting peace was impossible without a respect for human rights, and that human rights and good governance were important in the struggle for development. He placed *people* (rather than states) and their needs at the center of the UN's work. To do so, he used a variety of tools at his disposal: influential, sometimes provocative, speeches and other forms of advocacy, rigorous and thoughtful reports, high-level panels, and summits. He used the media to appeal to broader constituencies beyond states, including civil society and the business community. He was not reticent about speaking "above the heads of state" and appealing directly to the peoples of the world. He was an entrepreneur who was able to use the bully pulpit to generate and shape norms, such as R2P.

Annan tried to build networks with nonstate actors, including the private sector, civil society organizations, philanthropic foundations, universities and think tanks, as well as celebrities in order to promote human dignity without relying exclusively on state power and interstate cooperation. An understanding that his accountability was ultimately not to states but to the people they served informed his approach to global challenges. In pursuit of human dignity he worked, to an extent that no secretary-general had done before, to protect populations threatened by gross and systematic violations of human rights even in an era when many people had come to regard global institutions and universal norms as a threat to their particular identity or interests.

The agenda of human dignity is clearly important enough to warrant the further engagement of the current and future secretaries-general. The UN secretary-general must demonstrate the courage needed to tackle hard questions and to bring forward new thinking on the concept of human dignity, which is so central to the relations within and among states, and on the institutional means and partnerships to advance it. Annan was a quintessential norm entrepreneur, and like all successful entrepreneurs he translated an instinctive vision into an agenda for action that won the support of effective coalitions. The secretary-general must continue to serve as a catalyst for a new debate on the promotion of human dignity around the world because in the words of the Universal Declaration of Human Rights: "All human beings are born free and equal in dignity and rights."

Notes

For a detailed discussion about strategic planning in the Executive Office of the Secretary-General including, inter alia, issues of human dignity, see Abiodun Williams, "Strategic Planning in the Executive Office of the UN Secretary General," *Global Governance* 16, no. 4 (2010): 435–49.

1. The notion of "sovereignty as responsibility" did not emerge with the political crises of the 1990s but has philosophical antecedents coterminous with the very emergence of Westphalian sovereignty. Nevertheless, it was Annan who expressed the argument most forcefully and with the greatest resonance, providing the political as well as philosophical underpinnings for the Responsibility to Protect.

2. For a treatment of the Security Council's efforts to address atrocities and an emerging Responsibility to Protect norm, see Nancy Soderberg's chapter 2 in this book.

3. For a detailed assessment of the record of the Human Rights Council, see chapter 6 in this book by Mark P. Lagon and Ryan Kaminski on institutional evolution and efficacy in the area of human rights.

References

Annan, Kofi. 1997a. Annual Assembly of Heads of State and Government of the Organization of African Unity (OAU) (speech). Harare, Zimbabwe, June 2. http://www.un.org/News/ossg/sg/stories/statments_search_full.asp?statID=14.

———. 1997b. 50th Anniversary of the Universal Declaration of Human Rights (speech). University of Tehran, December 10. Accessed September 22, 2013. http://www.un.org/rights/50/dpi1937.htm.

———. 1998a. *The Causes of Conflict and the Promotion of Durable Peace and Sustainable Development in Africa*, Report of the Secretary General, Delivered to the Security Council and the General Assembly. UN Document S/1998/318-A/52/871, April 13.

———. 1998b. "Secretary-General Reflects on 'Intervention' in Thirty-Fifth Annual Ditchley Foundation Lecture." UN Press Release SG/SM/6613, June 26.

———. 1998c "The Quiet Revolution." *Global Governance* 4: 123.

———. 1999a. "Secretary-General Proposes Global Compact on Human Rights, Labour, Environment." UN Press Release SG/SM/6881, February 1.

———. 1999b. "Secretary-General Presents His Annual Report to the General Assembly." UN Press Release SG/SM/7136, September 20.

———. 2000a. *We The Peoples: The Role of the United Nations in the Twenty-First Century*. United Nations Publications.

———. 2000b. *Report of the Secretary-General on the Work of the Organization*. UN Document A/55/1, August 30.

———. 2004. "Secretary-General Launches Action Plan to Prevent Genocide in Speech to the Commission on Human Rights." UN Press Release SG/SM/9197, April 7.

———. 2005. *In Larger Freedom: Towards Development, Security and Human Rights for All*. UN Document A/59/2005, March 21.

———. 2006. "The Secretary General's Address to the Human Rights Council" (speech). Geneva, Switzerland, June 19. http://www.un.org/sg/statements/?nid=2090.

Annan, Kofi (with Nader Mousavizadeh). 2012. *Interventions: A Life in War and Peace*. New York: The Penguin Press.

Blair, Tony. 1999. "Doctrine of the International Community" (speech). Economic Club of Chicago, April 24. http://www.pbs.org/newshour/bb/international/jan-june99/blair _doctrine4-23.html.

Forsythe, David P. 1993. "The UN Secretary-General and Human Rights." In *The Challenging Role of the UN Secretary-General: Making "The Most Impossible Job in the World" Possible*, edited by Benjamin Rivilin and Leon Gordenker. Westport, CT: Greenwood Press.

Goulding, Marrack. 2004. "The UN Secretary-General." In *The UN Security Council: From the Cold War to the 21st Century*, edited by David M. Malone. Boulder, CO: Lynne Rienner Publishers.

International Commission on Intervention and State Sovereignty (ICISS). 2001. *The Responsibility to Protect*. Ottawa: International Development Research Centre.

Johnstone, Ian. 2007. "The Secretary-General as Norm Entrepreneur." In *Secretary or General: The UN Secretary-General in World Politics*, edited by Simon Chesterman. New York: Cambridge University Press.

Killie, Kent J. 2006. *From Manager to Visionary: The Secretary-General of the United Nations*. New York: Palgrave.

Mandela, Nelson. 1993. "Acceptance and Nobel Lecture" (speech). Oslo, Norway, December 10. http://www.nobelprize.org/nobel_prizes/peace/laureates/1993/mandela -lecture_en.html.

Norwegian Nobel Committee. 2001. "The Nobel Peace Prize 2001." Accessed September 22, 2013. http://www.nobelprize.org/nobel_prizes/peace/laureates/2001/press.html.

Report of the Panel on United Nations Peace Operations—Brahimi Report. 2000. UN Document A/55/305-S/2000/809, August 21.

Smith, Courtney B. 2007. "Politics and Values at the United Nations: Kofi Annan's Balancing Act." In *The UN Secretary-General and Moral Authority: Ethics & Religion in International Leadership*, edited by Kent J. Killie. Washington DC: Georgetown University Press.

Terlingen, Yvonne. 2007. "The Human Rights Council: A New Era in UN Human Rights Work?" *Ethics and International Affairs* 21 (2): 167–78.

Thakur, Ramesh. 2006. *The United Nations, Peace and Security*. New York: Cambridge University Press.

Traub, James. 2006. *The Best Intentions: Kofi Annan and the UN in the Era of American World Power*. New York: Farrar, Straus, and Giroux.

United Nations Peacekeeping Operations: Principles and Guidelines. 2008. New York: United Nations.

Urquhart, Brian, and Erskine Childers. 1990. *A World in Need of Leadership: Tomorrow's United Nations*. Uppsala, Sweden: Dag Hammarskjöld Foundation.

CHAPTER 4

Regional Security Organizations and Human Dignity

CHESTER A. CROCKER

Regional security organizations (RSOs) differ as actors in global politics in accordance with the differences among the regions in which they are based.[1] Regional history, culture, internal power structures, linkages to outside power centers, levels of development, and strength of state institutions all help to shape a region's ability to support RSOs and to determine their mandates and capacities (Williams and Haacke 2011). Hence, it follows that most efforts to capture generically the strengths and weaknesses of RSOs as diverse as the European Union, the Organization of American States, the African Union, the Gulf Cooperation Council, or the Collective Security Treaty Organization are less than totally satisfactory. Although the level of abstraction is too high for sweeping generalizations, this chapter, nonetheless, explores some visible trends concerning RSO performance, and it identifies actions that offer the prospect for greater RSO contributions to advancing the human dignity agenda.

There is a range of quite distinct roles that RSOs may play in contemporary world politics. They may be defenders of the sovereignty principle, seeking to protect the independence and security of states (and their regimes) from external intrusions, intervention and interference. They may serve as agents of regional stability, working to iron out interstate differences and solve problems among neighbors. RSOs may define themselves as advocates of a form of "regional sovereignty" for the purpose of defending certain values, promoting particular policy priorities, resisting external influences, and achieving strength in numbers vis-à-vis a threat or an adversary. RSOs may serve as platforms or transmission belts for the projection of the influence of particular members or groups of members. RSOs may see themselves as agents of good governance, using control of the process of admitting, expelling, or suspending members as a tool for spreading best practices and preferred norms. In sum, then, RSOs are capable of becoming agents of change or pillars of the status quo.

The question of legitimizing the salience of individuals and promoting their potential (their agency) in the name of dignity hinges on some intervening variables. States may still be the primary instrument for defending the dignity and rights of individuals and for extending the benefits of liberty and justice to them. But some governments have other priorities. In some cultures and societies, the rights of the group (however defined) and the value of social cohesion appear to trump the value of individual rights. To be sure, these claims are easily abused by authoritarians who seek to counter opposition of any kind. That said, however, it is hard to dismiss the notion that order and discipline are highly valued in places where the alternative may be factional strife or generalized mayhem. Some governments lack the capacity to defend and advance the rights of individuals effectively. In some directly relevant fields (e.g., political party development, professional education, skills training, women's empowerment, environmental protection, independent media, judicial reform, and prison), the real expertise may lie in civil society and the private sector. On top of these obstacles, RSOs may lack the resources and functional skills to advance the human dignity agenda through their programs of rights monitoring and conflict prevention and resolution. They may not be, in other words, the logical first responders.

This chapter explores some of the different roles that RSOs can play in support of human dignity and individual rights as well as the rights of identity groups and minorities. It argues that RSOs are beginning to play an increasingly significant role in security affairs and conflict management. Although this trend has implications for their capacity to be relevant to the human dignity agenda described in the Introduction, the substantial differences in RSO priorities shape whether they are, on balance, a positive or negative factor.

Even though RSOs differ in major respects, there are a few overarching points on which it is possible to generalize across the universe of RSOs. First, membership in RSOs is confined to states. The norms and principles embodied in an RSO's charter reflect the interests and priorities of its state parties, as articulated by member governments at the time of adoption. Charters also tend to reflect customary and conventional international law: that is, the law of interstate relations.

Second, it must quickly be added that neither international law nor states themselves are frozen in time. The relationship between international law and the strategies of states is an evolutionary and increasingly important one (Rostow 2012). Both are evolving in response to a host of political and normative influences, with the result that RSOs can no longer be understood to be exclusively concerned with interstate relations. Rather, they are situated along a dynamic continuum, ranging from those most interested in domestic governance concerns—including equal respect for the human dignity of all people—to those least respectful of their importance. Accordingly, it is important to understand why and how norms relevant to human security and dignity get diffused.

Third, it is axiomatic that the roles played by RSOs are directly related to the threat environment in which they operate. Where threats to individual rights and human dignity are most evident and best documented, RSOs are most likely to experience pressures to acknowledge the challenge. When indigenous civil society institutions are relatively strong and able to sustain their connections to external partners, RSOs are more likely to find that their member states are more positive about their becoming agents of good governance. Where instability and violent conflict take the form of civil wars—that is to say, wars conducted by regimes or armed factions against unarmed civilians or wars in which civilians are the primary casualties—basic human dignity is less likely to be privileged by political elites in RSOs.

Finally, where narco-trafficking networks and piracy have sunk their roots into corrupt, weak (or nonexistent) state institutions, it is a safe bet that parallel forms of illegal commerce threatening to human dignity will soon flourish (O'Regan 2012). In sum, diverse political and security environments lead to diverse RSO roles; these variations help to explain their differences over such issues as radical populism, resource nationalism, women's rights, gay/lesbian rights, HIV/AIDS programs, foreign involvement in Responsibility to Protect (R2P) issues and the role of the International Criminal Court (ICC), arms trafficking, freedom of information and internet access, and climate change.

Before proceeding to identify the changing roles of RSOs on issues of human dignity and human security, a few comments on how these terms are used is in order. The definition of human dignity offered in chapter 1 by the editors of this book is a highly developed and quite specific formulation: "Human dignity is the fundamental agency of human beings to apply their gifts to thrive. As such, it requires social recognition of each person's inherent value and claim to equal access to opportunity. To be meaningful, human dignity must be institutionalized in practice and governance."

Agency and recognition are the core ingredients. As argued below, these values depend for their realization on a prior condition of legitimate peace, which in turn is the precursor for decent governance.

For some, such as former UN secretary-general Kofi Annan, the term "human security" is preferred precisely because of its sweeping breadth and its concern with all the sources and manifestations of conflict. In his view:

During the cold war, security tended to be defined almost entirely in terms of military might and the balance of terror. Today, we know that "security" means far more than the absence of conflict. We also have a greater appreciation for nonmilitary sources of conflict. We know that lasting peace requires a broader vision encompassing areas such as education and health, democracy and human rights, protection against environmental degradation, and the proliferation of deadly weapons. We know that we cannot be secure amidst starvation, that we cannot build peace without alleviating poverty, and that we cannot build freedom on foundations of injustice. These pillars of what we now understand as the people-centered concept of "human security" are interrelated and mutually reinforcing. (Annan 2001)

Human security can also be conceived more narrowly and perhaps usefully as relating to vulnerability (or its opposite) to threats of physical violence. Astri Suhrke puts it this way:

The central task of a policy inspired by human security concerns would therefore be to protect those who are most vulnerable. . . . The philosophers do not tell us precisely who the vulnerable are, but it is self-evident that those exposed to immediate physical threats to life or deprivation of life-sustaining resources are extremely vulnerable. . . . Other persons can be placed in equally life-threatening positions for reasons of deep poverty or natural disasters. This gives us three categories of extremely vulnerable persons:

- victims of war and internal conflict;
- those who live close to the subsistence level and thus are structurally positioned at the edge of socioeconomic disaster; and
- victims of natural disasters.

In this schema, the condition of abject poverty or powerlessness is not qualitatively different from vulnerability to physical violence during conflict. (Suhrke 1999, 265–76)

These conceptions are not mutually exclusive. Given our focus here on institutions and governance, it is best to recognize the wide spectrum of definitions and to concentrate on what RSOs can realistically do to advance both human security and then, human dignity.

Why is the Role of RSOs Becoming More Important?

The study of regional security institutions rests on the prior assumption that regionalism is an important dimension of international security affairs. Modern regionalism traces its development from the negotiations that produced

UN Charter Chapter VIII, which is dedicated to relations between the global body and regional arrangements (i.e., RSOs). Buzan and Waever consider that a regionalist perspective is a major contending approach alongside neo-realist and globalist approaches because it underscores the territoriality inherent in security dynamics and it bridges between the local and global levels: "Acknowledging the regional level as an independent, and frequently powerful, factor in the security equation is essential to both sound theory and sensible policy" (Buzan and Waever 2003, 481).

RSOs typically arose in one of six contexts: (a) as an embodiment of Cold War alliance systems, (b) as an assertion of regional solidarity to bolster shared norms or to advance shared cultural or ethnic values, (c) in the wake of decolonization, as an expression of sovereign independence and resistance to neocolonial or superpower intrusion, (d) as a search for mutual support and cooperation in the face of a powerful neighboring adversary, (e) as an assertion of subregional competence in dealing with challenges more rapidly and purposefully than would a more distant, regionwide organization, and (f) as a post–Cold War act of balancing against existing global and Western-led bodies. But whatever their origins, RSOs are emerging as an increasingly significant vehicle for security cooperation.

The reasons for this are several. As argued elsewhere, regionalism and RSOs are becoming more important due to a widespread recognition that global institutions and the leading global so-called security exporters are already overstretched and are more likely to be retrenching than expanding their activities (Crocker, Hampson, and Aall 2012). Regionalism is emerging, in part, to fill an apparent gap. In recognition of this reality, it is noteworthy that global actors are not necessarily opposed to regional actors' emergence. On the contrary, the UN Secretariat has conducted extensive, multiyear engagements (e.g., conferences, publications, and capacity-building programs) on the topic of cooperation and coordination between the world body and regional organizations, especially in the field of peacekeeping and conflict management. Such activity has received support from various UN members. The United States has increasingly identified the advantages of partnering with multilateral institutions, a process that began during the second administration of George W. Bush and has expanded under Barack Obama and Secretary of State Hillary Clinton with a focus on a multipartner world, including increased emphasis on regional institutions. The process is symbolized by the appointment of US ambassadors to the African Union and to the Association of Southeast Asian Nations (ASEAN) in 2009 and 2011, respectively (Patrick 2012). This partnering can only work if there is a reciprocal willingness on the part of the relevant RSOs, as often appears to be the case.

In addition to these factors, RSOs are becoming more significant because of a self-conscious determination in some regions to assert ownership and a right of first refusal in the handling of regional security problems, even in cases where regional will to act far outstrips regional capacity for action. Such assertions of what might be called regional sovereignty have deep historical roots going back to the negotiations leading to the adoption of the UN Charter and its Article 52(2). The Indian scholar-diplomat P. N. Panikkar conceived of regionalism in the late 1940s in ways distinct from and broader than the Western conceptions of the day that tended to focus on narrow conceptions of security. As regionalism has developed since then, scholars have differentiated regionalism from regional integration and viewed the former as an assertion of autonomy from great power aspirations to control weaker neighbors (Acharya 2012). In arguing in the late 1960s for a Pax Africana, the Kenyan-American scholar Ali Mazrui made reference to a concept of racial sovereignty that would resist all forms of external rule or domination (Mazrui 1967). Such notions of regional self-assertion explain the more recent efforts since the 2002 inauguration of the African Union to upgrade the African regional security architecture, a long-standing goal of such leaders as Nigeria's Olusegun Obasanjo and South Africa's Thabo Mbeki (Engel and Porto 2010).

Regional ownership and buy-in offers legitimacy and helps to explain the growing support of powerful states for RSO roles. Interestingly, such support would likely strengthen to the extent that RSOs are receptive to the human dignity agenda; by the same token, their receptivity is likely to vary with the pressures and incentives received from more powerful actors. Not only are RSOs viewed to be closer to the issues culturally and geographically, they also provide cover against accusations that external security agendas are somehow being imposed. On the other hand, RSOs can sometimes provide a useful platform for regional hegemons to project their values and interests onto a regional stage. Weaker regional states may be wary of such influences but are also aware of their need for the protection afforded by being part of something much larger.

Another factor in the growing salience of RSOs is the increasingly ad hoc, a la carte character of conflict-management initiatives. The problem of overstretch, the changing nature of security challenges, and the risk-averse character of decision making in leading world capitals all point toward a quest for burden sharing and borrowed legitimacy. However challenged they may be in terms of tangible capacity, RSOs have become increasingly attractive partners for other actors. The result is a pattern of spontaneous, improvised security management in which RSOs are frequent participants in a wide range of hybrid arrangements. This pattern of collective conflict management may not be the answer to all challenges, but it may be the most likely pattern in the face of problems that no one actor wants to own (Crocker, Hampson, and Aall 2011).

What Can RSOs Contribute to a Human Dignity Agenda?

The most basic contribution of RSOs to human dignity is an indirect one: helping to create the bare minimum conditions in which the values of human dignity are recognized and human beings have at least some opportunity to achieve their potential. Absent those conditions—state institutions strong enough to impose a monopoly on the instruments of organized violence and sovereign enough to garner the respect of external actors—it is difficult to avoid local or regional anarchy. Individual agency in all its meanings cannot flourish during civil wars and intractable conflicts. Minimal security and some measure of civic order are preconditions for bringing war-torn states back from the abyss and crumbling states toward a chance for stable development. This helps to explain why most policy-related research on state building tends to focus on the security first approach, including the building of strong institutions, as Krasner has observed (Krasner 2011).

RSOs make security contributions to dignity in various ways. They may provide procedures and mechanisms for dispute settlement by offering facilitation, good offices, and mediation services to members. Member states may prefer that interstate conflicts are addressed under the aegis of an RSO rather than a global body, at least in the first instance. RSO founding charters and basic principles typically provide a normative framework that mirrors the UN Charter's prohibition on the use of force except for purposes of self-defense, offering another layer of support for members' independence and territorial integrity. As for intrastate conflicts, which form the vast bulk of the modern conflict universe, RSO practice varies but an increasing number are moving toward greater willingness to take up issues that affect the sovereignty and internal affairs of member states. Some RSOs, such as the Organization of American States (OAS), include in their remit specific commitments to the protection of democratically elected governments as well as sanctions that mandate the suspension of members experiencing coups or military putsches. Some like the European Union have elaborate programs aimed at strengthening observance of human rights by means of intergovernmental commissions charged with responsibilities in this area. In addition to these contributions, a few RSOs, such as the African Union, have developed a security architecture with the potential to mount peace observation and monitoring missions as well as more ambitious peacekeeping and peace enforcement operations in support of implementation of negotiated agreements within or among member states (Bercovitch and Jackson 2009, Chapter 9).

Beyond their security contributions, RSOs have the potential to block or alternatively to support the introduction of contemporary thinking on human dignity. Whether or not RSO members are consciously aware of the link, when they privilege peacemaking and conflict resolution they are also strengthening respect and recognition for individual human beings. Those precious things so eloquently discussed in the Introduction depend upon a measure of peace with justice. RSOs, of course, have no monopoly on the practice of peacemaking. But they are gradually becoming more central to the field.

To be sure, RSOs have the standing to go either way—to be a force for positive change or an obstacle. They are legitimizers of a region's consensus, and lowest common denominator outcomes are the frequent result. But, as noted above, many governments in various regions are themselves under pressure to evolve toward a greater respect for universal values—due to the influence of local advocacy and interest groups, global and local nongovernmental organizations (NGOs) and media, as well as the desire to appeal to overseas financial markets, investors, and donors. As they do so, RSOs will evolve with them. Holdouts will experience shaming as RSOs gradually become official megaphones for new thinking. Although RSOs serve at the pleasure of their members, they also have some capacity to discipline members that discredit a region's image.

It remains unclear whether the polarized debates over values and priorities outlined in the Introduction will endure or, alternatively, will be superseded at either the regional or the global level. Sterile debate over abstract principles is a favorite pastime of international organizations at both levels. It is interesting to consider the possibility that RSOs will rise above such value cleavages before the UN itself does. The Arab League and Gulf Cooperation Council (GCC) calls for action in Libya in 2011 eased the way for UN and then the North Atlantic Treaty Organization (NATO) to do something about Qaddafi, overcoming predictable resistance from Russia and China. A similar dynamic occurred in 2012 when African Union pressure helped overcome their resistance to threatening sanctions on Sudan and South Sudan when the recently separated neighbors edged toward another chapter in their decades-long trauma of warfare.

Another factor to be considered is lateral learning as well as possible rivalry between RSOs (and between them and global actors). The long-established democratic norms of the European Union (EU) and NATO were followed on September 11, 2001, by the adoption of the Inter-American Democratic

Charter, which empowered the OAS to suspend a member state's participation when there had been "an unconstitutional interruption of the democratic order." The Charter includes strong support for democratic institution-building and human rights protections. African RSOs, including the continental African Union (AU) have evolved in a parallel direction since the start of the twenty-first century, suspending the participation of states that experience military coups and mounting diplomatic missions, sanctions programs, and even coercive threats and actions directed at miscreants. Sovereignty under the AU's Constitutive Act is described in a recent study as "contingent on a government's willingness and capacity to deliver on human security" (Williams and Haacke 2011, 126). Whereas the results are mixed (as the recent cases of Mali and Guinea Bissau make clear), African armies no longer have a free hand to seize power without fear of significant consequences. This represents a shift in RSOs' commitment to advancing norms of governance bearing on basic dignity.

What Can Be Done to Strengthen the RSO Role?

The emergence of the human security paradigm as an important if not central focus of concern in international security studies marks a significant development for all interstate institutions, including regional ones. As Hampson et al. have argued, the arrival of people (i.e., individuals) as a reference point in assessing the presence or absence of international security represents an open-ended paradigm shift in the way we view international politics. To the extent that it becomes legitimized, the human security paradigm changes the environment in which all relevant actors operate, including governments and intergovernmental bodies (Hampson, Daudelin, Hay, Reid, and Marting, 2002, 38).

It is worth looking at a few examples of the variations among regions and RSOs. This will shed light on what is missing in many RSOs and what can be done about it. Members of the Inter-American institutional system place a high value on a shared legal tradition and diplomatic culture, and they have come together effectively to quarantine states experiencing military take-overs (Quinney 2011). Since the 1998 peace accords between Ecuador and Peru, interstate conflicts and arms races are generally a thing of the past. Yet, when it comes to mobilizing real capacity to prevent conflict by integrating the tools of democratic development, rights monitoring, and poverty alleviation, the system falls short.[2] Effective coordination of tools is hampered by the high value placed on consensus decision making and noninterference as well as by severe resource shortfalls (Baranyi 2005). In addition, capacity constraints and political divisions in the region also account for the system's unimpressive track record in combating some of the most important regional threats related to criminal networks; gang violence; trafficking in people, drugs and arms; and corruption of local officials.

Democratic norms and individual rights face more uphill challenges as one turns to the Middle East and much of Asia. Here the sovereignty norm continues to hold pride of place, enabling states with highly diverse political arrangements to get along as partners in regional organizations. East Asia's political diversity makes it almost impossible to imagine a values-based regional political order. Organizations such as the Collective Security Treaty Organization (CSTO) and the Shanghai Cooperation Organization (SCO) concentrate on such priorities as border security, combating crime, and counterterrorism. The less openly acknowledged priority is to strengthen the security of regimes, to defeat ethnic separatism and, for some members, to balance against other groupings such as the Organization for Security and Cooperation in Europe (OSCE) where Western democratic norms have stronger support. This appears to be the barren soil in which human dignity has to take root.

Everything hinges on the political balance and the trends within a given RSO. Lateral learning and peer pressure may have been a factor in pushing a statist RSO, such as the Organization of Islamic Cooperation (OIC), toward establishing in 2008 an Independent Permanent Human Rights Commission. The Commission acquired a governing statute in June 2011 that identifies the OIC's purposes as including promotion of civil, political, and economic rights enshrined in its own "covenants and declarations and in universally agreed human rights instruments, in conformity with Islamic values." OIC secretary-general Ekmeleddin İhsanoğlu states that OIC rules of procedure are inspired by member-state proposals and "the practices of international organizations." In a July 2010 interview, *İhsanoğlu* noted the goal of "striking a delicate balance" between Islamic declarations and international human rights instruments (Cismas 2011, 1148). Nonetheless, Ihsanoglu publicly positions the OIC as an institution committed to helping "the new governments in the Arab and Muslim world . . . bring about political stability and build a civil society based on human rights and social justice while ensuring the right to livelihood and the provision of economic growth and basic sustenance for their citizens." His public remarks have pointed to a diffuse array of OIC efforts in "humanitarian and human development programs in its Member States through concrete and practical programs, including poverty alleviation, education, science and technology, and empowering women" (OIC 2012).

Commenting on the inaugural meeting of the OIC Human Rights Commission in Jakarta in February 2012, Indonesian human rights advocates welcomed its emergence as evidence of a "paradigm shift in the Islamic world on human rights" but cautioned that the "Islamic values" caveat could be used to legitimize a reduction or dilution of universal principles (Wahyuningrum and Hafiz 2012). The Commission's mandate stresses such purposes as supporting the OIC position on rights, offering technical advice to members, and conducting studies and research rather than monitoring and reviewing member state reports. The mandate's narrow emphases distinguish its scope of action from sister commissions in the African and Western Hemisphere systems (Cismas 2011, 2). In sum, the OIC case suggests a process of adaptation and improvisation—embracing while also resisting global norms. Such improvisation is also evident in the varied interpretations of state legitimacy reflected in the decisions of the GCC in reference to Libya, Syria, and Bahrain during the 2011–12 period.

European interests in and potential capacity for engagement on issues of human dignity and security are striking. EU and NATO's commitment to governance and human rights standards for admission of new members have played a critical role in driving the reform process in post–Cold War Central and Eastern Europe. The European Union, acting through the Commission and the Council, manages a vast and complex architecture of organizations and programs related to conflict management, development, governance including rule of law, and humanitarian assistance. European engagement with RSOs in other regions (i.e., the AU, ASEAN) has set a high standard for interregional cooperation and capacity-building. The rhetorical commitments of European actors to the principles and best practices for enhancing human dignity are also impressive.

But Europe has arguably not optimized the output of its foreign, defense, and development policies for a variety of reasons including internal policy divisions, institutional rivalries between EU institutions, overlap between EU mandates and those of the OSCE and NATO, and what one expert describes as Europe's continued "obsession with national sovereignty" (Bailes 2011, 290–91). Disarray and inability to cooperate for common purposes were on painful display during the 2011 Libya crisis whose aftermath could have offered the organization an opportunity to redeem itself as a human security actor had not the earlier discord over the basic mission made such action impossible.

To be sure, the EU has conducted a wide array of human security missions starting in 2003, including some eighteen discrete military and civilian operations in five geographic regions. These missions offer a striking illustration of EU capacity and further potential to be a constructive global actor.

Effective missions in the Balkans, Africa, and Indonesia are cases in point (Martin and Kaldor 2012). The impact of such activity within the European space is uncontested. What is less clear is whether it will continue and flourish on a global basis in the wake of the Afghanistan experience and the multiyear economic crisis within the Eurozone itself. (For a skeptical forecast of future European action in conflict management activity beyond Europe's own home base, see de Jonge Oudraat [in Crocker, Hampson, and Aall 2011].)

The snapshots above underscore the wide range of relevant RSO activity. They also offer clues as to what must be done to improve their performance. There are several ways to strengthen the RSO contribution to advancing human dignity. The most promising avenues for democratic states to engage in promotion of this agenda include: (a) development of interregional (inter-RSO) programs, meetings, and exchanges of information and people, (b) cultivating diplomatic and capacity-building relationships between Western RSOs and their counterparts in other regions in order to enhance the latters' standing in the eyes of their own members and other political actors, (c) using UN, alliance, and bilateral networks with RSO officials in regions with autocratic or contested governance standards to press for improved performance, providing incentives where appropriate, (d) exploring new partnerships with RSOs—and their leading members—that might appear to value human dignity less than the United States and other Western states in order to test for areas of potential common ground on which to build, and (e) sharing with receptive RSOs the best practices and smart power tools for going after miscreants and hostile organizations that directly threaten human dignity.

There is circumstantial evidence that RSO officials are conscious of developments in sister organizations as well as in the UN that might be relevant to their own activities. Claims on the websites of newly arrived RSOs, such as the Russian-dominated CSTO or the newly refurbished OIC, suggest that the channels of cooperation are open. RSO officials, it appears, wish to communicate with their counterparts and to be seen cooperating laterally with them. Jointly planned ministerial meetings between EU officials and ASEAN and AU counterparts—mirrored and, to a degree, counterbalanced by similar events between the CSTO, SCO, ASEAN and the OIC—are examples of how formal, planned events offer a setting for networking, information sharing, and the development of assistance and capacity-building initiatives. This developing pattern may slowly increase the will and wherewithal to advance human dignity in an RSO.

Resource-constrained RSOs such as the AU have discreetly welcomed assistance from the UN, the EU, and the US Africa Command (Africom) and other bilateral sources. Whereas capacity-building and training are well established in the security sector, parallel activity can be encouraged in such fields as health, rule of law, rights monitoring, and conflict prevention/early warning.

As RSOs develop the habit of welcoming and accrediting envoys from other RSOs, the UN, and individual states—the latter assign experienced people to such missions—this practice opens a potentially important channel for advice and demarches as well as other forms of communication. To illustrate, if Washington seeks improved RSO performance on rights monitoring or prevention of gender-based violence, one way to support the goal is to assign active, senior diplomats to the RSO's so-called capital. Paying attention to the leading regional organizations demonstrates that they are taken seriously, which encourages others to do the same. It also elevates the organization in the eyes of media and civil society within the member states. Skillfully done, such attention should make it easier to press for information and transparency.

An interesting variant of this approach is the potential of RSOs to serve as building blocks for expanded security cooperation on a cross-regional basis where political and values differences are substantial. This principle explains the long-standing NATO program of security dialogues and programs with Russia and other individual members of the Commonwealth of Independent States (CIS) under NATO's Partnership for Peace (PfP) programs. In the case of Russia, these included joint exercises such as the Bold Monarch international submarine rescue exercise in 2012 and the Vigilant Skies exercise in 2011, the first ever airborne counterterrorism exercise; cooperation with Russia also took place in the fields of military medicine, logistics, bomb disposal and counterpiracy operations in the Horn of Africa.

Although these are admittedly illustrations of traditional security programming, they can also serve as a possible precedent and a foot in the door to broader initiatives in fields more directly linked to human security, such as cooperation against human and arms trafficking. What has not happened so far is a formal NATO relationship with the Russian-inspired CSTO on such issues as counter-narcotics trafficking, as Moscow has proposed. NATO members have been reluctant to take this step in order to avoid creating an imagery of equivalence between two such different organizations. By the same token, Russian officials have been reluctant to join or even tolerate governance programs of NATO, the EU, and the OSCE in some Balkan and Caucasus states. Zbigniew Brzezinski has argued that there could be a case for cross-RSO relationships if a NATO-CSTO "joint agreement for security cooperation in Eurasia and beyond were to contain a provision respecting the right of current nonmembers to eventually seek membership in either NATO or the CSTO—and perhaps, at a still more distant point, even in both" (Brzezinski 2009). Once again, the case depends on developing a conscious strategy for translating geopolitical common ground into expanded space for RSO roles on human dignity issues. This logic could then extend farther east to entail a form of cooperation with the Shanghai Cooperation Organization, five of whose six core members are also CSTO members.

Brzezinski's notion of NATO at the center of a web of institutions incorporating the security concerns of all Eurasia would have to start modestly, given vastly different conceptions of governance, human rights, and definitions of human security and dignity. Although the Web may share common concerns about terrorism and narco-trafficking, views on extremism and separatism, key CSO concerns, will differ sharply. Efforts of Eurasian autocrats to redefine cyberwarfare as an attempt by one state to use information to threaten the security of another in order to undermine its culture and political system only underscore the problem. However, the relevant point here is that interaction between and among RSOs can serve the interests of their members and create channels for shaping opinion and spreading ideas while also pursuing common interests. Failure to engage in dialogue and jawboning across the lines of values polarization will do little to advance human dignity. The world of RSOs is a competitive as well as cooperative arena, so Western democracies should not shy away from the competition.

A fifth avenue for strengthening the potential contribution of RSOs to the human dignity agenda is the sharing of best practices and tools that have been successful in other arenas. Specifically, the instruments and techniques developed in the fields of international police and judicial cooperation, counternarcotics trafficking, and counterterrorism are, in a general sense, fungible tools. The power they represent is transferable—between sectors, states, and RSOs themselves. If applied against clandestine arms dealers, human traffickers, or criminal warlords with some of the same zeal as was used in the case of financial sanctions against Iran over its nuclear policy, the effects could be striking. The use of counter-narcotics tactics and personnel to bring Russian arms merchant Viktor Bout to justice illustrates the general point. Tools developed to attack terrorist financial networks can serve other purposes as well. The ultimate objective in going after illicit operators is to shrink their freedom of action and limit the zone of ungoverned spaces where such people thrive at the expense of civilian populations. By doing so, it becomes possible to expand the space for concerted action on behalf of the rule of law (Asher, Comras, and Cronin 2011).

The obstacle to transferring such tools from one domain or jurisdiction to another is essentially political, but it also involves issues of intelligence sharing and concern about protecting sources and methods. Nonetheless, such tools have been at the forefront of US efforts not only to counter weapons of mass destruction (WMD) proliferators and terrorist networks but also to advance policy goals amidst the turmoil of the Arab awakening. And, US officials are becoming more outspoken about broadening the use of financial instruments of statecraft. As Daniel L. Glaser, assistant secretary for Terrorist Financing, US Treasury Department, stated in late 2011: "Within the Treasury Department, the mission of the Office of Terrorism and Financial Intelligence, known as TFI, is to marshal the Treasury Department's policy, enforcement, regulatory, and intelligence functions to sever the lines of financial support to international terrorists, WMD proliferators, narcotics traffickers, and other threats to our national security" (Glaser 2011). As the agenda of human dignity rises further up the priority list of foreign policy concerns of the United States and other like-minded powers, the application of smart power tools through regional organizations will predictably become more widespread.

Conclusion

This chapter has argued that RSOs can serve a range of political purposes and goals, reflecting the interests and priorities of member states as well as the histories and cultures of different regions. It further asserts that RSOs are becoming more important actors in international politics and security, as legitimizers, gatekeepers, and operational agents. While serving the interests of member states, they also reflect the broader universe of laws and norms, which are ever changing. The chapter makes the case that RSOs have the potential to be relevant players in advancing the agenda of human dignity. Although not often primary drivers, they do play an increasingly salient role in shaping the political and institutional environment in which issues of dignity are acted upon. Leading democratic states and intergovernmental bodies have possibilities for action to expand the scope for advancing human dignity if they set about it consciously. This chapter has identified a number of avenues for doing so and for strengthening the RSO contribution to building a more decent global order.

Notes

1. I am indebted to Georgetown University graduate student Stein-Ivar Eide for his research assistance in the preparation of this chapter.

2. I am indebted to Georgetown University graduate student Caitlin Fogerty for drawing my attention to these issues.

References

Acharya, Amitav. 2012. "Comparative Regionalism: A Field Whose Time Has Come?" *The International Spectator: Italian Journal of International Affairs* 47 (1): 3–15.

Annan, Kofi. 2001. "Foreword." In *Human Security and the New Diplomacy*, edited by Rob McRae and Don Hubert. Ottawa: Carleton University Press.

Asher, David L., Victor D. Comras, and Patrick M. Cronin. 2011. *Pressure: Coercive Economic Statecraft and U.S. National Security*. Washington, DC: Center for a New American Security.

Bailes, Alyson J. K. 2011. "Europe's Security: Attitudes, Achievements, and Unsolved Challenges." In *Rewiring Regional Security in a Fragmented World*, edited by Chester Crocker, Fen Osler Hampson, and Pamela Aall. Washington, DC: United States Institute of Peace.

Baranyi, Stephen. 2005. *Inter-American Institutions and Conflict Prevention*. Ottawa: Canadian Foundation for the Americas.

Bercovitch, Jacob, and Richard Jackson. 2009. *Conflict Resolution in the Twenty-First Century*. Ann Arbor: Michigan University Press.

Brzezinski, Zbigniew. 2009. "An Agenda for NATO: Toward a Global Security Web." *Foreign Affairs* 88 (5): 2–20.

Buzan, Barry, and Ole Waever. 2003. *Regions and Powers: The Structure of International Security*. Cambridge, UK: Cambridge University Press.

Cismas, Ioana. 2011. "Introductory Note to the Statute of the OIC Independent Permanent Human Rights Commission." *International Legal Materials* 5 (6): 1148–60.

Crocker, Chester A., Fen Osler Hampson, and Pamela Aall. 2011. "Collective Conflict Management: A New Formula for Global Peace and Security Cooperation?" *International Affairs* 87 (1): 39–58.

———. 2012. "Jumpstarting Conflict Management: Regional Organizations, Hybrid Groups and Security." Paper presented at the International Studies Association Annual Convention, April 1.

Engel, Ulf, and Joao Gomes Porto. 2010. *Africa's New Security Architecture: Promoting Norms, Institutionalizing Solutions*. Ashgate, England: Ashgate Publishing Ltd.

Glaser, Daniel L. 2011. Speech at the Washington Institute for Near East Policy. Accessed September 13, 2013. http://www.washingtoninstitute.org/policy-analysis/view /treasurys-response-to-the-arab-spring-financial-tools-for-international-sec.

Hampson, Fen Osler, Jean Daudelin, John B. Hay, Holly Reid, and Todd Marting. 2002. *Madness in the Multitude: Human Security and World Disorder*. Toronto: Oxford University Press.

Krasner, Stephen D. 2011. "International Support for State-Building: Flawed Consensus." *Prism* 2 (3): 65–74.

Martin, Mary, and Mary Kaldor, eds. 2012. *The European Union and Human Security: External Interventions and Missions*. London: Routledge.

Mazrui, Ali A. 1967. *Towards a Pax Africana: A Study of Ideology and Ambition*. London: Weidenfeld and Nicolson.

O'Regan, Davin. 2012. "Narco States: Africa's Next Menace." *New York Times*, March 12. http://www.nytimes.com/2012/03/13/opinion/narco-states-africas-next-menace .html?_r=0.

Organization of Islamic Cooperation (OIC). 2012. "OIC Is Vigorously Engaged in Bringing Political Stability in the Region, Said the Secretary-General at the US-

Islamic World Forum." OIC. Accessed May 30, 2013. http://www.oic-oci.org/topic _detail.asp?t_id=6890.

Oudraat, Chantal de Jonge. 2011. "Play It Again, Uncle Sam: Transatlantic Relations, NATO, and the European Union." In *Rewiring Regional Security in a Fragmented World*, edited by Chester Crocker, Fen Osler Hampson, and Pamela Aall. Washington, DC: United States Institute of Peace.

Patrick, Stewart. 2012. "The US and Global Conflict Management: UN, Regional and Ad Hoc Approaches." Paper presented at the International Studies Association Annual Convention, April 1.

Quinney, Nigel. 2011. "Culture Counts: A Diplomatic Perspective on Culture and Regional Conflict Management." In *Rewiring Regional Security in a Fragmented World*, edited by Chester Crocker, Fen Osler Hampson, and Pamela Aall. Washington, DC: United States Institute of Peace.

Rostow, Nicholas. 2012. "Grand Strategy and International Law." *Strategic Forum* 277. Washington, DC: National Defense University.

Suhrke, Astri. 1999. "Human Security and the Interests of States." *Security Dialogue* 30 (3): 265–76.

Wahyuningrum, Yuhun, and Muhammed Hafiz. 2012. "OIC, Human Rights and Indonesia's Role." *Jakarta Post*, February 24. http://www.thejakartapost.com/news/2012 /02/24/oic-human-rights-and-indonesia-s-role.html.

Williams, Paul D., and Jurgen Haacke. 2011. "Regional Approaches to Conflict Management." In *Rewiring Regional Security in a Fragmented World*, edited by Chester Crocker, Fen Osler Hampson, and Pamela Aall. Washington, DC: United States Institute of Peace.

CHAPTER 5

Inclusive Growth, Institutions, and the Underground Economy

ANOOP SINGH

The global surge in public protests against perceptions of bad governance and lack of inclusive growth are a reminder of the importance of developing strong institutions on the one hand and of expanding the benefits of the formal economy to encourage economic growth and opportunities on the other. The two challenges are interlinked: Good institutions depend on ample state capacity, which in turn depends on bringing economic activity into the ambit of the formal sector. A large informal economy limits state capacity, which may hinder institutional development, in turn discouraging expansion of the formal sector, limiting economic and financial inclusion, and thus restricting the benefits of a formal economy to relatively few participants. More fundamentally, the presence of large underground economies and weak domestic institutions lead to unequal access to economic opportunities and thereby hinder the freedom of individuals to thrive based on their capabilities, which are defined by Amartya Sen as the individual's opportunities and ability to generate outcomes that are valued by themselves.

Large underground economies pose problems for policymaking: A vicious cycle can be set off as governments with large informal or underground economies may raise tax rates to make up revenues, thereby encouraging further enlargement of the underground economy. This may erode the institutional capacity of the government even further. Fragile states are at heightened risk of falling into this vicious circle. Moreover, large informal economies render official statistics unreliable and incomplete, complicating the formulation of informed policies. In this bad equilibrium, benefits of a formal economy such as property rights protection and access to credit markets are not widely available, which may discourage economic growth and deny economic opportunities to many. The resulting lack of inclusiveness will adversely affect human dignity, which, as noted in the introduction, requires equal access to opportunities, which in turn would enable each individual to apply their capabilities to thrive.

The presence of a large underground economy and widespread corruption undercut access to justice and the agency to thrive, thereby impinging on human dignity. Evidence suggests that the underground economy, which includes both illegal and legal activities, constitutes a significant portion of the economy in a number of countries.[1] Smith (1994) defines the underground economy as the "market-based production of goods and service whether legal or illegal, that escape detection in the official estimates of GDP." This chapter, however, follows recent studies that adopt a narrower definition of the underground economy, "which includes all market-based legal production of goods and services that are deliberately concealed from public authorities to avoid the payment of income, value added or other taxes, to avoid payment of social security contributions, having to meet certain legal labor market standards, such as minimum wages, maximum working hours, and safety standards, and complying with certain administrative procedures" (Schneider, Buehn, and Montenegro 2010). The lack of social security contributions and the circumvention of labor standards could potentially undercut the dignity of the labor force employed in the shadow economy.

However, on the positive side, a large informal sector may be viewed as the nursery of future economic growth within the formal economy. It serves as an important buffer against economic uncertainty and underdevelopment in the formal sector by providing livelihoods to large sections of the population. This is particularly important when viewed from a development perspective, since poor and emerging countries have much larger shares of informal activity than do rich countries. What links underdevelopment and the shadow economy?

Hernando De Soto (1989) links the problem of underdevelopment with a key institutional weakness, namely that much of the potentially productive capital in poor countries is outside the system of formal property rights. Unlike in countries with mature property rights systems where assets can be leveraged easily into capital that can be employed for productive activity and thus grow the stock of capital, in poor countries it is often very difficult to establish clear rights to property in the first place. It is even more challenging to reap their benefits, such as the capacity to use property as collateral to invest and the protections afforded by them. The productive capacity of the economy is restricted due to this fundamental institutional weakness; therefore, wider participation in the formal economy is hindered, encouraging enclave-like development that benefits the few and leaves many out, leading to increased inequality and detracting from human dignity.

In De Soto's view, the establishment of institutions that create and protect property rights is the key that can unlock the potential for growth contained within the informal sector. Emerging economies in particular have been playing a more central role in boosting global growth, and the large size of the informal sector in these economies suggests that even higher rates of growth are potentially achievable once domestic institutions are strengthened, leading to greater inclusiveness.

In examining the determinants of the size of the shadow economy, several studies place importance on the centrality of institutions and link the size of the shadow economy more broadly to various measures of institutional development. This chapter seeks to build on this approach and is structured as follows. First, some methods to estimate the size of the underground economy are discussed and these estimates are analyzed. Next, the chapter discusses the determinants of the underground economy, with particular emphasis on the role of institutions and the rule of law. The chapter also examines the role of the International Monetary Fund (IMF) in combating the growth of informal economies. Intergovernmental institutions, including the IMF, have an important role to play as they help in strengthening domestic institutions, which should serve to promote dignity and prosperity more widely.

This chapter's findings confirm that economies characterized by weak institutions, in particular those with a high regulatory burden, weak rule of law, and high corruption, have larger shares of informal economic activity, which in turn undermine economic management, growth, and ultimately the broadened social inclusion and potential for individual agency upon which enlarged human dignity rests. The evidence may also be seen as conforming to the view that firms operating in such an environment have an incentive to hide their activities in the underground economy. As Daron Acemoglu and James Robinson argue in *Why Nations Fail*, the main difference between rich and poor countries is their man-made political and economic institutions, not their culture or geography. The book's compelling narrative shows that nations prosper when they put in place inclusive and pro-growth institutions, and they fail when their institutions become extractive and benefit the interests of a narrow elite instead of creating economic benefits and political power that are widely shared (2012). Thus, institutions that are oriented toward ensuring that a broad base of people has access to the opportunity to prosper economically are crucial. And international institutions have a role in catalyzing these national institutions, which is further explained later in this essay.

Measuring the Size of the Underground Economy

Estimating the size of the informal economy is a challenge as the purpose of operating in it is often to avoid detection and, in some cases, countries may lack the capacity to monitor underground activity. Although there are no direct measures of the size and composition of the underground economy, a number of indirect methods have been proposed, although each of these has drawbacks. The methods to estimate the size of the underground economy are:

- *A currency demand approach.* Since most transactions in the underground economy are conducted in cash, this approach estimates the size of the underground economy from the excess demand for cash.
- *An electricity demand approach.* This assumes that electricity usage is a good physical indicator of economic activity and estimates the growth of the underground economy based on the difference between the growth rate of electricity consumption and the official GDP growth.
- *A labor force approach.* This estimates the growth of the underground economy based on the decline in labor participation, assuming a constant labor participation rate.
- *A multiple indicators, multiple causes model (MIMIC model).* This estimates the size of the shadow economy based on multiple observed variables that are presumed to cause it, including the share of direct taxes, the size of the government, tax rates, the regulatory burden, and GDP per capita (Schneider 2004; Schneider, Buehn, and Montenegro 2010).

These approaches to measuring the size of the informal economy suggest that it is sizable in a number of countries (figure 5.1). Estimates based on the above estimation methods for 2006 suggest that the shadow economy in the most advanced countries ranges from 14 to 16 percent of GDP, whereas in the case of emerging market countries the range is 32–35 percent of GDP (figure 5.2). Underground economies are much larger in Latin America, Central America, and Africa, often greater than 40 percent of GDP. In contrast, in the Middle East and Developing Asia they range between 25 and 35 percent of GDP (figure 5.3).

The extent of informality may also vary by sector within countries, depending on the nature of the activity. For example, services sectors such as petty/street retail and household services and subsistence farming may be entirely informal, requiring little capital or low skill levels. Labor-intensive

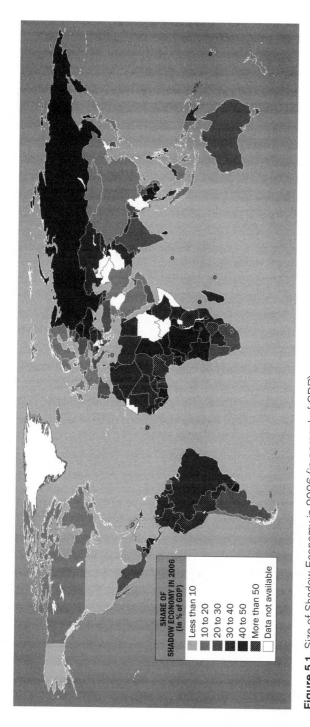

Figure 5.1 Size of Shadow Economy in 2006 (in percent of GDP).
Source: Friedrich Schneider, Andreas Buehn, and Claudio E. Montenegro. 2010. "New Estimates for the Shadow Economy All Over the World," *International Economic Journal* 24 (4): 443–61.

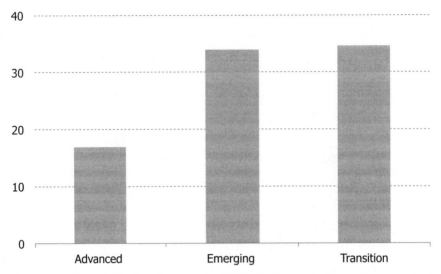

Figure 5.2 Size of Shadow Economy in 2006: By Economic Status (in percent of GDP).
Source: Friedrich Schneider, Andreas Buehn, and Claudio E. Montenegro. 2010. "New Estimates for the Shadow Economy All Over the World," *International Economic Journal* 24 (4): 443–61.

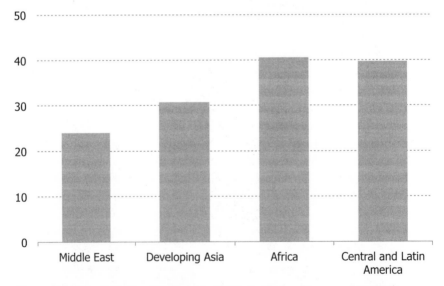

Figure 5.3 Size of Shadow Economy in 2006: By Region (in percent of GDP)
Source: Friedrich Schneider, Andreas Buehn, and Claudio E. Montenegro. 2010. "New Estimates for the Shadow Economy All Over the World," *International Economic Journal* 24 (4): 443–61.

manufacturing firms may also be highly informal. And activities requiring high levels of skill and capital are expected to be found primarily in the formal sector.

Determinants of the Size of the Underground Economy: Key Results from the Literature

There is considerable debate on the role of the burden of taxation in leading to increased underground economic activity. One strand of the literature finds that a more burdensome tax regime (including onerous tax rates and adminis-tration) is a key driver that leads to an increase in the share of the underground economy as firms move underground to evade taxes and boost profits. Esti-mates show that if the tax burden as perceived by firms (measured by the Global Competitiveness Survey) becomes more onerous (by one point on a scale of 1 to 7), the size of the shadow economy rises by 11.7 percentage points (Johnson, Kaufmann, and Zoido-Lobaton 1998), though once they control for log GDP per capita the coefficient changes to -6.5. Friedman and others (2000) find that higher taxes are associated with a smaller underground economy. Specifically, raising taxes by one point (on a scale of 1 to 5, using the Heritage Foundation's 2011 measure of tax rates, in which a higher score implies a more onerous taxation system) leads to a 9 percent fall in the size of the underground economy. The contention is that the higher tax rates lead to stronger revenues and better public goods provision, including a more robust legal environment, thereby encouraging firms to operate in the official sector.

Another strand of the literature argues that political, economic, and so-cial institutions are the main drivers of increased underground economic activity.[2] Using data from the 1990s for sixty-nine countries, Friedman and others (2000) find that higher taxes are not associated with a larger unofficial economy; rather, more bureaucracy, higher corruption, and weaker legal en-vironments are correlated with a larger unofficial economy. In particular, the regulatory burden faced by workers and firms is a more important factor that determines the size of the underground economy. Regulatory burden in-cludes costs related to complying with license restrictions and leads to increased costs for firms, which may encourage the move to the shadow economy. In-deed, more regulation is correlated with a larger shadow economy (figure 5.4), as a one point worsening of the regulation index (as measured by the Heritage Foundation in 2011) is associated with a 12 percent increase in the size of the underground economy (Friedman et al. 2000).

Cumbersome labor market restrictions often lead to an increase in the size of informal employment and thereby the underground economy. The International

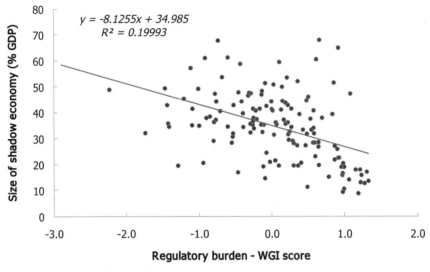

Figure 5.4 Size of Shadow Economy and Regulatory Burden.
Sources: Friedrich Schneider, Andreas Buehn, and Claudio E. Montenegro. 2010. "New Estimates for the Shadow Economy All Over the World," *International Economic Journal* 24 (4): 443–46; World Bank World Governance Indicators (WGI) Database.

Labor Organization (ILO) estimates that around half the workers in developing countries are employed in the informal economy, even though the share of the underground economy is much lower, around 35 percent of GDP (ILO 2011). Overly stringent labor market regulations have the unintended consequence of encouraging more informal labor arrangements as they raise the cost of hiring for firms. Labor regulations are designed in many cases to restrict hiring workers on flexible contracts, to place limits on maximum hours worked, and to create barriers to firing workers. Analysis using the World Bank's *Doing Business* database suggests that restrictions on hiring and firing intended to protect workers have instead discouraged firms from hiring in the formal labor market, as compliance tends to be expensive and cumbersome (World Bank 2004). Instead, firms hire informal workers, pay them under the table, and avoid providing health insurance and other benefits. The World Bank study finds that reforms that work well to create jobs include: increasing the length and scope of term contracts, introducing apprentice wages, allowing flexible working hours, and removing administrative approvals for dismissals.

Another drawback of operating in the informal sector is the loss of access to the formal financial sector for firms and individuals. In many developing countries, less than half the population has an account with a financial institution, and in some countries less than one in five households do. This lack of access to finance traps firms in low productivity operations and perpetuates inequality as poor individuals rely on their own limited resources to finance education or start businesses. Since the lack of access to finance is often the critical cause behind both persistent income inequality and slow economic growth, financial sector reforms that promote broader access to financial services are crucial. Government policies should focus on building sound financial institutions, encouraging competition, and establishing sound prudential regulation to provide the private sector with appropriate incentive structures and to broaden access (World Bank 2004). Governments should make lending attractive to banks by strengthening creditor rights, enabling securitized lending, and raising interest rate ceilings. The IMF and World Bank jointly prepare a comprehensive and in-depth analysis of a country's financial sector under the Financial Sector Assessment Program (FSAP). The FSAP provides an assessment of both the stability of the financial sector, with emphasis on the soundness of the banking and other financial sectors, and the development aspects of the financial sector, which focuses on the quality of the legal framework and financial infrastructure.

Relationship between the Underground Economy and Institutions: Empirical Analysis

Data and Methodology

The following empirically analyzes the determinants of the size of the unofficial economy using a more comprehensive and recent dataset than the papers discussed above. The key empirical question is the extent to which weaknesses in institutional quality create room for underground economic activity. Large underground economies and weak institutions, however, can be mutually reinforcing in theory, and institutions cannot be considered exogenous. From a policy perspective, it is important to gauge whether weak institutions lead to larger underground economies or whether the reverse effect predominates. To do this, this essay employs an instrumental variable regression in which a set of exogenous variables related to geographical and historical factors are used because they have been shown to influence institutional formation. This methodology can isolate and estimate the contribution of poor institutions in creating large underground economies.[3]

The analysis uses data on about one hundred countries and includes advanced countries, emerging markets, and developing countries. The dependent variable is the size of the shadow economy, which is estimated in Schneider, Buehn, and Montenegro (2010) based on the methodologies outlined in the previous section. Other independent variables include the top marginal income tax rate (Gwartney et al. 2011), real per capita GDP (World Bank 2012 WDI database), and Consumer Price Index inflation (IMF's IFS database).

The measures of institutional quality are drawn from the widely used World Bank's Governance database, which is based on Kaufmann, Kraay, and Zoido-Lobaton (1999) and Kaufmann, Kraay, and Mastruzzi (2009).[4] This data comprises six composite indicators, which measure perceptions of institutional quality: voice and accountability, political stability and the absence of violence, government effectiveness, regulatory quality, the rule of law, and control of corruption.[5] The overall institutional quality or governance indicator is the average of these six composite indicators. A higher value of these indicators corresponds to superior institutions. All these measures are highly correlated so only one can be used in the empirical analysis at a time to avoid misleading inference.

Results

The size of underground economies is influenced predominantly by the quality of institutions. As discussed in the previous section, a number of studies find that the underground economy accounts for a larger share of national income when there is more corruption and when the rule of law is weak. Figures 5.5 and 5.6 show that the size of the underground economy declines as the overall institutional quality and the rule of law improve. However, in the presence of large underground economies, we observe widespread corruption and a lack of governance, and economic opportunities are restricted to a few, which in turn hinders the promotion of human capabilities and dignity as defined in the introduction.

The three main findings of the regression analysis are contained in table 1 and are as follows:

> First, better institutions are associated with a significantly lower share of the shadow economy. If overall institutional quality improves by one standard deviation, an almost 11 percent reduction in the size of the shadow economy is achieved. Furthermore, a one standard deviation improvement in the rule of law score is associated with an 8 percent reduction in the share of the shadow economy. These results are robust across a number of different measures of institutional quality.
>
> Moreover, it is important to note that institutions are the most important determinant of the size of the underground economy. Once institutions are controlled for, taxes, inflation, and per capita income are no longer statistically significant. Therefore, it is not higher taxes per se

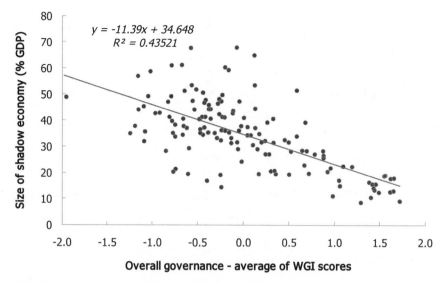

Figure 5.5 Size of Shadow Economy and Overall Governance.
Sources: Friedrich Schneider, Andreas Buehn, and Claudio E. Montenegro. 2010. "New Estimates for the Shadow Economy All Over the World," *International Economic Journal* 24 (4): 443–46; World Bank World Governance Indicators (WGI) Database.

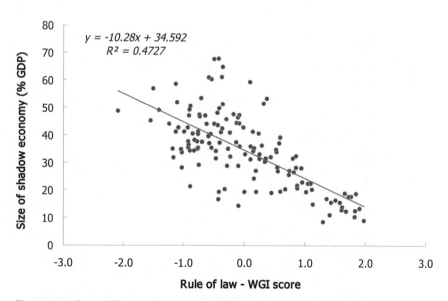

Figure 5.6 Size of Shadow Economy and Rule of Law.
Sources: Friedrich Schneider, Andreas Buehn, and Claudio E. Montenegro. 2010. "New Estimates for the Shadow Economy All Over the World," *International Economic Journal* 24 (4): 443–46; World Bank World Governance Indicators (WGI) Database.

Table 1. Determinants of the Size of the Shadow Economy

Dependent variable: size of shadow economy (in percent of GDP)[a]	(1)	(2)	(3)	(4)	(5)	(6)	(7)
Top marginal income tax rate[b]	-0.345*		-0.300*	-0.234*	-0.195	-0.191	-0.240*
Inflation[c]		0.674**	0.828**	0.059			
Per capita income (log)				-5.919**	-2.170	-2.517	-1.325
Rule of law[d]					-8.172*		
Control of corruption[d]						-7.077*	
Overall governance[e]							-10.725*
Constant	45.578**	27.615**	35.708**	88.258**	59.810**	62.185**	55.639**
Observations	94	135	91	91	82	82	82
R-squared	0.099	0.117	0.259	0.523	0.576	0.572	0.558

Notes and data sources:
Robust t-statistics in parentheses; ** $p < 0.01$, * $p < 0.05$.
[a] Average of estimates for 1999–2000, 2000–01, 2002–03, from Schneider (2005).
[b] Fraser Institute; data from the year 2000.
[c] CPI inflation in 2000.
[d] Kauffman, Kraay, and Mastruzzi, World Bank 2009; data are average from 1996–2008.
[e] Overall institutional quality is measured as the averaged of six institutional variables as in KKM 2009.

that lead to increased shadow economy but rather weak institutions and rule of law. Businesses have an incentive to go underground not to avoid high taxes but rather to reduce the burden of regulation, consistent with the findings of Friedman and others (2000) described in the previous section.

Third, countries with more corruption tend to have larger underground economies. A one standard deviation decrease in the corruption index leads to a 7 percent increase in the size of the shadow economy.

Policy Implications: The Role of the IMF in Reducing the Size of the Underground Economy

The underground economy is a significant part of many countries' economies and represents a vital growth opportunity, especially for developing countries. Due to the variety of problems facing informal economic activity, persistent large informal sectors can lead to low productivity and anemic growth in the sectors in which they prevail, necessitating policies to remedy the problem. Maximizing *inclusive* growth requires an understanding of the incentives motivating underground activity, bringing as many people as possible into the formal economy, and helping them to tap their capabilities and thrive, which in turn will promote human dignity as defined in the introduction. The literature offers some ideas as to how the informal sector can be unshackled and be integrated into the formal sector. For example, governments that wish to shrink the size of the shadow economy could focus on strengthening the rule of law, creating access to the formal economy, and strictly enforcing only the minimum necessary set of regulations.

Given the central role of institutions in preventing the enlargement of underground economies and more importantly in catalyzing long term economic growth, institutional development must take center stage. A strong culture of the rule of law, capacity to implement the rule of law in all sectors, government credibility, and a strong legal and judicial framework are critical priorities, as they form the basis for good institutions. Also it is important to give priority to the establishment and consolidation of economic institutions, which in turn have a powerful impact on macroeconomic stability, access to and security of property rights, and free trade. The IMF has been involved in strengthening economic institutions in the context of both the provision of surveillance advice and technical advice to the membership. The IMF has also been at the forefront of the reform of the financial regulatory and supervisory framework in the aftermath of the global recession with a view to strengthening domestic institutions and the global economy. Also, in order to directly combat the problem of the underground economy, the IMF's legal department (LEG) has been supporting member countries in areas of combating money laundering and implementing fiscal legal reforms.

A key enabling condition for private sector activity to flourish is a well-functioning property rights system. It catalyzes individuals' power to apply their capabilities and enjoy economic opportunity. Firms in the formal economy that enjoy these rights and protections are able to leverage assets into working capital and grow their businesses. As mentioned earlier, De Soto (1989) argues that recognizing the assets of the informal sector as property might help to convert these assets into capital that can be used for investment. In general, institutional reform should include measures to ease regulatory burdens where possible and strengthen the rule of law to effectively enforce a minimum necessary set of regulations. Country-specific and sector-specific circumstances will of course guide the precise path and desirable sequencing of policy measures, which will vary considerably.

The IMF and the Reform of Financial Regulation and Supervision

The IMF is playing a key role in the development of financial regulation and its implementation by national authorities.[6] It serves as a forum to ensure that reform efforts are appropriate, sustained, coordinated, and globally consistent. The IMF, with its knowledge of member countries' financial systems and its experience in monitoring global standards and codes, is well positioned to help ensure that a well-designed financial system benefits all its members, not just some. The resulting broader access to opportunity will strengthen dignity globally. The IMF is able to see the pros and cons of different regulatory structures, what has worked well, what has not, and what can help translate these assessments into practical regulation. The IMF could advise countries on the best placement of a mandate for financial stability, depending on each country's current financial architecture. Thus, the IMF could help minimize the collateral damage to households and firms that might otherwise take place if the necessary financial system reform fails to occur or occurs in an uncoordinated way, leading to an unlevel playing field. Through its surveillance activities, the IMF can help to bring peer pressure to bear on countries that fall short of conforming to international best practices. In so doing, it demonstrates the vital role of an intergovernmental institution to help strengthen the domestic legal framework in a fashion that will advance the ability of broad populations to count on consistent legal norms, make their own choices, and economically thrive.

To help foster a more stable global financial system, the IMF is taking steps to refine its surveillance of the financial system using a more global approach—by looking at the connections between the financial system and the macroeconomy (so-called macrofinancial linkages) and by removing data gaps that inhibit observance of various linkages. IMF policy advice is being strengthened by enhancing the interaction between multilateral and bilateral surveillance and through more targeted technical assistance in the areas of supervision, regulation, and crisis management. Assessment of contingent fiscal liabilities to the financial sector and their impact on systemic risk is becoming a particular focus.

The IMF already contributes to ongoing discussions on regulatory reform through its interactions with the financial sector standard setters (Basel Committee on Banking Supervision, the International Organization of Securities Commissions, International Accounting Standards Board, and the International Association of Deposit Insurers and the Financial Action Task Force). The IMF has been increasingly interacting with the Financial Stability Board (FSB) and the Bank of International Settlements (BIS) on topics of mutual interest. The roles of these bodies will become further intertwined as the FSB helps to advance the agenda for international financial regulatory changes, the BIS collects data and performs research, and the IMF brings to bear its members' experiences by tracking and encouraging the implementation of new standards and regulatory changes through its surveillance activities and technical assistance.

The IMF's ability to monitor implementation and enforcement through FSAP should help to spur reform efforts. To assure compliance with emerging regulations, best practices, or guidelines, the IMF has recently developed additional ways for reviewing the implementation of new standards and codes and has adopted proposals for making the FSAPs and Reports on the Observance of Standards and Codes (ROSCs) more flexible in their application and more targeted and timely in their delivery. In low-income countries, the FSAP also focuses on issues related to access to financial services by the broader population and development of financial markets. Actions to achieve these objectives result in wider participation in financial markets, which contributes to furthering human dignity through (1) social recognition of more groups as deserving of inclusion and (2) agency to thrive yielded to those people gaining access to financing.

Fiscal Legal Reforms and the IMF

The IMF's legal and fiscal work is related to reducing the size of the underground economy and focuses mainly on improving the tax system as well as increasing revenues and reducing corruption. Specifically, the IMF carries out a substantial program of technical assistance in tax policy, tax administration, and drafting of tax legislation. Among other things, this technical assistance seeks to establish tax regimes for small businesses that:

(1) involve minimum discretion, hence reducing the scope for corruption,

(2) employ tax accounting rules that minimize the compliance burden on businesses, and

(3) fix a tax burden on the informal sector that is reasonable but not concessionary, in turn providing small businesses an incentive to adopt more comprehensive accounting procedures. The latter might in some cases result in a lower tax burden than under presumptive regimes.

The IMF also works on reforms related to the drafting of tax procedure codes and implementation of tax administration reforms that support simplified registration procedures, thereby unleashing access to opportunity. One-stop shopping allows a small business to register without having to go to a multitude of government offices to obtain the necessary business licenses. The IMF's work in this area is coordinated with that of the International Finance Corporation (IFC), which facilitates tax and other administrative reforms to create a more supportive climate for small business. More broadly, the IMF collaborates with the World Bank, other regional development banks such as the Asian Development Bank and the African Development Bank, the World Trade Organization, UN agencies, and other international organizations on a number of issues to serve its membership and to work towards inclusive growth.

The IMF's Role in Promoting Financial Integrity

In part, recognizing that macroeconomic policy execution and, more abstractly, the fuller realization of individuals' dignity are impaired by the existence of unaccounted for economic transactions generated in the informal or illegal sectors, the IMF's legal department addresses a number of issues related broadly to underground economies.[7] Although the department's financial integrity group is providing increasingly meaningful support to IMF surveillance and programs, its primary role has been to provide technical assistance to member countries on policy for anti-money laundering and countering the financing of terrorism (AML/CFT) and on broader governance and institutional issues when large illicit or informal sectors are thought to have an impact on financial or economic stability. Specifically, the IMF implements a broad program of technical assistance designed to develop domestic institutions and help members build capacity in and strengthen AML/CFT law, legal frameworks, financial intelligence units, national risk assessments and strategies, training programs designed to improve on-site inspection procedures for banks and regulators, and implementation of a risk-based approach to supervision. IMF-managed technical assistance (TA) on these issues is supported by external donors and has taken place in countries such as Antigua and Barbuda, Armenia, Azerbaijan, Bolivia, China, Ghana, Indonesia, Iraq, Mauritius, Morocco, Nepal, Nigeria, Peru, Thailand, Tanzania, Uruguay and Zimbabwe.[8]

The IMF regularly advises members through technical assistance and AML/CFT assessments, which are an important part of the FSAP and ROSC programs, on areas within the IMF's mandate associated with underground economy (IMF 2009a and b). These activities have dual objectives related to reducing the size of underground economies: increasing the ability of governments to identify the source of all assets (including tax fraud) and reducing the size of the cash basis of an economy if it interferes with the ability to identify the source of funds in the economy.

Money laundering may be associated with tax fraud that can undermine financial or macroeconomic activity in important ways. As such, weak institutions, corruption, and criminal activity undercut the consistent legal norms and contribute to worsening inequality, which weakens the agency of individuals to thrive and hence weakens basic human dignity. Also, as discussed above, significant levels of tax fraud may affect a government's revenues and undermine the fiscal balance and prospects for long-term sustainable growth. Moreover, the injection of large amounts of so-called hot money arising from tax evasion may subject a country's banking system to volatile inflows and outflows that can threaten its stability. By limiting opportunities for the banking system to be used to launder the proceeds of tax evasion, a robust framework of AML/CFT controls can serve as an effective instrument in combating tax evasion (IMF 2009b).

AML legal and institutional tools can be used to detect and investigate the laundering of the proceeds of tax evasion, corruption, and fraud; prosecute offenders; and recover the proceeds of these crimes, including when they are hidden abroad. Assessing IMF members' compliance with the AML/CFT recommendations, advising on corrective actions, and providing technical assistance arguably contributes to reducing the size of underground economies by helping IMF member countries' work in regulating various relevant sectors with the economy.

An IMF paper (IMF 2009b) on this issue reflects recognition of the importance of AML/CFT as a component of the IMF's work on governance and addresses how the AML/CFT program should evolve in two areas:

(1) assessments that are part of the ROSC and FSAP programs, and (2) modular financial stability assessments, IMF Article IV surveillance (which is the regular consultation with members), and support for IMF financing programs. It was decided to maintain the mandatory inclusion of AML/CFT assessments in all FSAPs.

The legal department has been actively supporting surveillance and program work where underground or illegal economic activity leads to serious unwanted macroeconomic outcomes and has been making this work operational through targeted, systematic interventions under the terms of IMF programs.

Taken together, IMF-supported reforms in the areas of financial regulation, fiscal policy, and AML/CFT have an important role to play as they help to strengthen domestic institutions, which should serve to increase inclusiveness and access to economic opportunities, thereby promoting human dignity.

Conclusion

The underground economy constitutes a significant portion of the overall economy in a number of countries. A central finding of this essay is that when businesses are faced with onerous regulation and weak and inconsistent enforcement and corruption, they have an incentive to hide their activities in the underground economy. That context undercuts accountability and transparency upon which greater economic growth, shared prosperity, and the realization of human dignity rest. Another finding focuses on the importance of the rule of law in curbing shadow economic activity. The policy implication is that large reductions in tax rates or increasing the number of regulations will not shrink the shadow economy. Instead, governments should place emphasis on strengthening the rule of law, simplifying access to the formal economy, including improving access to financial services, and strictly enforcing a minimum necessary set of regulations, rather than increasing the plethora of regulatory requirements.

The IMF has been involved in strengthening domestic economic institutions in the context of both provision of surveillance advice and technical advice to member countries. Since the global financial crisis of 2008, the IMF has played a key role in the reform of the global financial regulatory and supervisory framework. Also, in order to directly combat the problem of the underground economy, the IMF has been supporting its members by providing technical assistance on combating money laundering and terrorist finance and on larger governance and institutional issues when large illicit sectors are thought to be seriously hindering favorable macroeconomic outcomes.

To sum up, the empirical examination in this chapter indicates that the absence of rule of law and widespread corruption inevitably allow underground economic activities to flourish, particularly in developing countries. Conversely, in order for the population to more fully flourish, domestic institutions must be strengthened, thereby protecting private property rights, regularizing financial flows, and ensuring full access to economic opportunities. Despite the recent emergence of new types of international groupings (from the G–20 to philanthropic foundations to public-private partnerships), the Bretton Woods institutions and the IMF in particular continue to play an important function to help countries strengthen domestic institutions. And as those domestic institutions become increasingly responsible and responsive to the needs of all members of society, citizens will have more consistent access to legal rights and a greater assurance that their capabilities, choices, and efforts will translate into a better life in practice. In short, intergovernmental institutions can and must help domestic institutions emerge; this will catalyze inclusive growth and the realization of the fruits of a life of dignity.

Notes

The views expressed herein are those of the author and should not be attributed to the International Monetary Fund, its Executive Board, or its management. The author would like to thank Sonali Jain-Chandra, Carine Chartouni, Jody Meyers, Adil Mohammad, Melissa Tullis, Victory Thuronyi, and Rhoda Weeks-Brown for their input and comments.

1. Also variously known as the informal, shadow, or parallel economy.

2. Institutions are defined as the formal and informal constraints on political, economic, and social interactions (North 1990).

3. The goal is to use a set of instruments that are correlated with the endogenous regressors, but not with the error term. This paper uses a standard set of instruments from the literature, including legal origins, language, ethno-linguistic diversity, and some geographical factors (for more details please see IMF 2003).

4. This essay also considers alternative measures of institutional quality, namely the Heritage Foundation's (2011) *Index of Economic Freedom*.

5. These aggregate indicators are based on hundreds of individual variables that measure various dimensions of governance and institutional quality derived from views of household and firm survey respondents. The paper then uses an Unobserved Components Model (UCM) to combine these individual indicators into the six composite measures of governance. The composite measures of governance generated by the UCM are in units of a standard normal distribution, with mean 0, standard deviation of 1, and running from approximately -2.5 to 2.5, with higher values corresponding to better institutional outcomes.

6. Based on Kodres and Narain (2010).

7. The work done by the IMF LEG's Financial Integrity Group as described in this chapter took place until mid-2006 and was completed jointly by staff in LEG and in the then Monetary and Financial Systems Department, who together now comprise the Financial Integrity Group.

8. This list includes all of the countries identified in figure 5.1 with shadow economies greater than 50 percent of GDP. Fund TA on AML/CFT targets economies and subject areas where TA can make the greatest impact.

References

Acemoglu, Daron, and James Robinson. 2012. *Why Nations Fail: The Origins of Power, Prosperity, and Poverty*. New York: Crown Business.

De Soto, Hernando. 1989. *The Other Path: The Invisible Revolution in the Third World*. New York: Harper Collins.

Friedman, E., S. Johnson, D. Kaufmann, and P. Zoido-Lobaton. 2000. "Dodging the Grabbing Hand: The Determinants of Unofficial Activity in 69 Countries." *Journal of Public Economics* 76: 459–93.

Gwartney, James, Robert Lawson, and Joshua Hall. 2011. *2011 Economic Freedom Dataset*, published in Economic Freedom of the World: 2011 Annual Report. Fraser Institute. http://www.freetheworld.com/datasets_efw.html.

Heritage Foundation. 2011. *Index of Economic Freedom*. Washington, DC: Heritage Foundation.

International Labor Organization (ILO). 2011. *Key Indicators of the Labour Market*. Geneva: ILO.

International Monetary Fund (IMF). 2003. "Growth and Institutions." *World Economic Outlook*, 95–128. Washington, DC: IMF.

———. 2009a. *AML/CFT Methodology with FATF 40 + 9: Recommendations, Interpretive Notes, and Best Practices*. Washington, DC: IMF.

———. 2009b. *Anti-Money Laundering and Combating the Financing of Terrorism (AML/CFT), Report of the Review of the Effectiveness of the Program*. Washington, DC: IMF.

Johnson, S., D. Kaufmann, and P. Zoido-Lobaton. 1998. "Regulatory Discretion and the Unofficial Economy." *American Economic Review* 88 (2): 387–92.

Kaufmann, D., A. Kraay, and M. Mastruzzi. 2009. "Governance Matters VIII: Aggregate and Individual Governance Indicators, 1996–2008." World Bank Policy Research Working Paper 4978. Washington, DC: World Bank.

Kaufmann, D., A. Kraay, and P. Zoido-Lobaton. 1999. "Aggregating Governance Indicators." Policy Research Working Paper Series 2195. Washington, DC: World Bank.

Kodres, Laura, and Aditya Narain. 2010. *Redesigning the Contours of the Future Financial System*. International Monetary Fund Staff Position Note SPN/10/10.

North, D. 1990. *Institutions, Institutional Change and Economic Performance*. Cambridge, UK: Cambridge University Press.

Schneider, F. 2004. "The Size of the Shadow Economies of 145 Countries All over the World: First Results over the Period 1999 to 2003." IZA Discussion Paper No. 1431. Bonn, DE: IZA. http://ssrn.com/abstract=636661.

Schneider, F., A. Buehn, and C. Montenegro. 2010. "New Estimates for the Shadow Economies All over the World." *International Economic Journal* 24 (4): 443–61.

Smith, P. 1994. "Assessing the Size of the Underground Economy: The Statistics Canada Perspectives." *Canadian Economic Observer* 7 (5).

World Bank. 2004. *Doing Business in 2005: Removing the Obstacles to Growth*. Washington, DC: World Bank.

———. 2012. *World Development Indicators Database*. Washington, DC: World Bank.

CHAPTER 6

The Global Human Rights Regime

Assessing and Renovating the Architecture

MARK P. LAGON AND RYAN KAMINSKI

Although the concept of human rights is abstract, how it is applied has a direct and enormous impact on daily life worldwide. It requires all people be recognized in practice as deserving equal access to justice and to the opportunity to make choices to apply their gifts and thrive. That is what human dignity entails. Yet millions have suffered crimes against humanity. Countless more toil in bonded labor. In the last decade alone, authoritarian rule has denied civil and political liberties to billions. The idea of human rights has a long history, but only in the past century has the international community sought to galvanize a regime to promote and guard them. Particularly, since the UN was established in 1945, world leaders have cooperated to codify human rights in a universally recognized regime of treaties, institutions, and norms (Farer and Gaer 1993).

An elaborate global system is being developed. Governments are striving to promote human rights domestically and abroad and are partnering with multilateral institutions, civil society groups, and even the private sector to do so. Together, these players have achieved some real success, though the institutionalization and implementation of different rights is progressing at varying rates. Acknowledging key exceptions, such as over 100,000 killed in Syria since 2011, response to mass atrocities has seen overall progress, even if enforcement remains inconsistent. The desire to stem critical threats to public health is strongly embedded across the globe, and substantial resources have been devoted to the challenge. The right to freedom from slavery and forced labor has also been integrated into international and national institutions and has benefited from high-profile pressure to combat these extreme abuses. Finally, the steady accumulation of human rights-related conventions has encouraged

123

most states to do more to integrate binding legislation in their constitutions and domestic statutes.

Significant challenges to promoting human rights norms remain, however. To begin with, the conceptual umbrella of human rights is massive. Freedom from slavery and torture, the imperative to prevent gender and racial persecution, and the right to education and health care are only some of a broad spectrum of issues asserted as human rights. Furthermore, nations continue to dispute the importance of civil and political versus economic, social, and cultural rights—two sides of human dignity. National governments sometimes resist adhering to international norms they perceive as contradicting local cultural or social values. Western countries—especially the United States—resist some international rights cooperation from a concern that it might harm business, infringe on autonomy, or limit freedom of speech. The world struggles to balance democracy's promise of human rights protection against its historically Western identification.

Moreover, some of the worst violators of human rights have not joined core rights treaties or institutions, undermining the initiatives' perceived effectiveness. Negligence of international obligations is difficult to penalize. The UN Charter promotes "fundamental freedoms," for example, but also affirms that nations cannot interfere with domestic matters. The utility of accountability measures, such as sanctions or force and under what conditions, is also debated by some. At times, to secure an end to violent conflict, negotiators choose not to hold human rights violators accountable. Furthermore, developing nations are often incapable of protecting rights within their borders, and the international community needs to bolster their capacity to do so—especially in the wake of the recent revolutions across the Middle East and North Africa. Finally, questions remain over whether the UN, regional bodies, or other global actors should be the primary forums to advance human rights, a focus in this book.

In the long term, strengthening the human rights regime will require a renovated UN human rights architecture complemented by other more nimble and accountable institutions as well as building partnerships between the heterogeneous array of international institutions today. A steady coalition between the global North and South to harmonize political and economic rights within democratic institutions will also be necessary. In the meantime, regional organizations and NGOs must play a larger role from the bottom up, and rising powers must do more to lead. Together, these changes are the world's best hope for durable and universal enjoyment of human rights, to meaningfully extend human dignity.

Human Rights: Heightened Attention, Uneven Regional Efforts, and Weak Global Compliance

The international human rights regime has made several welcome advances—including increased responsiveness in the Muslim world, attention to prevention and accountability for atrocities, and notably at the UN Security Council (UNSC), more pressure on great powers to avoid standing in the way of action. Yet, despite responses to emerging cases demanding action, such as Sudan and Libya, global governance in ensuring human rights has faltered, including in Syria in recent years.

Many experts credit intergovernmental organizations (IGOs) for making advancements, particularly in civil and political rights. These scholars cite the creation of an assortment of secretariats, administrative support, and expert personnel to institutionalize and implement human rights norms (Rubenstein 2004). Overall, the UN remains the central global institution for developing international norms and legitimizing efforts to implement them, but the number of actors involved has grown exponentially, creating the neomedieval context Lagon and Arend describe in this book.

The primary mechanisms include UNSC action, the UN Human Rights Council (UNHRC), committees of elected experts, various rapporteurs, special representatives, and working groups (Piccone 2012). War crimes tribunals—the International Criminal Court (ICC), tribunals for the former Yugoslavia and Rwanda, and hybrid courts in Sierra Leone and Cambodia—also contribute to the development and enforcement of standards. All seek to raise political will and public consciousness, assess human rights-related conduct of states and warring parties, and offer capacity-building advice to states on improving human rights.

However, these mechanisms are far from consistent. Generally, when they are effective, they change states' conduct more by publicizing abuses than by providing technical advice or applying punitive measures. For example, no global body was capable of forcing the United States to stop its mistreatment of detainees at the Guantanamo Bay Detention Facility, but mounting international pressure did encourage fundamental US reform of its detention and interrogation policies in 2009 (Warrick and DeYoung 2009). As a result, skeptics also counter that other grassroots movements or organizations may be more responsible for rights improvements than global institutions (Smith-Cannoy 2012). Furthermore, although progress has been significant in condemning and responding to atrocities, it has been limited in advancing civil and political rights. Many in the international community are reassessing economic, social, and cultural rights as IGOs increasingly link human rights to business practices and public health.

Of all UN bodies with a similar focus, the UNHRC receives the most attention. In its former incarnation as the Commission on Human Rights, it developed a reputation for allowing the participation—and even leadership—of notorious human rights abusers, which undermined its legitimacy. Reconstituted as the UNHRC in 2006, the new forty-seven-member body has a higher threshold for membership as well as a Universal Periodic Review (UPR) process, which evaluates the human rights records of states, including those on the Council. Nevertheless, the UNHRC's effectiveness has been uneven. On the one hand, the UNHRC took the unprecedented move of voting to recommend the suspension of one of its members (Libya) in 2011. In the same year, the organ also passed a pioneering resolution on sexual orientation. On the other hand, however, the UNHRC agenda maintains a disproportionate focus on Israel, ignores major abuses in other nations, and still includes serial rights abusers in its ranks.

The UNSC has more power to take action against human rights abusers (as discussed in Nancy Soderberg's chapter 1 in this book). It can impose sanctions, mandate peacekeeping operations, and authorize the use of force in extreme cases. Furthermore, UNSC deliberations are higher profile than UNHRC meetings and thus substantially elevate international attention to and pressure on rights violators. In particular, the UNSC deliberates on countries' abuses when they threaten international peace and security—but only when UNSC politics permit it. The five permanent UNSC members can all veto resolutions. France, the United Kingdom, and the United States tend to be the most vocal advocates for promoting human rights, though they at times subordinate such concerns to strategic interests. China and Russia, however, often veto human rights interventions and have stymied efforts at achieving international consensus regarding extreme human rights violations in Syria. Recently, major powers elected to the UNSC have been ambivalent on human rights, and none of the three seeking permanent membership (Germany, Brazil, and India) voted to authorize intervention in Libya in 2011.

Increasingly, the locus of activity on human rights is moving to the regional level but at markedly different paces from place to place. (See Chester Crocker's chapter 4 in this book on regional bodies and human security.) Regional organizations and powers contribute to advancing human rights protections in their neighborhoods by bolstering norms, providing mechanisms for peer review, and helping countries codify human rights stipulations within domestic institutions. Regional organizations are often considered the first lines of defense and are better able to address rights issues unique to a given area. This principle is explicitly mentioned in the UN Charter, which calls on member states to "make every effort to achieve pacific settlement of local disputes through such regional arrangements or by such regional agencies" before approaching the UNSC.

Major regional organizations in the Western Hemisphere, Europe, and Africa—such as the Organization of American States (OAS), the European Union (EU), and the African Union (AU)—have integrated human rights into their mandate and established courts to which citizens can appeal if a nation violates their rights. This has led to important rulings on slavery in Niger and spousal abuse in Brazil, for example, but corruption continues to hamper implementation throughout Latin America and Africa, and a dearth of strong leadership in African nations has slowed institutionalization (Duffy 2009; Canton, 2009).

Meanwhile, organizations in the Middle East and Asia, such as the Association of Southeast Asian Nations (ASEAN) and the South Asian Association for Regional Cooperation, focus primarily on economic cooperation and have historically made scant progress on human rights. The Arab League, however, departed from its indifference to human rights in 2011 by backing UN action against Libya and sanctioning Syria (Rice 2012).

Civil society efforts have achieved the most striking success in human rights through frequent engagements with international institutions and national governments. Nongovernmental organizations (NGOs) provide valuable data and supervision, which can assist both states and international organizations. NGOs also largely rely on international organizations for funding, administrative support, and expert assistance. Indeed, some 3,900 NGOs have been named as official consultants to the UN Economic and Social Council alone, and many more contribute to domestic and international human rights advocacy in more informal ways (ECOSOC 2013). Domestic NGOs understand needs on the ground far better than their international counterparts. That international NGOs are beginning to recognize this is clear in two recent developments: The first is financier-philanthropist George Soros's $100 million donation to Human Rights Watch to develop field offices staffed by locals, which enabled the organization to increase its annual operating budget to $80 million; and second, the number of capacity-building partnerships between Western-based NGOs and NGOs indigenous to a country is increasing. That said, NGOs have, to date, been more successful in advocacy—from achieving passage of the Anti-Personnel Mine Ban Convention to calling attention to governments' atrocities against their own citizens (Evans

2012). Yet NGOs devoted to implementing human rights compliance have been catching up—on issues from democratic transitions to gender empowerment to protecting migrants.

Norm and Treaty Creation: Prodigious but Overemphasized

The greatest strength of the global governance architecture has been creating norms. Myriad treaties, agreements, and statements have enshrined human rights on the international community's agenda, and some regional organizations have followed suit. These agreements lack binding clauses to ensure that action matches rhetoric, however, and many important violators have not signed on. In addition, states often attach qualifiers to their signatures that dilute their commitments.

The array of treaties establishing standards for human rights commitments is broad—from political and civil liberties to economic, social, and cultural rights to racial discrimination to the rights of women, children, migrant workers, and more recently the disabled (OHCHR 2011). Other global efforts have focused on areas such as labor rights and human trafficking (Perez Solla 2009). Regional organizations, most notably the Council of Europe and the Organization of American States, have also promulgated related instruments, although less uniformly. In addition, member states have articulated declarations and resolutions establishing human rights standards, and increasingly so in economic affairs. In 2011, the UNHRC, in a departure from the premise that states are to be held accountable for human rights conduct, passed formal guidelines for related business responsibilities (UNHRC 2011; Ruggie 2013).

On the other hand, states are under are no binding obligation to observe or implement rights resolutions unless passed—without a veto—through the UNSC or one of the few regional bodies with binding authority over member states. Similarly, although the proliferation of treaties, conventions, and protocols over the past fifty years implies significant advances in human rights norms, the true impact of these measures is questionable.

First, many of the conventions, such as the Rome statute or the Convention on the Rights of Migrant Workers and Their Families, have not been ratified by central players, such as the United States. Second, although calls for enhanced human rights norms have increased, consensus over implementation and compliance has not kept pace. In particular, whereas the global North has largely focused on advancing civil and political rights, the global South has tended to defend economic, social, and cultural rights. Third, even if a rights document is ratified, states often use reservations, understandings, and declarations (RUDs) to evade obligations, especially those of legally bind-ing documents. They do so to avoid negative press or the potential for imbro-glios from even moderately intrusive monitoring mechanisms. Saudi Arabia is an apt example. The country has ratified the Convention on the Elimination of All Forms of Discrimination against Women (CEDAW), but one RUD states that the convention is not applicable when it conflicts with sharia law, which allows Riyadh to continue denying basic rights to women.

To be effectively implemented, the language in international treaties must be incorporated into domestic legal structures, but this process is often quite slow and mere norm-building is too often overemphasized. Implemen-tation of existing rights treaties and agreements might have more concrete effect than expanded protection on paper. Human dignity depends on it.

Rights Monitoring: Proliferating Experts, Increasing Peer-Based Scrutiny

Monitoring is imperative to matching rhetoric with action. Over the years, human rights monitoring has matured and developed considerably, though serious challenges remain, such as ensuring freedom from torture for suspected terrorists and uniformly protecting and promoting human rights despite the biases of rights organizations or officials entrusted with doing so.

The original UN Commission on Human Rights and its successor the UNHRC both authorized a wide array of special procedures to monitor hu-man rights protection in functional areas and particular countries. Since the UNHRC was established in 2006, the number of country-specific and the-matic special procedures has swelled to more than fifty, with monitors ad-dressing economic and social issues outnumbering those addressing political and civil liberties. Similarly, the UNHRC has also established official com-missions of inquiry to examine particularly egregious cases of human rights violations.

In addition, each UN human rights treaty has an elected body of experts to which state parties must report at regular intervals on implementation (Keller and Ulfstein 2012). For instance, the Human Rights Committee (not to be confused with the Council) is charged with receiving reports about the imple-mentation of the International Covenant on Civil and Political Rights (ICCPR) and making nonbinding "concluding observations" about states' overall compliance (OHCHR "Committee Against Torture"). The Human Rights Committee can also receive complaints from individuals regarding state compliance with the accord. One of the UN Convention Against Torture's monitoring mechanisms, the Committee Against Torture (CAT), is similar but can also send representatives to inspect areas of alleged cases of torture being "systematically practiced." Very few parties to the Convention (e.g., China, Syria, and Israel) have exercised the "opt-out" provision to avoid these inspections. The Committee has exercised the mechanism eight times since 1988 (OHCHR "Convention Against Torture").

Some observers believe that this array of special procedures and treaty bodies, bolstered by the UPR of all member states, indicates a robust capacity to monitor human rights globally (Piccone 2012). This could, in turn, empower NGOs to raise information and engage governments in countries where they operate. Others question the strength of the system, noting that the quality and personal biases of experts vary dramatically and that as much time is spent in the UPR on liberal states as on systematic rights abusers, and that non–Western states often elevate praise over even constructive criticism when questioning peers (McMahon 2012). There is also the risk of stacking the deck during such reviews if government-friendly (or -sponsored) NGOs submit erroneous or misleading reports (Tamayo 2013).

Various regional bodies also monitor implementation of human rights. The Organization for Security and Cooperation in Europe (OSCE) and Council of Europe mechanisms are robust. The inter-American system is highly institutionalized but disinclined to address suspension of constitutional provisions by democratically elected leaders. The AU has a promising foundation in its peer review mechanism, but it is largely unrealized in the human rights area. Other regional organizations, such as ASEAN and the Gulf Cooperation Council, have no monitoring mechanisms to speak of, despite dramatic cases of abuses and public demand for better protections in their regions (Tavares 2009).

Capacity-Building: Vital but Underemphasized

Capacity-building—especially for human rights—is often expensive and daunting, viewed with suspicion, and the success of assistance is notoriously hard to measure. In many cases, national governments have signed international commitments to promote and protect human rights, and they earnestly wish to implement them but are incapable of doing so. For example, serious questions continue to surround the basic operability of Libya's judicial system following the collapse of Muammar Qaddafi's regime (ICG 2013). On the other hand, some states refuse assistance from NGOs and IGOs, suspecting that it might interfere with domestic affairs. On balance, it also remains far easier, and less costly, for the international community to condemn, expose, or shame human rights abusers rather than to provide the material aid for human rights capacity-building to tangibly advance dignity.

The international community has developed various ways to offer technical assistance. Most notable is the Office of the High Commissioner for Human Rights (OHCHR), established in 1993 (Farer and Gaer 1993). In addition to providing an institutionalized moral voice, OHCHR offers technical assistance to states through an array of field offices—for example, by providing training to civilian law enforcement and judicial officials through its country office in Uganda, strengthening the Cambodian legal and institutional framework for human rights, and assisting Mexico with development of a National Program on Human Rights. However, some member states prefer unilateral support for capacity-building (addressed below), others favor naming and shaming over capacity-building, and yet others perceive human rights capacity-building as either a threat to sovereignty or tantamount to neocolonialism.

Regional organizations such as the OSCE, Council of Europe, OAS, EU, and to some extent the AU, may be more effective than the UN in sharing best practices and providing capacity-building advice to states. Often capacity-building entails training human rights protectors and defenders, but it may also include legal framework-building or addressing countries' specific capacity deficits. The OSCE, for instance, collaborates with member states on election monitoring and offers training and education to human rights defenders through its Office for Democratic Institutions and Human Rights (see OSCE 2007). In another example, the OAS collaborates with European partners in its judicial facilitators program, which trains judicial officials in rural areas with limited access to justice, and assisted Haiti in establishing a civil registry. Still, opportunities for sharing resources and coordinating between IGOs and NGOs in capacity-building are limited. As mentioned, norm creation has outstripped both monitoring and implementing norms.

Some developed states, however, prefer providing bilateral assistance to working with IGOs and multilateral institutions because resources can be better monitored and projects more carefully tailored to support donor state interests. For instance, the US Foreign Assistance Act of 1961, which laid the basis for the creation of the US Agency for International Development (USAID), calls for the use of development assistance to promote economic and civil rights. Since its inception, USAID has provided billions of dollars to support good governance, transparency-building, and civil society projects worldwide—in effect advancing agency for millions. For instance, it recently gave hundreds of millions of dollars to Liberia to train judges, promote the rule of the law, and increase transparency.

Meanwhile, other multilateral institutions like the World Bank, International Monetary Fund (IMF), and World Trade Organization (WTO) also support human rights promotion, but tend to do so more indirectly, through poverty alleviation and community enhancement schemes. Together, though, these institutions face new constraints as the international community continues to grapple with the global financial crisis and unprecedented budget deficits.

NGOs, although indispensable actors in terms of implementing ground-level capacity-building, mostly operate at the pleasure of national governments and have little recourse if asked to cease operations or even leave a state entirely. Suspicious of NGO activity, some governments have attempted to pass laws limiting the activity of NGOs or requiring them to receive prior approval before engaging in capacity-building efforts. The March 2009 decision of Sudan's president, Omar al-Bashir, to order thirteen international NGOs to leave Sudan—in the aftermath of his indictment by the ICC—demonstrates that NGOs may be perceived as easy targets by governments seeking to gain political or diplomatic leverage when pressed on their human rights records.

As a whole, successful capacity-building forms the core of long-term efforts to improve human rights in countries. Regardless, ground-level human rights capacity-building is often underemphasized both in areas most in need as well as among countries or IGOs that are most in a position to help (Hafner-Burton 2013). Broad, crosscutting partnerships of international institutions are essential for such efforts to enjoy success and produce sustainable human rights reform.

Response to Atrocities: Significant Institutionalization, Selective Action

Atrocities of all sorts—whether war crimes, genocide, crimes against humanity, or ethnic cleansing—have been a major focus in the international community over the last two decades. A number of regional and country-specific courts, as well as the ICC, provide potential models for ending impunity (see chapter 2 by Tod Lindberg in this book). However, these courts have unevenly prosecuted violators of human rights, have been criticized for focusing on some abuses or regions while ignoring others, and have focused more on extended ex post facto accountability than on successful prevention.

Regional and hybrid courts have made some advances on accountability. In April, 2012, the hybrid Special Court for Sierra Leone convicted former Liberian president, Charles Taylor, of eleven counts of war crimes, including "acts of terrorism" and "sexual slavery." Taylor was sentenced by the court in May 2012 and is the first former head of state to be convicted of war crimes by an international judicial organ since the Nuremberg Trials, after World War II. Many hailed the ruling as an important step in national reconciliation for Liberia and Sierra Leone.

As for preventive action, former UN secretary-general Kofi Annan championed stronger norms for intervention against ongoing atrocities. In the wake of the Kosovo crisis, Annan cited the need for clarifying when international intervention should legally be used to prevent atrocities in states. In response, the Canadian-sponsored International Commission on Intervention and State Sovereignty (ICISS) promoted the concept of the Responsibility to Protect (R2P) in 2002 (ICISS 2002). Specifically, it placed the primary responsibility on states to protect their own citizens. When states failed, responsibility fell to the international community. Annan's *In Larger Freedom* report picked up on this concept, and R2P informed two paragraphs in the 2005 UN World Summit Outcome Document. The latter also included an emphasis on the importance of capacity-building assistance to help states meet their R2P obligations. As Nancy Soderberg notes in chapter 1, in the UNSC, the R2P doctrine has been invoked repeatedly—first generically affirmed, then raised in semi-germane cases in 2008 (in Myanmar after a cyclone and in Kenya during postelection violence), and then more conclusively in 2011 with UNSC Resolution 1973 on Libya (Bellamy 2009; UNSC 2011).

Sudan has also served as a bellwether for the international community's capacity to respond to instances of atrocities. In 2004, in response to the depredations of government-backed *Janjaweed* forces against the inhabitants of Darfur, the United States issued a legal determination that genocide had been committed. Rape of women venturing outside camps for the internally displaced, however, continued long after the UN became involved. A combined UN and AU peacekeeping force was also established to help mitigate the violence. In 2009, the ICC indicted Bashir but had neither the means to apprehend him nor the leverage to facilitate his capture. Sudan would officially split in 2011, with a new state, South Sudan, becoming the UN's 193rd member just five days later.

The geopolitical complexities of the Syrian conflict beginning in 2011, have presented a fresh challenge to the international community's response to atrocities. Although the UNSC was slow to respond, the UNHRC has established a commission of inquiry to help create a framework for accountability, and the UN General Assembly has moved more than once to condemn Damascus for human rights abuses. Elsewhere, the efforts of the World Food Program, UNICEF, and the UN High Commission for Refugees have been critical in bringing lifesaving aid to over a million people, composed overwhelmingly of women and children, affected by the situation.

In short, the international community has taken its greatest step by redefining sovereignty as answerable to legal international intervention should a state fail to shield its citizens from atrocities, or worse yet, sponsor them (Lagon and Shorr 2007). However, state practice has not matched these norms, and it remains to be seen whether consensus about Libya was sui generis.

Political Rights: Uneven Institutionalization, Backlash on Free Expression and Association

Treaties that define political and civil liberties are widely ratified, but many countries have not signed on to enforcement protocols, and many continue to violate the rights of their citizens regardless of treaties. In addition, the right of people to choose their leaders and to have freedom of the press, religion, and association has backslid in recent years. At the same time, however, people are increasingly demanding rights and attempting to bypass repression of illiberal regimes. New technology (such as cell phones, social media, and satellite television) is also providing unprecedented opportunities for social recognition and voice. Citizens publicize abuse and organize protests through platforms like Twitter and Facebook, though repressive regimes are closely following with practices to censor new technology.

States resisting the spread of political and civil liberties have been challenged more by civil society than by other states or by IGOs. Using information and communications technology, and with the support of global NGOs and occasionally the private sector, civil society has taken its demands to a new level. China's effort to control dissent, for example, has been greatly challenged by Uighur dissenters in Xinjiang, by Falun Gong groups, and by Google's decision to refuse to implement comprehensive censorship in China. However, international pressure remains relevant. For example, the Obama administration's October 2011 statement that censorship practices in China may violate WTO rules has increased pressure on China to reform (Kravets 2011).

In the UN, the number of member states, organs, and generic mandates related to freedom of expression and association has increased. For instance, the UN General Assembly adopted a resolution in 2007 calling for the end of capital punishment. In September 2010, the UNHRC adopted another resolution that created a special rapporteur on rights to freedom of peaceful assembly and of association. This occurred in the wake of a multiyear backlash against domestic NGOs and their international philanthropic and civil society backers in a series of autocracies (Gershman and Allen 2006).

Nonetheless, analysis has documented a five-year backslide in levels of democratic governance and other civil political liberties worldwide (Kurlantzick 2011). Moreover, ratifications of the First and Second Protocols of the International Covenant on Civil and Political Rights remain low. The latter, which attempts to ban the death penalty, has only eighty parties. Another more recent accord, the International Convention for the Protection of All Persons from Enforced Disappearances, came into force in 2010 but has not been ratified by states most commonly charged with executing such practices, including Russia and China.

Attacks on journalists have also increased, especially as the Arab revolutions swept through the Middle East and North Africa. And even as individuals and civic organizations have used social media and other online tools to exchange ideas and press their cause, authoritarian governments have taken advantage of the same technology to halt or reverse gains in freedom of expression. In July 2012, the UNHRC passed a resolution on internet freedom, advancing the notion that individuals retain their rights to expression whether online of offline.

In recent years, national debates about the relationship between terrorism and Islam have also increased the number of measures in IGO bodies like the UN and UNHRC on religious expression. Muslim-majority states have proposed resolutions to stem the "defamation" of religion. During the spring of 2011, however, the UNHRC shifted from the annual tradition of passing the controversial defamation of religion resolutions, which many rights groups and Western states believed opened the door to so-called religious blasphemy laws limiting pluralistic expression, to adopt a more authentically robust freedom of religion formula (Lagon and Kaminski 2013). The new balance, focusing on combating religious intolerance, was largely due to a compromise the United States struck with the Organization of the Islamic Conference, since renamed the Organization of Islamic Cooperation (OIC).

As a whole, although a large number of states continue to disregard or even retard the protection of political and civil liberties, expanding efforts on the ground and in multilateral bodies may prove most significant to enlarging *realized* human dignity in the long term.

Economic Rights and Business Responsibilities: Increased Focus and Engagement

A long-standing debate between the global North and global South has been over whether to prioritize negative obligations of states to avoid restricting political and civil liberties or positive obligations to deliver economic and social benefits. Indicators, however, show a subtle yet important shift in the last ten of the forty-year debate, indicative of the potential for a transcendent human dignity consensus.

Until the end of the twentieth century, international law frameworks placed human rights obligations on the shoulders of states. Not least through former UN secretary-general Kofi Annan's role as an ideas entrepreneur (which Abiodun Williams treats in this book), notions of the obligation of businesses on human rights have blossomed. First, in 2000, Annan and his adviser John Ruggie crafted the UN Global Compact, which enumerates voluntary principles for business related to human rights and environmental stewardship. The UN then created a mandate for a special representative of the secretary-general to assess state, business, and civil society stakeholders on business conduct and human rights, for which Ruggie was selected. As noted earlier, in July 2011, the UNHRC adopted guidelines that delineate state obligations to protect human rights, business obligations to respect them, and a joint role to provide remedies to people robbed of them (UNHRC 2011; Ruggie 2013). These successes do not come without challenges, however, as implementation will be a difficult next step.

Nevertheless, the decisions of businesses to uphold human rights standards remain largely voluntary and thus subject to market—rather than moral—forces. Even when businesses make commitments to corporate responsibility programs, no actor exists to enforce such commitments. Civil society can play a critical role in mitigating these challenges, however, by publicizing corporate human rights abuses and working directly with businesses on corporate responsibility. NGOs such as Human Rights Watch, the Institute for Human Rights and Business, the International Federation for Human Rights, Global Witness, and the International League for Human Rights exemplify these efforts. Additionally, even where businesses act in violation of domestic laws or international conventions protecting human rights, limited domestic law enforcement capabilities undermine the force of accountability standards.

The international community's efforts to address economic and social rights have accelerated. Some measures evidence a questionable redefinition of human rights, such as the special procedure mandate from the UNHRC on toxic waste. Some entail ambitious norm setting, such as the UN Convention on the Rights of Persons with Disabilities, negotiated during the George W. Bush administration and signed by the Obama administration, which ought to not spark controversy. Most important have been efforts to address economic and social rights with tangible programming. The Global Fund to Fight AIDS, Tuberculosis, and Malaria is a landmark achievement for bridging health, economic, and discriminatory ills; for mobilizing significant resources beyond regular assessed budgets of the UN; and for involving an array of UN, private sector, philanthropic, and civil society actors in a concerted partnership. It is worth noting that the global North (and its greatest skeptic on economic and social rights, the United States) has championed this effort, supplementing it heavily through the US President's Emergency Plan for AIDS Relief (PEPFAR).

Child labor, forced labor, human trafficking, and contemporary slavery have also become a focus of global governance efforts since the beginning of the twenty-first century (see Lagon's chapter 11 in this book). Such abridgments of freedom and autonomy signal a tragic combination of economic desperation, weak rule of law, and discrimination. The work of the International Labor Organization (ILO) to address forced labor and the most acute forms of child labor through conventions and preventive programs has now been supplemented by other efforts. New energy has been directed to mitigating the most coercive of labor practices as a result of the near simultaneous enactments of the Palermo Protocol to the UN Crime Convention on Trafficking in Persons (TIP) and the US Victims of Trafficking and Violence Protection Act in 2000.

The UNHRC has also authorized special rapporteurs on both human trafficking and contemporary slavery. States, IGOs, and NGOs have developed partnerships to address child labor, forced labor, and human trafficking. Businesses are also joining global governance efforts, moving from sector-specific partnerships (such as the travel and hospitality sector on child sex trafficking and chocolate companies on child labor in West Africa) to cross-sectoral ones (such as the Athens Ethical Principles and emerging thought-leader coalitions).

Women's and Children's Rights: Institutional Progress but Holdouts on Implementation

The rights of women have advanced incrementally. The UN system has moved beyond creating norms, such as the Convention on the Elimination of All Forms of Discrimination against Women and the Convention on the Rights of the Child, to more assertive leadership and calls for implementation efforts among national governments. However, despite marked success on various fronts, the UN estimates that women continue to make up less than 10 percent of world leaders and only about one-fifth of parliamentarians (UN Women 2013). Moreover, it remains to be seen whether the uprisings across the Middle East and North Africa will help or hinder the cause of gender equality—given Islamic parties' role. Efforts to enhance the economic and social well-being of women and children have also improved but remain at risk as a result of tightened national and international aid budgets.

Arguably, the decision of the UN Development Program (UNDP) to commission reports by Arab experts to link gender inequality and reduced development in the Arab world, published in 2005, was an important step forward (UNDP 2006). The formation of the UN Entity for Gender Equality and the Empowerment of Women (UN Women), amalgamating four existing agencies, received an additional boost when Chile's Michelle Bachelet was appointed its first leader. The remaining question is whether the consolidation of women's rights' functions will mainstream or silo them.

The essential role of women in peace and consensus-building has moved from statements like UNSC Resolution 1325, which recognized that women are not adequately consulted and integrated into peace processes, to reality. In December 2011, for example, the United States joined thirty-two other countries in publishing a National Action Plan (NAP) on Women, Peace, and Security designed to integrate governmental efforts to implement UNSC Resolution 1325. Ellen Johnson Sirleaf's leadership as the first woman elected head of state in Africa in postconflict Liberia, the July 2010 establishment of UN Women, and widespread agreement on the necessity of integrating gender empowerment in a proposed UN post–2015 development framework provide further evidence of the international community's improving recognition of the indispensable role of women in contributing to national prosperity.

Moreover, attention to the acute problem of violence against women has advanced, even if it has been significantly curtailed in practice. In 1998, the International Criminal Tribunal for the former Yugoslavia (ICTY), along with the Rome Statute, established the precedent that targeted rape is a crime against humanity, though the practice has continued largely unabated in Darfur, the Democratic Republic of the Congo, Burma, and Zimbabwe. The degree to which prostitution of girls and sex trafficking of women is an act of violence and gender commodification is beginning to be better understood around the world.

Despite several conventions addressing the issue of human trafficking and antitrafficking laws in many countries, it remains a nearly $32 billion industry (UNODC 2012). Although exact statistics are difficult to obtain, a 2012 ILO report estimated that at least 20.9 million people are victims of forced labor and human trafficking (ILO 2012). Over the past decade, the United States and the UN have devoted greater resources to monitoring and prosecuting trafficking by means of the UN Office of Drugs and Crime's human trafficking case law database and the US Department of State's annual *Trafficking in Persons Report*. Additionally, in 2010, the UN established a trust fund to assist victims of human trafficking, and the UN General Assembly adopted a global plan of action to combat trafficking (see Lagon's chapter 11 in this book on institutional partnerships and human trafficking). Girls are substantially less likely to attend and complete basic education, especially in South Asia and sub–Saharan Africa. Moreover, the World Bank reports that this situation is unlikely to change through economic development alone. Although girls' education has received more attention in recent years, much work remains. Gender parity in primary and secondary education was among the Millennium Development Goals (MDGs) originally targeted for achievement by 2005. In support of this goal and its original 2005 deadline, the UNICEF launched the "25 by 2005" initiative, which brought greater awareness to girls' educational needs in twenty-five countries of concern. However, the international community failed to reach the 2005 MDG target—60 percent of countries still lack gender parity in education—and it remains on the list of MDGs targeted for 2015 (UNDP 2010). Nevertheless, NGOs like the public-private Education for All-Fast Track Initiative have successfully implemented country-specific approaches. A dignitarian agenda requires such efforts to facilitate agency to thrive without societal discrimination.

Awareness and official standards for the rights of children have also expanded, but implementation has lagged. The near-universally ratified Convention on the Rights of the Child and its two optional protocols—on child soldiers and on the sale and sexual exploitation of children—have set crucial norms. Partnerships of states, IGOs, NGOs, and the private sector have begun to address the subjects of these two protocols in particular. International organizations have heightened focus on postconflict rehabilitation and reintegration of child soldiers in various regions, from the Democratic Republic of Congo to Sri Lanka. NGOs, media, and authors have raised international public awareness, and increasingly, using child soldiers is seen as human trafficking. As for child prostitution, diverse groups such as UNICEF, ILO, UN Interagency Project on Human Trafficking, International Center for Missing and Exploited Children, the secular nonprofit End Child Prostitution and Trafficking, the faith-based nonprofit World Vision, and Body Shop Corporation have forged partnerships to identify and assist victims. However, the problem of prostituted children being treated by local authorities as disposable or criminal, rather than as victims, persists globally, even in major democracies like the United States, Japan, and India.

In large segments of the developing world, children are seen as breadwinning assets, sometimes abandoned to degrading exploitation when they are too much of a burden to families. Among those capable of responding to this problem, UNICEF is arguably the best run, most respected, and most able to secure donations. In a related effort, the World Health Organization has encouraged linking immunizations to human rights as a part of its Decade of Vaccines program, which spans 2011 to 2020, though financial support will likely be constrained as a global economic downturn continues.

Other Group Rights: Heightened Focus, Selective Bias

Dedicated efforts to address the rights of particular groups have advanced for some, but stalled for others. Racism and other forms of xenophobia have been a major focus. OAS members have been negotiating over an antiracism convention proposed by Brazil since 2005, to follow in the footsteps of the UN Convention on the Elimination of All Forms of Racism and monitoring regime. The UN process, despite the 1991 repeal of UN General Assembly Resolution 3379 (classifying Zionism as a form of racism), has been sidetracked by the issue of Israel and its occupation of Palestinian territories. The 2001 UN World Conference against Racism in Durban came close to declaring Israel racist, and follow-on efforts, such as at the 2009 Review Conference, had a similarly skewed focus. In practice, however, certain great exemplars of antiracism have transcended past discrimination, from South Africa's reconciliation under Nelson Mandela to Barack Obama's election in a nation in which segregation was widely institutionalized a half century earlier. Sadly, many varied instances of racism and xenophobia remain, from anti-Semitic violence in Europe to antiwhite land seizure policies in Zimbabwe.

Indigenous peoples have been the subject of elaborate, extended dialogue and expert monitoring in the UN and inter-American system of IGOs but remain subject to discrimination. After establishing the Convention on the Rights of Indigenous and Tribal Peoples in 1989, the UN General Assembly voted to adopt the Declaration on the Rights of Indigenous Peoples in 2007. Although Australia, New Zealand, the United Kingdom, and the United States initially opposed the declaration, they ultimately voted in favor. Other ethnic minorities are the targets of discrimination (such as Dalits, who make up the vast majority of the estimated forty million bonded laborers in India despite a 1976 law against the practice) or state-led political and cultural repression (such as Tibetan Buddhists and Uighur Muslims in ostensibly autonomous territories of China) (Kethineni and Humiston 2010). Ethnic rights abuses remain one of the major sources or pretexts for armed conflict.

Sexual minorities have begun to gather increased attention in IGO forums, in resolutions, and in national practice. Focus has ranged from being subjects of violence to securing freedom from discrimination. Brazil has spearheaded confronting rights abridgments in the UN and OAS, as it did on homophobia. African and Middle Eastern states and the Vatican have led opposition to sexual minority rights in the UN. Western and Latin American states have increasingly swung toward supporting these rights, which culminated in the UNHRC passing the first UN resolution on the protection of sexual minorities in June 2011. A November 2011 follow-up OHCHR report mandated by the resolution concluded that discrimination and violence toward sexual minorities persists in all regions of the globe (OHCHR 2011).

In short, an increasing number of groups have sought and, in turn, have been recognized as deserving equal access to justice by multilateral bodies, states, and publics. Implementation efforts are spottier. Second, cultural legacies of prejudice may persist as more and more groups lobby for rights.

Strengthening the Global Human Rights Regime in the Near Term

United States and international action are needed to extend the tangible impact for people's dignity of the global human rights architecture. These recommendations for how international institutions can advance dignity specifically in the area of human rights fall into two time frames: near-term and long-term.

In the near term, the United States and its international partners should consider the following initiatives:

Empowering Regional Organizations and NGOs to Act

Global IGOs are important but alone are not enough to advance the fullest realization of human rights. Regional organizations and NGOs have also become important actors. The United States, in concert with other leading powers and global IGOs, should actively cultivate a more robust role for regional institutions and NGOs.

Compared to regional organizations, human rights action in global IGOs and institutions commonly falls prey to regional and North-South bloc politics, procedural logjams, and the need to compromise among far too many competing interests—in effect rendering a final outcome document toothless. In contrast, working through regional organizations involves fewer actors and may work best in terms of ensuring legitimacy and building consensus. Institutions like the EU, Council of Europe, and OSCE have advanced human rights in transitional states seeking to be members of the institutions in good standing. The inter-American system of IGOs has highly developed human rights mechanisms. The AU has also developed good governance and a promising peer review mechanism.

Rather than host conferences to share best practices, the United States should seek to deepen the already strong efforts of regional organizations, such as that of the OSCE for technical assistance and monitoring, and to bolster their capacities, such as that of the AU to support UN-authorized military operations (which could, for instance, help alleviate the ongoing crisis in Somalia and Mali). Promising but slowly developing efforts, such as AU and the New Partnership for Africa's Development's peer review mechanisms, should be encouraged, especially by other regional organizations and leading African powers. Stalled efforts, such as the Inter-American Democratic Charter, signed in Santiago, Chile in 2001, should be resuscitated. In the Charter, OAS members are committed to helping prevent other members from backsliding from democracy, but no mechanism exists to ensure a response to several states' executives revising constitutions by fiat—including lengthening their terms (Trujillo 2012). Regional organizations that have largely ignored human rights, such as the ASEAN, should be encouraged to integrate them into their charters.

The United States should also encourage Mexico, Japan, and India among other leading liberal powers to trust, rely on, and fund NGOs as partners where applicable, both within their own territory and internationally. The United States should also help IGOs find inventive ways to sidestep member state politics to empower NGOs. A model to scale up and replicate is the UN Democracy Fund (UNDEF), which funds responsible and reliable civil society organizations to advance a wide array of political, civil, economic, and women's rights.

Technical Assistance to States

The United States should make a concerted effort to urge IGOs to devote more time and resources to help developing countries expand their capacity to protect human rights on the ground. Although they must not abandon roles of speaking truth to power, condemning rank abuses of human dignity, and authorizing experts to monitor human rights, IGOs' finite resources would be best spent on technical assistance.

As such, the United States should also push other IGOs to prioritize technical assistance rather than relying solely on explicitly rights-oriented institutions. For instance, the UN Office on Drugs and Crime should provide more resources in the form of technical assistance to help countries enforce the Palermo Protocol on Trafficking in Persons, rather than only help them draft suitable laws. A vital aspect of this strategy is ensuring that relevant mechanisms for disseminating capacity-building and technical assistance are adequately resourced.

A Global Trust for Rule of Law

That said, forty different UN organs contribute to rule of law efforts in one capacity or another in over 110 countries. A study on the UN's rule of law efforts from New York University's Center on International Cooperation concludes, "As it stands, each UN department and entity has its own tools and mechanism to develop benchmarks and indicators and to monitor and measure progress, but these tend to be superficially consultative, focus narrowly on program outputs rather that the attainment of broader goals, and are seldom based on a theory of change" (Kavanagh and Jones 2011, 15). But the need is great. Poor implementation of rule of law in developing and least developed parts of the world ensures that countless people will not enjoy tangible agency to economically thrive and actually enjoy their rights on paper (Haugen and Boutros 2010; Khan 2009).

Based on the urgent need for concerted rule of law capacity-building, the United States—in partnership with likeminded developed and developing countries, international institutions, NGOs, and private sector actors—should create a Global Trust for Rule of Law (Global Trust). Similar to the Global Fund to Fight AIDS, Tuberculosis, and Malaria (Global Fund), the Global Trust would be an autonomous funding body run by a diverse board of donor states, philanthropists, rule of law experts, and civil society representatives. Its primary function would be to provide grants and technical advice to NGOs and governments strictly tied to enlarging access to legal rights and to rule of law capacity. The Global Trust would, for instance, support projects training lawyers or prosecutors, helping citizens gain access to existing justice institutions, or spreading awareness about corruption.

Lessons from the Global Fund include involving foundations and private sector actors to mobilize their resources and comparative advantages, and not giving lead responsibility to a single UN entity (like the World Health Organization) with vested interests. Lessons from the lesser-known UNDEF include budgetary insulation from score-settling member state politics of IGOs, while still offering the legitimacy and imprimatur of a highly respected body. Most important, UNDEF favors nimble non-UN implementers and civil society organizations, which receive a minimum of 85 percent of its total grants as a policy. Based on these models, a Global *Trust* for Rule of Law would stand as the globe's most nimble catalyst to build *trust* in societies in veritable access to justice and economic opportunity (Lagon 2012).

Strengthening the Global Human Rights Regime in the Long Term

More forward-looking objectives should also be prioritized. This goal includes not only a focus on institutional reform but also efforts to rethink conventional approaches to the fulfillment of universal human rights that can transcend typical political, social, and cultural fault lines. As such, thought leaders and policymakers on the front lines of the advancement of dignity need not interpret "long-term" goals to mean unattainable.

Further Renovation of the Human Rights Council and Global Institutions

In the long run, the global human rights architecture needs to be reformed to advance the agency and social recognition in practice on which dignity depends. Some argue that advances from the UN Commission on Human Rights to the UNHRC should not be risked by reopening dialogue on structural and procedural issues. Two reforms, which should not be objectionable to the developing world, are critical.

First, the UNHRC should move to New York, where all member states already field delegations, to better inform the work of the UNSC, UNDP, UN Women, and UNICEF, and to shield the Geneva-based OHCHR from micromanagement by a proximate political body. Second, the United States could also call for boosting the direct role of regional organizations to shape the work of the global ones without the latter dictating or limiting the former. Despite OAS inertia, increased AU and Arab League capacity will justify this step.

Rethinking Economic and Social Rights

In the long run, the United States can advance the efficacy of the human rights regime by encouraging the global North and South to rethink economic, social, and cultural rights. The United States, for instance, has been even less inclined than more social democratic states in the North to embrace the justifiability of economic, social, and cultural rights. However, recent US policy priorities—such as the push to ratify the UN Convention on the Rights of Persons with Disabilities within the Senate as well as combating human trafficking and HIV/AIDS through the PEPFAR initiative—

demonstrate the inseparability of weak rule of law, discrimination, poverty-induced desperation, and poor public health.

Aspects of human dignity cannot be compartmentalized. The United States should work with the global North to mobilize more support for political and civil liberties in the South—notably among rising liberal powers—by demonstrating more openness to economic, social, and cultural rights. So too, the United States should engage the global South to accept limits on these rights—focusing on equal opportunity and access to food, education, health care, housing, and decent work conditions, rather than equality of outcomes or unrealistic mandates. Finally, the United States should encourage the global South, and again particularly rising liberal global powers, to de-link their calls for economic, social, and cultural rights from efforts to sidetrack multilateral focus on political and civil liberties, which are, in fact, enablers of the latter (see Lagon and Schulz 2012).

Democracy as a Touchstone of Multilateral Human Rights Policy

Human rights and democracy are not exactly one and the same. Human rights can be incrementally improved in contexts lacking elements of democratic governance. Yet, in the long run, the global human rights regime should be premised on the idea that democratic governance is the best foundation for durable human rights protection, and in our opinion, human dignity. Without regular free and fair elections and core democratic institutions, it is too easy for even benevolent autocrats to violate the rights of their populations. The onset of the Arab revolutions is serious evidence that democracy can be considered a universal aspiration. Building democracy is the best way to ensure peace, as many studies have suggested that democracies tend not to fight one another.

In short, multilateral institutions should premise their declaratory, diplomatic, and aid policies on democracy as the foundation, as the UNDP did between 1999 and 2005 (Malloch-Brown 2011; Newman and Rich 2004). The effective implementation of human rights stems not only from good governance but also particularly from democratic governance advancing horizontally among states and vertically by planting institutionalized roots within states.

Use of Global Economic Institutions to Promote Rights

Global economic institutions, given adequate political will, can also help promote and protect human rights. In particular, these institutions should promote the notions of equal access to justice, real-time freedom of information, and ultimately the concept of agency as mutually reinforcing catalysts for economic development. For instance, the World Bank, IMF, and regional development banks should extend their anticorruption and good governance work to promote equal access to legal rights for all groups with the objective of expanding developing nations' productivity and prosperity (see Anoop Singh's chapter 5 on the rule of law and the role of the IMF in strengthening domestic institutions).

This effort should include streamlining and expanding projects related to rule of law, bolstering emerging judicial institutions, and promoting the functioning of civil society within countries. A good example is an ambitious effort by the World Bank to quantify the domestic economic impact of homophobic exclusion of sexual minorities (Kim 2014).

The Way Forward

Despite many achievements enumerated herein, the global human rights regime exhibits skewed priorities and lagging implementation, retarding *both* essential elements of human dignity that Lagon and Arend identify: (1) agency to thrive and (2) societal recognition of the equal inherent value of all groups. Many of the logjams on progress involve states clinging to parochial interests and blocking traditional IGOs—especially the UN and others of global scope—from contributing to human rights being realized in practice.

The short- and long-term recommendations above focus on the opportunity offered by the emergence of a mosaic—albeit messy—multilateralism of complementary, partnering, and hybrid institutions. That opportunity is to break through this implementation-related gridlock. Empowering regional organizations and civil society institutions, creating a Global Fund for Rule of Law, and in the longer term engaging international financial and trade institutions more in rights promotion would harness that mosaic multilateralism to good effect. Moreover, rethinking the false dichotomies of political versus socioeconomic rights and of human rights versus democracy as priorities, as well as the UN human rights institutions themselves, could meaningfully advance human dignity. They build upon the human rights tradition and existing institutions to advance dignity in the lived experiences of people worldwide.

Notes

This chapter draws significantly from the Council on Foreign Relations' International Institutions and Global Governance (CFR IIGG) program's Global Governance Monitor (GGM) Global Human Rights Regime Issue Brief. Specifically, it reflects and builds upon the conclusions reached by Mark P. Lagon and Stewart M. Patrick. The project was a direct result of the generous support of the Robina Foundation, as well as the work of the CFR IIGG staff. The human rights component of the GGM—along with other components on major global governance issues, can be found at http://www.cfr.org/global-governance /global-governance-monitor/p18985.

References

Bellamy, Alex J. 2009. *A Responsibility to Protect*. Malden: Polity.

Canton, Santiago. 2009. "The Inter-American Commission on Human Rights: 50 Years of Advances and the New Challenges." *Americas*. Summer.

Duffy, Helen. 2009. "Slavery Unveiled by ECOWAS Court." *Human Rights Law Review* 9: 151–70.

ECOSOC (Economic and Social Council). 2013. "Basic Facts about NGO Status." ECOSOC. Accessed August 17, 2013. http://csonet.org/index.php?menu=100.

Evans, Gareth, 2012. "The International Crisis Group: The Role of a Global NGO in Preventing and Resolving Deadly Conflict." Gareth Evans Professional Webpage, May 17. http://www.gevans.org/speeches/speech471.html.

Farer, Tom J., and Felice Gaer. 1993. "The UN and Human Rights: At the End of the Beginning." In *United Nations, Divided World: The UN's Roles in International Relations*. 2nd ed. Edited by Adam Roberts and Benedict Kingsbury. New York: Oxford University Press.

Gershman, Carl, and Michael Allen. 2006. "The Assault on Democracy Assistance." *Journal of Democracy* 17 (2).

Hafner-Burton, Emilie M. 2013. *Making Human Rights a Reality*. Princeton, NJ: Princeton University Press.

Haugen, Gary and Victor Boutros. 2010. "And Justice For All: Enforcing Human Rights for the World's Poor." *Foreign Affairs*. May/June.

ICG (International Crisis Group). 2013. "Trial by Error: Justice in Post-Qadhafi Libya." Brussels: International Crisis Group Headquarters.

ICISS (International Commission on Intervention and State Sovereignty). 2002. "The Responsibility to Protect: The Report of the International Commission on Intervention and State Sovereignty." Ottawa: IDRC Books.

ILO (International Labor Organization). 2012. "New ILO Global Estimate of Forced Labour: 20.9 Million Victims." ILO. June. http://www.ilo.org/global/about-the-ilo /newsroom/news/WCMS_182109/lang–en/index.htm.

Kavanagh, Camino, and Bruce Jones. 2011. "Shaky Foundations: An Assessment of the UN's Rule of Law Support Agenda." New York: New York University Center on International Cooperation.

Keller, Helen, and Geir Ulfstein. 2012. *UN Human Rights Treaty Bodies: Law and Legitimacy*. Cambridge: Cambridge University Press.

Kethineni, Sesha, and Gail Diane Humiston. 2010. "Dalits, the 'Oppressed People' of India: How Are Their Social, Economic, and Human Rights Addressed?" *War Crimes, Genocide, and Crimes against Humanity* 4.

Khan, Irene. 2009. *The Unheard Truth: Poverty and Human Rights*. New York: W. W. Norton and Company.

Kim, Jim Yong. 2014. "Discrimination By Law Carries a High Price." *Washington Post.* February 27.

Kravets, David. 2011. "Feds Say China's Net Censorship Imposes 'Barriers' to Free Trade." *Wired.* Accessed April 14, 2014. http://www.wired.com/2011/10/china-censorship-trade-barrier/.

Kurlantzick, Joshua. 2011. "The Great Democracy Meltdown." *The New Republic.* June 9. http://www.newrepublic.com/article/world/magazine/88632/failing-democracy-venezuela-arab-spring.

Lagon, Mark P. 2012. "A Global Trust for Rule of Law." Council on Foreign Relations Policy Innovation Memorandum (26). Accessed September 1, 2013. http://www.cfr.org/rule-of-law/global-trust-rule-law/p29170.

Lagon, Mark P., and Ryan Kaminski. 2013. "Clash of Elites: What Lies Behind the Defamation Debates." *Georgetown Journal of International Affairs* 14 (1).

Lagon, Mark P., and William F. Schulz. 2012. "Conservatives, Liberals, and Human Rights." *Policy Review* (171): 23–32.

Lagon, Mark P., and David Shorr. 2007. "How to Keep from Overselling or Underestimating the United Nations." In *Bridging the Foreign Policy Divide,* edited by Derek Chollet, Tod Lindberg, and David Shorr. New York: Routledge.

Malloch-Brown, Mark. 2011. *The Unfinished Global Revolution: The Pursuit of a New International Politics.* New York: Penguin Press.

McMahon, Edward R. 2012. "The Universal Periodic Review: A Work in Progress: An Evaluation of the First Cycle of the New UPR Mechanism of the United Nations Human Rights Council." Berlin: Friedrich-Ebert-Stiftung Dialogue on Globalization.

Newman, Edward, and Roland Rich. 2004. "Building Democracy with UN Assistance: From Namibia to Iraq: Has the United Nations Found the Right Formula for Promoting Democracy?" *UN Chronicle* 41 (4).

OHCHR (Office of the High Commissioner for Human Rights). 2014. "Committee Against Torture." Accessed April 14, 2014. http://www.ohchr.org/EN/HRBodies/CAT/Pages/CATIntro.aspx.

———. 1984. "Convention Against Torture, and Other Cruel, Inhuman or Degrading Treatment of Punishment." Accessed April 14, 2014. http://www.ohchr.org/EN/ProfessionalInterest/Pages/CAT.aspx.

———. 2011. "Discriminatory Laws and Practices and Acts of Violence against Individuals Based on Their Sexual Orientation and Gender Identity." New York: Office of the High Commissioner for Human Rights.

OSCE (Organization for Security and Cooperation in Europe). 2007. "Human Rights Defenders in the OSCE Region: Our Collective Conscience." Warsaw: OSCE Office for Democratic Institutions and Human Rights.

Perez Solla, María Fernanda. 2009. "Slavery and Human Trafficking: International Law and the World Bank." World Bank. Social Protection and Labor Discussion Paper.

Piccone, Ted. 2012. *Catalysts for Change: How the U.N.'s Independent Experts Promote Human Rights.* Washington: Brookings Institution.

Rice, Susan. 2012. "Testimony of Ambassador Susan E. Rice, U.S. Permanent Representative to the United Nations, House Subcommittee on Appropriations for State, Foreign Operations, and Related Programs." United States Mission to the United Nations. March 20. http://usun.state.gov/briefing/statements/186080.htm.

Rubenstein, Leonard. 2004. "How International Human Rights Organizations Can Advance Economic, Social and Cultural Rights: A Response to Kenneth Roth." *Human Rights Quarterly*. 845–65.

Ruggie, John. 2013. *Just Business: Multinational Corporations and Human Rights*. New York: W. W. Norton and Company.

Smith-Cannoy, Heather. 2012. *Insincere Commitments: Human Rights Treaties, Abusive States, and Citizen Activism*. Washington, DC: Georgetown University Press.

Tamayo, Juan. 2013. "Watchdog Group: Cuba Cheated on Its UN Human Rights Review." *Miami Herald*. May 3. Accessed April 14, 2014. http://www.miamiherald.com /2013/05/02/3377370/watchdog-group-cuba-cheated-on.html.

Tavares, Rodrigo. 2009. *Regional Security: The Capacity of Regional Organizations*. New York: Routledge.

Trujillo, César Gaviria. 2012. "The Inter-American Democratic Charter at Ten: A Commitment by the Americas to the Defense and Promotion of Democracy." *Latin American Policy* 3 (1).

UNDP (UN Development Program). 2006. "The Arab Human Development Report 2005: Toward the Rise of Women in the Arab World." United Nations Development Program, Regional Bureau for Arab States. Amman: National Press.

———. 2010. "15 Years after Landmark Gathering, Women Still Lack Equal Rights." March 1. New York: United Nations.

UNHRC (United Nations Human Rights Council). 2011. "UN Human Rights Council Resolution 17/14: Human Rights and Transnational Corporations and Other Business Enterprises." Geneva: United Nations.

UNODC (United Nations Office on Drugs and Crime). 2012. "Human Trafficking, Organized Crime and the Multibillion Sale of People." Vienna: United Nations. Accessed September 3, 2013. http://www.unodc.org/unodc/en/frontpage/2012/July/human -trafficking_-organized-crime-and-the-multibillion-dollar-sale-of-people.html.

UNSC (UN Security Council). 2011. "UN Security Council Resolution 1973." New York: United Nations.

UN Women. 2013. "Facts and Figures: Leadership and Political Participation." UN Women. Accessed August 17, 2013. http://www.unwomen.org/en/what-we-do/lead ership-and-political-participation/facts-and-figures.

Warrick, Joby, and Karen DeYoung. 2009. "Obama Reverses Bush Policies on Detention and Interrogation." *Washington Post*. January 23. Accessed April 14, 2014. http:// articles.washingtonpost.com/2009-01-23/news/36920354_1_executive-orders-de tention-and-interrogation-task-force.

CHAPTER 7

The Human Dignity Lens on Terrorism and Counterterrorism

ANTHONY CLARK AREND

One of the most dramatic challenges in today's neomedieval world has been the increasing use of political violence by nonstate actors, often in the form of terrorism. Whereas some scholars would trace the roots of terrorism back to groups like the Zealots of the first century CE,[1] the destructiveness of terrorism in the late twentieth century and early twenty-first century has risen to a whole new level. Following the terrorist attacks of September 11, 2001, global institutions have had to engage the problem of terrorism to an unprecedented extent. Indeed, in the early years after September 11, some officials spoke about the existence of a global war on terrorism.

With terrorism and counterterrorism playing such a prominent role on the global stage, it is not surprising that terrorism has been analyzed from multiple perspectives—the philosophical, the political, the sociological, the ethical, and the legal. Each of these lenses adds to our understanding of the phenomenon we call terrorism. But what would the lens of human dignity suggest? How would human dignity advance our understanding of terrorism, and what would it suggest for actions by global institutions?

In order to address these questions, this chapter will do three things. First, it will set forth a basic definition of terrorism. Second, it will offer several propositions about terrorism that can be derived from a human dignity perspective. Third, it will make several concrete recommendations for global institutions.

What Is Terrorism?

Over the years, the international community has repeatedly sought to develop a definition of terrorism. But after many lengthy debates at international conferences and in other fora, states, intergovernmental organizations (IGOs), and other major actors have still not been able to reach a consensus on a legal definition. For purposes of this work, however, I would offer the following definition: Terrorism is the threat or use of force undertaken for political purposes by a nonstate actor that intentionally targets civilians and other noncombatants in violation of existing law relating to the conduct of hostilities (Arend 2002).

This definition, in my view, captures the essence of what we commonly call terrorism. First, terrorism involves force—either threatened or realized. This requirement is inherent in the violent nature of terrorism. Second, this threat or use of force is undertaken for political purposes. This is an important criterion that differentiates terrorism from criminal activity, which is undertaken for private gain. Third, terrorism is something undertaken by a nonstate actor. It is true that there can be state-sponsored terrorism, but there must be some nonstate group involved. Fourth, terrorism means the targeting of civilians or other noncombatants in violation of law. One of the hallmarks of terrorism is that it attacks legally protected persons and places—civilians, commercial airliners, subways, commuter trains, shopping malls.

It should be noted that this definition of terrorism does not include forcible actions by nonstate actors when they are directed against legitimate military targets. There is a long philosophical tradition of a right of revolution—allowing persons to use force against their government.[2] Indeed, the American Declaration of Independence specifically acknowledges this right. If such forcible actions are taken against military targets, such actions do not constitute terrorism.

Propositions about Terrorism and Counterterrorism

I. Terrorist Acts Violate Human Dignity

A first proposition about terrorism is that terrorist acts always violate human dignity. This may seem to be an obvious conclusion. But over the years, there has frequently been a claim that "one person's terrorist is another person's freedom fighter." In other words, if one agrees with the political goals of the group involved, it is not a terrorist group, whereas if one does not agree, then the group is a terrorist group. A human dignity lens would reject this. Viewed from the perspective of human dignity, violent acts against innocent civilians and other immune targets are wrong irrespective of motive. Terrorism, in essence, uses innocent people as policy tools and in so doing deprives human agency and removes the recognition of their status, which is necessary to assure their dignity.

II. Distinguish between Terrorist Acts, Terrorist Groups, and Terrorists

A second proposition is that it is important to draw distinctions between terrorist acts, terrorist groups, and terrorists. What does this mean? First, terrorist acts are those described above. Second, a person that commits one of those acts may be described as a terrorist. Third, a terrorist group is a nonstate actor that, as a part of its identity, advocates and engages in terrorist acts. It would not seem logical to designate a group as a terrorist group if some of its members had committed isolated terrorist acts that were generally rejected by the leadership of the group. An analogy may serve to illustrate this distinction. Over the years, some members of the US military have committed war crimes; the behavior of US personnel at My Lai in Vietnam or Abu Ghraib in Iraq come immediately to mind. But although those persons found responsible for committing those atrocities can be labeled as "war criminals," the US military or the United States itself as a whole cannot be so labeled. The same principle would apply to nonstate actors.

It is also important to note that a group that previously engaged in terrorist acts could undergo a fundamental change and come to eschew terrorism. The Irish Republican Army (IRA) is an example of such a group. Although it previously supported acts against protected persons, the IRA ultimately rejected such a tactic.

It is also useful to differentiate terrorists from those persons who have some connection with a terrorist group but do not themselves advocate or engage in terrorist actions. A person may be a spouse or a friend of a terrorist, but that does not make that person a terrorist. Similarly, a person who provides food or shelter to a terrorist—especially when the person providing such assistance is not aware of the acts of the terrorist or when the person is forced to provide such assistance—should not be considered a terrorist. Indeed, one of the great difficulties of the legal category adopted by the United States of "providing material support" to terrorism is that it potentially conflates this type of support with terrorism itself.[3] A human dignity lens requires that these distinctions be made, because a fundamental corollary of human dignity is that all persons are of equal worth and should be treated justly. This means that the state should only punish offenders in a manner proportionate to the gravity of their offenses.

III. Forcible Response to Terrorism Is Permissible

As noted above, terrorist acts by definition violate the human dignity of persons. Consequently, it is incumbent upon the international community to take action to prevent, and if prevention fails, to stop terrorism. This means that the use of military force can rightfully be used for prevention and abatement of terrorism. But such force must meet criteria that are established under international law. In particular, such force must meet the *jus ad bellum* criteria of necessity and proportionality and the *jus in bello* criteria of discrimination and avoidance of unnecessary suffering.

The "jus ad bellum" is the law relating to the recourse to force (Arend and Beck 1993, 2). Under Article 51 of the UN Charter, states have an inherent right of self-defense if an armed attack occurs. Although the Charter was written when other states were thought of as the perpetrators of armed attacks, the international community has come to recognize that nonstate actors can also commit armed attacks and be subject to forcible response to such attack. In fact, following the terrorist attacks of September 11, 2001, the Security Council adopted Resolution 1373 that explicitly acknowledged the right of self-defense in the wake of an attack by al-Qaeda, a nonstate actor.

In order for such a response to be lawful, it must meet two criteria: necessity and proportionality (Arend and Beck 1993, 18, 72). First, it must be demonstrated that it is necessary to use military force. With respect to an ongoing terrorist operation, this criterion is easily satisfied. Thus, for example, following the al-Qaeda actions against the United States beginning in the early 1990s, the necessity requirement was met, and US forces were empowered to take forcible actions to stop the ongoing activities of al-Qaeda. With respect to a preventative action, it is a bit more complex. If a state believes that a group is contemplating terrorist acts, the state (or states) that is likely to be the target must demonstrate that an attack is truly about to occur. Under traditional international law, the state must demonstrate that an attack is imminent.

Second, the forcible response must be proportionate to the threat. The goal of using force against terrorism is to stop the terrorist threat. This means that force can be used in a manner that is calculated to end the threat. There is no necessity for a tit-for-tat response. In other words, if a terrorist were to kill a national of the target state, the victim state is not limited to the same level of action. The victim state is empowered to take action to end the threat. But the victim state is limited to only that amount of force that could reasonably be considered necessary to end the threat.

In addition to these jus ad bellum criteria, forcible responses to terrorism must also meet the requirements of the jus in bello, also referred to as the laws of war, the laws of armed conflict, and international humanitarian law (Dinstein 2004). The jus in bello emerged under customary international law and has been codified in numerous treaties, including The Hague Conventions of 1899 and 1907 and the Geneva Conventions of 1949. Whereas these agreements set forth a number of specific requirements—including some that will be discussed in the next section—two principles are particularly noteworthy when discussing a forcible response to terrorism: discrimination and unnecessary suffering.

First, the use of force must discriminate between legitimate and illegitimate targets. Under the laws of war, military force can only be employed against military targets—active combatants, weapons systems, military installations and equipment, and other such force components. Force cannot be used against civilians who pose no military threat, military personnel that are surrendering, and troops that are wounded and pose no threat. Similarly, force cannot be used against nonmilitary targets, such as hospitals, places of worship, or undefended population centers. Any counterterrorist action must discriminate in this fashion. Indeed, one of the distinctive characteristics of terrorism itself is that terrorist acts *intentionally* target these protected persons and places.

Second, under the jus in bello, all parties to an armed conflict are to avoid methods of combat that are calculated to cause unnecessary suffering. While it might seem that any use of force causes unnecessary suffering, under international law, there is a specific prohibition on both weapons that always cause gratuitous suffering and the use of methods that would produce such suffering. Thus, for example, jagged-edged bayonets and hollow-point bullets are not allowed in combat because they cause injuries beyond that which is necessary to neutralize an enemy. In engaging in a counterterrorism operation, military forces are bound not to take any action that would violate this prohibition on producing unnecessary suffering.

IV. Terror Suspects Must Be Treated Humanely

Given the horrific nature of terrorism, there has frequently been a tendency on the part of those apprehending terrorists to claim that those individuals somehow forfeit their humanity by virtue of their actions. Human dignity, however, requires that irrespective of the heinous nature of terrorism and any particular terrorist act, individuals that are captured under suspicion of being terrorists must be treated humanely, with international humanitarian law setting the minimum standard for this treatment.

Concretely, this requirement means several things. First, it means that terror suspects that have surrendered cannot be killed, tortured, or otherwise treated with disrespect. Following the US Supreme Court decision in *Hamdan v. Rumsfeld* from 2006, the legal standard articulated in Common Article 3 of the 1949 Geneva Convention serves as a good baseline. It provides:

In the case of armed conflict not of an international character occurring in the territory of one of the High Contracting Parties, each Party to the conflict shall be bound to apply, as a minimum, the following provisions:

1. Persons taking no active part in the hostilities, including members of armed forces who have laid down their arms and those placed hors de combat by sickness, wounds, detention, or any other cause, shall in all circumstances be treated humanely, without any adverse distinction founded on race, colour, religion or faith, sex, birth or wealth, or any other similar criteria. To this end, the following acts are and shall remain prohibited at any time and in any place whatsoever with respect to the above-mentioned persons:
    (a) violence to life and person, in particular, murder of all kinds, mutilation, cruel treatment, and torture;
    (b) taking of hostages;
    (c) outrages upon personal dignity, in particular humiliating and degrading treatment;
    (d) the passing of sentences and the carrying out of executions without previous judgment pronounced by a regularly constituted court, affording all the judicial guarantees which are recognized as indispensable by civilized peoples.
2. The wounded and sick shall be collected and cared for.

Although these requirements might seem straightforward, during the so-called war on terror, there were significant disputes about the definition of torture. As is well-known, the US Justice Department produced a series of legal memoranda that set an extremely high threshold for torture, allowing for the conduct of waterboarding and a number of other tactics that were widely criticized (Greenberg and Dratel 2005). Moreover, although the Supreme Court concluded that Common Article 3 applied to terror suspects, there is not necessarily universal agreement on that determination.

Looking at the treatment of terror suspects through the lens of human dignity does not provide an authoritative list of dos and don'ts with respect to treatment, but it does demand that when in doubt, a harsh technique should not be undertaken. Human dignity would encourage an interrogator to err on the side of the suspect and to refrain from actions that any reasonable person would consider an affront to human dignity. Practices such as waterboarding, for example, clearly violate human dignity.

A second conclusion drawn from the requirement that terror suspects be treated humanely is that the practice of indefinite detention is by nature problematic. With the potential exception of Common Article 3, the Geneva Convention on the Treatment of Prisoners of War really only applies to persons who meet the definition of a prisoner of war contained in Article 4 of that Convention. Because terrorists by definition do not follow the laws of war, they cannot be considered prisoners of war (POWs) and thus are not entitled to the full protections of the Convention. One area addressed by the Convention is the length of detention. POWs must be repatriated at the end of the conflict. But what about terror suspects?

There are several problems here. First, although in a traditional war there is a much clearer sense as to when the conflict is over, when would a war on terror be over? Unlike in traditional wars, where repatriated POWs are unlikely to continue the conflict with the enemy, terror suspects may continue to challenge the state that captured them even if the terrorist group with which they were associated no longer exists. Second, POWs can be tried for violations of the laws of war and, if found guilty, imprisoned. Certainly, a terror detainee could also be tried and if found guilty imprisoned for the length of the sentence, including presumably life. But what if a terror suspect is captured and detained and due to the circumstances surrounding the capture of the person, there is either insufficient evidence to try and convict the person or the evidence was obtained through techniques that would prevent such evidence from being admissible in court? Can that person simply be indefinitely detained because those capturing him or her reasonably believed he or she committed war crimes?

This is a serious problem here. A human dignity lens would counsel against detaining a person indefinitely without any trial and subsequent conviction. As noted earlier, when we acknowledge the inherent value of all persons, justice requires that persons only be subjected to punishment in proportion to their offense. But if the offense has not been adjudicated, how can the person be indefinitely detained? Part of the problem is the law. This is clearly a lacuna in the Geneva Convention that needs to be addressed.

V. The International Community Needs to Address the Root Causes of Terrorism

Whereas much of the focus in recent years has been on counterterrorism and efforts to prevent terrorist attacks and capture individual terrorists, a human dignity perspective suggests that the international community should seek to understand and address the root causes of terrorism. By addressing the root causes, it is hoped that the incidence of terrorism could be greatly reduced, even if it's never eliminated. But what causes human beings to become terrorists? In order to attempt to answer this question, it is important to recognize distinctions among different types of terrorism and different types of terrorists.

When continental Europe was being hit with a wave of terrorist activities in the 1970s, the German scholar Claus-Dieter Kernig drew the distinction between what he called "terrorism with a goal" and "terrorism without a goal" (Kernig 1978). Into the first category, he placed groups that had clear, identifiable policy goals. These groups adopted terrorist tactics as a means to achieving those goals. Thus, for example, ETA, the Basque group, had the explicit goal of establishing an independent Basque state. The Palestine Liberation Organization and the IRA had similarly concrete goals. Indeed, when al-Qaeda was created, its leadership articulated a series of demands that undergirded their raison d'être.

The designation of the second type of terrorism, terrorism without a goal, should not be taken too literally. If the leaders of these groups were to be asked, they would undoubtedly describe a series of goals. The main difference here is that the goals these groups articulate seem to translate into a desire for a complete overhaul of the entire established political, economic, or social system. Such groups would include the Baader-Meinhof Group, the Red Brigade, the Red Army, Aum Shinrikyo, and even the Symbionese Liberation Army. These groups seemed to engage in terrorism to rage against the system as a whole. Even if public officials wanted to respond to address their concerns, there would be no way to effectively address their demands.

Another critical distinction to make when attempting to understand the root causes of terrorism is the distinction between the leadership and the foot soldier. On one side are the Osama Bin Ladens and the Mullah Omars, and on the other is the fifteen-year old with a bomb strapped to her body. Although the leaders may be motivated by an established ideology or clear political goals, foot soldiers may not be. Foot soldiers may be coming from a society that is ungoverned and rife with poverty, unemployment, and political corruption. They might feel disenfranchised and lost. Indeed, to use the theme of this book, such people may feel that their human dignity has been stripped. They may feel a loss of agency and the inability or unwillingness of society to grant recognition to their personhood. Then, into such people's seemingly hopeless lives comes a group that promises to give life meaning and a sense of belonging. Although it is impossible to draw a definitive conclusion, such a motivation could indeed be an important reason that many join a terrorist cause.

In efforts to address the causes of terrorism, these distinctions need to be considered. First, for groups that have concrete political goals, international institutions and states need to seek to understand these goals. And although they should not feel an obligation to yield to terrorist blackmail, they should realistically deliberate on the political goals that have led groups to engage in terrorist tactics and seek a resolution that is ultimately just and fair. Second, given that many foot soldiers may be less motivated by a concrete ideology or specific political goals and more inspired by their need to reclaim their human dignity, the international community needs to address the conditions in society that have led persons to feel powerless and without dignity.

Recommendations for Global Institutions

One of the implications of these propositions is that in order for human dignity to be given effect, institutions—both traditional and emerging—must take a holistic approach to the problem. In the past, states and IGOs have understandably tended to focus their attention on the more immediate aspect of terrorism—counterterrorism—and have not focused on the more systemic problems that lead to terrorism. To effectively promote human dignity in the wake of terrorism, however, both the immediate challenge and the underlying problems must be addressed. Accordingly, I would make these recommendations for action by a variety of global institutions.

I. A New Geneva Convention

The International Committee on the Red Cross and Red Crescent (ICRC) is a nongovernmental organization (NGO) headquartered in Geneva, Switzerland. Since 1864, the ICRC has been the leader in promoting the development of international humanitarian law. As warfare has evolved over the years, the ICRC has convened a series of conferences to update the Geneva Conventions. It is time for another such conference.

The goal of the new Geneva Conference would be to either adopt an additional protocol to the 1949 Conventions or produce a completely new convention that would address the lacunae in the existing Conventions. It is hoped that several specific issues would be addressed. First, although at present an argument could be made that Common Article 3 of the Conventions applies to terror suspects—indeed, as noted earlier, the US Supreme Court has ruled that it does—its applicability still remains unclear and its provisions minimal (Lagon and Schulz 2012). A new convention could provide clarity to the rights given to terror suspects. Second, a new treaty could explicitly set forth the level of evidence that is necessary to convict a person of war crimes for various acts of terrorism. The convention might also draw distinctions between the leaders of terrorist operations and persons who could be considered foot soldiers and other actors who fall somewhere in between. Whereas foot soldiers cannot be absolved of a war crime, a mitigating factor could be their level of involvement in the planning and the extent to which they may have been coerced into committing the terrorist act. Third, a new convention could address the problem of indefinite detention in cases where there is insufficient evidence to convict a person of a war crime. As noted earlier, although traditional POWs can be held until the armed conflict is over, that same standard is problematic regarding terrorism. When is the war on terror over? When individuals are committed to using terrorist tactics against a state, do they no longer become a threat when their organization is no more? A convention could address this issue—perhaps with an arrangement such that persons detained as terror suspects would be subject to periodic review to determine whether they continue to be a threat, perhaps even with a provision that requires their release after a certain period of time in any case.

II. An Early Warning System for Terrorism

What if we could predict terrorism before it occurs? In theory, this is the goal of each state's intelligence agencies. And although the successes of such efforts are generally not known, the failures are all too public. In the aftermath of the terrorist attacks of September 11, 2001, for example, numerous commissions made it clear how the intelligence community in the United States failed to connect the dots to prevent 9/11. But would the lens of human dignity suggest an additional approach?

As noted earlier, some individuals may be motivated to take up a terrorist cause when they feel that they have been stripped of their dignity due to adverse conditions in their state. Confronted with challenges such as abject poverty, the lack of a fair governance structure, and a general sense of hopelessness, disenfranchised persons may seek some sense of meaning in a terrorist group. Accordingly, it would make sense to seek to identify the early onset of these conditions that might lead persons to join terrorist groups. In order to do this, two actions are necessary. First, clearer correlations need to be established between adverse conditions and the incident of terrorism. Second, once such correlations are determined, so called big data needs to be used to predict those factors in the global system that are likely to produce conditions conducive to terrorism. A word can be said about each of these tasks.

First, although much has been written about the root causes of terrorism, it makes sense to attempt to develop an international consensus on conditions that *historically* have led to disenfranchised persons joining terrorist groups. To accomplish this task, state governments and private foundations can play the primary role by funding social science research that models terrorism based on past actions and proposes a variety of conditions that leads to terrorism. The goal is to develop hypotheses that can then be discussed and evaluated at international fora, perhaps under the sponsorship of the UN Education, Science, and Culture Organization (UNESCO).

Second, once a set of conditions are formulated, NGOs and IGOs could use available big data to explore the development of these conditions. Much as organizations like the World Health Organization can use big data to predict outbreaks of diseases, so too could the proper use of big data be able to predict the early emergence of conditions that are likely to create fertile ground for terrorism.

There is likely more art than science in such an approach to predicting terrorism. But if there were to be an institutionalized mechanism for promoting the examination and discussion of conditions potentially leading to terrorism, it would at the very least ensure that there is a regular exploration of emerging conditions that are destructive to human dignity. Such exploration would, it is hoped, help the global community focus on the problem before it manifests itself into full-blown terrorism.

III. A Global Trust for Governance

Although there are many adverse conditions that potentially create the environment for disaffected persons to become terrorists, undoubtedly one of those conditions is poor governance or lack of governance completely. A state where corruption is rampant, the judicial system decidedly unfair, and a government that cannot deliver even on the most basic services necessary for survival is a likely breeding ground for the foot soldiers of terrorism.

One way to address some of these governance issues is to establish a Global Trust for Governance. This recommendation draws upon a proposal made by co-editor Mark P. Lagon for a Global Trust for the Rule of Law (Lagon 2012). Modeled after the Global Fund to Fight AIDS, Tuberculosis and Malaria, the Global Trust for the Rule of Law would be a partnership of states, NGOs, other nonprofits, IGOs, and private sector actors. As Lagon explains, "Its purpose would be to build developing nations' capacity to implement rule of law and unleash the potential of marginalized groups worldwide, promoting not only human dignity but, crucially, global economic growth" (Lagon 2012). It would do this by "provid[ing] grants and technical advice to NGOs and governments dedicated to enlarging access to legal rights and rule of law capacity where both are weak" (Lagon 2012). In particular, "[a]mong other activities, it would support projects to train lawyers or prosecutors, help citizens gain access to justice institutions, and spread public awareness about corruption" (Lagon 2012). Donors to the Trust could include states, multilateral institutions, nonprofits, large foundations, private corporations, and even individual persons. Importantly, "It would have an autonomous governing board composed of representatives from developed and developing countries, the UN and international financial institutions, NGOs, relevant foundations, representatives of the private sector, and civil society institutions. A regional representation allotment would allay concerns about a Western bias. Funding from and decision-making influence of any single donor—including the United States—would be limited (e.g., a 10 percent ceiling), with no veto power for any board member. A technical committee of experts across cultures charged with evaluating grant applications would report to the board" (Lagon 2012).

My suggestion is to expand this to a Global Trust on Governance and the Rule of Law. Under such an arrangement, it would address all the issues Lagon raises and would expand to other areas. These could include funding and training to develop governmental institutions that provide basic social services—education, health care, child services, safety regulations and such. In particular, proper funding and training could help those institutions develop in such a way as to reduce corruption and increase efficiency. Although such a fund is certainly no magic bullet, it could help improve agency and recognition—and hence justice and prosperity—in states and perhaps reduce the chances of disenfranchised persons becoming terrorists.

IV. Joint Action by Faith-based Institutions

As noted earlier, it is not unusual for terrorist groups to be motivated by certain ideologies. Unfortunately, some groups draw upon religion to justify their terrorist actions. Fundamentalists of a variety of different religious traditions have engaged in many of the most destructive terrorist acts in history. From the Zealots to al-Qaeda to groups that bomb abortion clinics, terrorists have frequently made religious arguments to support violence.

A claim that we make in this book is that virtually all mainstream religions value human dignity—even if they may not use that term or may implement it differently in their own cultural contexts. Accordingly, it is logical that faith-based institutions at all levels could play a major role in engaging in a dialogue on human dignity and terrorism. In particular, these institutions could work to make it clear to their adherents that terrorist methods are *always* at odds with the affirmation of human dignity. And indeed, religious groups have spoken out against terrorism and condemned specific terrorist acts. But there is still more that can be done.

One suggestion is to encourage interreligious conferences aimed specifically at developing common approaches to terrorism. Such common approaches could not only involve formulating common statements on terrorism but could also include common actions relating to alleviating the underlying conditions that may be conducive to terrorism. Joint efforts by religious organizations—especially in communities with great religious diversity—to address poverty, health care, and education could go a long way to addressing some of the root causes of terrorism. Joint efforts could also demonstrate a level of cooperation among different religious groups that could help mitigate the problem of demonization of one religious group by another.

Conclusion

Sadly, violence by nonstate actors in pursuit of political aims seems to be a permanent feature of the twenty-first century. Far too often, however, discussions of terrorism get lost in ideological or even legal debates and a fundamental point is missed: Terrorism by definition is an affront to human dignity. When viewed through the lens of human dignity, the negative effects of terrorism on the agency and affirmation of persons is clear. At the same time, a human dignity lens allows us to affirm that the terrorists themselves—as well as those who live with and care for them—are still persons, worthy of having their dignity preserved.

In order to combat terrorism in the short and long term, it is necessary that both traditional and nontraditional institutions act in partnership. Actions by states alone are not sufficient—nor are actions by more traditional IGOs such as the UN. Those actors frequently have limited recourses, circumscribed geographic reach, and in some cases insufficient legitimacy. Instead, states, IGOs, NGOs, and hybrid institutions need to work in partnership to both combat contemporary acts of terrorism and to address the global conditions that set the stage for future terrorists to emerge. Human dignity demands it.

Notes

1. I am indebted to Dr. Elizabeth Grimm Arsenault for her lectures on the origins of terrorism.

2. We tend to think of John Locke as one of the great philosophers supporting a right to revolution, but several medieval political thinkers, such as John of Salisbury, argued that violence could be permissibly undertaken against a tyrant.

3. One applicable section of US federal law can be found at 18 USC § 2339A: providing material support to terrorists. It holds:

> (a) Offense. Whoever provides material support or resources or conceals or disguises the nature, location, source, or ownership of material support or resources, knowing or intending that they are to be used in preparation for, or in carrying out, a violation of

section 32, 37, 81, 175, 229, 351, 831, 842 (m) or (n), 844 (f) or (i), 930 (c), 956, 1091, 1114, 1116, 1203, 1361, 1362, 1363, 1366, 1751, 1992, 2155, 2156, 2280, 2281, 2332, 2332a, 2332b, 2332f, 2340A, or 2442 of this title, section 236 of the Atomic Energy Act of 1954 (42 USC 2284), section 46502 or 60123 (b) of title 49, or any offense listed in section 2332b (g)(5)(B) (except for sections 2339A and 2339B) or in preparation for, or in carrying out, the concealment of an escape from the commission of any such violation, or attempts or conspires to do such an act, shall be fined under this title, imprisoned not more than fifteen years, or both, and, if the death of any person results, shall be imprisoned for any term of years or for life. A violation of this section may be prosecuted in any Federal judicial district in which the underlying offense was committed, or in any other Federal judicial district as provided by law.

(b) Definitions. As used in this section, the term "material support or resources" means any property, tangible or intangible, or service, including currency or monetary instruments or financial securities, financial services, lodging, training, expert advice or assistance, safehouses, false documentation or identification, communications equipment, facilities, weapons, lethal substances, explosives, personnel (one or more individuals who may be or include oneself), and transportation, except medicine or religious materials.

References

Arend, Anthony Clark. 2002. "International Law and Rogue States: The Failure of the United Nations Charter Framework." *New England Law Review* 36 (4): 740.

Arend, Anthony Clark, and Robert J. Beck. 1993. *International Law and the Use of Force: Beyond the United Nations Charter Paradigm*. London: Routledge.

Dinstein, Yoram. 2004. *The Conduct of Hostilities under the Law of International Armed Conflict*. Cambridge: Cambridge University Press.

Greenberg, Karen J., and Joshua L. Dratel, eds. 2005. *The Torture Papers: The Road to Abu Ghraib*. Cambridge: Cambridge University Press.

Kernig, Claus-Dieter. 1978. "Theorie und Praktisch der Terroristischen und Anarchistischen Bewegungen [Theory and Practice of Terrorist and Anarchist Movements]" (lecture). Universität Trier. Fall.

Lagon, Mark P. 2012. "A Global Trust for the Rule of Law." Policy Innovation Memorandum No. 26. Council on Foreign Relations. Accessed November 4, 2013. http://www.cfr.org/rule-of-law/global-trust-rule-law/p29170.

Lagon, Mark P., and William F. Schulz. 2012. "Conservatives, Liberals, and Human Rights." *Policy Review*, 171.

PART II

EMERGING INSTITUTIONS

P art II treats what this volume terms "emerging institutions." These include various private sector, philanthropic, civil society, and hybrid institutions. While some of these institutions have been in existence for some time, such as the Roman Catholic Church or multinational corporations, in today's neomedieval world they are properly considered emerging because they have become engaged in new, innovative ways in promoting human dignity.

On one hand, the next seven chapters show the impact of actors separate from international government organizations, such as chapter 12 by Thomas Banchoff, who focuses on the Catholic Church and other major faith traditions; chapter 13 by Nicole Bibbins Sedaca, who addresses faith-based, programmatic, nongovernmental organizations; and chapter 14 by Michael Samway, who discusses multinational corporations. On the other hand, two chapters show emerging institutions collaborating with traditional ones—such as chapter 8 by Rosalía Rodriguez-García, who considers UNAIDS and the Global Fund to Fight AIDS, Tuberculosis and Malaria; and chapter 11 by Mark P. Lagon, who treats institutional partnerships to combat human trafficking.

Human dignity inspires the work of these emerging institutions. For instance, chapter 9 by Raj Desai and Homi Kharas explores how lenders to developing world entrepreneurs are moved and themselves empowered by new private sector institutions employing crowdsourcing. So too, Banchoff's and Bibbins Sedaca's chapters reveal the mobilizing power of dignity in faith-based institutions' work.

Finally, the chapters in part II reveal important yet different types of impacts on human dignity. Some emerging institutions help marginalized people seize agency and social recognition, such as the nimble private sector development entities that Desai and Kharas examine. Others can stop threats to dignity or reduce complicity in such threats, such as the institutional reforms to help stateless persons—a category of human beings denied access to justice—as proposed in chapter 10 by Benjamin Boudreaux. Samway enumerates internet companies' due diligence measures to avoid helping states infringe on civil liberties. Still other institutions can reverse the stigma or blame placed on those victimized. Here, Lagon shows how multistakeholder partnerships can stop human trafficking victims from being reflexively treated as criminals or from being deported, and Rodriguez-García shows how UNAIDS and the Global Fund overcome the social stigma on populations most vulnerable to HIV/AIDS. Emerging institutions show promise to avert a shameful double denial of individuals' dignity.

CHAPTER 8

Transcending HIV/AIDS Social Stigma

Putting Human Dignity Center Stage in Global Institutions

ROSALÍA RODRIGUEZ-GARCÍA

Global institutions, both intergovernmental and multistakeholder partnerships, have for three decades grappled with the dignity-negating effects of discrimination in the AIDS (acquired immunodeficiency syndrome) pandemic. Slowly, they have dealt with the social stigma of vulnerable and affected groups as a barrier to their interventions. The cases of the Joint UN Programme on HIV/AIDS (UNAIDS) and the Global Fund to Fight AIDS, Tuberculosis, and Malaria show how gaps between discourse and action and between global commitments and impact on individuals must be bridged to tangibly serve human dignity.

The first cases of an unusual type of immune deficiency not seen before were found in the United States among gay men in 1981. When the US Center for Disease Control and Prevention (CDC) issued its first official report on HIV (human immunodeficiency virus), few could have foreseen that HIV, the virus identified as the cause of AIDS, would become the most severe epidemic of modern times. In the early 1980s the disease was confined primarily to high-income countries and among the gay population. Little did the global health community realize that HIV had been spreading unnoticed for decades among the general population, first in sub–Saharan Africa and then in different regions. By the year 2000 HIV affected every region in the world and the number of people living with HIV rose from less than one million to an estimated 27.5 million (UNAIDS 2011).

AIDS was first and foremost a health catastrophe, but soon it was also seen as a national security issue. Public health arguments for AIDS engagement were made even more urgent by arguments that emphasized how the vicious circle of poverty, often leading people to engage in commercial sex to survive,

167

maximized the risk of HIV infections and AIDS, thereby creating social instability. The concern for security was fueled by the fact that in the decade of 1990–2000, the number of countries in a preconflict, conflict, or postconflict status had tripled (Global Development Alliance 2001) and populations at war were often subjected to human rights abuses and sexual violence, all of which facilitated HIV transmission (Gostin 2003). This situation was compounded by the fact that the security sector (i.e., armed forces, law enforcement) in many countries were hit with high rates of HIV infection, and thus, AIDS became part of the military lexicon (Rodriguez-García 2002).

Not since ancient times with diseases like leprosy had a disease fueled the imagination and fear of people as AIDS did due in great part to its undertones of illegality, same-sex acts, and sure death. Some people when confronted with same-sex relationships experience a deep aversion or disgust. Nussbaum (2010) argues that disgust has long been among the fundamental motivations of those who are fighting for legal discrimination against lesbian and gay citizens. As Nussbaum argues, the politics of disgust must be confronted directly, for it contradicts the basic principle of the equality of all citizens under the law.

In the emergency response mode that defined the early stages of the epidemic (around 1981) the application of public health measures of isolation or mandatory testing, such as the US practice of detaining HIV-positive Haitian refugees at Guantánamo and Cuba's forcible quarantine of its own HIV-positive citizens, was controversial and bitterly criticized by health practitioners and human rights advocates (Stemple 2008). This position was not as farfetched then as one may think now, as in the early times of the epidemic AIDS was a fatal disease.

However, by the late 1980s health officials recognized that discrimination against people with AIDS or who were HIV positive was counterproductive, and by 1988 the World Health Organization (WHO) adopted a resolution, which stated that addressing discrimination was an essential element of HIV prevention programs. This principle of nondiscrimination was consequently incorporated into the governance and practice of the first HIV/AIDS Strategy of the WHO. If the first phase of the HIV epidemic (in the early 1980s) saw the international community applying a public health approach to HIV prevention, and the second phase (in the late 1980s) decrying the need to fight discrimination, the third phase of the epidemic in the early 1990s underscored the concept of vulnerability and the fundamental connection between HIV and human rights. By then it had become clear that a lack of respect for human dignity was a major contributor to the HIV epidemic (Gruskin, Hendriks, and Tomasevski 1996).[1]

The development of the health and human rights framework at the UN coincided with the beginning of the rapid spread of HIV/AIDS. Whereas in previous epidemics the spread of disease was fueled largely by lack of scientific knowledge, the spread of HIV was fueled by social and human determinants. Discrimination (singling out a person with the result that the person is treated unfairly and unjustly) and disregarding human dignity contributed to the spread and exacerbated the impact of the disease, while at the same time HIV itself undermined progress in the realization of human rights. This link is apparent in the fact that the overwhelming burden of the epidemic today is borne disproportionately by low income countries, the poor, and vulnerable populations—mainly sex workers (SWs), men who have sex with men (MSM), and injecting drug users (IDUs).

Thus, since the beginning of the global response to HIV/AIDS, human rights and human dignity accompanied the dialogue about prevention, treatment, care, and mitigation. Jonathan Mann, who headed the first HIV/AIDS program of the WHO (1986–1990), worked unceasingly to garner consensus among world leaders against the exclusion of people living with AIDS from everyday life, including from housing, employment, and travel (Gostin 1998).[2] This was not easily addressed, as it turned out, not even in high-income countries. Case in point: It would take twenty years for the United States to end a ban against HIV-positive people entering the United States. In the words of President Obama: "I was so proud to also announce that my administration was ending the ban that prohibited people with HIV from entering America" (Obama 2011).

Despite significant expansion of knowledge about HIV transmission, treatment, and preventive regimes, it was only in 1996 that regulatory approval was given for antiretroviral therapy (ART). Several more years would pass before ART treatment was available in low- and middle-income countries due to its high cost. Concomitantly, global resources available for HIV in low- and middle-income countries rose from about US$1 billion in 2001 to more than US$16 billion by 2009 (UNAIDS 2011).

This dramatic increase in the level of global investments on one single disease was facilitated by the creation of the UNAIDS in 1995 and later, in 2001, by the UN General Assembly Declaration of Commitment on HIV/AIDS, which acknowledged AIDS as a global epidemic (United Nations 2001). This recognition led to the creation of the two major financiers of HIV/AIDS today: The Global Fund to Fight AIDS, Tuberculosis, and Malaria (the Global Fund) in 2002 and the US President's Emergency Plan for AIDS Relief (PEPFAR) in 2003.[3] In the 1980s and 1990s the major leader and financier of HIV/AIDS programs had been the World Bank. UNAIDS and the Global Fund are archetypical examples of the impactful hybrid, multistakeholder institutions highlighted in this book. Thus, how do the international community and particularly the major international agencies working on HIV/AIDS address human rights and human dignity issues?

Despite these unprecedented global actions the disease is experienced at a very personal level that affects the HIV-positive person's relation with family, friends, coworkers, and community. Indeed, in the early phases of the epidemic, a diagnosis of AIDS carried a double burden: It was a death sentence physically, and it was a death sentence socially, the latter fed by fear of abandonment and societal discrimination, marginalization, and exclusion. People living with HIV were, and in many countries still are, denied the most basic care and support; they are seen as no longer productive members of society, and their value is expressed in societal costs and not in societal contributions, thereby dehumanizing them. Many of those infected and affected by HIV/AIDS see their human rights violated, their social value withdrawn, and their human potential crushed by the enormity of the disease and by the societal fears that result in the condemnation and penalization of many of the behaviors that are considered to heighten HIV risk. Stigma and discrimination curtail individuals' political and economic freedoms, civil rights, social opportunities and autonomy (Sen 1999). Applying the definition of human dignity provided by Lagon and Arend in the introduction of this book, one could say that the quality of life of these populations is undermined by lack of individual respect, social recognition, and power to achieve their full potential; that is, denial of human dignity.

This chapter posits that to advance the human dignity agenda one needs to balance the inherent tensions that both propel and hamper progress: (1) the tension between discourse and action at the global and national levels, and (2) the tension between global commitments and the national and individual nature of human rights impacts (see figure 8.1).[4]

But first, a word about the scope of this chapter and how human rights and human dignity are understood herein. "Human rights" refer to the basic rights and freedoms that all people are entitled to regardless of nationality, sex, national or ethnic origin, race, religion, language, or other status as discussed elsewhere in this book.[5] Individual human rights are a concept of modern societies, though. It came forth in the wake of World War II driven by the principle of respect for the individual and respect for human life, which culminated in the document called the Universal Declaration of Human Rights (UDHR) in December 1948, from which international human rights conventions and law have flowed. In this declaration, the term "human dignity" is used to express the basic principle upon which human rights are understood to rest (Lebech 2004).

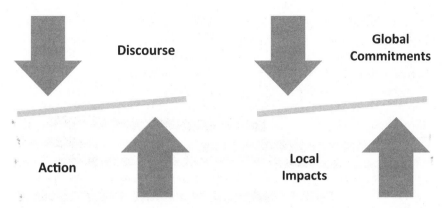

Figure 8.1 AIDS and Human Dignity: Competing Tensions.

In addition to this macro-level view of human rights, this chapter suggests a micro-level view based on a causal-logic theory of change.[6] This theory asserts that the restoration of human dignity is the desirable outcome of human rights actions, whereby human dignity is a result of human rights inputs—action leading to local impacts (i.e., international guarantees and treaties, national laws and legislation, and importantly, their implementation). Although the basic principles of human dignity might be readily agreed upon in most cases, it is the *application* of these principles and the expectation of concrete and measurable results in the improvement of people's lives that underlines the tensions between global discourse and action and between global commitments and local impacts. Rights spring from inherent dignity at the macro level, whereas at the micro level, especially when human dignity has been suppressed or attacked, the application of human rights would aim at restoring dignity.

Major Players, Pathways, and Milestones in HIV/AIDS and Human Dignity

In their definition of human dignity in this book, Lagon and Arend also posit that to be meaningful, human dignity must be institutionalized in practice and in governance. Accordingly, this section examines the degree to which UNAIDS and the Global Fund address human dignity in their corporate governance and in their practices. UNAIDS does so through primarily a convening and normative role and the Global Fund through a financing one.

UNAIDS was established in 1994 by Resolution 1994/24 of the UN Economic and Social Council and launched in January 1996 with the objective of providing global leadership for a nationally and internationally coordinated and accountable response to the HIV/AIDS pandemic.[7] Although the UNAIDS resolution did not explicitly include human rights or human dignity language, it de facto adopted the UN rights-based approach to HIV/AIDS. Furthermore, the UNAIDS charter did include language that at the time many considered revolutionary by making explicit civil society participation at the policy and programmatic levels. Specifically, the resolution indicates that in fulfilling its objectives the UNAIDS program would collaborate not only with national governments and intergovernmental organizations but with *nongovernmental organizations (NGOs) and groups of people living with HIV/AIDS*. This decision enabled a path towards action on human dignity by involving from the start those groups that could better express the voices of the marginalized and the vulnerable. And indeed civil society has played a pivotal and constant role at all levels as a conduit of information on abuses and as defenders of human dignity, effectively shifting from the naming and shaming approach of the early phases of the HIV epidemic to becoming the accountability watchdogs for AIDS and the voices of the affected (Meernik, Aloisi, Sowell, and Nichols 2012).

Despite these good intentions, it would take another five years before the lofty objectives of UNAIDS took root. According to Peter Piot, UNAIDS' first executive director, during the first five years, "countries were under-spending on AIDS, there was no effective treatment, and people living with HIV had to battle stigma and discrimination" (UNAIDS 2011, 23).

This situation began to change in September 2000 when the UN General Assembly adopted the UN Millennium Declaration, giving birth to the Millennium Development Goals (MDGs). For the first time high-level decision makers (donors, governments, private sectors, and NGOs) supported specific goals and measurable targets on a global scale (United Nations 2000). Two MDGs are directly concerned with HIV: (1) to halt and begin to reverse the spread of HIV and to achieve universal access to treatment, and (2) to provide assistance to children orphaned by HIV/AIDS. Three other MDGs are related to HIV/AIDS: (1) to halve the proportion of those whose income is less than one dollar a day, (2) to ensure that girls and boys have equal access to all levels of education and are able to complete a full course of primary schooling, and (3) to reduce maternal and under-five child mortality. These linkages point to the two pillars that ground the definition of human dignity offered in this book: respect or recognition and agency. (For instance, access to schooling by boys and girls, even those orphaned by AIDS, is seen as a pathway to get out of poverty, gain recognition, and flourish.)

Other global meetings followed and by June 2001 the UN General Assembly Special Session (UNGASS) on HIV/AIDS was pivotal to rally broad political commitment in support of a global response to HIV and to galvanize civil society and the private sector as partners. And by then, evidence was beginning to show HIV preventive measures and treatment regimes that worked. But these programs needed to have much higher coverage of affected populations to show impacts on the epidemic, and thus required much more significant resources. The further realization that halting the epidemic would require an unprecedented amount of resources, including resources that could move quickly from donors to recipients, led to the creation of the Global Fund in 2002, an experimental financial mechanism to get funds quickly on the ground.

Since 1986 the World Bank had been the major financier of HIV/AIDS programs. Through the African Multi-country AIDS Program (MAP) alone, the World Bank allocated US$500 million in 2000–2006 (World Bank 2000). The MAP approach required strong political commitment, institution building, multisectoral partnerships, and community engagement, all of which the MAP funded. By September 2006, the World Bank had committed US$1.32 billion to the AIDS response (World Bank 2007a). By 2007 most financing was on grant terms (World Bank 2007b).

The Global Fund was created as a multistakeholder international financing institution dedicated to disbursing additional resources to combat HIV/AIDS, tuberculosis and malaria. It was funded based on a set of principles related to its role as a financial instrument not an implementing entity. These principles guide everything it does, from governance to making grants. It is telling that none of the principles addressed issues related to the recipient countries or the potential beneficiaries of the funds. The Global Fund principles can be assumed to be anchored, although not explicitly, on the UDHR, which guides agencies such as UNAIDS.

The Global Fund has followed its core principles, which reflect its comparative advantage as a financial institution, not a technical agency. As a financial instrument the Global Fund has become the world's largest financier of AIDS, tuberculosis, and malaria programs. By mid–2012 it had approved funding of US$22.9 billion to support more than 1,000 programs in 151 countries. In 2010, the Global Fund accounted for around 20 percent of international public funding for HIV that included providing AIDS treatment for some 6.7 million people in 147 countries, among which twenty-one countries reported more than 60 percent coverage of those in need, with a total of US$12.4 billion in approved HIV funding since 2002 (Global Fund 2012). For normative criteria and technical quality assurance, the Global Fund relies on UNAIDS, WHO, and other partners.

It was 2007 when the Global Fund recognized the imperative of addressing some of the crucial social underpinnings of AIDS: gender issues. This realization resulted in the Gender Equality Strategy, which focuses on the vulnerabilities of women and girls and on sexual minorities (MSM, transgender people, and female, male, and transgendered SWs). Gender equity was followed in 2009 by the strategy on sexual orientation and gender identities (SOGI) (Global Fund 2008, 2009). In 2011 the Global Fund released an Information Note on HIV and Human Rights advising applicants to ensure that human rights principles were applied to Global Fund processes (Global Fund 2011a).

In its 2012–2016 corporate strategy, the Global Fund makes explicit linkages between equity and human rights of sexual minorities through the encouragement of in-country participatory equity. This is important because if the Global Fund encourages a human-rights approach in country proposals, it means that it is ready to finance measurable actions (i.e., to prevent stigma, encourage equity, and thus restore human dignity), heightening the plausibility of achieving local impacts. In this way the Global Fund can also support countries to apply UNAIDS and WHO normative guidance in concrete ways, which these agencies do not always have the resources to do.

Of note is the Global Fund's acknowledgement of the importance of partnerships not only with civil society but with UN and other institutional players by proposing to roll out a partnership and advocacy plan for 2012–2016 in support of key global initiatives, such as the joint UNAIDS accelerated action plan for women and girls or the UN secretary-general's global plan for the elimination of mother-to-child HIV transmission (Global Fund 2011b).

Despite the significant financial contribution of the Global Fund to the global AIDS response, the institution is not without controversy, from the ups and downs in its own institutional development to facing corruption in some of its recipient countries. And the media continues to note how donations have dwindled because of the financial crisis and reports of mismanagement (Economist 2012). Still, it is hard to move so much money to so many countries and not face some controversy. What matters most is how the institution responds to such challenges and the Global Fund seems to have learned from experience.

Some of the criticisms are not without basis. Despite the global consensus that gave birth to the institution, early on the Global Fund was slow in seeking the assistance of established agencies and was often a reluctant player in international cooperation. It is remarkable that in a letter former Global Fund general manager Gabriel Jaramillo sent on his last day at the job, he described that among the accomplishments of the Global Fund under his watch was bringing "rigor to our model by working with partners to introduce three Disease Committees, and by allowing our technical partners to participate in our Grant Approval Committee, [and] that collaboration in the field with the Global

Fund's major bilateral partners had improved, and that the results were already visible" (All Africa 2013).[8] The statement was backhand recognition that this collaboration was wanting for more than ten years.

In their Informational Note on HIV and Human Rights, the Global Fund adopted UNAIDS and WHO recommendations that national HIV responses include programs to overcome stigma, discrimination and violence; increase access to justice; sensitize law enforcement agents and law and policymakers; train health care workers in nondiscrimination; monitor and reform laws, regulations and policies; and empower affected populations by increasing their legal and rights literacy (UNAIDS/WHO 2010).

Human dignity was also affirmed in the declaration of universal access, which UNAIDS formally launched in 2006 and reaffirmed in the political declaration of HIV/AIDS adopted by the UN General Assembly in June 2011 (United Nations 2011). Although voices for human dignity had been audible in the global HIV/AIDS discourse, the actions to address the threats to human dignity were less visible and more complex, especially at the national and group-specific levels, namely among the drivers of the epidemic and at-risk populations. For instance, in 2011 past UN secretary-general Kofi Annan continued to urge leaders to "tackle social barriers and affirm human rights as key planks in the AIDS response" (UNAIDS 2011, 47), and former president Clinton exhorted "stakeholders around the world [to] focus more on high-impact prevention efforts that reach the most vulnerable populations, including those affected by political bias and social stigma" (UNAIDS 2011, 35). Although succeeding to increase and make visible global leaders' commitment to human rights and human dignity in HIV/AIDS, the actions to achieve these aspirational goals were less successful due in large part to the fundamental tensions between the global, the national, and the individual domains and the lack of attention to the need for balancing and rebalancing these tensions.

The initiative for universal access to prevention, treatment, care, and support re-energized countries and civil society, the private sector, and people living with HIV/AIDS, guided by the principle, which says: "HIV and AIDS services and products must be accessible, acceptable, affordable, available, of good quality, and sustainable to all people in need, regardless of their status and free from any form of stigma or discrimination" (UNAIDS 2011, 77). To channel efforts on these principles, UNAIDS developed a plan of action, the outcomes of which reflect the vision articulated by UNAIDS in 2010: zero new HIV infections, zero discrimination, and zero AIDS-related deaths. Finally, thirty years after the first cases of AIDS were reported, stigma and discrimination had become one of three critical goals of the HIV/AIDS response. In the words of Michel Sidibé, executive director of UNAIDS: "We have made tremendous progress in stabilizing rates of new infections in nearly sixty countries, but this success only highlights the rampant stigma and discrimination that contributes to rising infections rates among key populations at higher risk and to the vulnerability of women and girls. We can end the discrimination and inequality that blocks access to prevention, treatment, care and support. We can stop the criminalization of people living with and at risk of HIV" (UNAIDS 2011, 11).

Tension between Discourse and Action at the Global and National Levels

There is an inherent tension in HIV/AIDS between human dignity discourse based on the declaration of principles that govern international institutions on the one hand and the actions that are taken to apply those principles at the policy and programming levels on the other hand. Part of this tension sprang from the fact that international human rights declarations are nonbinding. The UN cannot impose penalties on violations like other entities, such as the World Trade Organization, can do. However, these declarations provide a mechanism for good governance related to HIV/AIDS and could be used as conditions for international development aid, although such conditions are not always feasible or desirable.

UNAIDS has not been idle in efforts to move the human dignity agenda from discourse to action. It leveraged its convening and normative roles to prepare guidelines on the application of international human rights law to HIV/AIDS (UNAIDS 2006).[9] By setting time-bound targets for prevention, access to essential medicines, and eliminating discrimination, these guidelines often act as an accountability tool. For NGOs and advocacy groups, human rights law provides a basis and tools to monitor countries' HIV/AIDS performance, take action to redress public health policies that violate rights (Patterson and London 2002), and hold decision makers accountable for their global commitments and their actions.

Historically, the UN has provided an impartial venue for discussion and dialogue about human rights and human dignity. Civil society has been both spurring and contributing to the global response, asking for action, not just words, and demanding that institutions apply those principles that underpin their missions in their own governance and practice. A statement by the International Red Cross/Red Crescent Federation to the 58th UN General Assembly in September 22, 2003, underscores the thinking at the time showing some of the key aspects of this tension between discourse and action and demanding that action serve real people and not focus on only money and statistics. They said:

Much has been said already about the social and economic impact of the HIV/AIDS epidemic and the threat that it represents for security and stability in the world. The projections are truly frightening: HIV/AIDS will kill more people this decade than all the wars and disasters in the past 50 years. There is no doubt that the pandemic is a global disaster of catastrophic proportions. But this simply must not become a cold debate around numbers and figures. Instead we must make this an ethical debate and move away from the ethics of mere survival to the ethics of dignity. . . . The fact that the discourse has turned into discussion on how much money is needed or what types of interventions we should or should not do is indecent and an affront to the dignity of every person who is living with or has been affected by HIV/AIDS. (International Federation of Red Cross and Red Crescent Societies 2003)

Undoubtedly, this is not an either/or matter. Halting the epidemic does require addressing the economic, financial, and programmatic dimensions of the epidemic as well as addressing human rights, which cannot be disassociated from a discussion of the laws that penalize certain behaviors of people who are HIV positive or most at risk of infection.

The internal governance and practices of global institutions can provide a proxy indicator of their ability to move from discourse to action and from action to impact. Balancing these tensions within institutions is reflected in how they undertook to address HIV in their hiring and human resources practices, from combating stigma and discrimination to providing testing and treatment. For instance, in their job announcements, the Global Fund stresses that "all appropriately qualified people regardless of sex, sexual orientation and/or gender identities and individuals who are living with HIV are encouraged to apply." UNAIDS asserts that "applications from people living with HIV are particularly welcome. Applications from women and from nationals of non- and underrepresented member states are particularly encouraged."[10]

Another proxy indicator is the engagement of UN employees in advocacy, which gave birth to UN Plus, the UN systemwide advocacy group of staff living with HIV. It was established in March 2005 as part of UN reform. It brings together HIV-positive staff from across the region and from other agencies in "solidarity, equality, and acceptance of people living with HIV within the UN system through awareness raising, policy change and advocacy" (UN Plus 2013). This approach has been adopted at the local level. Liberia, Mozambique, Swaziland, Rwanda, and Ghana launched Friends of UN Plus as part of their efforts to achieve a work environment that is free from stigma for all UN staff living with HIV and their families. Thus, UN Plus helps HIV-positive employees to gain respect and enables them to assert their agency to live fulfilling lives—crucial to what Lagon and Arend contend human dignity rests upon.

The Global Fund in its 2011 HIV and Human Rights Note underscores "individual agency," namely empowering individuals to be proactive in taking care of their health needs. Further, demonstrating the mutually reinforcing roles of different rights, it says that: "[A] focus on human rights can help minimize the impact of harmful social norms and violations including discrimination, harassment, or violence. It can empower individuals to claim and exercise their rights and be proactive in taking care of their health and welfare. For example, women living with HIV are more likely to be able to safely disclose their HIV status, adhere to treatment, and discuss HIV with their children if they have equal access to property and inheritance, are protected from violence, and have equal rights in marriage and divorce" (Global Fund 2011a, 4).

The UNAIDS strategy for 2011–2015 goes a step further towards action in that it heightens the importance of promoting and enforcing the rights of those infected and affected by HIV/AIDS and decries the harmful impact of stigma, social and legal exclusion, and gender inequality, which deepens the vulnerability of women, girls, and people living with HIV/AIDS. This strategy brings action closer to discourse. It places discrimination at the forefront, recognizing that stigma must be overcome to reach universal access to HIV prevention, treatment, care, and support and to achieve the MDGs by 2015.

Social transformation is at the heart of the HIV/AIDS response.[11] Social transformation requires positive changes in social, legal, gender, and economic inequalities that continue to weaken access to services by those who need them. At the end of the day the international community and country governments must view actions directed to qualitatively safeguard and restore human dignity with the same ardor as expanding services by allocating budgets to implement context-appropriate strategies. Hence, the Global Fund's move to encourage human rights-based approaches in country proposals is a major milestone—a critical catalyst to transform the pathway from discourse to concrete actions that are funded, leading to local impacts.

Tension between Global Commitments and the Individual Nature of Human Dignity

In addition to the tension between discourse and action, there is an inherent tension between the national and global levels, as states assert national sovereignty over the laws that govern their societies (i.e., those related to equal access to services, police violence, drug use, or sex work, among others), which are sometimes at odds with the commitments governments make in the global arena. This tension is even more acute between national laws and the experience of AIDS, which is unique at the personal, family, and community levels. Thus, despite progress, there have been important setbacks in ensuring the right type of policy and legal changes occur and that those changes result in positive impacts at the societal and individual levels.

Nobody questions that the global response to the AIDS epidemic has been remarkable. Over 8 million people living with HIV were receiving treatment in 2011, a 20 percent increase from 2010, with coverage reaching 54 percent of those infected. There was 19 percent increased treatment coverage in sub–Sahara Africa alone. By 2011, new infections among children had declined for the second year in a row. Fifty-seven percent of the estimated 1.5 million pregnant women living with HIV in 2011 received treatment to prevent mother-to-child transmission, up from 48 percent in 2010. Increased treatment coverage has added 14 million life-years in low- and middle-income countries since 1995 and declining death rates means that there are 34.2 million people living with HIV, more than ever before; the HIV epidemic is shifting from a death sentence to a chronic disease. With the focus on treatment expansion, UNAIDS estimates that "the world is nearly on track to having 15 million people living with HIV on antiretroviral treatment by 2015" (UNAIDS 2012, 18). This is an optimistic estimate. Such a level of coverage would require more and better access to treatment precisely by those populations that are most vulnerable to discrimination: SWs, MSMs, and IDUs. In many countries, these populations remain sadly marginalized and often neglected. Discrimination robs these groups of their human dignity and any prospects of a fulfilled life. Thus, despite significant progress, there are setbacks in reaching the goals of zero discrimination and universal access to HIV prevention, treatment care, and support. These setbacks feed the gap between global commitments and local impacts.

First, the 2001 Declaration of Commitment on HIV/AIDS did not specify these populations as needing special protection. And the UN Assembly applied the term "vulnerable groups," which many advocates renounced as vague and undefined, leaving room for countries to avoid real commitments to these politically unpopular groups (Gruskin 2002).

The UN was criticized again when the 2006 Political Declaration on HIV/AIDS (United Nations 2006) failed to concretize the steps that could lead to lasting change, which civil society interpreted as a missed opportunity for heightened action by countries (Africa Science News Service 2006). HIV/AIDS advocates argued that by refusing to name specific vulnerable groups and by failing to set new benchmarks for measuring success, countries were hampering the AIDS response (IGLHRC 2007). And it was only in 2011, as previously noted, that the Global Fund released an Information Note on HIV and Human Rights advising applicants to ensure human rights principles were applied to Global Fund processes (Global Fund 2011a).

In 2012–2013 several milestones converged: PEPFAR released its Blueprint for Creating an AIDS-free Generation, the Global Fund rolled out its new funding model, and the Institute of Medicine released its congressionally mandated evaluation of PEPFAR. Together, these landmarks paint a picture of remarkable alignment between PEPFAR and the Global Fund. They also show how complementary the two organizations are as they pursue the same mission: saving lives (Derrick 2013).

Although the funding for HIV/AIDS programs worldwide has continued to increase, funding from domestic public sources in low- and middle-income countries grew by more than 15 percent between 2010 and 2011, supporting more than 50 percent of the global response. Bilateral donors, banks, and philanthropy contributed about 25 percent, and the US Government and the Global Fund together accounted for 25 percent of contributions or US$5.5 billion in disbursement (UNAIDS 2012).

This level of support carries influence, as many HIV/AIDS national budgets rely heavily on external funding. Thus, when the United States, the largest single bilateral donor, launched PEPFAR in 2003 with its own set priorities, their approach to treatment and prevention services was the subject of sustained critique by some lawmakers, scholars, and advocates (Dietrich 2007). For example, the antiprostitution pledge requirement forced countries and agencies that received PEPFAR money to adopt a written policy opposing prostitution, which in the view of many were counterefforts against stigma and discrimination of SWs. Despite the condom's confirmed effectiveness in HIV prevention, one-third of PEPFAR's prevention funding was directed to programs that promoted abstinence and faithfulness and were not required to provide any information about condoms (Kay and Jackson 2008; IGLHRC 2007).

Given the above criticisms, it is worth noting that the evaluation of PEPFAR, conducted by the US Institute of Medicine (IOM) of the National Academy of Sciences over a period of four years and released on February 20, 2013, has given PEPFAR a glowing assessment in terms of improving and saving lives and, overall, being globally transformative in the way it envisioned and implemented health assistance. The IOM evaluation report applauds PEPFAR's emphasis on gender-based violence, as an underlying driver of vulnerability, and acknowledges that biomedical approaches are important but not sufficient (IOM 2013). The evaluation of PEPFAR has implications for the global HIV/AIDS community in terms of investments, measurement, country ownership, and collaboration.

A commentary published by the *Lancet* on the same day PEPFAR's evaluation report was issued highlighted the need for PEPFAR to maintain its support for interventions that target all modes of HIV transmission but that it falls short of identifying specific population groups (Black 2013). Summers (2013, 1) goes a step further when he underscores an evaluation finding saying that "PEPFAR continues to emphasize treatment and clinical care over prevention, and often *fails to address the challenges patients face in accessing and retaining HIV/AIDS services, including prevention.* Key among these challenges is discrimination and social stigma which hampers access to services" (emphasis added). For UNAIDS, the report's assessment "reinforces the strong synergies between UNAIDS' vision of zero HIV infections, zero discrimination, and zero AIDS-related deaths with the US goal of an AIDS-free generation" (UNAIDS 2013).

At the national level, the need for concrete legal changes persists. Although the number of countries that reported programs to reduce HIV-related stigma increased from 39 percent in 2006 to 92 percent in 2012, many of these programs lack adequate budgets and therefore had little impact (UNAIDS 2010). The tension between commitments to principles and actual changes in country policy from discriminatory to dignity enabling is daunting. It can be socially explosive, requires sophisticated policy and political know-how at the country level, and cannot be accomplished without a sound plan and concomitant resources. It requires the support of parliamentarians, communities, and people living with HIV themselves.

Decision makers need evidence to support their policies, yet, although there is a plethora of strong anecdotal evidence, hard evidence is only recently beginning to be available. A recent study of HIV prevalence among MSMs shows that of the eleven countries with the highest HIV prevalence rates studied in sub–Sahara Africa, seven punished male-to-male relationships with ten years of imprisonment and two with the death penalty. Only South Africa provides legal protection. (There was no legal data on one of the countries.) (World Bank 2011). As the authors assert, "while legal status alone does not guarantee protections or enabling environments, it is a parameter for understanding social tolerance and the space for rights advocacy at country level" (306). It permits the type of social interventions that can enable the agency in human dignity.

Although global institutions foster a multistakeholder approach to achieving local impacts, the very nature of these institutions makes them less agile for engaging in swift actions at the local level, hence, necessitating the critical role of nonstate actors. Community activism has been instrumental in enacting laws to protect key populations (e.g., Chile's May 2012 antidiscrimination law and India's 2009 decriminalization of same-sex relations). Activism and community-led initiatives had been driving forces behind the significant expansion of HIV prevention and treatment of the last decade along with decreases in stigma, discrimination, and domestic violence (UNAIDS 2012; Rodriguez-García et al. 2013).

A recent portfolio of studies conducted by the World Bank on the local HIV/AIDS impacts of community responses demonstrate that social and structural interventions can result in improved agency. One study in India found strong association between empowerment of female SWs and MSM/transgender individuals and social change, where being a member of a sex worker community group was associated with access to social entitlements (p<.05), reduced violence (p<.001), and reduced police coercion (p<.001). Access to justice and legal services is empowering for people, the more so for marginalized populations. The same study found that although the prevalence of sexually transmitted infections (STIs) had decreased among female SWs, it did not decrease among MSM/transgender (MSM/T) populations. One explanation is that, in this case, real and perceived stigma toward MSM/T decreased their use of health services and therefore, very few were tested for STIs (Rodriguez-García et al. 2013, 8, 71–73). This finding is interesting given the High Court of Delhi, India decriminalizing consensual same-sex relations in 2009, which shows the limited impact of laws alone. Another study in Lesotho found that fear of discrimination deterred men from being tested, and if tested, from collecting the results. The higher the stigmatizing attitudes at the work place and within the household, the less likely individuals would seek the results of the HIV test and therefore, would be treated if needed (Rodriguez-García et al. 2013, 76–77).

The epidemic has evolved since the 1980s and 1990s and many advances in HIV/AIDS prevention, treatment, care, and support, and mitigation have given the international community a sense that the MDG of halting new HIV infections is within reach. But this goal cannot be achieved without reaching the populations that are most at risk and who are driving the current phase of the epidemic. Some of their behaviors (i.e., drug use or sex work) cause them to be often penalized and criminalized by national laws, discriminated against by employers, marginalized by society and ostracized by family and community. Addressing the legal environment alone involves not one but many actions on several fronts: legislation, law enforcement, and access to justice.

Whereas more countries are recognizing the need to implement programs to reduce HIV/AIDS-related stigma, progress remains inadequate. More than fifty-six countries have laws that specifically criminalize HIV transmission or exposure, with the majority of prosecutions reported in high-income countries; 116 countries criminalize some aspects of sex work; seventy-nine countries criminalize consensual same-sex sexual relations; and thirty-two countries have laws that penalize with the death penalty drug-related offenses. Laws such as these increase peoples' vulnerabilities and isolation and deter many of them from seeking much needed services (UNAIDS 2011). Using the HIV Stigma Index, a study of people living with HIV/AIDS in nine countries found 53 percent of Rwandans and 33 percent of Zambians have been verbally abused; 20 percent of Rwandans and 25 percent of Colombians who participated in the survey have experienced physical violence.[12] What is even more appalling is that many "people internalized this stigma: More than 60 percent of people living with HIV in Bangladesh, China, Myanmar and Scotland said they felt ashamed of being HIV-positive" (UNAIDS 2012, 68).

Not only is the agency of people affected by HIV not supported at the country level, but the legal and societal norms that result in stigmatization and discrimination prevent these population groups from being recognized and respected by their social peers, assaulting their human dignity. In short, if left unbalanced, the tensions between discourse and action and between global commitments and local impacts will hamper restoration of the dignity of every person affected by HIV/AIDS.

Conclusion

Looking back at the early writings on AIDS and human dignity one is struck by the challenge of appraising progress. There has been progress in human rights and human dignity, but it has been slow and patchy.

On the one hand, there is a deeper understanding of what Mann named the societal nature of the pandemic and the societal preconditions for HIV vulnerability (Mann 1999, 223). One could argue that by being responsive to the needs of people they are meant to serve—enabling them to improve their *agency*—UNAIDS and the Global Fund are positioned to work with stakeholders and country governments to achieve positive change in countries.

On the other hand, significant local impacts are still elusive. Stating that discrimination must end is not enough. To the extent that UN resolutions are not legally binding, it falls on national policymakers to introduce concrete changes in their sociolegal system. A few have succeeded, but in many countries the legal environment related to HIV/AIDS has changed relatively little in the past twenty years. Purposeful action on a broad scale is needed to repeal discriminatory laws and replace them with antidiscriminatory ones. If the international community is serious about zero discrimination, the work on AIDS and human dignity must be implemented with evidence, realizable goals, sound strategies, and significant resources—in other words, on a scale more typical of biomedical interventions (Stemple 2008).

Among the many challenges that scaling up faces, two are critical. One, as mentioned above, is adequate funding. If actions to improve the legal environment and to undertake concrete programs are not adequately funded, it will be difficult to see impact on human dignity. The other critical challenge is political will. It is usually easier to commit to broad principles globally than to take action on those principles locally, and those policymakers who take action face serious obstacles when they try to uproot long-held national laws and societal practices that penalize certain behaviors. This is compounded by the fact that activists in civil society, a key instigator of change at the local level, often have their own hands tied by belonging to groups who themselves might be penalized by local laws. This chapter argues that human rights need to be taken as seriously in HIV/AIDS programming and funding as biomedical and prevention programs in order to see tangible results for human dignity.

This look at HIV/AIDS and human dignity shows that for global institutions there will always be tension between the need to bring stakeholders together globally around fundamental principles and the imperative to translate these principles into concrete actions to achieve local impacts. Some national governments have demonstrated the wisdom to devise and implement changes to safeguard or restore human dignity. Global institutions can make a difference by recognizing and supporting these efforts with adequate resources, normative guidance, and good practices. Equally important, they can empower civil society to engage in those countries that are more recalcitrant regarding legal and societal changes and provide adequate support.

Despite slow progress, active multilateral partnerships, unprecedented engagement of civil society, UNAIDS's explicit goal of zero discrimination, and the Global Fund's support of human agency taken together appear to be paving a path toward improvements in human dignity. Global institutions are going beyond protecting people who are vulnerable to HIV to empowering them.

Notes

The author thanks Mark P. Lagon and Matthew Carnes for their valuable inputs and comments.

1. This book is recommended reading for anyone interested in the evolution of HIV/AIDS and human rights.

2. Jonathan Mann was particularly interested in the effect of health policies on human rights, the health impact of human rights violations, and the inextricable connection between promoting and protecting health and rights.

3. In January 2003, under President George W. Bush the United States committed US$15 billion over five years to address the international AIDS epidemic. Full implementation of PEPFAR began in June 2004 and by 2012 the United States was a leading financier having invested over US$37 billion in bilateral funding and over US$7 billion in the Global Fund. Fact Sheet, November 29, 2012. Washington, DC, http://www.state.gov/r/pa/prs/ps /2012/11/201195.htm.

4. In this chapter "tension" does not imply "opposite." It refers to the forces that influence possibly equally important demands. Different actors balance these tensions differently, which in turn affects the evolution of HIV/AIDS, human rights, and human dignity.

5. See Lagon and Kaminski's chapter 6 in this book.

6. A "theory of change" is a specific and measurable description of a social change. It depicts a causal outcomes-based model that articulates underlying assumptions and hypotheses about why something will cause something else. Theories of change capture complex initiatives. They often start with a goal and then link outcomes and activities to explain how and why the desired change is expected to come about. Consult: http://www.theoryofchange.org.

7. UNAIDS brings together the resources of its Secretariat (based in Geneva) and eleven UN system organizations: ILO, UNDP, UNESCO, UNHCR, UNICEF, UNFPA, UNODC, UN Women, the World Bank, WFP, and WHO, http://www.unaids.org/en/aboutunaids/un aidscosponsors/.

8. Gabriel Jaramillo was an able general manager of the Global Fund during 2012. Since January 2013, the executive director of the Global Fund is Mark Dybul, who in 2006–2009 served as the US global AIDS coordinator, which includes PEPFAR.

9. Publications that bring human rights thinking together with sound public health policy in a clear and consistent way are: *The International Guidelines on HIV/AIDS and Human Rights 1998* (HR/PUB/98/1) and *2006* (consolidated version) (http://www.unaids.org) and *The AIDS Pandemic: Complacency, Injustice and Unfulfilled Expectations*, by Lawrence O. Gostin (University of North Carolina Press, 2004).

10. See the web pages of these agencies under jobs or employment.

11. Social transformation refers to individual and societal processes. Within the social system, transformation refers to large-scale social change leading to cultural reforms. At the individual level it refers to a reciprocal relationship whereby people are correctly identified with the cultural expectations of their particular class membership. It requires that individuals have their social position be validated by others.

12. The People Living with HIV Stigma Index is a research tool used to capture data on HIV-positive people's experiences and perceptions regarding stigma and discrimination, http://www.stigmaindex.org.

References

Africa Science News Service. 2006. "International Civil Society Denounce UN Meeting on AIDS as a Failure." Accessed September 26, 2013. http://africanscience.blogspot .com/2006/06/international-civil-society-denounce.html.

All Africa. 2013. "Africa: Most Reforms Already Implemented, Jaramillo Says in Farewell Letter." *All Africa*. February 18. http://allafrica.com/stories/201302180614.html.

Black, Robert. 2013. "The Future of the US Response to Global HIV/AIDS." *Lancet* 382 (9894): 751–53.

Derrick, Deborah. 2013. "Better Than Ever, Together." *The Huffington Post*. April 1. http://www.huffingtonpost.com/deborah-derrick/better-than-ever-together_b_2992982.html.

Dietrich, John W. 2007. "The Politics of PEPFAR: The President's Emergency Plan for AIDS Relief." *Ethics & International Affairs* 21 (3): 277–92.

Economist. 2012. "The Global Fund Heal Thyself: Grappling with a Controversial Malaria Programme." *Economist*, November 24. http://www.economist.com/news/science-and-technology/21567054-grappling-controversial-malaria-programme-heal-thyself.

Global Development Alliance. 2001. "USAID: Strategies for Conflict Prevention." Discussion paper.

Global Fund. 2008. *Strategy for Ensuring Gender Equality in the Response to HIV/AIDS, Tuberculosis and Malaria*. Geneva: The Global Fund to Fight AIDS, Tuberculosis and Malaria.

————. 2009. *Strategy in Relation to Sexual Orientation and Gender Identities (SOGI)*. Geneva: The Global Fund to Fight AIDS, Tuberculosis and Malaria.

————. 2011a. *Information Note: HIV and Human Rights*. Geneva: The Global Fund to Fight AIDS, Tuberculosis and Malaria.

————. 2011b. *Response to the Evaluation of the Global Fund's Gender Equality and Sexual Orientation and Gender Identities (SOGI) Strategies*. Geneva: The Global Fund to Fight AIDS, Tuberculosis and Malaria.

————. 2012. *Strategic Investments for Impact: Global Fund Results Report*. Geneva: The Global Fund to Fight AIDS, Tuberculosis and Malaria.

Gostin, Lawrence O. 1998. "A Tribute to Jonathan Mann: Health and Human Rights in the AIDS Pandemic." *Journal of Law and Medical Ethics* 26 (3): 256–58.

————. 2003. "The Global Reach of HIV/AIDS: Science, Politics, Economics, and Research." *Emory International Law Review* 17: 1–54.

Gruskin, Sofia. 2002. "The UN General Assembly Special Session on HIV/AIDS: Were Some Lessons of the Last 20 Years Ignored?" *American Journal of Public Health* 92 (3): 337–38.

Gruskin, Sofia, Aart Hendriks, and Katarina Tomasevski. 1996. "Human Rights and Responses to HIV/AIDS." In *AIDS in the World Two*, edited by Jonathan M. Mann and Daniel Tarantola. New York: Oxford University Press.

IGLHRC. 2007. *Off the Map: How HIV/AIDS Programming Is Failing Same-Sex Practicing People*. New York: International Gay and Lesbian Human Rights Commission.

Institute of Medicine (IOM). 2013. "PEPFAR Evaluation Brief." IOM. Accessed September 26, 2013. http://www.iom.edu/Reports/2013/Evaluation-of-PEPFAR.aspx.

International Federation of Red Cross and Red Crescent Societies. 2003. "HIV/AIDS, Human Dignity, Global Fund—How to Respond to the Challenge of HIV/AIDS." Accessed September 26, 2013. http://www.ifrc.org/en/news-and-media/opinions-and-positions/speeches/2003/hivaids-human-dignity-global-fund—how-to-respond-to-the-challenge-of-hivaids/.

Kay, Julie F, and Ashley Jackson. 2008. *Sex, Lies and Stereotypes: How Abstinence-Only Programs Harm Women and Girls*. New York: Legal Momentum.

Lebech, Mette. 2004. "What is Human Dignity?" *Maynooth Philosophical Papers*. 59–69.

Mann, Jonathan M. 1999. "Human Rights and AIDS: The Future of the Pandemic." In *Health and Human Rights: A Reader*, edited by Jonathan M. Mann, Michael A. Grodin, Sofia Gruskin, and George J. Annas. New York: Routledge.

Meernik, James, Rosa Aloisi, Marsha Sowell, and Angela Nichols. 2012. "The Impact of Human Rights Organizations on Naming and Shaming Campaigns." *Journal of Conflict Resolution* 56 (2): 233–56.

Nussbaum, Martha. 2010. *From Disgust to Humanity: Sexual Orientation and Constitutional Law (Inalienable Rights)*. United Kingdom: Oxford University Press.

Obama, Barack. 2011. "Remarks by the President on World AIDS Day." Washington, DC: White House. Accessed September 26, 2013. http://www.whitehouse.gov/pho tos-and-video/video/2011/12/01/president-obama-world-aids-day#transcript.

Patterson, David, and Leslie London. 2002. "International Law, Human Rights and HIV/AIDS." *Bulletin of the World Health Organization* 80 (12): 964–69.

Rodriguez-García, Rosalía. 2002. "Can Diplomacy Serve as a Bridge for Peace?" *International Affairs Review* 11 (1): 111–12.

Rodriguez-García, Rosalía, René Bonnel, David Wilson, and N'Della N'Jie. 2013. *Investing in Communities Achieves Results: Findings from an Evaluation of Community Responses to HIV and AIDS*. Washington, DC: The World Bank.

Sen, Amartya. 1999. *Development as Freedom*. New York: Alfred A. Knopf Inc.

Stemple, Lara. 2008. "Health and Human Rights in Today's Fight against HIV/AIDS." *AIDS* 22 (2): S113–S121.

Summers, Todd. 2013. "The IOM's PEPFAR Evaluation: Implications for the Global Fund." Global Health Policy Center at Center for Strategic and International Studies. Accessed September 26, 2013. http://www.smartglobalhealth.org/blog/entry/the -ioms-pepfar-evaluation-implications-for-the-global-fund/.

UNAIDS. 2006. *International Guidelines on HIV/AIDS and Human Rights*. Consolidated version. Geneva: United Nations Cosponsored Programme for HIV/AIDS and the UN Office of the High Commissioner for Human Rights.

———. 2010. *UNAIDS Global Report*. Geneva: United Nations Cosponsored Programme for HIV/AIDS.

———. 2011. *AIDS at 30: Nations at the Crossroads*. Geneva: United Nations Cosponsored Programme for HIV/AIDS.

———. 2012. *Together We Will End AIDS*. Geneva: United Nations Cosponsored Programme for HIV/AIDS.

———. 2013. "Feature Story: Four-Year Evaluation of PEPFAR Concludes." UNAIDS. Accessed September 26, 2013. http://www.unaids.org/en/resources/presscentre/fea turestories/2013/february/20130225iompepfar/.

UNAIDS/WHO. 2010. *Technical Guidance Note for Global Fund HIV Proposals: Reduction of HIV Stigma and Discrimination*. Geneva: United Nations Cosponsored Programme for HIV/AIDS and World Health Organization.

United Nations. 2000. UN Millennium Declaration. Accessed September 26, 2013. http://www.un.org/en/development/devagenda/millennium.shtml; http://www.un .org/millenniumgoals/.

———. 2001. "Declaration of Commitment on HIV/AIDS." United Nations General Assembly Special Session on HIV/AIDS, June 25–27. Accessed September 26, 2013. http://www.unaids.org/en/media/unaids/contentassets/dataimport/publications/irc -pub03/aidsdeclaration_en.pdf.

———. 2006. "Political Declaration on HIV/AIDS." United Nations General Assembly A/Res/60/262, June 15.

————. 2011. *Report of the UN Secretary-General—Uniting for Universal Access: Towards Zero New HIV Infections, Zero Discrimination and Zero AIDS-related Deaths.* New York: United Nations, March 28.

UN Plus. 2013. "Missions and Objectives." UN Plus. Accessed September 10, 2013. http://www.unplus.org/wp/about-unplus/what-we-do.

World Bank. 2000. *Intensifying Action against HIV/AIDS in Africa: Responding to a Development Crisis.* Washington, DC: The World Bank.

————. 2007a. *The Africa Multi-Country AIDS Program 2000–2006.* Washington, DC: The World Bank.

————. 2007b. *Legal Aspects of HIV/AIDS: A Guide for Policy and Law Reform.* Washington, DC: The World Bank.

————. 2011. *The Global HIV Epidemics among Men Who Have Sex with Men.* Washington, DC: The World Bank.

CHAPTER 9

The New Global Landscape for Poverty Alleviation and Development

Foundations, Ngos, Social Media, and Other Private Sector Institutions

RAJ M. DESAI AND HOMI KHARAS

Following the end of the Second World War until very recently, international development assistance aid was mainly provided by two types of institutions: donor agencies of richer countries and multilateral development banks whose capital was contributed largely by governments of richer countries. But between 2000 and 2011, international private giving by US-based corporate and independent foundations and individuals more than doubled. Along with foundations, nongovernmental organizations (NGOs), religious groups, and charities in the United States contributed $39 billion to development causes in 2011. By comparison, the World Bank lent about $43 billion and the United States disbursed about $31 billion in economic assistance (World Bank 2011; Hudson Institute 2013). Our chief aim here is to examine the implications of this dramatically changed aid landscape for global poverty alleviation as well as for human dignity in international affairs. We argue that although there remains some uncertainty about the effects of private aid on development and on the motivations of private aid givers, there is reason to believe that private aid advances the centrality of personal agency as the focus of donor-recipient aid transactions both for individual taxpayers and for beneficiaries. For taxpayers, private aid most obviously offers opportunities for greater control over funding and allocation that is not possible through the normal route that official aid takes in being transferred from rich-country taxpayers to poor-country beneficiaries. For recipients, private aid fundamentally involves dignity-enhancing, person-to-person relationships that often trump sovereign considerations of strategic and commercial interest in allocating of funds.

Private Aid: New Players, New Directions

Both official aid and private international giving have risen strongly in the United States over the last decade. In the United States private giving for international development now exceeds official development assistance by 30 percent. Whereas time series data on private giving volumes is limited, the sheer number of private foundations grew from 40,100 in 1995 to 71,000 in 2005, with more than 650 US foundations making grants for international affairs (Lawrence, Austin, and Mukai 2007; Renz and Atienza 2006). Meanwhile, international NGOs quadrupled from 6,000 to 26,000 in the 1990s, before increasing again to 40,000 by the end of the 1990s (Keohane and Nye 2000). The growth in private aid is all the more striking because survey data suggests that public opinion overestimates the size of official aid by significant amounts. In the United States, 69 percent think the US government gives more than other countries in international aid as a share of their gross domestic product (Ramsay et al. 2009).

Meanwhile, new global institutions have emerged in the last two decades. Growth in private, nonofficial aid is seen at all levels, from the largest charities, such as the Gates, Ford, MacArthur, Rockefeller, and Hewlett Foundations, to transnational NGOs, such as CARE, Oxfam, Médecins Sans Frontières, and Save the Children, to hundreds of smaller foundations, to the small-scale philanthropy of millions of individuals who have at their fingertips a variety of mechanisms for delivering donations or microloans to developing countries.

Despite this growth, relatively little is known about the allocation and effectiveness of private aid. Private aid's defenders argue that private development assistance is more effective than official development assistance due to lower overhead costs, less susceptibility to corrupt practices, less leakage due to public-sector inefficiencies, a stronger need-based orientation, and fewer funds being funneled back to consultants and contractors in rich countries, as is the case for much official technical assistance (Dreher et al. 2009; Koch et al. 2008). Research on the allocation and selectivity of private aid is still of recent vintage; information on the impact of private aid remains in its infancy.

Although evidence on the workings of private aid may be preliminary, there is reason to believe that private aid, by putting a human face on those whose dignity will be served through their economic empowerment, advances the centrality of human agency as the analytical centerpiece of relationships between donors and recipients. It does this in two separate but related ways: (1) through a sometimes dramatic shortening of the route between donor and recipient, thus potentially reducing both transaction and agency costs of aid, and (2) through a reliance on person-to-person relationships that are, increasingly, abetted by social media and internet technology.

The Long and Short Routes
of Development Aid

The new forms of private aid offer different answers to the traditional models of charity. First, official aid and private aid face different collective action constraints. For the former, taxpayers who support foreign aid in principle may be insufficiently mobilized relative to particular interest groups. Even philanthropically minded individuals may free ride on the efforts of larger private donors. For the latter, private giving offers an opportunity for individual action rather than collective action. Aid is an act of altruism. Second, the path that official aid takes—from taxpayers to government coffers to aid agencies to governments in developing nations to public agencies or private organizations in the field—is long and winding. And whether accurate or not, this course is often perceived by taxpayers in donor countries to be costly and susceptible to corruption and leakage as funds move from donor countries to beneficiaries in recipient countries. Private aid offers a more direct connection between giver and recipient. Third, donor-country individuals may want to help and recipients may want input into funding decisions, but both recognize that they need to act through one or more intermediaries (usually governments or NGOs)—parts of a global foreign-aid apparatus that may be simply too insulated or centralized to incorporate the individual preferences (see, e.g., Easterly 2005; Roodman 2006). Private giving offers many more opportunities for choosing the kind of intermediation platform with which donors and recipients feel most comfortable.

Coordination

The public economics literature suggests that collective action problems may block private giving for worthy causes because each individual, behaving rationally, tries to free ride on others' generosity. Governments can overcome the collective action problem by taxing everyone and providing grants to the causes to which individuals would want to give. One common empirical approach is to test whether individual donations are smaller in areas where government grants are larger. Such crowding out is evidence of collective action problems at work.

A review of the literature by Bekkers and Wiepking (2007) finds evidence that crowding out in domestic charities is significant. Their summary looks mostly at cross-section studies. Garrett and Rhine (2007) analyze time series for 1965–2003 and reach the same conclusion. In the long run, cointegration tests show that increased government spending crowds out charitable giving, especially in the education sector. In the short run, however, the effects are weaker and not significant. The authors suggest that it may take time for individuals to get full information on what the government is doing.

Andreoni and Payne (2008) also confirm the crowding-out effect in a large sample of charities. They demonstrate that crowding out occurs through two channels: classic crowding out (where donors feel less willing to give) and fundraising crowding out (where grant-receiving organizations reduce their activity to collect donations). Their evidence suggests that fundraising crowding out accounts for 68 percent of the observed crowding-out effect.

This evidence, however, relates to giving through NGOs compared to government tax-and-spend programs. It does not directly look at new forms of private giving. For these newer types of private assistance, the premise is that the act of individual giving gives pleasure directly to the donor—that is, assuming that giving is altruistic. If so, it would suggest that the collective-action constraint to international aid is minimal.

The Chain of Official Aid

If one were to follow the money of a bilateral aid transaction, it would look something like this. Taxpayers in rich countries pay taxes that are collected by a revenue-raising agency and are then allocated to the foreign aid agency or department. Within the foreign aid agency, project officers, through a series of interactions with their counterparts in various line ministries in developing countries, design aid programs to be funded that are subject to managerial approval (and in some cases may require interagency authorization) before the funds can be transferred to the recipient governmental agency. In accordance with program design, the recipient ministry may rely on extant procedures for accounting and use of the received funds (the country systems approach), or it may establish new, specialized units within the ministry for the specific purpose of managing the use of program funds (the project-implementation unit approach). In either case, a portion of funds may be used for a variety of incidental expenses, including salary supplements for civil service. According to procedures thus defined, the ministry then allocates the funds to a frontline agency or organization—for instance, a regional government or a provider of public services. The frontline agency, similarly, may use some funds to pay or supplement the salaries of specific staff members responsible for administering the funds. Finally, the frontline agency spends the funds remaining on the intended project, such as a vaccination effort, a new school, improved sanitation, or other such areas.

Foreign aid delivered through these official channels, obviously, does not provide direct connections between citizens and recipients. Citizens pay their taxes to the government, which in turn allocates resources to other governments to fund myriad public programs, among them programs that benefit poor individuals around the world. There is no face-to-face contact between an individual taxpayer and the final recipient, and insofar as taxpayers have inaccurate perceptions of how their government spends development aid, there are few concrete expectations of impact, return, or reward.

Official aid travels a long route, with costs at each stage. The first stage is the cost of tax collection when money is transferred from individuals to the treasury. In this stage, costs consist of the direct administrative costs of tax collection as well as deadweight losses from taxation. These costs can be substantial. For example, Alm (1985) found deadweight losses on US taxes could approach nine percent. In the second stage, official donor agencies transfer funds to recipient country governments to support specific development projects and programs. The administrative costs of these agencies have averaged between 4 to 5 percent according to statistics reported by the Organization for Economic Co-operation and Development's (OECD) Development Assistance Committee. The third stage involves costs associated with transferring the money from the recipient government to final beneficiaries through project implementation.

Administrative costs of the project, corruption, and other leakages mean that only about *half* the funds actually reach their stated end purpose. One study, based on surveys in Ghana, Tanzania, and Rwanda concludes that, "approximately half of the overall amount allocated to clinics and hospitals did not actually reach them" (Lindelow, Kushnarova, and Kaiser 2006, 30). Similar figures appear in other studies. According to the Paris monitoring survey, in 2011 some $62 billion was disbursed by donors to 78 percent of the recipients who participated in the survey. But only $42 billion was received by these recipients; between the aid agencies of donor countries and the government budgets of these recipient countries, some $20 billion was lost (OECD 2011). The US Government Accountability Office (GAO), in its recent analysis of the Millennium Challenge Corporation was able to identify the allocation of 59 percent of in-country disbursements as transaction costs in the nine compact countries that are currently operational.[1] Of this, 32 percent was for direct project-related expenses, and 27 percent was for administrative, audit, fiscal, and procurement expenses (GAO 2007). Adding all these together, transaction costs on official aid could amount to 60 percent or more.

Some of the most venerable, older international development charities traditionally operated in a similar manner. Individuals (sometimes prompted by tax rules allowing charitable contributions to be deducted from taxable income) directed resources to an organization (e.g., the Red Cross or Child-Fund[2]), with which the taxpayer identified or otherwise to trusts, and the organization in turn allocated resources to various programs and operational expenses. Some organizations allowed varying forms of sponsorship, where donors received updates from recipients (e.g., updates from a child recipient) or selected a level of donation that corresponded to different types of the organizations' activities (e.g., a donation to allow the charity to purchase vaccines). Donors were not typically able to select which child they sponsored and funds received were not usually earmarked.

These traditional modes of aid delivery were designed to cope with three principal challenges: Most donors did not have enough information on the specific causes of poverty or on the types of programs that could be designed to address these causes—not just to treat the symptoms; small-scale donations that might otherwise be fragmented or insubstantial needed to be coordinated; and agency costs needed to be addressed. Aid agencies or some more traditional charitable organizations provided an institutional basis for reducing the taxpayer-specific burden of acquiring information on specific program and project possibilities and, by pooling resources, avoided the coordination problem that atomistic donor-taxpayers faced.

Private Aid as a Direct Transaction

Private aid in the last decade, however, has removed the advantage that official aid (and older private aid) held in overcoming these challenges. In part, this has been accomplished through the expansion of a particular type of global institution that is not an intergovernmental entity but one that is attached to private philanthropists: the mega-charity. With charities whose endowments have been established at the bequest of individual billionaires, such as the Gates Foundation, Hewlett Foundation, and Google Foundation, there is little coordination problem in making aid-allocation decisions. Regarding the information challenge, moreover, the operating principle of many of these larger charities is to direct large amounts of funds to programs and sectors that individual philanthropists themselves have chosen as priorities. Reflecting the dot-com boom that created the wealth of these new philanthropists, many hold an abiding faith in the capacity of innovation, technology, and modern management methods to solve problems of extreme poverty. And there is an emphasis on blurring the line between nonprofit and for-profit approaches, as the new philanthropists seek to invest in income-generating activities. Google.org (a for-profit charity aiming to address issues of global health, disease, poverty, and climate change) and the for-profit Omidyar Network are prime examples.[3] Rather than funding a medical clinic, for example, the new philanthropists invest in biotech companies working on tropical diseases. Rather than fund the distribution of drugs, the new philanthropists seek to invest in and create incentives for drug companies to operate in poor regions.

As a consequence of this, there are three arguments to be made that new private aid may be, on the margins, more effective than official aid. First, private aid may be less susceptible to so-called leakage due to corruption and bribes. Because it usually avoids public-sector ministries or government agencies in recipient countries and is instead transferred directly to frontline NGOs and development projects, it can avoid problems associated with weak or fragile public institutions. Second, smaller portions of private aid are typically spent on overhead costs or on technical assistance that often funds contractors in donor countries. Most foundations and charitable organizations typically lack a (costly) network of field offices with international staff and instead tend to rely on local staff and partnerships with frontline NGOs. They also tend to depend more extensively on the input of end-user beneficiaries. Third, although official donor allocations are strongly influenced by strategic or commercial relations with recipient countries, private aid allocations appear to be more heavily influenced by recipient need and human dignity, as defined by Mark P. Lagon and Anthony Clark Arend at the outset of this book.

This is not to suggest that private aid is not without its drawbacks. Although there are certainly reasons to believe that private aid may be more cost saving and that larger portions of private aid than official aid actually reach the poor, in contrast to the extensive evaluation of official-aid effectiveness there is very little comparable information on the cost efficiency of private aid. Self-evaluations of NGOs may be positive, but these are rarely conducted according to accepted standards of reliable impact evaluation.

Moreover, private aid givers are not subject to the same standards of budgetary and governance oversight or accountability as are official aid agencies.[4] The use of taxpayer funds naturally raises demands for financial accountability, which can encourage risk-averse strategies when compared to private funds, which can be less risk-averse. Finally, private aid cannot, of course, promote liberalization, institution building, fiscal reforms, governance reforms, or any of dozens of other key elements of an effective development strategy.

Crowdfunding Aid

As we have seen, official aid, although funded by taxpayers, gives citizens little say over aid allocations. Compared to official aid, private aid is by definition more sensitive to the preferences of philanthropic-minded individuals who determine allocations across countries and, within countries, across sectors, projects, and individuals; in short, the aid giver is empowered. In recent years, private development aid has been facilitated by the availability of peer-to-peer, internet-based platforms, which bundle large amounts of small, individual contributions for investments, grants, or loans. The bundling of funds is generally done through internet-based social networks. From the United States, internet-based companies such as Global Giving, Kiva, Wokai, and Zidisha, have channeled millions of dollars to individuals and partner organizations in developing countries.

Crowdfunded private aid also offers the promise of a much shorter route from giver to recipient. Internet-based platforms offer a direct matching between the two. Although there are some differences in approach across platforms (e.g., Kiva focuses on individuals or entrepreneurs whereas Global Giving highlights the worthiness of the projects they are proposing for funding), all enhance social recognition of the beneficiaries' worth and catalyze their agency. Donors contribute directly to those activities rather than to individuals. In both cases, the flow of funds route is short. The money goes from an individual to the internet-based bundler, where it is pooled and transferred to a financial or project intermediary in the recipient country that then disburses it to the final beneficiaries. The long route of passing through government bureaucracies is avoided.

Private Aid and Personal Agency

From the perspectives of both individual taxpaying donors as well as end-user beneficiaries, channeling funds through official aid agencies has the drawback that it is the agency, rather than the donor or recipient, that decides what projects to fund. For some, this may not be a cost but a benefit. If an official agency learns about what works in development, has an active evaluation mechanism, strong project review and implementation structures, and appropriate financial controls, it may provide valuable services to both the individual donor and recipient. On the other hand, if the official agency chooses projects on a different basis from what individual donors or recipients would choose or imposes conditions on its giving, there may be agency costs. In the past, one large source of agency costs came from tied aid, a practice where procurement was linked to the country of origin of the funds. It is unlikely that altruistic individual donors would care about whether a particular good or service was procured from a specific country, whereas it is more obvious why a national government may care about such linkages. Estimates of the cost of tied aid vary, but they averaged between 15 and 30 percent. For some types of aid, like technical cooperation, the costs of tying may be even higher.

A further source of agency costs comes from differences in approach about what makes for an effective aid intervention. Individual donors and recipients may have views about project size, sector, and other characteristics that differ from official agency views. The greater the difference, the greater the agency costs of transferring aid through official channels. To the extent that private aid establishes—and to a great extent relies upon—the personal connection of individual donors and recipients, there is reason to believe that new forms of private aid facilitate the placement of individual agency of both the donor and recipient as a main driver of efforts to alleviate global poverty.

One approximation of the relative benefit of personal agency over official agency, then, is to examine whether the preferences of individual donors and recipients match the allocative decisions of official aid agencies. There is a considerable body of analysis of the general effects of public opinion on foreign policy. Although early research suggests that the effects of public opinion on foreign policy are weak or indeterminate, recent studies indicate that public opinion often has a measurable impact on, for instance, international security (Hartley and Russett 1992; Hill 1998; Sobel 2001; Wlezien 1995), trade (Kono 2008; Mansfield and Mutz 2009), and immigration policies (Facchini and Mayda 2008).

Several authors, similarly, find that foreign aid increases with public support for international assistance in rich countries (Lumsdaine 1993; Tingley 2007; Chong and Gradstein 2008). But although there is evidence that public opinion affects aid levels, we know little of how citizen preferences shape aid allocation. Of course, where individual preferences must be articulated through interest groups, political parties, or representative institutions, ideology and group affiliation will filter those preferences for aid allocation. Thus Tingley (2009), for example, finds that although one would expect conservative individuals in rich countries less inclined than their liberal counterparts to support foreign aid, right-wing and left-wing governments show no difference in aid to middle-income countries. Only with low-income recipient countries is there an ideological bias, with right-wing governments giving less aid to these poorer nations. Similar effects have been seen with respect to legislative voting on aid allocation (Fleck and Kilby, 2001; Milner and Tingley, 2010).

In the framing of this book, of course, the perspectives of recipients are as important—indeed, more important—than those of donors. What do the citizens in recipient countries think of official aid? Few, if any, systematic studies of citizens' views of aid in recipient countries have been conducted. Official donors occasionally run market-research-style surveys, but results are rarely released to the public. One of the few field experiments on a nationally representative sample (in Uganda), for example, finds that citizens do like aid, want more of it, but want greater say in its use. In fact, 80 percent of respondents reported that they themselves have not directly benefited from aid, and nearly two-thirds of participants believed that more than half of aid dollars were not spent as intended (Milner, Nielson, and Findley, 2013).

Public opinion regarding aid allocation may also shape decisions of foundations, NGOs, and other private aid organizations. But private humanitarian and development aid has been little studied by social scientists, and the limited research that exists has focused exclusively on larger organizations. Financial records of the most prominent US-based international development NGOs, for example, show that these NGOs allocate funds raised from private sources based on strong humanitarian motives principally to projects that provide or improve education, health care, safe drinking water, sanitation, sewage, and emergency relief in poor countries (Büthe, Major, and de Mello e Souza 2012). Information on the allocative preferences of individuals however, is nonexistent. Examining contributions by large numbers of individuals to international charitable causes can provide a more direct understanding of citizen preferences regarding aid allocation.

Taking the example of charitable crowdfunders, we can assume that crowdfunders who participate in global philanthropy are likely to be representative of larger populations of individuals who, in the United States at least, now account for 75 percent of all private donations to international charitable causes (Giving USA 2012).

Person-to-Person Aid: The Case of Kiva

Kiva is a nonprofit organization that operates an internet-based, peer-to-peer, crowdfunding platform connecting microlenders to microentrepreneurs in developing countries. Founded in San Francisco in 2005, Kiva operates through its internet portals, through which anyone with a credit card or PayPal account can lend to microentrepreneurs who post requests online. Prospective borrowers must post their projects through one of several affiliated microfinance institutions (MFIs). Prospective microlenders, once they have registered, can select projects based on region, country, and project objective.

Once the preferred traits have been selected, a microlender is shown a list of project requests matching the preferred project criteria. Alternatively, microlenders can select most recent projects that have been newly listed, or they may have the Kiva website randomly select a project. It is this flexibility in matching donor preferences to recipient requests that, through platforms such as Kiva's, support personal agency as well as the empowerment and hence dignity of beneficiaries, along with donors.

Selecting any particular project reveals more information: the amount of the loan (up to a maximum of $5,000), the loan duration in months (up to a maximum of two years), the name and risk-rating of the MFI, the number of borrowers (if the borrower is a group), the gender of the borrowers, and a short narrative written by the microentrepreneur as to the specific purposes for which the funds will be used. Finally, the project information also includes an indication of how much of the project amount requested has been funded thus far.

Once a project is selected, microlenders can contribute funds in any amount (above a required minimum of $25) up to the full amount requested. Using a PayPal account or a direct payment from a credit card, microlenders then transfer funds in the pledged amount. Projects accumulate funds from lenders in this manner until they are fully funded. When microloans reach maturity, their principal is to be repaid to the original lender's account; lenders receive no interest, and thus the cost of capital is borne by the lender. Zero-interest loans, moreover, allow Kiva to operate as a nonprofit 501(c)3 organization under US law instead of as a regulated commercial bank.

Once microlenders choose to lend (i.e., once they become crowdfunders), they are notified periodically of the progress of the microentrepreneurs' effort. Kiva's field partners may post business journals identifying how the loan is being used or what effect it has had on the business owner. This reporting is not required, thus the flow of information from recipients can be erratic and the information provided is very rarely financially detailed (Bonbright, Kiryttopoulou, and Iversen 2008). Nevertheless, Kiva platforms provide enough information to make a personal connection between the donor and the recipient. The information enhances *social recognition* of the recipient as the other pillar of dignity in addition to *agency*, as posited by Lagon and Arend in this book. Yet a key problem for both organizations is to decide on exactly what (and how much) information to provide to permit informed choices without overwhelming an individual donor.

Beneficiaries' agency, of necessity, is not without limits. Kiva restricts both loan size and time on the website. Until the end of 2007, individual loan requests by potential beneficiaries could not exceed $1,200; that limit has since been raised to $2,000. The maximum request for group loans remains

$5,000. All requests by microentrepreneurs must be made through partner MFIs, and all requests made to Kiva enter a queue. After a preliminary screening, they are posted on the website for a maximum of thirty days, after which they are pulled from the site if they have not been funded. Kiva has occasionally had to cap individual lenders' contributions because of the lack of fundable projects.

What Motivates Private Philanthropists?

Indirect evidence of the funding preferences of private philanthropists may be inferred from data on crowdfunded microloans through Kiva. The behavior of private aid givers has been little examined to date, despite the increase in private development aid. There are three possibilities: crowdfunders act as rational charitable contributors, making funding decisions based on project-specific risks and incentives; crowdfunders behave like official foreign-aid agencies, funding projects based on a combination of country need and institutional quality; or crowdfunders are motivated by the social networks connecting them to countries in which projects take place. Because Kiva crowdfunders expect to have their principal repaid, Kiva's project data affords us an opportunity to test the risk-aversion of crowdfunders. Because Kiva's projects span some eighty developing countries, we can also examine whether aid flowing through Kiva is as selective as official development assistance.

Analysis of funding rates for Kiva projects—on the assumption that faster-funded projects are more aligned with donors' individual preferences about project characteristics—finds weak support for the view that crowdfunders are risk-averse with respect to microcredit in developing countries. Kiva's crowdfunders preferred loaning to women for shorter duration and smaller amounts. However, they reject the group-liability approach of traditional microfinance and only weakly prefer lending through lower-risk partner microfinance institutions. We find almost no consistent support for the hypothesis that crowdfunders act selectively towards projects based on the poverty or institutional quality of the country.

By contrast, there is strong support for the argument that crowdfunding is essentially an expressive act that enables individuals to connect with microentrepreneurs much in the same way that individuals can sponsor children in developing countries through a number of NGOs. Again, the social recognition of the recipient is arguably part of the benefit. In this regard, we find the nature of social relations that developing countries are able to rely upon in richer countries, in particular, through their communities of migrants has a strong effect on the funding rates of Kiva projects. Kiva crowdfunders prefer to lend to countries that claim larger numbers of more recent, wealthier immigrants and to which a large number of refugees also come. One possible reason for this is that immigrants themselves participate as crowd-funders. (Kiva lending, however, is unaffected by remittances, which would be unlikely were immigrants themselves largely responsible for Kiva funding to their home countries.) Another possibility is that immigrant communities, through their social ties with native-born populations, provide information about their home countries to prospective crowdfunders.

In sum, Kiva and its feedback mechanisms and other information are principally geared towards establishing a connection between people rather than between sovereign entities or between multilateral organizations and a sovereign entity. Kiva in many ways is highly representative of the changes in international private philanthropy that have taken place in the past decade, for example, an increasing amount of aid, global accessibility, and real-time information about recipients and their use of funds.

These findings have implications for official aid policy. In contrast to years past, the collective-action costs of private aid appear to be minimal, especially with the proliferation of internet-based crowdfunding platforms. Moreover, internet technology appears to have superseded the earlier advantage that official agencies once held in terms of minimizing the transaction costs of disbursing aid. Finally, private aid now has significant advantages over official aid in promoting personal agency now that private aid givers can give money to recipients in developing countries in a much more direct way. Indeed, the rapid growth of crowdfunded, private aid may be attributed to the attractiveness of this short route to giving.

Not all recipient countries, however, are organized to take advantage of this spread of private aid. Another obvious conclusion is that aid recipient countries would do well to organize themselves to take advantage of new forms of private aid. In some countries like India, MFIs must first obtain approval from the Reserve Bank of India before they can borrow abroad—an obvious barrier to accessing private loans from Kiva. These findings also suggest that the design of projects can be fine-tuned to make them more attractive to donors. As an example, it is probably more effective to invest in providing assistance to entrepreneurs to allow them to develop project ideas than to invest in building the capacity of microfinance intermediaries. Private lenders seem not to care too much about the rating of these agencies.

The phenomenal growth of internet-based giving is testimony to the potential for private aid to reach a scale which can be significant in global terms, an institutional arrangement rivaling in scale that of national institutions' and multilateral development banks' funding. What has not been shown is that organizing aid in this fashion is more effective for development, which many would argue could more robustly advance the human dignity of aid recipients in the long term. A comparison of development effectiveness between public and private aid platforms is an important direction for future research. Time and future research will reveal if this represents a new dominant institutional arrangement for aid provision and whether it is effective. Yet to the degree it appears to affect agency of donors and recipients—connected more directly to one another—this institutional trend is dignity-building and ought to be facilitated.

Conclusion

In this chapter we have argued that, in the new aid landscape, newer forms of private aid enhance the personal agency of both donors and recipients in aid transactions. Donors, who are better able to select countries, sectors, projects, and in many cases individuals to whom funds (and loans) can be given, are afforded greater control over allocative decisions. Beneficiaries who can provide input and information directly to donors are better able to influence funding decisions and have greater flexibility in the timing and disbursement of funds, that is, accorded agency. Through these institutions, they are accorded social recognition too, helping them realize dignity. For both groups, these person-to-person relationships constitute a shorter route than official aid normally takes. The result can economize on coordination, transaction, and agency costs of official aid.

Private aid can make a difference, but it is by no means a panacea for all that ails the world's poor. For all the amounts that have been granted, there has been little evaluation of the cost-effectiveness of private aid, and there are few examples of privately-funded programs being expanded in ways needed to make a dignity-building dent in global poverty. The history of global charity has also had its share of scandals involving misappropriations of funds and theft. And the universe of foundations, charities, educational organizations, and private and voluntary organizations may be too crowded and too fragmented to make a real difference on a large scale.

There are four possible implications of the spread of private aid for the alleviation of global poverty. First, private aid functions best as a complement to, rather than a substitute for, official aid. Indeed, there are many things that private aid cannot support in recipient countries; development strategies, debt reduction, and so on are generally beyond the scope of private aid modalities. Private aid also raises separate (but related) issues of accountability compared to official aid.

Second, private aid is supported by new types of global institutions that rely principally on multilayer connectedness between individuals—linked through social networks that, supported by internet technology and social media, now span the globe—rather than on bilateral or multilateral intergovernmental relations. Although many of the longer-term implications of the expansion in influence of these global private institutions are uncertain, the private sector has grown from a small player in development assistance to a major, dynamic force. Yet the world has little noticed. Annually, approximately 800 press credentials were issued for the World Bank-IMF annual or spring meetings. Meanwhile, at the Global Philanthropy Forum (GPF), few if any members of the press were on hand. This lopsidedness is unfortunate. The fact is that the attendees who meet at the GPF will soon give more aid to the world's poor than the Bretton-Woods institutions.

Third, although at present private aid is not connected to policy reforms in the way official aid is, it is plausible that the proliferation of private aid will encourage governments in recipient countries to reform in order to permit individual or group beneficiaries to take advantage of these new forms of aid. Pressures to permit greater cross-border capital flows, for example, can be driven by citizens who do not wish to be deprived of the benefits of peer-to-peer financial flows—whether they are remittances, microloans, or private grants.

Fourth, it is also possible that private aid will make foreign aid more competitive. For decades, poor developing nations have faced a take-it-or-leave-it attitude from international financial institutions and official donors and were forced to deal exclusively with a particular official bureaucracy on development projects. Private aid now can offer alternative channels for development assistance. But to make this competition work, recipient countries must be free to choose whether aid is channeled through an official government project or through a more efficient NGO provider. Recipients of aid must also be able to rely on benchmarks that compare the effectiveness of private and official aid programs.

But a competitive aid system also requires a better understanding of what works and what doesn't. Neither the demand side—the priority needs of the underserved—nor the supply side—who is doing what and for which communities—has been mapped out at the country level. Without that, it is inevitable that both public and private aid providers will fail to provide systemic change and will fail to help poor nations develop their own capabilities, both of which are needed for sustained poverty reduction and greater realization of dignity in practice. These are the efforts to which the global development community should dedicate itself—not to the maintenance of the current inflexible foreign aid system but to its transformation into a system of global institutions that are both flexible and dignity enhancing for both donors and recipients.

Notes

The authors thank Mark P. Lagon and Michael Morfit for valuable comments on earlier drafts.

1. The remaining 41 percent of funds have still not been classified by use.
2. Formerly known as Christian Children's Fund.
3. See the treatment of Omidyar-funded Humanity United underwriting NGO partnerships to combat human trafficking in chapter 11 in this book by Mark P. Lagon.
4. On these problems, see Wenar (2006).

References

Alm, James. 1985. "The Welfare Cost of the Underground Economy." *Economic Inquiry* 23 (2): 243–63.

Andreoni, James, and A. Abigail Payne. 2008. "Crowding out Both Sides of the Philanthropy Market." Mimeo. Accessed September 22, 2013. http://econ.ucsd.edu/~jan dreon/WorkingPapers/andreoni_payne2.pdf.

Bekkers, Rene, and Pamala Wiepking. 2007. "Generosity and Philanthropy: A Literature Review." Mimeo. Accessed September 22, 2013. http://papers.ssrn.com/sol3/pa pers.cfm?abstract_id=1015507.

Bonbright, David, Natalia Kiryttopoulou, and Lindsay Iversen. 2008. *Online Philanthropy Markets: From 'Feel-Good' Giving to Effective Social Investing?* London: Keystone.

Büthe, Tim, Solomon Major, and Andre de Mello e Souza. 2012. "The Politics of Private Foreign Aid: Humanitarian Principles, Economic Development Objectives, and Organizational Interests in the Allocation of Private Aid by NGOs." *International Organization* 66 (44): 571–607.

Chong, Alberto, and Mark Gradstein. 2008. "What Determines Foreign Aid? The Donors' Perspective." Journal of Development Economics 87 (1): 1–13.

Dreher, Axel, Peter Nunnenkamp, Hannes Oehler, and Johannes Weisser. 2009. "Acting Autonomously or Mimicking the State and Peers: A Panel Tobit Analysis of Financial Dependence and Aid Allocation by Swiss NGOs." Working Paper No. 2617. Munich: CESifo.

Easterly, William. 2005. "How to Assess the Needs for Aid?" Paper for the 3rd AFD/ EUDN Conference. Paris, December 14.

Facchini, Giovanni, and Anna M. Mayda. 2008. "From Individual Attitudes towards Migrants to Migration Policy Outcomes: Theory and Evidence." *Economic Policy* 23 (56): 651–713.

Fleck, Robert, and Christopher Kilby. 2001. "Foreign Aid and Domestic Politics." *Southern Economic Association* 67 (3): 598–617.

Garrett, Thomas, and Russell Rhine. 2007. "Does Government Spending Really Crowd Out Charitable Contributions? New Time Series Evidence." Working Paper No. 2007–012. Federal Reserve Bank of St. Louis.

Giving USA. 2012. *Annual Report on Philanthropy.* Chicago: Giving USA Foundation.

Government Accountability Office (GOA). 2007. "Analysis of Millennium Challenge Corporation Compact Disbursements through March 2007." Letter to congressional committees, May 14.

Hartley, Thomas, and Bruce Russett. 1992. "Public Opinion and the Common Defense: Who Governs Military Spending in the United States?" *American Political Science Review* 86 (4).

Hill, Kim Quaile. 1998. "The Policy Agenda of the President and the Mass Public: A Research Validation and Extension." *American Journal of Political Science* 42: 1328–34.

Hudson Institute. 2013. *The Index of Global Philanthropy and Remittances.* Washington, DC: Center for Global Prosperity.

Keohane, Robert, and Joseph Nye, Jr. 2000. "Introduction." In *Governance in a Globalizing World,* edited by Joseph Nye, Jr. and John Donahue. Washington, DC: Brookings Press.

Koch, Dirk-Jan, Axel Dreher, Peter Nunnenkamp, and Rainer Thiele. 2008. "Keeping a Low Profile: What Defines the Allocation of Aid by NGOs." Working Paper No. 191. Zurich: KOF Swiss Economic Institute.

Kono, Daniel. 2008. "Does Public Opinion Affect Trade Policy?" *Business and Politics* 10 (2): 1224–26.

Lawrence, Steven, Aglernon Austin, and Reina Mukai. 2007. *Foundation Growth and Giving Estimates.* New York: The Foundation Center.

Lindelow, Magnus, Inna Kushnarova, and Kai Kaiser. 2006. "Measuring Corruption in the Health Sector." In *Global Corruption Report 2006.* Cambridge: Transparency International/Cambridge UP.

Lumsdaine, David H. 1993. *Moral Vision in International Politics: The Foreign Aid Regime, 1949–1989.* Princeton, NJ: Princeton University Press.

Mansfield, Edward, and Diana Mutz. 2009. "Support for Free Trade: Self-Interest, Sociotropic Politics, and Out-Group Anxiety." *International Organization* 63 (3): 425–57.

Milner, Helen, Daniel Nielson, and Michael Findley. 2013. "Which Devil in Development? A Randomized Study of Citizen Actions Supporting Foreign Aid in Uganda." Mimeo. Accessed October 4, 2013. http://papers.ssrn.com/sol3/papers.cfm?abstract_id=2134409.

Milner, Helen, and Dustin Tingley. 2010. "The Political Economy of US Foreign Aid: American Legislators and the Domestic Politics of Aid." *Economics and Politics* 20 (2): 200–32.

Organization for Economic Cooperation and Development (OECD). 2011. "Aid Effectiveness 2005–10: Progress in Implementing the Paris Declaration." Paris: OECD.

Ramsay, Clay, Steven Weber, Steven Kull, and Evan Lewis. 2009. "American Public Opinion and Global Health." College Park, MD: Program on International Policy Attitudes.

Renz, Loren, and Jose Atienza. 2006. "International Grantmaking Update." New York: Foundation Center.

Roodman, David. 2006. "Tax Policies to Promote Private Charitable Giving in DAC Countries." Working Paper No. 82. Washington: Center for Global Development.

Sobel, Richard. 2001. *The Impact of Public Opinion on US Foreign Policy since Vietnam: Constraining the Colossus.* Ithaca, NY: Oxford University Press.

Tingley, Dustin. 2007. Preferences over Foreign Aid Funding: Survey Evidence from Norway. Working paper. Princeton University.

———. 2009. "Donors and Domestic Politics: Political and Economic Influences on Foreign Aid." *The Quarterly Review of Economics and Finance* 50 (1): 40–49.

Wenar, Leif. 2006. "Accountability in International Development Aid." *Ethics and International Affairs* 20 (1): 1–23.

Wlezien, Christopher. 1995. "The Public as Thermostat: Dynamics of Preferences for Spending." *American Journal of Political Science* 39 (4): 981–1000.

World Bank. 2011. *Annual Report 2011.* Washington, DC: The World Bank Group.

CHAPTER 10

Statelessness, Sovereignty, and International Law

Promoting the "Right to Have Rights"

BENJAMIN BOUDREAUX

Hannah Arendt, in *The Origins of Totalitarianism* (1973), argues that states often deny persons rights in two general ways: not only by various forms of oppression and discrimination of the kind frequently catalogued by human-rights organizations but also by denying them the very precondition of having rights at all. She argues that the latter situation, faced by persons who are stateless, is one of complete vulnerability. The stateless lack membership in a political community, she claims, and live on their own in a prepolitical state of nature. In her words, the stateless are denied "the right to have rights." They find themselves in the unique and unfortunate situation in which "their plight is not that they are not equal before the law, but that no law exists for them; not that they are oppressed but that nobody wants even to oppress them" (Arendt 1973, 295).

Arendt's point was not simply to draw attention to a vulnerable group but to show the hollowness of the modern human-rights regime. According to Arendt, human rights are practically meaningless because states that profess allegiance to them frequently violate them and more fundamentally, because rights *require* states to begin with. Although supposedly grounded in universal human quali-ties such as a human's inherent dignity, rights are only grounded "from within the nation" (Arendt 1973, 299). The state is the protector, enforcer, and recog-nizer of human rights, and without a state, one is denied these protections. For Arendt, this was not only a matter of access to rights or enjoying the exercise of rights but a matter of having rights at all. As Arendt put the point, "the stateless people were as convinced . . . that loss of national rights was identical with loss of human rights, that the former inevitably entailed the latter." She continued, "the restoration of human rights . . . has been achieved so far only through the restoration or the establishment of national rights" (Arendt 1973, 299). Paul Weis, a former UN High Commissioner for Refugees (UNHCR), legal scholar, and a contemporary of Arendt, echoed her words. In his view, a court's decision was that "a State . . . does not commit an international delinquency in inflicting an injury upon an individual lacking nationality, and consequently no state is empowered to intervene or complain on his behalf either before or after the injury" (Weis 1956, 162). In other words, according to Weis and Arendt, international law in the mid-twentieth century permitted states to treat stateless persons as cruelly as they liked.

Despite Arendt's assertion that legal rights are dependent on states, the world today might appear quite different. She was writing at a time when a wide array of international actors and efforts were taken to denationalize rights by establishing a universal foundation decoupled from the state. Over the sixty-plus years since the Universal Declaration of Human Rights (UDHR), human rights have become substantially more embedded throughout international law and practice. Indeed, states have claimed and even actualized the right to intervene in the domestic affairs of other states to protect foreign citizens. Such intervention can be justified only by appeal to rights that transcend origin in the national sovereignty of the state that violates them. And states have legally bound themselves through accession to international conventions that generate obligations. Nonstate actors also play an increasingly important role, advocating for those denied rights and sometimes even providing some of the protections typically associated with a state.

Notwithstanding these developments, the problem of statelessness highlighted by Arendt over fifty years ago remains dire: Stateless persons continue to live an extremely vulnerable life and face an array of daily indignities, and their numbers are vast, depending on one's definition of who counts as stateless, a number that ranges between ten to hundreds of millions of persons.

This chapter analyzes the plight of the contemporary stateless. In particular, it assesses the various efforts made to fill the still-present gap that Arendt identified within the human-rights regime, by examining the conceptual complications of statelessness, the halting development of international legal instruments, and the role of other institutions in protecting this vulnerable population. Addressing the problem of statelessness, I argue, requires joint action by states and nonstate actors in the short term and in the long run nothing less than a transformation of some of the most basic and venerable international norms. This often overlooked problem shows both how the sovereign state system fails to properly take responsibility for persons and how states are still necessary in a messy neomedieval world to provide the conditions in which persons can live with dignity; it thus suggests an imperative for further transforming the state-based system.

This chapter begins, first, by pointing to a tension in international law that informs and yet complicates the problem of statelessness. Second, it grapples with an ongoing debate about what exactly statelessness consists of, noting some of the enduring conceptual challenges. Third, it discusses ongoing efforts to address the problem but points to continuing gaps in protection. Finally, it offers recommendations to further protect and reduce the stateless.

A Tension in International Law

A point of conflict embedded within international law illuminates the problem of the stateless and the challenge of an effective international response. Consider the tension between a state's interest in protecting its sovereignty and a basic humanitarian concern for all persons. States maintain that the right to determine who is a citizen is a fundamental component of their sovereignty. Stemming from the very beginnings of the state system following the Treaty of Westphalia, the right is justified in part by the state's role in protecting and stabilizing a particular ethnonational community. The principle asserting that states determine their own citizens has been enshrined and advanced by international law, from at least the 1930 Hague Convention on Nationality onward and has been further developed and applied in judicial cases, such as the *Nottebohm* case adjudicated in 1955 by the International Court of Justice, which claims that "nationality is within the domestic jurisdiction of the State."[1] Even given today's emergence of global institutions and other nonstate actors, no nonstate institutions have the authority to make determinations of citizenship other than states themselves.[2]

Whereas states have maintained the right to determine who is a national, they have also recognized the basic right of all persons to a nationality. This right appears most prominently as Article 15 of the UDHR, which states that "everyone has a right to a nationality and no one shall be arbitrarily deprived of his nationality." Although the UDHR is not binding international law, the same right appears in treaties with legal force, including the International Covenant on Civil and Political Rights and the Convention on the Rights of the Child.[3] All told, nearly every state has endorsed at least one of these tools, thereby recognizing the right.

At least three reasons justify the right of every person to a nationality. First, a basic humanitarian principle stresses that citizenship is a necessary means for persons to live with dignity. In the introduction, Mark P. Lagon and Anthony Clark Arend define two pillars of dignity—the agency of a person to realize his or her potential and public recognition of the person's inherent value and equal access to opportunity—that seem to require that a state protect and acknowledge an individual. The absence of a nationality, as Arendt suggests, is akin to living in a Hobbesian state of nature, where life is "solitary, poor, nasty, brutish, and short" (Hobbes 1994, chapter 13). This justification of the right is a cross-cultural, universal factor because it is grounded in conditions that all of humanity shares.

A second justification is based within states' pragmatic calculations and, in particular, the potential instability that stems from the existence of unacknowledged and unaccounted-for persons. These persons seem to threaten the very foundations of the state system by putting at risk the notion that states have ultimate juridical authority over the entire human population. As US officials state, "the United States government cares about statelessness as an issue that carries repercussions for regional stability and economic development" (Green and Pierce 2009).

Third, and perhaps somewhat cynically, certain political considerations seem to support inclusion of the right to a nationality in the UDHR and in legally binding conventions as a way for some states to occupy the moral high ground against irresponsible states that exclude or discriminate against certain groups. Consider the development of the refugee regime, developed during the Cold War, in which arguably democratic states sought to gain an upper hand against their ideological opponents (Loescher 1996).

Despite the latter two state-based justifications and contra Arendt, the right to a nationality is prima facie grounded in the inherent worth of all persons.[4] All humans are presumably vested with this right, even if they have no state to protect them; the right supposedly precedes the state, rather than vice versa.[5]

Whatever the merits of these proposed justifications, the tension between the legal rights of states and of persons is straightforward: A person's right to a nationality amounts to nothing if no state exercises its right to bestow nationality upon him or her. If states have the sovereign right to determine who is or is not a national, then no state is required to actualize an individual's right to a nationality, and thus persons might be unable to exercise their right. In the terminology of rights-theory, the right to a nationality is a positive or claim right that requires some other party to take deliberate action to protect it. But the right to a nationality is a claim right that does not identify a party responsible to act. In fact, there is a conflicting right held by the only parties that could actualize the right that explicitly gives them the right *not* to provide protection.[6]

Consider how this tension plays out in the case of stateless persons. A state has an interest in responding to the problem of statelessness not only out of a humanitarian concern for stateless persons but also because the stateless are a potentially destabilizing force. Those without a state live an exceptionally insecure life but also potentially increase the insecurity of the state in which they reside. Although states have an interest in diminishing and addressing the problem of statelessness, they might not perceive that they have an interest in granting a particular stateless group citizenship. Indeed, it appears that many states would rather persuade other states to take responsibility rather than face the costs and potential political backlash of nationalizing new groups of persons. Given that statelessness is a practical problem for states, they have a clear incentive to minimize the existence of the problem even in the absence of a legal requirement to respond. The UNHCR legal scholar Weis made this point sharply: "To the extent that there are no rules of international law imposing a duty on States to confer their nationality, nor, in general, rules denying or restricting the right of States to withdraw their nationality, one may say that statelessness is not inconsistent with international law" (Weis 1956, 166).

The tension between the rights of states to determine their citizens and the right of persons to a nationality underscores Arendt's point about the surpassing importance of the state in securing a person's dignity. The right to a nationality is grounded in the notion that persons need a state to live well, whereas the right of states to determine who is a national is similarly grounded in the importance of the state for human well being. Of course, it is not surprising that when looking at a state-based legal regime, states are of central importance. However, this feature of international law makes the problem of the stateless seemingly intractable.

Of course, the right to a nationality is not entirely feckless; to be sure, it has motivated international law and domestic analogs that oblige states to provide nationality under certain circumstances. For instance, the Convention on the Nationality of Married Women requires that states not deprive women of their nationality in the event of divorce or if the husband changes his nationality (Article 1). Likewise, the Convention on the Rights of the Child states that children "shall be registered immediately after birth and shall have the right from birth to a name, the right to acquire a nationality" (Article 7).

Above all, the tension in international law illustrates that responding to the problem of the stateless requires a fundamental transformation of traditional elements of the state-based system. In particular, either the sovereign right of states to determine who is a national must be limited, thereby requiring them to give nationality to stateless persons, or the world must change in such a way that nationality is no longer a necessary means for the exercise of basic human rights and the possibility of a life of dignity.

Before discussing these options more fully, we should clarify the precise components of statelessness.

What Is Statelessness?

My brief discussion of Arendt and international law has already indicated to what extent statelessness is a significant affront to one's dignity and quality of life. It is worth exploring, however, the array of vulnerabilities the stateless face in order to emphasize the stakes in failing to protect them. First, there is the fundamental connection highlighted above between the state and the protection of a person's rights. The stateless generally lack all political rights and thus submit to a government for which they have had no voice or influence. In addition, they often lack the economic rights associated with property and employment as well as the mobility rights to travel or to reenter their country of habitual residence once they leave. They are frequently the victims of discrimination in such crucial aspects of life as housing, education, police protection, or even when opening a bank account. Further, there is an important connection between a state and a person's identity: Persons often identify with their state as a valuable cultural community and, moreover, by registering one's birth and issuing an identity card, the state is most often literally the source of one's official identity. According to classical theorists like Plato and Aristotle, social contract theorists of modernity, such as Hobbes and Locke, and contemporary political thinkers like Sen, the state is a necessary precursor to enjoying important capabilities and living well (Sen 1999).

Depending on one's definition, the numbers of stateless range greatly, and different definitions imply different gaps in protection. The crucial consideration when defining the stateless is whether one considers only the de jure or legally stateless or whether one also includes the de facto stateless, those who possess some legal nationality, but do not have an effective nationality.

De Jure Statelessness

The most widespread and established definition in international law stems from the 1954 Convention Relating to the Status of Stateless Persons, the first major international treaty that focused exclusively on the stateless. Article 1 offers this definition: "'[S]tateless person' means a person who is not considered as a national by any State under the operation of its law." This definition is a de jure definition as it is based exclusively on the legal status of a person as determined by sovereign states. The 1954 Convention, framed on the heels of the 1951 Convention Relating to the Status of Refugees, was motivated by the stateless population that emerged after World War II. Those who designed the Convention believed that this definition would fully close all gaps in protection without overlapping this category of persons with refugees protected by the 1951 Refugee Convention. Besides minimizing overlap, this de jure definition enjoys the advantage of simplicity: A person's status comes down to how states identify the person, a presumably ascertainable legal fact. And it focuses the problem of statelessness on a relatively small and manageable group of persons who lack a basic legal right resolvable through legal means. Given these advantages and its place in the international stateless regime, this definition guides most international action.

According to the de jure definition, the UNHCR counts approximately twelve million persons as stateless (UNHCR 2010a).[7] These persons become stateless in a variety of complex ways, including through explicit state discrimination and through accident. The sovereign state system is one in which states determine nationality according to their own standards: some by jus soli or citizenship by birth in the territory, whereas others only by jus sanguinis or blood ancestry. But cracks between these laws create situations in which one has no nationality whatsoever: One might be born in a state that does not have jus soli citizenship or one might lack the ability to claim citizenship through descent.[8]

Other laws that cause statelessness include gender-discriminatory laws that pass citizenship exclusively through patrilineal descent, like those in Jordan, the Gulf Arab States, and over twenty states across Africa. If one is born in these states to a female citizen but a male noncitizen, then one lacks a de jure nationality. Indonesia's citizenship laws are also gender-discriminatory, holding that if one is born out of wedlock to a citizen mother but a noncitizen father, one is denied Indonesian citizenship.

Statelessness also results from laws that specifically exclude groups on ethnonational grounds. The Bihari Urdu speakers in Bangladesh are denied Bangladeshi citizenship because of doubts about their national loyalties. Similarly, almost a million mostly Muslim Rohyngya are denied nationality by the ruling junta in predominantly Buddhist Myanmar. Further, more than 3 million persons in Cote d'Ivoire, ethnic Nepalese in Bhutan, Nubians in Kenya, and people of Slavic origin in Latvia are all denied citizenship because of ethnic exclusion (Blitz 2009). Each group is a victim of discriminatory laws that seem to violate the UDHR's guarantee that "no one shall be arbitrarily deprived of his nationality."

Others become de jure stateless simply through the difficulties of registering births. The UN estimates that 36 percent of total annual births go unregistered for practical or cultural reasons, mostly in South Asia and sub–Saharan Africa, and many of those persons legally lack nationality of any state. State succession can also lead to statelessness. During the break-up of the Ottoman Empire and the USSR, for instance, millions were left without a state.

The overall number of de jure stateless is particularly difficult to determine. The UNHCR's twelve million estimate relies heavily on the numbers provided by state governments. The Department of Homeland Security, for instance, has estimated that the de jure stateless in the United States is a mere 4,000 persons. But the stateless are a particularly difficult group for states to identify given the fact that, by definition, they live without state recognition. Determining the number of stateless is made even more difficult by the fact that most states do not have specific procedures by which to identify or process the stateless. Stateless determinations are typically done through the refugee process, and persons are thus identified as stateless on an ad hoc basis when and if they apply for asylum (Batchelor 1998). What's worse, some states have an incentive to undercount the number of domestic stateless, minimizing the problem to deflect negative international attention. There is therefore good reason to believe that the UNHCR estimate is not an accurate count; indeed, the UNHCR itself calls the number a "guesstimate."[9]

Despite possessing the advantage of simplicity, the de jure definition has been attacked for posing an excessively high hurdle. To be considered de jure stateless, a person must prove a negative—that none of the over 190 states in the international system claim him or her as a citizen. This burden of proof falls on the applicant, but many candidates are unable to prove they have no legal state because the transactional costs can often be prohibitively high, other states might not cooperate with the investigation, or the state in which they have had strong links no longer exists (e.g., Yugoslavia). Consider also the difficult situation of thousands of persons of Haitian descent living in the Dominican Republic. The Dominican Republic does not grant them citizenship, claiming that they have Haitian citizenship even though the Haitian government also does not grant them nationality. Although they have no citizenship, these persons are not considered stateless by the Dominican Republic because it treats them as being Haitian citizens.

An additional drawback of the de jure definition is that it excludes many persons who, although they might be claimed as a citizen by some states, in practice reside and have strong attachments to a state that does not recognize them. Consider the case of persons who have a nationality but because of severe conflict are forced to flee to other states where they develop social attachments. These persons are not identified as stateless by the customary de jure definition nor are they refugees according to the 1951 Refugee Convention. Nonetheless, such persons might still face the same affronts to their dignity as the de jure stateless, vulnerable to exploitation and without any of the protections accorded by either their state of residence or state of nationality. This consideration suggests that although international legal instruments have largely focused on the de jure stateless, the specific affronts to dignity seem to apply equally to both the de jure and other persons who, although they may have some nationality, lack an *effective* nationality. From the person's perspective, the vulnerabilities of de jure and de facto statelessness are equivalent. The customary de jure definition enshrined in international law is blind to this reality as the definition was developed from the perspective of the states that contain the stateless, rather than the perspective of the stateless themselves. The assumption of the de jure definition seems to be that a de facto stateless person can be repatriated or otherwise could seek the protection of their state of nationality, whereas a de jure stateless person cannot and thus the latter should be granted special protection. This, however, simply raises a further question. How should states identify the persons mentioned above who claim some nationality but cannot be repatriated? Their right to a nationality is ineffective, as the mere fact of nationality de jure includes with it no protections.[10] Moreover, because they already have a nationality, the solution to their plight is not simply to give them a legal nationality; hence, there is no obvious legal remedy.

The UNHCR, the organization vested with the most expansive international mandate to grapple with the problem of statelessness, seems to agree with these considerations. In the Information and Accession Package to the Stateless Conventions, they state:

> It is now apparent that there are those who do not qualify as refugees but whose nationality status is unclear. The situation of such a person in terms of a lack of national protection may be identical to that of a de jure stateless person. (UNHCR 1999)
>
> On this basis, the UNCHR accepts a responsibility to accommodate the de facto stateless. Likewise, the Final Act of the other major international convention dealing with statelessness, the 1961 Convention, "recommends that persons who are stateless de facto should as far as possible be treated as stateless de jure to enable them to acquire an effective nationality." (UNHCR 1999; UNHCR 2006)

Although the UNHCR seems to accept a mandate to address the problem of the de facto stateless, it itself does not however offer a clear definition of what this concept means and who actually counts, an issue to which I now turn.

De Facto Statelessness

A de facto definition of the stateless includes a broader category of persons who might have some legal nationality but nonetheless lack an *effective* nationality.

There is no consensus on how best to understand this category of persons; indeed, some have even suggested that there is no such thing. Nehemiah Robinson, for instance, argues that "nationality is a legal concept; therefore de facto statelessness is a somewhat illogical term" (Robinson 1955; Hudson 1952). Robinson's point is that the de facto stateless do not face a problem solvable through juridical means as they already have a legal nationality. If they have a nationality, how are they stateless? Others, however, have been struck by the vulnerabilities of and significant gaps in protection for these persons. Even the UNHCR, as noted above, argues that the de facto stateless should be treated as far as possible as stateless. I consider below several alternative definitions, pointing to the potential advantages and disadvantages of each; rather than argue for a particular view, my goal is to demonstrate the need for a consistent and operational definition.

One definition of de facto statelessness takes seriously the perspective of persons living without a state rather than the perspective of the states administering nationality laws. According to this definition, persons are stateless if they are not accorded the protections of citizenship from their state. Weissbrodt and Collins offer one version: "De facto statelessness can occur when governments withhold the usual benefits of citizenship, such as protection, and assistance . . . persons who are de facto stateless might have legal claim to the benefits of nationality but are not, for a variety of reasons, able to enjoy these benefits. They are, effectively, without a nationality" (2006, 251–52).

The UNHCR offers a similar definition in its *Handbook for Parliamentarians*, stating: "[D]e facto stateless persons . . . technically, still hold a nationality but do not receive any of the benefits generally associated with nationality, notably national protection" (UNHCR 2005, 25).[11] For Weissbrodt and Collins and in this UNHCR publication, then, de facto statelessness occurs when persons fail to possess certain legal protections of their state.

This definition has come under significant fire. First, the definition requires a clear explanation of what it means for a person to lack the usual protections of citizenship, and which protections, if denied, cause statelessness. Consider the myriad examples of persons in conflict with their state—Tibetans in China, for instance, the Syrian opposition, or internally displaced persons worldwide. Others are denied legal protections generally thought of as basic human rights, such as women in Taliban-era Afghanistan or present-day Saudi Arabia. These persons are in some sense denied state protections, but is this sufficient to render them stateless? Weissbrodt and Collins claim that "most persons considered de facto stateless are the victims of state repression," which suggests that persons in conflict or otherwise repressed by their state should count as de facto stateless (Weissbrodt and Collins 2006, 263). After all, they lack the benefits usually associated with nationality.

But, to recall Arendt's argument, these persons are oppressed in the sense that their rights are not respected, though this does not entail that they are genuinely stateless. The genuinely stateless, according to Arendt, do not merely face oppression, but they do not possess the very preconditions of receiving protection. Compare UNHCR Senior Legal Adviser Hugh Massey's treatment, who argues that the "right to a nationality is distinct from the rights attached to nationality . . . and the violation of one does not necessarily entail a violation of the other" (Massey 2010, 38). So even if the Assad regime violates rights usually associated with the nationality of the Syrian opposition, this does not entail that they have no nationality—they are, after all, still Syrian. Massey goes even further in rejecting this definition: "[T]o argue that persons who are deprived of their nationality are de facto stateless, and that all de facto stateless persons should be treated as de jure stateless, would be doing a grave disservice to persons who should be treated as the nationals that they are, rather than as stateless persons" (Massey 2010, 39). One is not stateless so long as one has a nationality, even if this nationality does not offer the protections that might ideally be associated with it; the definition severely overstretches the term "stateless."

One problem with Arendt and Massey's distinction is that the right to a nationality means little unless it is attached to rights accorded to being a national. The right to a nationality is a means to live well, not an end on its own. Thus, the cost of keeping their distinction intact is potentially to neglect all those who, even if they have some nominal nationality, do not enjoy even the most basic protections and thereby seem to live a life of de facto statelessness. That said, it is important to keep in mind Arendt's and Massey's distinction between not having a state (and therefore being stateless) and not enjoying protections provided by the state and to not make the problem of statelessness completely unmanageable. The definition of de facto stateless that is under consideration significantly enlarges the numbers: Depending on the withheld rights that are deemed the crucial benefits of nationality, the number of de facto could be hundreds of millions or more, constituting perhaps all persons living in irresponsible states (Goldston 2006). This massive scale alone precludes an effective international response. Moreover, by what methods can the international community respond to persons denied these benefits of nationality? If the UNHCR takes seriously the stated definition of de facto stateless, and they seek to treat the de facto similarly to the de jure, this might involve major intervention within sovereign states, potentially enlarging UNHCR's purview to protect all those oppressed globally.

Consider, then, a second potential definition that has also been promulgated by the UNHCR: A person is de facto stateless if they do not have a nationality from the state in which they have a "genuine and effective" link. In their words: "Governments must acknowledge, formally and in practice, that they do not have the right to withdraw or withhold the benefits of citizenship from individuals who can demonstrate a genuine and effective link with the country" (UNHCR 2005, 3). If governments do withdraw or withhold benefits, then those persons are de facto stateless. Being de facto stateless is not a matter of failing to be protected; rather, it is that one lacks nationality from the state in which one lives. The *Nottebohm* case and other international instruments have also invoked this account of nationality through attachment—sometimes referred to as *jus connectionis*, or the law of connectedness.[12]

However, this definition likewise raises a variety of questions that are problematic for its applicability. First, what more precisely is the genuine and effective link, and how might it be determined? Standard international practice and law, such as the *Nottebohm* case, leaves this to state discretion, and states typically deny that persons without a proper jus soli or jus sanguinis connection have a "genuine and effective" link. Even relatively welcoming states, such as the United States, have been unwilling to give citizenship to persons on the basis of social attachment. Taking the UNHCR's suggestion seriously might require that states radically alter their citizenship laws, thereby greatly affecting their right to make their own determinations of nationality. Although ideally jus connectionis might best promote human dignity worldwide, this principle surely is not what drives UNHCR action nor will it likely guide state action in responding to the particular issue of statelessness.

A third definition responds to one problem with the de jure definition, holding that persons are de facto stateless when they have a nationality but cannot prove it. As indicated above, administrative, technical or other reasons might make this proof difficult if not impossible to obtain, and as a result many persons live without the preconditions for basic protection. This definition is significantly more narrow than previous definitions, excluding many irregular migrants or those systematically oppressed by their state. It thereby tries to balance the perspective of the state and the perspective of the vulnerable person while acknowledging the extent to which many who have de jure nationality should be treated as stateless.

Although this definition seeks to balance the perspective of states and of persons, it might be challenged from either side. Many vulnerable persons might be able to prove their nationality yet still lack all of their state's protections and thus might live identical lives as those who are de jure stateless. This definition might not therefore be sufficiently strong to give teeth to the notion that all persons have a right to a nationality.

But a state might also challenge this designation because it enables persons to qualify as de facto stateless if they still reside in their state of nationality. States might object that the concept of statelessness must only apply to persons who are outside of their own state. Although this might not matter for the persons themselves, some might believe that this is crucial to limiting the definition to a manageable group to which the UNHCR and states might provide response.

Consider now a fourth alternative definition of de facto statelessness: "Persons who are outside the State of their nationality and lacking in that State's protection, the protection in question being diplomatic and consular protection and assistance (as opposed to protection on the territory of the State of nationality itself)" (Massey 2010, ii). This definition, stemming from the 1946 Memorandum on Statelessness by the Intergovernmental Committee on Refugees and recently promoted by UNHCR Senior Legal Adviser Massey, is sufficiently narrow and does not include those who are systematically oppressed by their own state. Its criteria require that one be outside one's state of nationality and that one's state of nationality fails to provide protection in specific diplomatic or consular functions. According to Massey, this failure to provide protection must be the result of one's state refusing to provide it rather than being unable to provide protection, or if there is simply an absence of diplomatic recognition (Massey 2010).

But this definition likewise seems too limited to characterize persons who live functionally equivalent lives as those who are de jure stateless. One's de jure state might provide diplomatic or consular services, though one might live with strong attachments in a different state that provides none of the protections essential to living well. From the perspective of the person, this definition thus fails to capture something crucial about the right to nationality. And surely what matters for a definition of statelessness, if it is to be made operational to fill a protection gap, is to capture the lived experience of the unprotected person. To further bolster this point, it might be asked, why would it matter from a person's perspective whether one's de jure state fails to provide protection simply because it does not have diplomatic relations with one's de facto state? This is a trivial distinction, perhaps meaning something to the respective states but not the vulnerable person left out of all protections in their de facto residence simply because they have some de jure connection to a state that does not protect them. On this definition, the right to a state is thus divorced from the rights associated with having a state; the former might be granted without any provision of the latter.

As should be clear by now, the major potential definitions of de facto statelessness are subject to scrutiny. Without fully arbitrating this dispute, this discussion does hopefully suggest the difficulties of defining statelessness in a way that reasonably balances the concerns of states and the vulnerabilities of persons who fall into a protection gap and points again to a solution that requires breaking through the basic tension in international law that animates this dispute. I offer my own approach to broker this tension in the recommendation section below. But, before making recommendations and with these conceptual complications in mind, I turn now to efforts taken by states to address the problem.

The Development of an Anti-Stateless Regime: State-Sponsored Protection

The origin of an anti-stateless regime can be traced to the League of Nations and Fridtjof Nansen's work as the League's high commissioner for refugees. However, it was only following World War II that states began to distinguish the stateless from refugees. During discussions in the development of the 1951 Refugee Convention, a provision was offered to extend the 1951 convention to include de jure stateless persons who did not also qualify as refugees, but states declined, and the stateless were sidelined without protection until specific instruments were developed.

The 1954 Convention Relating to the Status of Stateless Persons

The first such instrument, the 1954 Convention Relating to the Status of Stateless Persons, attempted to fill the protection gaps faced by the de jure stateless by acknowledging the problem and promoting basic rights. It offers the now standard definition of the de jure stateless and contains thirty articles granting them rights at least as strong as the rights granted to other foreign nationals. Although excluding persons already receiving UN protection (such as the Palestinians in the United Nationals Relief and Works Agency zone of operation) and those convicted of criminal acts, the de jure stateless are guaranteed some basic rights on par with nationals of the state, such as religious freedom, the right to elementary education, and the right to court access, along with other rights on par with nonnationals, such as the right of association, the right to housing, and the right to property. In addition, Article 27 provides the stateless with the right to an identity document from their state of habitual residence, and Article 28 provides travel documents that enable them to leave and return.

Despite the provision of these rights, the Convention provides weaker rights for the stateless than the 1951 Convention's rights for refugees because it only applies to stateless persons who are lawfully within the country. If the person was not legally admitted, then none of the rights are guaranteed; of course, it is for states themselves to determine when a person is a lawful resident. It also does not prohibit penalties for unlawful entry into a state and thus a de jure stateless person fleeing conflict might be penalized for crossing the border. Further, there is no explicit obligation of states not to return the stateless to their country of origin. In comparison with the much stronger provisions of Articles 31 and 22 of the Refugee Convention, the protections of the stateless are quite weak.

Moreover, the Convention inherits the basic tension in international law between the right of states to determine nationality and the right of persons to a nationality. The Information and Accession Packet itself acknowledges that, despite the protections guaranteed by the convention, "there is no replacement for nationality itself." But the Convention does not require that states grant nationality to stateless persons, merely that it "facilitates" their naturalization, and thus it in no way restricts the right of states to grant nationality at their discretion (Article 32).[13] In addition, the Convention neither reduces the existing population of the stateless by providing a path to citizenship nor does it try to prevent future populations of stateless by closing loopholes in nationality laws. And it does not otherwise prohibit laws that discriminate against women or specific ethnic groups. And of course, it only applies to the de jure stateless, excluding potentially millions of de facto stateless who lack an effective nationality and thus are accorded no rights at all.

Given these limitations, it is no wonder that Arendt calls the 1954 meeting that led to the convention "no more than a mere gesture: to gather the representatives of at least twenty states, but with the explicit assurance that participation in such a conference would entail no obligations whatsoever" (Arendt 1973, 280). The 1954 Convention clearly fails to resolve the problem of the stateless over the long term. Indeed, given that it neither provides the stateless with a path to citizenship nor requires states to change their nationality laws to prevent future statelessness, one might argue that the Convention recognizes a permanent and second class of persons, thereby sidestepping the entire problem.

The 1961 Convention on the Reduction of Statelessness

The international community was not blind to the gaps remaining from the 1954 Convention and worked to develop an additional instrument in the 1961 Convention on the Reduction of Statelessness. The Convention employs the de jure definition of the 1954 Convention, and seeks to reduce their overall numbers by providing a path to citizenship for those who would otherwise be stateless. In particular, it obliges states to provide nationality to children born on their territory if those children have no other nationality. So, in jus sanguinis states, the Convention requires states to apply jus soli rules to persons who would otherwise be stateless; in jus soli states, the Convention requires states to apply jus sanguinis rules to provide a nationality to children who would have no other nationality (for instance, if they migrated to the state but were not born there). It thereby seeks to break free of the legal tension and restricts a state's discretion to determine nationality. The 1961 Convention also tries to reduce statelessness by prohibiting the renunciation or deprivation of citizenship if the person would otherwise be stateless, and in general, it prohibits states from depriving persons of nationality on racial, ethnic, religious, or political grounds (Articles 8 and 9).

The 1961 Convention strives to reduce the stateless population but is nonetheless quite limited. First, as usual, it applies exclusively to the de jure stateless, thereby leaving out an entire population that lacks an effective nationality.[14] Second, it only provides a path to nationality in limited contexts: One has to apply in the right age range and has to reside in the country for a specified period of time (Articles 1.2.a and 4.2.a, and 1.2.c and 4.2.c). Outside of this age range, states are under no obligation to provide an otherwise stateless person nationality. Moreover, the Convention provides a path to nationality if one is born in the state and would otherwise be stateless, but it does not give a path to citizenship for those who are already stateless outside of the age range. Thus, it reduces future populations of stateless but does nothing to accommodate the current population. What's more, these provisions only apply if one can prove both that one has no other nationality (a burden for all de jure stateless) and that one was born within the contracting state. As noted above, approximately fifty million births annually go unregistered, and the convention would thus potentially exclude these persons from receiving benefits. In general, it is beset by the overarching aspiration that if a state ratifies the Convention it will take responsibility for its stateless population by giving them citizenship, but the very existence of the stateless is itself the result of the ongoing failure of states to accommodate this group. Even a commitment to the Convention does not therefore mean that states will actually take responsibility.

Beyond the limitations within the Conventions is the basic problem that very few states have ratified them. Currently there are seventy-two state parties to the 1954 Convention and forty-three parties to the 1961 Convention, with almost all of Asia, Eastern Europe, and Africa being nonparties to both, whereas most of Europe remains a nonparty to the 1961 Convention. Many states with significant populations of de jure stateless are nonparties, including Bangladesh, India, the Gulf Arab States, and the Dominican Republic. Although some states, such as the Philippines, have domesticated the laws without becoming a party, most states have simply ignored the Conventions.

States offer a variety of reasons for not ratifying, with some claiming that statelessness is not a problem at all. Other rationales have also been employed. Think of the explanation offered by US officials, who claimed that because the United States is a jus soli state, it "does not contribute to the problem of statelessness" (Green and Pierce 2009, 35). Of course, there remain thousands (and, depending on one's definition, perhaps millions) of stateless persons in the United States who lack protection and a path to citizenship. One might further argue that by not ratifying the Conventions, the United States contributes to the problem of statelessness by setting a bad precedent for other states that have larger stateless populations and far fewer means to address the problem.

US officials argue that the Conventions conflict with other aspects of their nationality laws, such as Americans' right to freely renounce their nationality, because the 1961 Convention prohibits renunciation if it would result in statelessness (Green and Pierce 2009, 35). But again this justification faces a serious objection: The whole point of the Conventions is to shape states' nationality laws to reduce statelessness. The only way the population will eventually be accommodated is if states are willing to accept modifications to their existing nationality laws. If states are unwilling to modify their laws, then the stateless population will never be reduced.

Other states, including India and countries in Europe, have concerns about encroachments on sovereignty and their perceived duty to protect a particular ethnonational group that has seemingly precipitated these countries' failure to ratify the conventions. However, even these justifications can be challenged by the responsibility of all states to ensure the conditions under which persons can live with dignity and, in this case, to help persons realize their right to a nationality.

Recommendations: Who Is Ultimately Responsible?

The problem of statelessness is worsened by ongoing conceptual complications and the many causes of statelessness. Solutions must therefore be similarly complex to address an array of challenges. The following recommendations are divided between short-term and long-term solutions.

In the short term, more international attention needs to be directed at the plight of stateless persons. The stateless are too often an afterthought in the international community, which, for political and other reasons, has tended to focus more on refugees. But, as should be clear, although not all stateless persons qualify as refugees, many of them live with similar indignities, though they lack equally strong legal protections. The work by Refugees International and other advocacy groups to help publicize the plight of particular stateless groups has effectively placed the problem within an international agenda. But more must be done both to identify particular groups and to resolve the conceptual difficulties that complicate and confuse many discussions. It bodes poorly for effective international engagement if even the organizations whose mandate it is to respond to statelessness cannot come to a consensus about what statelessness is. Stateless persons cannot be identified, much less protected, if there is no clear definition and no sense of their numbers.

Second, states should accede to the Conventions relating to statelessness. Despite their limitations, they do put statelessness on the international agenda and provide some protection. At UNHCR's ministerial conference in December 2011 to mark the fiftieth anniversary of the 1961 Convention, eight states ratified at least one Convention, and twenty others pledged to ratify soon. One advantage is that states have a genuine self-interest in diminishing the stateless population and providing them with protection. No state is well served by wasted economic talent and an invisible population. States that have recently ratified the Conventions have seemingly recognized their self-interest in ratification, and they should set an example for other states.

Even states like the United States, who are so-called noncontributors, should demonstrate that they take this problem seriously by ratifying the Conventions. If states continue to resist, strong pressure should be applied by the international community to at least adopt the basic framework of each Convention as an element of domestic legislation.

Third, continued emphasis should be placed on birth registration, especially across sub–Saharan Africa and South Asia. The UN Children's Fund and other actors should continue to work with nongovernmental organizations (NGOs) and should emphasize to states the importance of using mobile clinics and other forms of outreach. Although fewer persons will be stateless if more births are registered, birth registration will not solve the problem of a lack of legal identity on its own. As a result, humanitarian organizations should also promote access to some form of alternative identity documents for persons who are stateless. Either the UNHCR should pressure states to offer alternative identity documents, or the UNHCR itself should consider issuing a kind of identity document that might allow the stateless access to a bank account, health care, and other basic services. This is of course no substitute for a legal national identity, but it might alleviate some of the daily indignities faced by the stateless.

Fourth, NGOs and other nonstate actors should consider alternative tools to protect the stateless outside of traditional state protections. Some American cities have already taken the lead as so-called sanctuary cities that will not use municipal funds or other resources to cooperate with federal immigration law.[15] Some cities have even taken steps to offer protections at the city level that are typically associated with the state—San Francisco, for instance, offers city-based health care coverage. By providing the stateless some of the protections typically associated with nationality, without offering them nationality itself, cities and smaller organizations could also seek to decouple protections from the state.

These short-run fixes might alleviate the plight of some individuals, but they do not solve the problem itself. In the long run, the only surefire way to prevent the indignities of the stateless is to radically change our conceptions of citizenship and sovereignty. In particular, two transformative ideas that are already gaining traction should be furthered to fundamentally improve the situation.

First is a reconceptualization of the notion of sovereignty that expands the states that have a responsibility to persons within their territory, sometimes referred to as "sovereignty as responsibility." Embraced by the UN General Assembly in the Outcome Document of the 2005 World Summit and reaffirmed by the Security Council in 2006 as Pillar 1 of the so-called Responsibility to Protect, the idea is that states have the responsibility to protect their population from threats, including genocide, war crimes, and crimes against humanity.[16] This notion of sovereignty requires that states be able to justify their actions over their population to both an internal and external audience. Although there are some states that have taken steps to resist this changing conception of sovereignty—in particular, Russia, China, and India—there are efforts to strengthen and apply the norm. Roberta Cohen, former US state department deputy assistant secretary, UN special adviser, and someone with experience negotiating with states regarding the concept of sovereignty as responsibility, notes that: "No government has ever challenged the concept of sovereignty as responsibility. . . . Governments can no longer persuasively argue that sovereignty allows them to deny life-sustaining support to their citizens. More traditional and absolute notions of sovereignty have given way to notions of accountability to one's domestic constituency and to the international community at large" (Cohen 2003). Despite fundamentally transforming the traditional notion of sovereignty, then, states have at least purported to accept it. Indeed, it is difficult for even the most authoritarian state not to acknowledge publicly its responsibility to its citizens.

How might this transformative norm be applied to the situation of the stateless? As a model, consider how sovereignty-as-responsibility has been employed in the development of guiding principles to mold international action in response to the more than twenty-five million internally displaced persons (IDPs) worldwide. Dr. Francis Deng, among others, recognized that IDPs were fundamentally unprotected under existing international law (indeed, they were not even defined as a distinct category of vulnerable persons) and employed this norm of sovereignty to develop a definition and principles that would guide state response. The guiding principles have been successful insofar as IDPs now command more international attention, some states have taken greater responsibility for them, and some have even incorporated the nonbinding principles into domestic law. Cohen observes the role of states in responding to the principles but also notes the role of the array of other actors characteristic of the neomedieval world: "In the forefront of promoting the use of the Principles around the world have been local NGOs, lawyers' groups, women's associations, academics, and other members of civil society" (Cohen 2003). Getting states to take responsibility more readily for stateless populations will require a similarly pluralistic set of actors encouraging states to consider all persons over whom they have jurisdiction. States should be encouraged to take responsibility for the dignity of all within their borders. Other actors might have a role filling in protections and exercising their own sovereignty where states have failed.

A transformative conception of citizenship has developed in conjunction with this reconceptualization of sovereignty. Theoretical justifications of nationality and of the very existence of the state system come down to the principle that the kind of legal community constituted by the state is a necessary means for persons to live well and with dignity. So long as this is true, the focus of nationality and the function of the state should be about what is best for the person within a state rather than what is best for the state itself. In this regard, the idea of jus connectionis, the law of attachment, fundamentally captures the value of citizenship in a multipolar world. Persons should be able to enjoy the protections of citizenship where they live the most significant portions of their lives. This principle makes citizenship fundamentally about a current social attachment, the ongoing experience of a lived humanity, rather than some inert historical fact about birth or ancestry implicit within jus soli or jus sanguinis. With this principle in play, all stateless persons would have the right to nationality in the state in which they undertake the sorts of activities that constitute the valuable aspects of their lives. It would deal with gender discrimination in nationality laws, prohibit citizenship laws that exclude ethnic groups, correct for cracks in state laws, and resolve practical problems, such as a lack of birth certificates. This would also work as a proposal to resolve the definitional quandary facing the UNHCR regarding de facto statelessness: A person is stateless if they are not granted state protection from the state in which they have their most significant social attachments. This is the definition the UNHCR and other advocacy groups should use because it captures the most fundamental feature of what it is to lack the right to have rights.

These two ideas in tandem—sovereignty as responsibility and jus connectionis—would fundamentally transform international relations. Together they resolve the tension between the right of all to a nationality and the right of states to determine who is a national—decidedly against the latter and with the former. As moral thinkers have emphasized for centuries, humans are fundamentally of value and thus precede the artificial and arbitrary political grouping of the nation-state. Notwithstanding the practical problems of actually implementing these proposed norms, they would serve as an ultimate solution to the problem of the stateless. Persons have a right to nationality where they are most attached. States are sovereign only so far as they take responsibility for persons socially connected and living their lives within their borders. The result is a world in which states help persons enjoy the rights associated with nationality where it means the most to them. This change would mark nothing less than a reconfiguring of the normative landscape, putting humans ahead of states as the fundamental moral touchstone.

Conclusion

How would Arendt assess our progress on the problem of statelessness? Given the ongoing challenges and the enduring gaps in protection, she would likely not be satisfied. She herself understood how difficult the problem would be and the sort of massive transformation of the state system required to fully address it. In her view, half steps and subtle reforms, like international conventions, were bound to fail: They remained too close to a state-based system. She writes, "[F]or, contrary to the best intentioned humanitarian attempts to obtain new declarations of human rights from international organizations, it should be understood that this idea transcends the present sphere of international law which still operates in terms of reciprocal agreements and treaties between sovereign states; and for the time being, a sphere that is above the nations does not exist" (Arendt 1973, 298).

Although I have not followed her lead by proposing a sphere above nations to resolve the problem—that is, I have not proposed a suprastate that gives all nationality—I have sought to eliminate a debilitating tension in international law by reconceptualizing state sovereignty and nationality in a way that better suits the array of actors in the neomedieval world and better protects stateless persons. Arendt would perhaps find these suggestions too optimistic in their tendency to make states responsible for persons. But they remain the best step forward in creating a world without the stateless.

Notes

1. The 1930 Convention on Certain Questions Relating to the Conflict of Nationality Laws Article 1 states: "It is for each State to determine under its own law who are its nationals. This law shall be recognised by other States in so far as it is consistent with international conventions, international custom, and the principles of law generally recognised with regard to nationality." The *Nottebohm* case (Liechtenstein v. Guatemala) holds that nationality "is a legal bond having as its basis a social fact of attachment, a genuine connection of existence, interest and sentiments, together with the existence of reciprocal rights and duties." Note that although the latter part to the claim seems to limit the right, the genuine effective link is up to states to determine and includes birth or descent.

2. I use the concepts of "citizenship" and "nationality" interchangeably. For one canonical definition of nationality, see (Weis 1956): Nationality guarantees "the allocation of individuals, termed nationals, to a specific State—the State of nationality—as members of that State, a relationship which confers upon that State under customary international law rights and duties in relation to other States."

3. The International Covenant on Civil and Political Rights, Article 24.3: "Every child has the right to acquire a nationality." The Convention on the Rights of the Child, Article 7.1: All children "shall be registered immediately after birth and shall have the right from birth to a name, the right to acquire a nationality."

4. The Preamble to the UDHR makes this explicit: "Whereas recognition of the inherent dignity and of the equal and inalienable rights of all members of the human family is the foundation of freedom, justice, and peace in the world."

5. Consider for instance how Eleanor Roosevelt, in working to develop the UDHR, argued that the rights of the individual are above the rights of the state. See the account in (Glendon 2002).

6. This tension supports Lagon and Arend's attempt in the introductory chapter of this book to move beyond stalemated debates within the discourse of "rights" to establish a new normative foundation for assessing institutions.

7. The UNHCR also notes that they do not have "comprehensive statistics on stateless populations worldwide" (UNHCR 2010b).

8. Some analysts point to jus sanguinis as the central contributor to the problem. For instance, Blitz argues that, "the principle of membership on the basis of blood origin has historically locked many minority groups out of the right to citizenship in their habitual state of residence" (Blitz 2009).

9. "This number is a 'guesstimate'. It has been very difficult for organizations to collect comprehensive data on the number of stateless persons because the concept of statelessness is disputed among countries, because governments are often reluctant to disclose information about statelessness, and because the issue of statelessness is not high on the international community's agenda" (UNHCR 2005, 3).

10. Compare the special rapporteur to the International Law Commission Roberto Codova, who wrote in 1954: "It seems to the Special Rapporteur that the most important aspect of this problem of statelessness is not the technical question of nationality only, but the real situation. . . . Needless to say that the Commission is not only obliged to deal with juridical statelessness, but is also under the solemn obligation to provide juridical solutions for the situation of thousands of human beings who are in a much worse position than those only are de jure stateless" (Codova 1954, 30).

11. They also report that, "the individual is thus unable to demonstrate that he/she is de jure stateless, yet he/she has no effective nationality and does not enjoy national protection. He/She is considered to be de facto stateless" (UNHCR 2005, 11).

12. The *Nottebohm* decision states: "Nationality is a legal bond having as its basis a social fact of attachment, a genuine connection of existence, interest and sentiments, together with the existence of reciprocal rights and duties." But this raises the question: Is one stateless if one has strong social attachments but no rights?

13. Article 32 states: "The Contracting States shall as far as possible facilitate the assimilation and naturalization of stateless persons. They shall in particular make every effort to expedite naturalization proceedings and to reduce as far as possible the charges and costs of such proceedings."

14. As mentioned earlier, Resolution No. 1 of the Final Act states, "The Conference recommends that persons who are stateless de facto should as far as possible be treated as stateless de jure to enable them to acquire an effective nationality." This resolution, however, is a recommendation rather than an obligation.

15. There are thirty-one cities of this sort in the United States, including New York, Los Angeles, and Chicago.

16. The World Summit text reads: "Each individual State has the responsibility to protect its populations from genocide, war crimes, ethnic cleansing and crimes against humanity. This responsibility entails the prevention of such crimes, including their incitement, through appropriate and necessary means. We accept that responsibility and will act in accordance with it. The international community should, as appropriate, encourage and help States to exercise this responsibility and support the UN in establishing an early warning capability."

References

Arendt, Hannah. 1973. *The Origins of Totalitarianism.* 5th ed. San Diego, CA: Harcourt, Brace, Jovanovich.

Batchelor, Carol. 1998. "Statelessness and the Problem of Resolving Nationality Status." *International Journal of Refugee Law* 10: 156.

Blitz, Brad. 2009. *Statelessness, Protection, and Equality.* Oxford, UK: Refugees Studies Centre, University of Oxford. Assessed on April 17, 2014. http://www.refworld.org /docid/4e5f3d572.html.

Codova, Roberto. 1954. "Nationality, Including Statelessness—Third Report on the Elimination or Reduction of Stateless." Extract from the Yearbook of the International Law Commission 1954 vol. 2. A/CN/4/81. Accessed September 13, 2013. http:// untreaty.un.org/ilc/documentation/english/a_cn4_81_corr1.pdf.

Cohen, Roberta. 2003. "Sovereignty as Responsibility: The Guiding Principles on Internal Displacement." Public Lecture at the Calcutta Research Group and the Refugees Studies Centre. December 5. Calcutta, India.

Convention on the Nationality of Married Women. 1958.

Convention on the Rights of the Child "Convention" Article 7.1. 1990.

Convention Relating to the Status of Refugees. 1951.

Convention Relating to the Status of Stateless Persons. 1954.

Glendon, Mary. 2002. *A World Made New: Eleanor Roosevelt and the Universal Declaration of Human Rights.* New York: Random House.

Goldston, J. A. 2006. "Holes in the Rights Framework: Racial Discrimination, Citizenship, and the Rights of Noncitizens." *Ethics & International Affairs* 20 (3): 321–47.

Green, Nicole, and Todd Pierce. 2009. "Combatting Statelessness: A Government Perspective." *Forced Migration Review Journal* 11 (32).

Hobbes, Thomas. 1994. *Leviathan: With Selected Variants from the Latin Edition of 1668.* 3rd ed. Edited by Edwin Curley. Cambridge, MA: Hackett Publishing.

Hudson, Manley O. 1952. "Report on Nationality, Including Stateless" Extract from the Yearbook of the International Law Commission vol. 2. A/CN.450. Accessed September 13, 2013. http://untreaty.un.org/ilc/documentation/english/a_cn4_50.pdf.

Loescher, Gil. 1996. *Beyond Charity: International Cooperation and the Global Refugee Crisis.* New York: Oxford University Press.

Massey, Hugh. 2010. "UNHCR and De Facto Statelessness." *Legal and Protection Policy Research Series.* Geneva, Switzerland: UNHCR.

Nottebohm Case. 1955. (Liechtenstein v. Guatemala [second phase]). *Judgment of April 6.*

Robinson, Nehemiah. 1955. *Convention Relating to the Status of Stateless Persons: Its History and Interpretation.* New York: World Jewish Congress. Reprinted by the Division of International Protection of the UN High Commissioner for Refugees, 1997.

Sen, Amartya. 1999. *Development as Freedom.* New York: Alfred A. Knopf.

UNHCR (UN High Commissioner for Refugees). 1999. "Information and Accession Package: The 1954 Convention Relating to the Status of Stateless Persons and the 1961 Convention on the Reduction of Statelessness." Geneva, Switzerland: UNHCR.

———. 2005. *Nationality and Statelessness: A Handbook for Parliamentarians.* Inter-Parliamentary Union.

———. 2010a. *Statistical Report 2009: Trends in Displacement, Protection, and Solutions.* UNHCR. Accessed September 13, 2013. http://www.unhcr.org/4ce532ff9.html.

———. 2010b. *UNHCR Action to Address Statelessness: A Strategy Note.* UNHCR. Accessed September 13, 2013. http://www.unhcr.org/4b960ae99.html.

UNHCR Executive Committee. 2006. "Conclusion on Identification, Prevention and Reduction of Stateless and Protection of Stateless Persons." UNHCR. Accessed September 13, 2013. http://www.unhcr.org/453497302.html.

Weis, Paul. 1956. *Nationality and Statelessness in International Law.* New York: Frederick A. Praegar.

Weissbrodt, David S., and Clay Collins. 2006. "The Human Rights of Stateless Persons." *Human Rights Quarterly* 28 (1): 245–76.

CHAPTER 11

Fighting Human Trafficking

Transformative versus "Cotton-Candy" Partnerships

MARK P. LAGON

B oth the UN treaty and US law devoted to fighting human trafficking as a modern form of slavery have the same touchstones for areas of action. Completed in 2000, both the Palermo Protocol to the UN Convention on Organized Crime and the US Trafficking Victims Protection Act (TVPA) established norms around three *P*'s: *prosecution* of traffickers, *protection* of victims, and *prevention* of the offense. A fourth *P* was added by former secretary of state Hillary Clinton, who emphasized *partnerships* between governments, multilateral organizations, nongovernmental organizations (NGOs), and the private sector as a vehicle to seek an end to human trafficking (Clinton 2009).

In truth, partnerships have been at the heart of antitrafficking efforts since their inception. For instance, if it were not for strange-bedfellow partnerships between feminists, conservative Christians, legislators, and others, there would be no TVPA, no State Department antitrafficking office, and no annual global *Trafficking in Persons (TIP) Report* in the United States. Since the Bush Administration instituted it, the State Department office under administrations of both parties has devoted as much effort to funding NGOs and international organizations as partners as to preparing the global report as a diplomatic tool to spur change.

Moreover, a particular type of alliance—public-private partnerships—has been a feature of the Clinton, Bush, and Obama administrations as well as the UN Office on Drugs and Crime (UNODC) and the International Labor Organization (ILO) antitrafficking efforts (Report on the Vienna Forum 2008; ILO 2008). These partnerships involve businesses that are fighting the enabling environments for trafficking—from sex tourism in the travel sector to supply chains tainted by forced labor and onerous child labor.

Still, overall progress in fighting slavery appears less than transformative. Although over two-thirds of the world's nations have enacted comprehensive antitrafficking laws, laws on paper are not enough. According to the *TIP Report*, only 7,705 traffickers were prosecuted and 4,746 convicted in 2012 (levels which have remained fairly constant since 2004). Furthermore, only 1,153 were prosecuted and 518 convicted for labor-related (as opposed to sex-related) trafficking, although, encouragingly, those figures were up from 508 and 302 respectively in 2011. The victim protection P is arguably even more important to advancing dignity than the prosecution P. Yet in a world with at least 20.9 million trafficking victims, as estimated by the ILO (ILO 2012), the number of victims identified worldwide in 2012 was merely 45,570 (TIP Report 2013)—up from the previous year (41,210).

This book advocates the notion of institutions advancing agency and social recognition as the bases of dignity in tangible ways—beyond the norm setting, which intergovernmental organizations have emphasized. Some of the most crucial of the partnerships between actors to provide governance on (against) human trafficking are:

- between law enforcement and social service agencies of governments;
- between national, state/provincial, and local authorities within countries;
- bilaterally between governments of source, transit, and destination countries of transnational trafficking;
- between governments and intergovernmental organizations (IGOs);
- between IGOs (e.g., different agencies of the UN);
- between law enforcement and NGOs, where there is mutual lack of trust, even in democratic countries;
- between international NGOs and national NGOs, struggling over ownership and expertise;
- between NGOs in coalition in a nation (e.g., the Alliance To End Slavery and Trafficking, or ATEST, in the United States);
- between businesses, either with one sector (e.g., cocoa/chocolate, apparel, or travel/hospitality) or across sectors (e.g., the global Business Coalition Against Human Trafficking, or gBCAT);
- between businesses and governments or businesses and IGOs (public-private partnerships); and
- between businesses and NGOs.

This sheer variety of relationships drives home both the opportunities for leveraging capacities and the challenges from friction between stakeholders in hybrid global institutions. It is time to assess what kind of partnerships are vital to reduce the recognition- and agency-robbing effects of human trafficking and to progress down a path to its eradication. Some partnerships are more like cotton candy—big, airy, colorful, and sweet but of little actual substance—whereas others are truly effective and potentially transformative.

Specific examples of international partnerships that have had more or less impact for each focus yield some overall lessons. These lessons could make the difference between a disjointed, if energetic, global movement against trafficking and multistakeholder institutional arrangements capable of veritable international governance—namely, to reduce and ultimately marginalize trafficking as an obstacle to the realization of dignity. To make this assessment, it is important to unpack eight focus areas related to the 3 *P*'s. One is understanding the nature and extent of the problem. Three relate to protection of victims—identifying them, providing immediate care, and fostering longer-term economic re-empowerment. Another is prosecution of perpetrators, which also yields dignity to victims. Two relate to prevention—initiatives to promote awareness and training on the one hand and attention to demand forces for labor and sex trafficking on the other. (Some would argue that antipoverty programs dealing with a major root cause of trafficking is another area, but those efforts are too diffuse to explore in a short chapter.) Finally, mobilizing and coordinating monetary and other resources is an eighth antihuman trafficking focus area.

As a note on my empirical approach, these examples of stronger and weaker partnerships will sometimes be more empirically conclusive and at times will reflect heuristic or suggestive assessments based on my own work situated in government, an NGO, and business sectors, which will merit all the more rigorous future validation. Moreover, the examples herein typically are institutional actors in major powers—such as India, Brazil, and the United States. The rationale for this choice is that if partnerships in such resource-rich major powers reveal limitations, those limitations are likely to be all the more acute in actors operating in settings with lesser capacity and fewer resources.

Partnerships for a Baseline for Action

Focus #1: Researching and Mapping the Problem

To address the problem of human trafficking and to tangibly advance the dignity of its actual and potential victims, institutional partnerships need qualitative and quantitative information about the phenomenon. Importantly, those institutional partnerships need baselines to see if the problem is growing or diminishing and in what respects and whether interventions pursued (in all the other seven focus areas) are making a difference. The human trafficking field has suffered from weak statistics and baselines. Obviously, one of the major problems faced by researchers and organizations combating human trafficking stems from the fact that accurate accounting remains difficult given that, "[M]ost of the populations relevant to the study of human trafficking, such as victims/survivors of trafficking for sexual exploitation, traffickers, or illegal migrants are part of a 'hidden population', i.e., it is almost impossible to establish a sampling frame and draw a representative sample of the population" (Tyldum and Brunovskis 2005, 18).

Indeed, no advances in sampling techniques will adequately overcome this intractable problem. With that said, there have been both notable successes and stumbles associated with researching and mapping the human trafficking problem.

The ILO in its most recent report of June 2012 found that there were an estimated 20.9 million individuals at a minimum trapped in jobs or occupations that they cannot leave. It further found that 90 percent, or 18.7 million were in the private economy, where the ratios of chiefly labor to chiefly sexual exploitation was 3:1, adult-to-child victims was 3:1, and female to male victims was 11:9 (ILO 2012; Solis 2012). The ILO itself suggests that, "the numerical results of the 2012 estimation are not comparable to those derived in 2005" when it did a previous survey (Mehran and de Cock 2012, 11). And although their statistics are more robust, the statisticians, in explaining the decreased proportion in the incidence of state-imposed forced labor, demonstrated this most recent study still relies heavily upon available data. Indeed, they wrote, "state-imposed forced labor represents a lower proportion of the total, at around 10 percent. This could be due in part to the fact that far fewer data are available on state-imposed forced labor relative to the other forms, pointing to a need for further research in this area" (17). At its base, the ILO sampling uses a commonly used statistical method of capture-recapture sampling. This sampling allows researchers to calculate elusive populations, like the number of fish in a lake, where there are no sampling boundaries available. The major margin for error associated with the sampling in this case is that it relies upon reported cases as its base. Indeed, the ILO sampling is almost wholly reliant upon secondary sources (reports from NGOs, the media, government agencies, academics, and trade unions as partners). That said, based on these partnerships, notably academics as validators such as Siddharth Kara of Harvard University, this estimate is a substantial increase over the 27 million estimated by scholar Kevin Bales in 2004, ubiquitously cited by the US government, the UNODC, and NGOs worldwide (Bales

2004). And it is a huge leap forward from the aforementioned 2005 ILO estimate of 12.3 million based on weaker methodology and a propensity to undercount veritable human trafficking victims who are adults in the sex industry, or who have not crossed international borders.

The State Department *TIP Report* is perhaps the most significant example of research and mapping of the problem.[1] Still, the *TIP Report* "using information from US embassies, government officials sharing statistics, nongovernmental and international organizations, published reports, news articles, academic studies, research trips to every region of the world, and information submitted to tipreport@state.gov" (TIP Report 2012), is not designed to provide a baseline for the incidence of human trafficking. Rather, it is designed to evaluate efforts on a state-by-state basis to legislate and combat human trafficking, which places those states into four tiers. Indeed, those tiers are based not on the extent of the human trafficking phenomenon in countries but rather on the will and activity of the government to address the problem. Once again, the methods have been criticized by some for being undisclosed and subject to pressure on the basis of geopolitics. Yet the tiers offer their own baseline as states move between tiers. Thus far, the *TIP Report*, with admittedly less than transparent methods, offers the international community the most consistent reporting on the status of individual countries. It has significantly raised awareness of governments and publics. Judith Kelley of Duke University and Beth Simmons of Harvard University have established a robust causal relationship between the Report's ranking and enactment of antitrafficking laws (Kelley and Simmons 2014).

Another example of mapping is the International Organization for Migration (IOM). The IOM focuses on supporting specific projects or networks of NGOs in regional hot spots, whether in the Volta region of Ghana or Vietnam, to serve international human trafficking victims. The US State Department antitrafficking office supports these programs and encouraged IOM to form a comprehensive database of information on trafficking survivors. IOM's Counter-Trafficking Module Database that "facilitates the management of all IOM direct assistance, movement and reintegration on processes through a centrally managed system, as well as mapping victims' trafficking experiences," provides a useful tool for identifying potential hotspots. The problem with this database, however, is that it is dependent on host government cooperation, and sources of funding to scale up its work. Moreover, it provides after-the-fact data that does not serve the purpose of mapping the scale of the problem.

UNODC and its former Executive Director (2002–2010) Antonio Maria Costa aspired to produce a global human trafficking report as an analog to its annual *World Drug Report* to offer an ostensibly more legitimate multilateral counterpart to the US *TIP Report*. It has produced only two editions of the *Global Report on Trafficking in Persons* (2009 and 2012), and those two editions have pulled their punches regarding criticizing the UN member states and exhibited gaps in information and data larger than in the imperfect, if influential, US *Report*. The 2009 and 2012 reports feature individual country profiles with very limited statistics and graphics for each, which although illustrative, are not consistent across countries and are significantly more limited than the US *TIP Report*. Even the most recent 2012 report has profiles of only two-thirds of the nations of the world.

In an emerging area of mapping, there is great ardor on the part of business, NGOs, and the US Department of Homeland Security (DHS) to apply cutting-edge aspects of geospatial and investigative modeling using recent advances in big data analytics pioneered by, for example, Google, Deloitte, and Palantir (Skibola 2012). Yet this approach's success relies on robust and large datasets, integrated dialogue between enthusiastic experts on human trafficking, and equally enthusiastic technicians in the data analytics industry, which, quite simply, do not exist today. Moreover, if there are plans to use baselines to preempt interventions to address particular human trafficking hotspots, then standardization of data appears necessary—say, between known hotspots such as the Mekong region in Southeast Asia and the Amazon Basin in Brazil.

In a broader sense of mapping, the Organization for Security and Cooperation in Europe (OSCE), the world's largest regional security organization, comprised of fifty-seven states spanning from Vancouver to Vladivostok, hosts a multistakeholder partnership: the Alliance against Trafficking in Persons (Alliance). The first OSCE special representative and coordinator for Combating Trafficking in Human Beings (SR), Helga Konrad, proposed establishing an informal platform among IGOs and NGOs active in fighting trafficking. Consultations with the OSCE's chairperson-in-office and secretary general, member states, and heads of other IGOs spurred the Alliance's formation in July 2004. Konrad and her successors as SR have since chaired the Alliance, which is now comprised of some forty stakeholder institutions (OSCE 2014). The first meeting of the Alliance embraced an informal model for exchange of information and best practices. Input from other IGOs led to establishment of a smaller group of experts, the Alliance Expert Coordination Team (AECT), representing the same organizations at the working level, which meets twice a year in Vienna to share trends, methods, and avoid duplication. AECT meetings have yielded common understandings on such issues as protection and shelters for victims, national rapporteurs, and the protection of migrant, unaccompanied, and asylum-seeking children.

The annual Alliance conference facilitates a high-level dialogue between national authorities, civil society, and other stakeholders in the OSCE region. The tenth Alliance meeting focused, for instance, on a particularly hidden form of trafficking, domestic servitude (OSCE 2014). That the Alliance members pay their own way to meetings and events shows how concretely they value the forum.

This array of some of the most promising and potential efforts reinforces the huge need for the research and mapping of trafficking in order to advance human dignity and its elusive realization.

Partnerships for Protection

Focus #2: Victim Identification

In terms of dignity, one might say that the most morally urgent focus of antitrafficking work (even more than prosecution and prevention) is the protection of known, suffering victims. To offer protection, one has to first find victims. This is no easy matter as human trafficking is an underground economic and criminal activity. Moreover, victims are often treated as criminals acting on their own volition (e.g., in prostitution or undocumented migration) and worthy of detention, deportation, scorn, or apathy. Perpetrators use this fact to intimidate victims into not fleeing from their literal or psychological grip—suggesting if they do flee, they will only be treated as criminals or deportable, irregular migrants. And because victims are frightened of law enforcement and immigration officials, these officers need institutional partners to assist in their efforts.

For instance, Brazil has a substantial forced labor problem, most notably in the Amazon region, where victims clear fields to raise cattle and produce charcoal to heat pig iron for making steel. The Ford Motor Company uncovered the latter problem, which arose when it was discovered this activity had been contaminating steel supplies for its cars (Ford 2010-2011). Cognizant of its legacy of colonial slavery, Brazil's government has partnered with NGOs, businesses, and the ILO to address human trafficking for labor-related exploitation. With dedicated US funding support for Brazil, which was among eight target countries under a Bush presidential initiative, and long-term technical advice from the ILO, Brazil's Ministry of Labor has created mobile inspection teams to find and liberate forced laborers—5,016 in 2008, 3,769 in 2009, 2,617 in 2010, 2,428 in 2011, and 2,560 in 2012 (TIP Reports 2009, 2010, 2011, 2012, 2013). Despite the overall decline in numbers, this is a remarkable effort to identify and assist victims.

Another example is a partnership of government, NGOs, and the business community. The US Department of Health and Human Services (HHS) contracted with an NGO to run the primary national hotline for human trafficking. After awarding its first contract to an NGO partner that provided only limited language services and had an inadequate capacity for reliably answering calls, HHS awarded and renewed the contract twice to the Polaris Project during both Republican and Democratic presidential administrations. Its National Human Trafficking Resource Center (NHTRC) hotline (1-888-373-7888) offers not only information and training but also a place for victims, or those suspecting they have come across victims, to call. The hotline can quickly connect the latter to law enforcement. The LexisNexis Group made an in-kind contribution to Polaris by designing and building an elaborate searchable database allowing the NHTRC to refer callers to law enforcement and service providers countrywide—applying a comparative competency to extend the capacity of HHS and Polaris (LexisNexis 2009). Now Google has funded Polaris to share its model for setting up hotlines for victim identification in countries around the world. The statistics for the number of calls and victims assisted have grown markedly (Polaris Project 2011).[2]

A more troubling case on victim identification was in Cambodia, roughly between 2005 and 2007. The US *TIP Report*, by design of the US Congress in the TVPA, assesses other governments' efforts to combat trafficking by assigning one of four possible rankings: Tier 1 (best), Tier 2, Tier 2 Watch List, and Tier 3 (representing minimal government will or effort to address the problem). It can spur action in other governments to combat human trafficking by threatening sanctions and limiting nonhumanitarian aid to countries with the lowest tier ranking of Tier 3. The TVPA (and the Palermo Protocol to the UN Convention on Organized Crime, also finalized in 2000) emphasizes prosecution of victims. Thus, when Cambodia received Tier 3, its illiberal government interpreted it to mean they needed to lock up more criminals in the sex trade, which sadly included many prostituted girls and women (Doyle 2006). As a result, some institutional arrangements have not only advanced victim identification but also have temporarily hindered victim identification. Clearer US diplomacy and partnership with and training of Cambodian law enforcement in international agencies and NGOs, such as International Justice Mission, have improved the situation (earning Cambodia Tier 2, the second highest possible ranking in the last five years, 2008–2012).

In short, partnerships for victim identification need government will, the understanding of and training on the nature of who is a victim, and actors outside the public sector extending capacity beyond law enforcement, whose officers are sometimes intimidating to victims. If institutions lack these qualities, they cannot help victims reclaim their dignity by the necessary first step: finding them.

Focus #3: Survivors' Immediate Care

In addition to providing safety from traffickers, victim protection is typically interpreted as furnishing housing, food, and medical and counseling services for physical and psychological traumas induced by trafficking. Numerous global partnerships have emphasized immediate care and service (vice longer term empowerment), given the connotation of the word "protection" embedded in the Palermo Protocol and many States-Parties' national laws conforming to it.

One domestic example is the Salvation Army STOP-IT Program, a Chicago-based initiative that works with national and Chicago-area organizations to provide psychological treatment, residential placement, and support services for victims of sex trafficking. One of STOP-IT's most productive partnerships resulted in the success of Operation Little Girl Lost, a yearlong, undercover investigation undertaken by Chicago law enforcement working in concert with social service providers. Officers from the Cook County Sheriff's police vice unit, the US Attorney's office, the federally created High Intensity Drug Trafficking Area (HIDTA) program, the Federal Bureau of Investigation (FBI), and the State Attorney's federally funded Human Trafficking Unit—together constituting the Chicago Task Force on Human Trafficking—worked to target street gang members who had sex-trafficked women and children (Alvarez 2011). Although this collaboration had important prosecution-related dimensions (arrests of more than fifty customers and nine offenders trafficking women in the Chicago area), the immediate victim protection is noteworthy. Working alongside law enforcement, STOP-IT and the International Organization for Adolescents (IOFA) joined numerous raids to promptly address the needs of the recovered victims, synthesizing efforts by government and nongovernment local service providers to more efficiently allocate resources and training (Salvation Army 2013; Sweeney 2012). In this case, one sees not only a key role of an NGO in a governance partnership within this focus area but a faith-based actor, as discussed by Nicole Bibbins Sedaca in chapter 13 in this book.

Another energetic diplomatic actor besides the United States has been the Government of the Philippines. Citizens of the Philippines are migrant workers from all over the world, and the remittances to family members are the second highest in Asia, accounting for some 9 percent of the nation's GDP

(Huang, Rahman, and Yoeh 2005). Most embassies of the Philippines in nations with a substantial number of Filipino citizens run shelters for human trafficking victims who are running away from their exploitation—from domestic servitude to construction work. This is true in Gulf Arab States where placement fees to labor recruiters, sponsorship laws, holding of passports by employers, and treatment of foreigners and women as lesser human beings make legal, documented guest workers vulnerable to human trafficking. By running shelters and engaging the host government about their citizens (rather than ignoring the problem as numerous other governments do for fear of bad relations with host governments, which could hinder contracting access for work visas and hence remittances), these diplomatic entities extend global governance and the realization of dignity. It cannot be called ad hoc because it is the concerted policy of the Government of the Philippines, which moreover forms complementary relationships with NGOs offering immediate care for victims.

These varied cases show that immediate victim care requires more than physical shelters, benefits from nimble NGO cooperation with governments, and even benefits from governments engaging one another.

Focus #4: Survivors' Long-Term Economic Viability

Finding, sheltering, and offering basic services to trafficking victims are not enough. Re-empowerment requires survivors to be capable of making a living wage and re-integrating themselves into the population and society.

The Emancipation Network (TEN), also known as Made by Survivors, provides projects to this end through education and economic empowerment. By working closely with a dozen partner agencies in Nepal, India, Thailand, Cambodia, Uganda, and the United States, TEN offers employment to over one thousand survivors and education to two hundred former victims as well as their children.

TEN has a partnership with a local Indian NGO called the Rescue Foundation. Their shelter in Boisar, India, houses one hundred young slavery survivors on a forty-acre farm an hour from Mumbai, India, where Rescue Foundation—the largest child rescue agency in India as an NGO accredited by Government of the State of Maharastra—pulls hundreds of minors each year from that megacity's Kamathipura red light district. Finding sustainable employment for older girls and young adults is difficult, given the stigma surrounding prostitution and the lack of local jobs for poor, untrained women. The partnership trains survivors in renewable energy management, agriculture, and animal husbandry to help them reintegrate into their communities.

They work in a biogas plant designed to recycle dung from the farm's cattle. The complex, in turn, provides dairy products and fuel for the shelter. Surplus energy and dairy products are subsequently sold locally to provide sustainable income for the survivors and the shelter. This holistic approach gives survivors tools to thrive in the long term—to apply their agency—and gives them a stake in the robust sustainability of their community.

Another institution in India has advanced long-term economic empowerment to survivors of modern-day slavery. The *Pragati Gramodyog evam Samaj-kalyan Sansthan* (PGS) is a nonprofit organization that offers comprehensive services to stonebreakers in debt bondage to help achieve sustainable freedom. To accomplish this objective, PGS has partnered with the international nonprofit Free the Slaves (FTS) while working closely with the government of India and local banks.

PGS partnerships have been particularly successful in helping hundreds of families free themselves from enslavement in stone quarry sites located within the Allahabad province. For example, PGS has created self-help groups (SHGs) that include freed laborers as well as others who are at risk of falling prey to the debt-bondage phenomenon. Once the groups are in place, PGS engages the local government to acquire cooperative quarry lease licenses for this newly formed community. When leases are issued, the laborers are then able to capitalize on the skills they have already developed, collectively manage the sites, and generate their own incomes. To facilitate these efforts, PGS assists SHG members to persuade village leaders to purchase stones quarried by nonbonded laborers for local projects. In the village of Rajgarh, this particular model enjoyed a tangible impact. There, bonded stonebreakers were encouraged to escape their slaveholders to work on a SHG quarry site, where they finally earned salaries three times what they were paid by their previous employers (Free the Slaves 2014).

Prior to these interventions, breaking free from debt bondage was virtually impossible. If families fled, they met the harsh reality of acute poverty; opportunities for these landless and unskilled workers were almost entirely absent (Singh and Tripathi 2010). By leveraging resources and linking these individuals to government employment programs, trafficking survivors have been empowered to start small businesses and other income-yielding activities. Collaboration between PGS, the SHGs, banks, and the District Development Office has helped over 1,900 SHG members assert their inherent value by providing them with the economic, legal and social tools, as well as opportunities they need to thrive. The agency, prosperity, and dignity of this population have been extended (Free the Slaves 2014).

In this focus area, there is a clear need for businesses to train and hire survivors of human trafficking. ManpowerGroup, a global labor placement firm focusing on neutralizing scurrilous labor recruiters who lure victims into human trafficking situations, can play a significant role. Yet many businesses without these special motivations can offer jobs as partners of government and NGOs. Businesses' aversion to the risk ascribed to hiring a trafficking survivor is as unfortunate as it is predictable. US antitrafficking Ambassador Luis Cde-Baca envisions NGOs and businesses maintaining a joint database to help match jobs with the specific skill sets of victims. Businesses should audit their supply chains for signs of trafficking and commit marketing resources for raising awareness, but they especially should not lose sight of the fact that they are in a unique position to offer survivors the key to a new life: employment.

Partnerships for Prosecution

Focus #5: Bringing Traffickers to Justice

A key aspect of helping trafficking survivors reclaim their dignity is to bring to justice those who sought to rob that dignity. This *P*—prosecution—is emphasized above all other goals in the Palermo Protocol and TVPA.

To this end, the International Justice Mission (IJM) has had great success partnering with local authorities in the Philippines as a part of their Project Lantern. Over five years, IJM has sought to document that, when antitrafficking laws are enforced by well-trained and equipped police and courts, children are less vulnerable to traffickers. As a major global institution (as seen in its work to address HIV/AIDS, treated elsewhere in this book), the Bill and Melinda Gates Foundation funded a new IJM office in Cebu to work in tandem with the local police to have one hundred suspected traffickers arrested and successfully charged in that metropolitan area. External researchers found that the number of minors available for exploitation in the commercial sex industry in the Cebu metro area dropped 79 percent from what their initial study showed four years earlier, just before IJM began its casework in partnership with Cebu authorities (Haugen and Boutros 2014, 244). They also found measurable increases in law enforcement activity that addressed sex trafficking cases and in the commitment of law enforcement officers trained through the project to resolving the cases. IJM is replicating the project in Manila and Angeles City (in northern Luzon) and hopes to continue its work worldwide (IJM 2010). These local efforts reveal how partnerships not only yield greater prosecutions but also tangibly contribute to the crime's prevention (Haugen and Boutros 2014).

On the other hand, the Government of Brazil has had an anemic record on bringing perpetrators of forced labor to justice. Unfortunately, the active partnerships between the Ministry of Labor and ILO discussed above to identify victims have not yielded punishments for those responsible for forced labor. There are three reasons for this. First, powerful landholding interests continue to influence the legislative and executive branches of Brazil's government. As a result, although 2,560 victims of forced labor were rescued by government personnel in 2012, only 10 percent of those victims had a prosecution launched to hold a perpetrator to account. Second, the Brazilian judicial system does not move cases through its courts quickly—whereby justice delayed is justice denied. Third, judges sentencing perpetrators of forced labor tend to suspend or reduce sentences. In 2012, for example, thirty-nine people were convicted of slave labor (*trabalho escravo*), which includes more general forms of exhausting and degrading labor broader than human trafficking. Of these sentences, many were commuted to community service while others were given short terms in halfway houses (vice prisons). While convictions rose from 2011 to 2012, the figures remain minuscule compared to the thousands of victims rescued and the over 25,000 total victims estimated in the 2011 US *TIP Report* (TIP Reports 2011, 2012, 2013). Regrettably, efforts of the Brazilian Labor Ministry, ILO, NGOs, and enlightened businesses do not seem to be galvanizing law enforcement, prosecutors, and judges to yield prosecutions and especially convictions. This is a gaping hole in progress.

A last example is the partnership between States-Parties to the Palermo Protocol and the UNODC. UNODC, under Executive Director Antonio Maria Costa, emphasized a UN Global Initiative to Fight Trafficking (UN.GIFT), largely an exercise in holding conferences funded by princes of Gulf Arab States with problematic records on addressing human trafficking (Report of the Vienna Forum 2008). (To his credit, Costa stressed that partnerships should be the fourth *P*, beyond those cited in the Palermo Protocol, prior to then secretary of state Hillary Clinton's statement to the same effect.) His successor in 2010, Yuri Fedotov, has championed a Voluntary Trust Fund for Victims of Human Trafficking. This admirable idea seems clearly outside the core competency of a UN agency devoted to law enforcement against transnational organized crime. To the degree UNODC advances prosecution, it is through urging UN member states to sign and ratify the Palermo Protocol and to implement laws conforming to that treaty based on model laws UNODC and UN.GIFT have developed (Brusca 2011, 8–20). Yet, what appears to fit its core competency but be grossly underemphasized is technical assistance to states for implementing those laws once they are in place. As

Gary Haugen and Victor Boutros of the United States and Irene Khan of Bangladesh have noted, the gap between rule of law on paper (treaties and legislation) and enforced justice is acute (Haugen and Boutros 2010; Khan 2009).

Partnerships could contribute more to holding traffickers accountable in two ways. First, victim rehabilitation is crucial to successful prosecutions. Stabilizing survivors wracked by physical and psychological trauma is not only important in and of itself, but it makes for more willing witnesses to assist law enforcement with investigating, prosecuting, and convicting perpetrators. There is a temptation to use leverage on victims, for example, detaining them and withholding immigration relief from migrants until they cooperate with law enforcement. This is flatly wrongheaded. Instead, law enforcement needs well-resourced government and NGO social service providers to support witnesses so their traffickers can be held accountable.

Second, governments need labor inspectors to partner with law enforcement personnel, who often work only in isolated bureaucratic silos. Although victim rescue and protection is a moral imperative, law enforcement bodies need to be given access to evidence for a prosecution. Otherwise, a victim's access to justice will never be fully realized. While serving as US antitrafficking ambassador, I met Burmese girls victimized in the seafood-processing industry in Thailand. I subsequently urged collaboration in Thailand between labor inspectors and law enforcement, which appears to have taken place (TIP Reports 2010, 2011, 2012, 2013). Similar cooperation in Brazil could help advance the heretofore lagging punishment of traffickers.

Partnerships for Prevention

Focus #6: Preventive Awareness and Training Initiatives

Of the three pillars of the UN Palermo Protocol on Trafficking in Persons, beyond prosecution and protection, is prevention. A sixth focus area in which to examine the capacity of global institutions and partnerships in the major area of prevention is awareness campaigns and training.

For instance, the goal of World Vision Cambodia (WVC) is to empower communities to build a better future for Cambodia's children. To target human trafficking, WVC began collaborating with DHS. The work of these partners is a component of the DHS initiative called The Blue Campaign. The Blue Campaign is the banner under which the DHS unites its various antitrafficking programs. One element of the Blue Campaign attempted to prevent trafficking by publicizing the legal consequences for human traffickers. WVC coordinated this effort to illustrate the illegality of child sex tourism and created billboards within the country that evocatively showed why travelers should not participate in this industry. Captions read: "Abuse a child in this country, go to jail in yours," and "I am not a tourist attraction." This second caption is superimposed over a black and white photo of a child. These signs make it clear that child predators will be caught, which alludes to the training of law enforcement officials and newly enacted legislation that protect vulnerable youth throughout the world. The billboards also include a twenty-four-hour hotline number staffed by operators who are prepared to receive any reports of suspicious activity. This engages the entire community in preventative efforts by establishing a venue for reporting suspected trafficking.

This effort, coupled with the work of the Cambodian antitrafficking forces, international regulations, and the large-scale work by both World Vision and the US Office of Immigration and Customs Enforcement, prompted a crackdown on child sex tourism following its implementation. The arrest of at least eight alleged foreign pedophiles in 2006 demonstrated to the world Cambodia's commitment to decreasing the impunity for sex traffickers within the country. Though these highly publicized arrests and the very visible billboards show that traffickers will be prosecuted, these efforts have not been enough to come close to eradicating the practice within Cambodia. An IJM investigator and Chanthol Oung, executive director of the Cambodian Women's Crisis Center, said that the recent arrests—although causes for celebration—have prompted increased sophistication on the part of traffickers. Oung said that the government will need to allocate much greater amounts of legal and physical resources to convict the child predators (Naly 2004).

 manpowerGroup is a major global labor placement, multinational corporation helping employers with both long-term and short-term workforce solutions. It specializes in training to improve the competitiveness of its talent pool. ManpowerGroup partners with the nonprofit organization, Verité. By working directly with individual companies to ensure that their supply chains employ fair labor recruitment practices, this partnership decreases the incidence of human trafficking (ManpowerGroup 2012).

Verité created the initiative Help Wanted to research the ways in which current labor recruitment practices can lead to human trafficking. Help Wanted publicizes this research so that the private sector, civil society organizations, and governmental institutions can stem trafficking. Its publications outline a fair hiring framework for businesses and a template for winnowing exploitative practices in supply chains (Verité 2013). Help Wanted research demonstrates how continued profits are dependent upon maintenance of fair, nonexploitative labor practices, in order to avoid legal risk, harm to brand value and company reputation, and threats to investment and financing (Verité 2010). The Verité model is based on working with businesses and establishing profit-driven interests as well as moral bases of combating trafficking. The vitality of a Manpower-Verité collaboration compared to most business-NGO partnerships lies in the similarity of premises and goals, and the complementarity of assets.

A problematic example of an awareness campaign has been MTV Exit, an NGO that seeks to raise awareness of human trafficking in Asia through music, films, and concerts. Because it is not formally part of the MTV corporation, MTV corporate resources do not fund the project—it just lends its brand name. Its partners (i.e., funders) have included the US Agency for International Development (USAID), the counterpart agency Australian Aid, and the Association of Southeast Asian Nations (ASEAN). Circa 2005–2008, MTV Exit's video and film messaging was distinctly murky with regard to sex trafficking demand. In that period, USAID funded MTV Exit videos and public service announcements in India, which suggested that if a viewer was a purchaser of commercial sex that he or she should not contribute to human trafficking.[3] One does not need to wholly equate prostitution to human trafficking to recognize that a basic problem of commercial sex is the enabling environment of sex trafficking (prostitution for all minors, seen under the law as lacking meaningful consent and for adults being subjected to force, fraud, or coercion). (This is not to mention MTV as a separate entity simultaneously celebrating imagery and language of pimps in videos, again in the enabling environment of sex trafficking.) Since then, MTV has sought to mobilize young activists through live and filmed concerts, featuring major music and acting entertainers as headliners. Although it spurs younger people to engage in social media on this issue, it is not clear where the MTV Exit content creates textured awareness, as human trafficking is a classic case of the perils of knowing a little (such as incorrectly thinking that it is chiefly about children, when the ILO suggests they are only 25 percent of its victims; that it is abduction; that it refers to human smuggling; or that it requires physical violence). By comparison, CNN's Freedom Project (sponsored by corporate partners), which aired news stories and documentary films since 2011, including highlighting best practices of changemakers, offers qualitative awareness. As a function of ASEAN sponsorship, the content has also downplayed the responsibility and accountability of states in Asia—given the so-called ASEAN way—as an operating mode not interfering in the sovereign political decision making of its member states (Tavares 2009).

In short, to be transformative, institutional partnerships for awareness and training need partners unanimously committed to systematically reducing human trafficking's impact, forming useful content, targeting suitable audiences of the content, and giving those audiences a meaningful way to act to incrementally contribute to the advancement of dignity.

Focus #7: Preventive Anti-Demand Efforts

The cases of WVC, MTV Exit, and Verité point to a second area of preventive work for antitrafficking partnerships: addressing the demand side of the equation. WVC in part sought to deter those euphemized as "child sex tourists" from creating demand for child sex trafficking. MTV Exit's messaging in part condoned sex buying and failed to address demand. Verité's training materials recognize how consumer demand for lower prices militates companies to look for cheap labor, requiring them to put in place robust vetting of labor recruitment practices. Preventive demand reduction represents a seventh focus area of its own.

Returning to the rich case of Brazil, the Brazilian government publicizes a so-called Dirty List of companies implicated in forced labor, which are denied both public and private financing. This stigma uses market demand to force the companies to change. The knowledge to the consumer in Brazil of companies responsible for such forced labor—heightened by denial of financing— applied a market force against the dignity-denying practice. The Ford Motor Company discovered that forced labor in the Amazon was applied to making charcoal, which in turn was used to smelt pig iron, which in turn was used to make steel for export to the United States in Ford automobiles. With the stick of the Dirty List and the carrot of support from the ILO and a Bush presidential funding initiative, Brazilian businesses established a partnership to inspect supply chains for forced labor—the Citizen's Charcoal Institute. This is one of the best-documented case studies of how businesses, NGOs, authorities, and the ILO have worked together to counteract the demand for cheap inputs and labor feeding into its supply chain (Ford 2010/2011).

There are a number of examples and assessments of child sex trafficking demand prevention efforts in the developing world (Vidyamali and Burton 2007). Yet let us take an example in the United States, pertinent worldwide to the trend of sex trafficking moving from the street and brothel setting to being sold via the internet. "Adult services" advertisements on Craigslist.com and Backpage.com have been proven to enable trafficking of young women and girls, as testimonies of survivors validate. After weathering a similar wave of popular disapproval and pressure from state-level attorneys-general, Craigslist.com eliminated this section of its website. However, because the *Village Voice* makes an estimated $22 million from these advertisements and has seen profits rise as it gained Craigslist.com's business, it has resisted following suit (Pompeo 2012).

A multistakeholder partnership focused on both legal and publicity dimensions has worked to shrink an enabling environment for trafficking. The Coalition Against Trafficking in Women (CATW), an advocacy NGO, operates in fifteen countries and every major region of the world. It sponsored multiple protests in front of the *Village Voice* headquarters, coordinated and catalyzed other groups' calls for the elimination of *Backpage*'s adult ads, and encouraged two sets of key public officials to call for the same (CATW 2011, 2012; Office of Koster 2012). First, attorneys general from forty-eight states issued a statement describing Backpage.com as a sex trafficking hub (notably for minors) and called for the organization to reform its practices (Office of Blumenthal 2012; Office of Kirk 2012). Second, a bipartisan coalition of US senators issued a Sense of the Senate resolution calling on Village Voice Media to end its facilitation of human trafficking by eliminating the adult services section of their website. The senators also wrote to forty companies to inform them that their advertising host (*Village Voice*) owns *Backpage*, that *Backpage* facilitates trafficking, and that they should leverage their economic influence to force *Village Voice* to change *Backpage* policy (Powers 2012). Shortly after this letter was distributed, six major companies indicated that they would discontinue their advertisements with Village Voice Media in response to the senators' letters. This partnership of NGOs and public officials brought the leverage of a third actor, the corporate sector, to bear.

Another partnership is slaveryfootprint.org, created by musician and filmmaker Justin Dillon. Based on consumer awareness of their "carbon footprint" affecting their demand for climate change-inducing goods and services, Dillon consulted Stanford scholars on how to create a website and app related to human trafficking. As one of its signature efforts since 2010, the US State Department antitrafficking office has funded the demand-focused prevention effort. One enters the website, answers a few questions about one's lifestyle, gets an estimate of the number of slaves (human trafficking victims) that that lifestyle relies upon, and is then encouraged to contact companies and urge them to strengthen their antitrafficking supply chain auditing. I asked Notre Dame undergraduate research assistant Nicole Michels to go on the website, and she wrote to me:

> [T]hrough the use of simple animations, colorful graphics and sets of questions about consumption and lifestyle, slaveryfootprint.org is able to guide the consumer to a state of reflective self-analysis. However, it's not clear what to do after finishing the quiz. I was informed that fifty-two slaves contributed

to my lifestyle and then had the option to click on the "take action" button. . . . [W]ould-be advocates can call for antislavery reform by sending a note to companies, spreading the word through social networks, donating money to antislavery campaigns, and lobbying government representatives. The entire process relies on cursory questions to connect lifestyles to their consequences when really the problem is much deeper.

Although it aptly addresses demand, slaveryfootprint.org as an NGO partnership with a government agency falls short for two reasons. First, the back of the envelope calculation of the number of slaves supporting a lifestyle is the antithesis of the research and baselines Focus Area #1 requires. Second, antidemand partnership needs to choose between working with companies (e.g., Verité) or challenging them publicly (e.g., CATW); it is unclear which slavery footprint represents, if either.

Although these last two examples are merely suggestive (if highly so) as opposed to being empirically conclusive about potential impact on dignity in truly global multistakeholder partnerships, one can see some lessons for preventive antidemand partnerships. To succeed, partnerships require both addressing the demand forces propelling gross and violent exploitation in labor (e.g., charcoal in producing pig iron) and sexual (e.g., child prostitution) domains. They must apply the capacity of complementary actors in the public sector, corporate, and civil society to create transformative leverage.

Partnerships for Resources

Focus #8: Marshaling and Coordinating Funding

Finally, it requires resources for collective action against human trafficking to tangibly impact dignity—empowering those people already victimized, reducing its incidence based on baselines, and ultimately abolishing it as a modern form of slavery. Moreover, efforts and resources must be coordinated. Here, two cases of partnerships are instructive.

Humanity United is a philanthropy underwritten by Pierre and Pamela Omidyar, based on money made in the growth of eBay, for which the former helped lead. Imbued with a Silicon Valley ethic of metrics, engaging the private sector, and encouraging social entrepreneurship, it funds efforts in two areas: (1) fighting mass atrocities and their aftermath through postconflict peace building, and (2) human trafficking. Its basic model is the same in both areas: funding specific projects of NGOs globally and once an NGO proves to be a change-maker, funding its general operational budget with no strings attached but one. That one condition is membership in an NGO coalition designed to coordinate interventions, speak with a unified voice to government entities about their own policy and funding priorities, and avoid competition with each other based on a fundraising imperative.

In the human trafficking area, the result is ATEST. This alliance includes organizations with varied comparative competencies—in trafficking globally or in the United States, involving migrants or countries' citizens of countries, for labor or sexual exploitation, of adults or other minors. Perhaps ATEST's success over time is not just coordinating the resources of its own members (grantees) but encouraging other key actors to markedly increase resources (e.g., the US government or the Gates Foundation to address this problem as the latter addresses HIV/AIDS) and to coordinate their application with others (O'Connor 2012).

Let us return to the example of UNODC and the UN.GIFT initiative it launched as a global partnership to combat human trafficking. After the 2000 Palermo Protocol (for which UNODC is bureaucratically responsible) came into effect in 2003, UNODC chaired the established UN interagency group related to combating human trafficking, including, for instance, other agencies such as the UN Children's Fund (UNICEF) and the ILO, which address particular dimensions of the problem. UNODC launched the UN.GIFT Initiative ostensibly to better coordinate efforts to fight human trafficking, based on seed money from the United Arab Emirates. Officials of their partner agencies in UN.GIFT, such as the ILO, IOM, or the Organization for Security and Co-operation in Europe (OSCE), have told me they did not experience enhanced resource or programmatic coordination from UNODC. Major resources were not mobilized, other than from the United Arab Emirates, eager to be seen backing multilateral efforts as the trafficking problem festered at home, as it still does today according to the UN Special Rapporteur on the issue (UNOHCHR 2012). The product was chiefly conferences, model laws, trainings for businesses and legislators, and some dedicated reports.

The examples of Humanity United and UN.GIFT suggest that global partnerships can mobilize and coordinate use of resources if parochial institutional interests can be bridged with an ethic of complementarity and growing the pie. In global efforts to address human trafficking, the former does more of that (albeit chiefly with US-headquartered actors), and the latter has not.

Partnerships Which Advance Dignity

Of the antitrafficking partnerships discussed above, some have proven to be more fruitful than others. What distinguishes between a limited impact, higher impact, and a truly transformative partnership, in terms of the two fundamental elements of human dignity, which global institutions should advance (as raised in Anthony Clark Arend's and my introduction to this book) are: agency and social recognition. To advance the agency and social recognition that victims or potential victims of human trafficking enjoy, there are four common denominators or four *M*'s.

First, market mechanisms matter. A partnership must account for the supply of trafficking victims (e.g., children detached from family and regular and irregular migrants) and demand (for cheap products, cheap labor, and purchased sex). Brazil's Dirty List and CATW engage the latter, while slaveryfootprint.org and MTV Exit do so poorly. Moreover, it needs to account for the natural competition between actors—international organizations or NGOs seeking leadership roles, prominence, or funding at the expense of others. Humanity United has done this well, UN.GIFT has not.

Second, metrics matter. Collective action needs to have a sense of the problem and its extent in order to choose interventions and measure progress. Other activities need a serious empirical basis. If actionable big data does not exist, and mutual empirical understanding fails to bridge specialists respectively in data analytics and human trafficking, dreams of disrupting trafficking networks will founder. Or, in borrowing the powerful concept of carbon footprint from the sustainability field, if slaveryfootprint.org offers only the roughest of estimates of how many human trafficking victims support a consumer's lifestyle based on a handful of questions, it is not a very sustainable means for affecting consumer demand.

Third, matching missions matter. For a multistakeholder institution to succeed, its partners need to have aligned goals. For instance, Verité as a nonconfrontational NGO and the ManpowerGroup as a global human resources company both had interests and normative values that converged.

Finally, motives matter. Not only must the partners (governments, international organizations, NGOs, foundations, businesses) have matching intent, but they need good and sound intent. Unsound intent is seen in a business pursuing window-dressing corporate social responsibility or discrete philanthropy without addressing human trafficking in its business operations or supply chains; an NGO more focused on fundraising, celebrities, and galas than programmatic impact; or an international organization seeking to raise money from dubious sources and places itself at the front of a parade of sister organizations. Lacking the determination to do more, partnerships pursuing worthy interventions fall short of transformative impact. For instance, Brazil's government devoted labor inspectors to find and rescue some 2,560 forced labor victims in 2012 but did not partner the inspectors with law enforcement successfully enough to prosecute the victims' tormenters more than 10 percent of the time in order to better serve the social recognition and hence the dignity of those victims.

This book relies upon a number of Kantian notions. It focuses on the value of embedding rule of law and participatory governance in global institutions. Moreover, Kant's idea that all people have inherent and equal value and must never be treated as mere means animates the proposal that human dignity should be the primary aim of those global institutions. Yet here, another concept from Immanuel Kant's ethics is pertinent: actions should be judged by their intent. Institutional partnerships should be as well.

In short, the fourth of the four *P*'s to fight human trafficking—partnerships—need these four *M*'s. A partnership that is attentive to market forces, takes metrics seriously, has matching missions, and exhibits sound motives is more likely to be transformative—to help survivors reclaim dignity and actually reduce or abolish the ongoing threat to potential victims. A partnership lacking one or more of these qualities is increasingly likely to resemble cotton candy—sweet, colorful fluff.

Notes

Many thanks go to Mathew Caldwell, Nicole Michels, and Andrew Reddie for superb research assistance and input into this chapter.

1. In full disclosure and regarding objectivity, I edited and supervised the production of this report for two years.

2. As the former CEO of Polaris and later a LexisNexis adviser, I may not be the source to offer a wholly unbiased assessment of the impact of the hotline.

3. As State Department antitrafficking director from 2007 to 2009, I raised concerns but the partnerships with MTV Exit continued.

References

Alvarez, Anita. 2011. "State's Attorney Announces Charges in Joint Undercover Human Trafficking Investigation: Operation 'Little Girl Lost' Targets Chicago Street Gang Members." Office of Cook County State's Attorney, August 24. http://www.statesattorney.org/index2/press_littlegirllost01.html.

Bales, Kevin. (1999) 2004. *Disposable People: New Slavery in the Global Economy*. Berkeley: University of California Press.

Brusca, Carol S. 2011. "Palermo Protocol: The First Ten Years after Adoption." *Global Security Studies* 2 (3): 8–20.

Clinton, Hillary Rodham. 2009. "Partnering Against Trafficking." *Washington Post.* July 17. http://articles.washingtonpost.com/2009-06-17/opinions/36784296_1_sexual-exploitation-prostitution-human-rights.

Coalition Against Trafficking in Women (CATW). 2011. "Join Us to Protest Backpage .com's Facilitation of Sex Trafficking in Front of Its New York City Headquarters."

Coalition Against Trafficking in Women (CATW). Accessed September 1, 2013. http://action.web.ca/home/catw/readingroom.shtml?x=131995&AA_EX_Session=b c14d6e2771b697ba391122c2ade1e41.

———. 2012. "Leading Human Rights Groups CATW & PRE to Protest Village Voice Media in NYC on 6/20/2012." Coalition Against Trafficking in Women (CATW). Accessed September 1, 2013. http://action.web.ca/home/catw/readingroom.shtml ?x=133517.

Doyle, Kevin. 2006. "Cambodia's Child Sex Crackdown." *Time Magazine*, October 5. http://www.time.com/time/world/printout/0,8816,1543174,00.html.

Ford Motor Company. 2010/2011. "Case Study: Forced Labor in the Pig Iron Supply Chain in Brazil." Ford Motor Company. Accessed September 1, 2013. http://corporate.ford.com/microsites/sustainability-report-2010-11/issues-supply-materials-brazil.

Free The Slaves. 2014. "Our Work: Frontline Partners—India." Accessed April 9, 2014. https://www.freetheslaves.net/india/.

Haugen, Gary, and Victor Boutros. 2010. "And Justice for All: Enforcing Human Rights for the World's Poor." *Foreign Affairs* 89 (3): 51–62.

———. 2014. *The Locust Effect: Why the End of Poverty Requires the End of Violence.* New York: Oxford University Press, 242–57.

Huang, Shirlena, Noor Abdul Rahman, and Brenda S. A. Yoeh, eds. 2005. *Asian Women as Transnational Domestic Workers.* Singapore: Marshall Cavendish Academic.

International Justice Mission (IJM). 2010. "Project Lantern: Game-Changing Results in the Fight against Trafficking." International Justice Mission. Accessed September 1, 2013. http://www.ijm.org/projectlantern.

International Labour Organisation (ILO). 2008. *Combating Forced Labour: A Handbook for Employers and Business.* Geneva: International Labour Organization.

———. 2012. "New ILO Global Estimate of Forced Labour: 20.9 million victims." International Labour Organization. June 01. http://www.ilo.org/global/about-the-ilo /newsroom/news/WCMS_182109/lang–en/index.htm.

Kelley, Judith, and Beth Simmons. 2014. "Politics by Number: Indicators as Social Pressure in International Relations." *American Journal of Political Science.* Forthcoming.

Khan, Irene. 2009. *The Unheard Truth: Poverty and Human Rights.* New York: W. W. Norton and Company.

LexisNexis. 2009. "Polaris Project and LexisNexis Form Public-Private Partnership to Fight Human Trafficking." LexisNexis. May 27. http://www.lexisnexis.com/risk/news events/press-release.aspx?Id=1256036772792737.

ManpowerGroup. 2012. "Ethical Framework for International Labor Recruitment." ManpowerGroup. Accessed September 1, 2013. http://www.manpowergroup.com /wps/wcm/connect/manpowergroup-en/home/social-responsibility/social-impact /human-trafficking/ethical-framework-for-international-labor#.UhUMv5KkobE.

Mehran, Farhad, and Michaëlle de Cock. 2012. "ILO Global Estimate of Forced Labour: Results and Methodology." Geneva: International Labour Office–Special Action Programme to Combat Forced Labour (SAP-FL).

Naly, Sok. 2004. "Abuse a Child in this Country—Go to Jail in Yours." World Vision Cambodia. July 8. http://www.worldvision.org.kh/newsdet_25.html.

O'Connor, Clare. 2012. "Inside eBay Billionaire Pierre Omidyar's Battle to End Human Trafficking," *Forbes.* November 08. http://www.forbes.com/sites/clareoconnor/2012 /11/08/inside-ebay-billionaire-pierre-omidyars-battle-to-end-human-trafficking/3/.

Office of Missouri Attorney General Chris Koster. 2012. "State Attorneys General Reject Backpage Demand." Office of Missouri Attorney General Chris Koster. May 23. http://ago.mo.gov/newsreleases/2012/State_attorney_generals_reject_demand/.

Office of Senator Mark Kirk. 2012. "Senators Call for Backpage to End Ads Promoting Child Prostitution." Office of Senator Mark Kirk. May 2. http://www.kirk.senate.gov /?p=press_release&id=479.

Office of Senator Richard Blumenthal. 2012. "Senators Call on Backpage to End Human Trafficking through Adult Services Advertising." Office of Senator Richard Blumenthal. Accessed September 1, 2013. http://www.blumenthal.senate.gov/newsroom /press/release/senators-call-on-backpage-to-end-human-trafficking-through-adult -services-advertising.

Organization for Security and Cooperation in Europe (OSCE). 2014. Accessed May 8, 2014. http://www.osce.org/secretariat/107221.

Polaris Project. 2011. *Increasing Awareness and Engagement: Strengthening the National Response to Human Trafficking in the US* Polaris Project. Accessed September 1, 2013. http://www.polarisproject.org/resources/hotline-statistics.

Pompeo, Joe. 2012. "Meet Liz McDougall, the Unlikely-Seeming Lawyer Defending Village Voice Media in Backpage Controversy." *Capital New York*. April 26. http://www .capitalnewyork.com/article/media/2012/04/5773538/meet-liz-mcdougall-unlikely -seeming-lawyer-defending-village-voice-med.

Powers, Kirsten. 2012. "Boycott Village Voice Media? Senators and Clergy Push for Action on Backpage.com." *The Daily Beast*, April 19. http://www.thedailybeast.com/articles /2012/04/19/boycott-village-voice-senators-push-for-action-on-backpage-com.html.

Report on the Vienna Forum to Fight Human Trafficking (presentation). 2008. UN Global Initiative to Fight Human Trafficking (UN.GIFT). Vienna, Austria, UN Document E/CN.15/2008/CRP.2. Submitted to the UN Commission on Crime Prevention and Criminal Justice, seventeenth session. Vienna, April 14–18. http://www.unodc .org/documents/treaties/COP2008/CTOC-COP-2008-CRP-1-E.pdf.

Salvation Army. [2013. "STOP-IT Initiative Against Human Trafficking." Accessed September 1, 2013. http://sa-stopit.org/.

Singh, Sunit, and Rama Charan Tripathi. 2010. "Why Do the Bonded Fear Freedom? Some Lessons from the Field." *Psychology and Developing Societies* 22 (2): 249–97.

Skibola, Nicole. 2012. "Technology, Business, and Anti-Human Trafficking Innovation." *Forbes–Corporate Responsibility Blog*. January 4. http://www.forbes.com/sites /csr/2012/01/04/technology-business-and-anti-human-trafficking-innovation/.

Solis, Hilda L. 2012. "Statement by Secretary of Labor Hilda L. Solis on Statistics Updated by International Labour Organization Regarding Forced Labor." International Labour Affairs Bureau. June 1. http://www.dol.gov/opa/media/press/ilab/ILAB20121144.htm.

Sweeney, Annie. 2012. "New Task Force Targets Traffickers Who Force Children into the Sex Trade," *Chicago Tribune*. May 14, 2012. http://articles.chicagotribune.com /2012-05-14/news/ct-met-human-trafficking-20120514_1_chicago-police-traffickers -law-enforcement.

Tavares, Rodrigo. 2009. *Regional Security: The Capacity of International Organizations*. New York: Routledge.

TIP Report. 2009. *Trafficking in Persons Report*. US Department of State.

———. 2010. *Trafficking in Persons Report*. US Department of State.

———. 2011. *Trafficking in Persons Report*. US Department of State.

————. 2012. *Trafficking in Persons Report*. US Department of State.

————. 2013. *Trafficking in Persons Report*. US Department of State.

Tyldum, Guri, and Anette Brunovskis. 2005. "Describing the Unobserved: Methodological Challenges in Empirical Studies on Human Trafficking." *International Migration*, 43 (1–2): 17–34.

UN Office of the High Commissioner for Human Rights (UNOHCHR). 2012. "United Arab Emirates: UN Expert Urges Further Action to Protect Victims of Trafficking." United Nations Office of the High Commissioner for Human Rights (UNOHCHR). April 17. http://www.ohchr.org/en/NewsEvents/Pages/DisplayNews.aspx?NewsID=12068&LangID=E.

Verité. 2010."Forced Labor & Trafficking, Help Wanted: Hiring, Human Trafficking, and Slavery." Accessed September 1, 2013. http://www.Verité.org/forced-labor.

————. 2013. "A Framework for Action: What Can Suppliers Do?" Accessed September 1, 2013. http://www.Verité.org/helpwanted/toolkit/suppliers.

Vidyamali, Samarasinghe, and Barbara Burton. 2007. "Strategizing Prevention: A Critical Review of Local Initiatives to Prevent Female Sex Trafficking." *Development in Practice* 17 (1): 51–64.

CHAPTER 12

Religion and the Global Politics of Human Dignity

The Catholic Church and Beyond

THOMAS BANCHOFF

The idea of human dignity can serve to cultivate shared moral and political ground in a world divided along religious, social, economic, and ideological lines. At the same time, the ambiguity of the concept is a challenge. Unlike human rights, human dignity has not been codified. Human rights, although contested, have been the object of a structured conversation for more than half a century. Specific rights are set down in treaties, conventions, and other legal instruments. Professionals the world over—including lawyers, judges, activists, civil servants, and scholars—apply them in their work.

The concept of human dignity does not have these robust institutional foundations, but it does have a political force that human rights lacks. The language of rights is legal, whereas the idea of dignity has deep emotional resonance. Rights are adjudicated and balanced against one another, whereas human dignity is, by definition, inviolable. To claim that something violates human dignity is to assert that it contradicts basic moral precepts and must be remedied. Over the past two centuries, struggles against slavery, colonialism, racism, sexism, and the oppression of minorities have deployed the idea of human dignity—and revulsion at its violations—in building coalitions and bringing about change. Since the turn of the twenty-first century, the idea of human dignity and its implications for economic, social, and political life in a global era has informed an ambitious human development agenda around poverty, health care, and education.

The emotional pull and political force of the idea of human dignity has shaped, and been shaped by, the public role of religion in world affairs (Casanova 1994). The idea that human life is sacred—widely shared across the world's major traditions—adds a powerful expressive layer to the politics of human dignity. Violations of human dignity are viewed (and felt) as affronts to both a moral and a cosmic order. The call of religious leaders to advance human dignity and human rights is construed and experienced as a response to God or some ultimate concern. From Mahatma Gandhi to Martin Luther King Jr. and the Dalai Lama, faith leaders have mobilized members of their own and other communities around a wide range of human rights agendas. In a world of state competition for material power and advantage, religious communities do not dominate the politics of human dignity and human rights. But they have contributed to human rights coalitions by infusing the emotional power of the idea of human dignity with a spiritual dimension (Banchoff and Wuthnow 2011; Witte and van der Vyver 1996).

This chapter explores the religious politics of human dignity in the case of the Roman Catholic Church, the most influential formally organized religious community in the world. After an overview of the evolution of the idea of human dignity in world politics, it tracks the Church's shift towards a human dignity and human rights agenda at the Second Vatican Council (1962–1965) and its wider impact since. A concluding section sketches the idea of human dignity in two other leading traditions, Islam and Confucianism, as one way to explore the potential of interfaith and intercultural dialogue and collaboration to strengthen the international human rights regime.

Human Dignity in World Politics: Paths to the Present

Historically, the term "human dignity" has had two broad meanings. The original Latin *dignitas* signified something noble or worthy; it did not attach to all human beings, but only the most exemplary. This first sense is still present in the word "dignified." Human dignity, so understood, is something that some people have and others do not. The second meaning of human dignity extends to all people; it refers to an inherent worth possessed by members of the species *Homo sapiens*. Human dignity, so defined, cannot be taken away. It is something valuable to be protected and nurtured, recognized and respected (Kateb 2011; Rosen 2012; Waldron 2012).

This second, universal understanding of human dignity has emerged as a political force only in the modern era. Although it has deep historical roots—for example in the Hebrew and Christian scriptures, Stoicism, and Renaissance humanism—the idea of human dignity first took on a strong political (as well as philosophical and religious) complexion during the Enlightenment of the eighteenth century (Joas 2013). Among philosophers, Immanuel Kant emphasized human rationality as foundational for dignity; as free, reasoning moral agents, he argued, we should respect the inherent dignity of others (Kant 1797). In setting out their social and political visions, Jean-Jacques Rousseau and Adam Smith placed greater emphasis on the emotional foundations of the idea of human dignity. Rousseau's *pitié* (Rousseau 1754) and Smith's "moral sentiments" (Smith 1759) informed the idea of a common humanity and of obligations of mutual recognition and respect. Among Christian thinkers of the era, the Methodist John Wesley stood out for his invocation of human dignity, grounded in humanity's creation and redemption through God, as both theological precept and impetus for social reform (Wesley 1757).

The idea of human dignity—and moral and political outrage at assaults against it—had an eventful subsequent political career. It was deployed effectively by American, French, and other national revolutionaries in the eighteenth and nineteenth centuries, as well as by socialists, abolitionists, and anticolonialists, among others. Thomas Paine contrasted "the natural dignity of man" with "the attempt to govern mankind by force and fraud" (Paine 1791, 88), whereas Karl Marx and Friedrich Engels lamented the condition of workers, treated as "a commodity, like every other article of commerce" and an "appendage of the machine" (Marx and Engels 1848, 227). The Latin American revolutionary Simón Bolívar, like many other abolitionists, condemned slavery as a "shameless violation of human dignity" (Bolívar 1826, 148). At the turn of the twentieth century, the height of the imperialist era, anticolonialists in Asia and Africa invoked the principles of human dignity, freedom, and equality in their appeals for national self-determination (Simpson 2004).

Two world wars and the Holocaust proved a turning point in the global politics of human dignity. The Preamble to the 1945 Charter of the UN drew a close connection between violations of human dignity and the mission of the new world organization, expressing a determination "to save succeeding generations from the scourge of war, which twice in our lifetime has brought untold sorrow to mankind, and to reaffirm faith in fundamental human rights, in the dignity and worth of the human person, in the equal rights of men and women and of nations large and small." Other foundational UN documents also connected revulsion at violations of human dignity to the imperative of more effective global governance. For example, the constitution of the 1945 UN Educational, Scientific and Cultural Organization (UNESCO) refers to a "great and terrible war . . . made possible by the denial of the democratic principles of the dignity, equality and mutual respect of men, and by the propagation, in their place, through ignorance and prejudice, of the doctrine of the inequality of men and races."

The founding document of the contemporary human rights regime, the 1948 Universal Declaration of Human Rights, draws the clearest connection between the violation of human dignity and the imperative of human rights. Its Preamble asserts that "recognition of the inherent dignity and of the equal and inalienable rights of all members of the human family is the foundation of freedom, justice and peace in the world" and claims that "disregard and contempt for human rights have resulted in barbarous acts which have outraged the conscience of mankind." Several subsequent articles elaborate the human dignity–human rights connection. Article 1 states that "all human beings are born free and equal in dignity and rights" and that "they are endowed with reason and conscience and should act towards one another in a spirit of brotherhood." Article 22 is more specific, relating the idea of human dignity to development and to the "economic, social and cultural rights indispensable for his dignity and the free development of his personality," whereas Article 23 goes on to relate human dignity to "just and favorable remuneration ensuring for himself and his family an existence worthy of human dignity" (UN General Assembly 1948).[1]

From the beginning, critics of this dignity language and of the Universal Declaration and the emergent human rights regime attacked its conceptual ambiguity, internal tensions, and ineffectiveness in practice. Amid the political and ideological contradictions of the Cold War, human rights declarations and conventions proved an ineffective mechanism for countering violations of human dignity in the Soviet bloc or in autocracies allied with the United States. Nevertheless, a fuller human rights regime developed, gradually and unevenly, on the basic understanding of human dignity and human rights embodied in the UN Charter and the Universal Declaration. Two hallmarks were the International Covenant on Civil and Political Rights and the International Covenant on Economic, Social and Cultural Rights in 1966 (Lauren 2011).

From the 1970s onward, social and political changes in advanced industrial democracies, much of Eastern Europe and Latin America, and parts of Africa, Asia, and the Middle East transformed the global politics of human dignity and human rights. The extension of the idea of full human dignity and equality to women, children, and members of all races and religious and ethnic groups—the complex product of underlying economic, cultural, and political shifts—supported efforts within the UN to formulate and endorse a further set of human rights instruments, including the 1979 Convention on the Elimination of All Forms of Discrimination against Women; the 1984 Convention against Torture and Other Cruel, Inhuman or Degrading Treatment or Punishment; and the 1989 Convention on the Rights of the Child. Over the same time period, national and transnational human rights coalitions mobilized against violations of human dignity and in favor of human rights, contributing to waves of democratization in Latin

America and Eastern Europe and the end of apartheid in South Africa (Huntington 1991). With the collapse of Soviet communism, the end of the Cold War, and the accelerating globalization of the world economy, the idea of human dignity has been increasingly invoked in the context of global human development. Although the UN declared a Development Decade in the 1960s, major efforts in the 1970s and 1980s to address global poverty and shortages of health care and education ran up against East-West ideological confrontation and an emphasis on macroeconomic stabilization (structural adjustment) that often involved cuts in social services for the neediest. The first in a series of UN Human Development Reports, published in 1990, signaled a shift of emphasis. In the midst of the Eastern European revolutions, its authors suggested that "we are rediscovering the essential truth that people must be at the centre of all development" (UN Development Programme 1990, iii) and that "the basic objective of development is to create an enabling environment for people to enjoy long, healthy and creative lives" (9). The 2000 report made an even clearer connection between human rights, human dignity, and development: "Human rights and human development share a common vision and a common purpose—to secure, for every human being, freedom, well-being and dignity. Divided by the cold war, the rights agenda and the development agenda followed parallel tracks. Now converging, their distinct strategies and traditions can bring new strength to the struggle for human freedom" (UN Development Programme 2000).

Over the course of the 1990s, the first concrete efforts took place to adopt and pursue specific development targets within the UN system—a trend that culminated in the adoption of the Millennium Development Goals. In 1995, the World Summit on Social Development in Copenhagen created momentum for a wider UN development agenda. The following year, an influential Organisation for Economic Co-operation and Development (OECD) report noted the magnitude of the challenge: an "enduring concern for the human dignity and well-being of others" coupled with the fact that "more than one billion people still live in extreme poverty" (OECD 1996, 19). In the run-up to the turn of the millennium, UN agencies developed five ambitious development goals to be achieved by 2015, incorporating poverty reduction, primary education, child mortality, maternal health, and multisector cooperation. In endorsing these and other Millennium Development Goals at their Millennium Summit in September 2000, world leaders reiterated the close connection between human dignity, human rights, and development, recognizing "a collective responsibility to uphold the principles of human dignity, equality and equity at the global level" (UN General Assembly 2000).

From the eighteenth up through the twenty-first century, the idea of human dignity has supported a widening human rights and human development agenda. The idea that all human beings, whatever their origins, are entitled to basic recognition and respect has historical roots in diverse philosophical and religious traditions but only rose to political prominence with the first national and democratic revolutions in Europe and the Americas. Over subsequent centuries, revulsion at perceived violations of human dignity—through slavery, industrialization, colonialism, dictatorship, racism, war, and genocide; the subjugation of women, children, and minorities; and persistent poverty and lack of access to basic health care and education—has fed political mobilization around a diverse and widening set of human rights. The emotional force of the idea of human dignity has had a political impact from the Age of Revolution through today's global human development agenda.

The Case of the Catholic Church

As the world's largest centrally organized religious community and most influential nongovernmental organization, the Roman Catholic Church has both shaped and been shaped by the global politics of human dignity over the centuries. The Second Vatican Council (1962–1965) marked a turning point: a break with the Church's long-standing opposition to secular modernity and its full embrace of democracy, religious and other freedoms, and interreligious dialogue (O'Malley 2010). The idea of human dignity proved an important pivot—a concept with deep historical roots and theological and emotional resonance that could also be articulated in a more secular human rights idiom. Since the 1960s, successive popes have engaged public authorities and other religious traditions more actively around a range of national and international social and political challenges. Their espousal of human dignity and human rights—through appeals to reason, emotion, and faith—has facilitated the emergence of the Church as an effective advocate for democratization around the world and, more recently, as an influential proponent of a global human development agenda.

The steep decline in the Church's political fortunes in the eighteenth and nineteenth centuries was reinforced by its passionate and fruitless efforts to stem the tide of Enlightenment modernity. At a theological level, popes rejected the idea of reason, delinked from faith, as the arbiter of truth. They viewed secular reason as a rebellion against God's authority and against the authority of the Church, God's representative on earth. At a political level, the Vatican rejected democracy and civil liberties as absolute values, insisting that the best political system would give Catholicism a privileged institutional status and allow moral constraints on the freedom of citizens. From the point of view of Pius IX (1846–1878), the dominant pope of the nineteenth century, opposition to secular modernity was a defensive response to growing attacks on the Church and its prerogatives. His famous *Syllabus of Errors* (1864) was directed against atheistic, nationalist, liberal, and socialist forces. It was not an assault on human reason or human dignity as such, but was against efforts to conceive them outside of a Catholic religious framework.

The Vatican's first effort to articulate its own positive vision of human dignity and its social and political implications was the 1891 encyclical *Rerum novarum* of Leo XIII (1878–1903). Under the title "Of New Things," Leo provided an overarching analysis and critique of industrialization and its excesses. He decried both liberalism and socialism for their underlying atheism and materialism and the neglect of the spiritual needs of the burgeoning working classes. And he took a decisive step further, criticizing the material conditions of the proletariat and advocating social and economic change, including the freedom for workers to organize trade unions. For the first time, the Church systematically applied the idea of human dignity, traditionally a theological concept bearing on the human person's divine origins and eternal destiny, to wider economic, social, and political conditions. In a key passage, the encyclical criticized employers who "laid burdens upon their workmen which were unjust, or degraded them with conditions repugnant to their dignity as human beings" (Leo XIII 1891, 36).

The first half of the twentieth century saw a further development of the idea of human dignity as the cornerstone of Catholic Social Teaching. Catholic intellectuals like Jacques Maritain developed a Christian humanism that combined appeals to the authority of Catholic thinkers such as Thomas Aquinas with reflection on the implications of human dignity for contemporary economic, social, and political affairs (Maritain 1947; Amato 1975). During the Depression, Pius XI (1922–1939) issued his encyclical *Quadragesimo anno* on the fortieth anniversary of *Rerum novarum* in 1931, condemning the excesses of both industrial capitalism and state socialism and praising social legislation designed "to protect vigorously the sacred rights of the workers that flow from their dignity as men and as Christians" (Pius XI 1931, 28). In his 1942 Christmas message, Pius XII (1939–1958) went a step further. Looking with hope to prospects for a peaceful postwar order, he made the "dignity of the human person" and the "dignity of labor" two of the "five points for ordering society" (Pius XII 1942).

Through the 1950s, the Church's influence on the emergent global human rights agenda remained constrained by its ongoing opposition to principles of liberal democracy, including the nonestablishment of religion and full religious freedom.[2] Pius XII stayed close to the view that the ideal form of government should guarantee the Church's privileged status as the bastion of the one true faith and the arbiter of public morality. Relations with liberal and socialist parties and with other Christian denominations—not to mention other faiths—remained strained. It was only under John XXIII (1958–1963) and with the Second Vatican Council that the Church abandoned its defensive stance. In his opening Council address to bishops assembled from all over the world in October 1962, John called on Church leaders to address the needs of the present day by "demonstrating the validity of her teaching rather than by condemnations." While recalling a theological view of the human person as created and redeemed by God, he acknowledged that non-Catholics the world over were "ever more deeply convinced of the paramount dignity of the human person and of his perfection as well as of the duties which that implies" (O'Malley 2010, 94).

At the Council, the concept of human dignity served as a pivot between the Catholic tradition and an opening to a wider human rights agenda. Three authoritative documents issued in 1965 played a critical role. The declaration *Dignitatis humanae*—Of Human Dignity—abandoned the Church's historic opposition to religious freedom and endorsed individual liberty as both a gift of God and an expression of human dignity. "A sense of the dignity of the human person," the declaration began, "has been impressing itself more and more deeply on the consciousness of contemporary man" (Paul VI 1965a, 1). The declaration *Nostra aetate*, an opening to interfaith dialogue, abandoned the principle of "no salvation outside the Church" and condemned "discrimination against men or harassment of them because of their race, color, condition of life, or religion" (Paul VI 1965c, 5). *Gaudium et spes*, the Pastoral Constitution on the Church and the Modern World, included a section on "The Dignity of the Human Person," underscoring the far-reaching social and political implications of the concept, as well as its emotional force. "The Church knows that her message is in harmony with the most secret desires of the human heart," it proclaimed, "when she champions the dignity of the human vocation, restoring hope to those who have already despaired of anything higher than their present lot" (Paul VI 1965b, 21).

In the decades following the Council, the Church emerged as a powerful advocate for human rights and development on the world stage. The historic address of Paul VI (1963–1978) to the UN in New York in 1965 was a critical juncture. "What you proclaim here are the fundamental rights and duties of man, his dignity, his freedom, and above all his religious freedom," he told the General Assembly. "We feel that you are the interpreters of what is highest in human wisdom, We would almost say, of its sacred character" (Paul VI 1965d,

241). In his 1967 encyclical *Populorum progressio*, Paul set out the idea of "integral human development" designed "to eliminate every ill, to remove every obstacle which offends man's dignity" (Paul VI 1967, 6). The Pope linked the Church's passion for the imperative of human rights back to "the ferment of the Gospel," which "has aroused and continues to arouse in man's heart the irresistible requirements of his dignity" (32). But he also addressed emotional appeals to protect and advance human dignity beyond the Church faithful in his writings and on his trips to the Americas, Africa, and Asia.[3]

The global diplomacy of Pope John Paul II (1978–2005) intensified this trend. Through his numerous encyclicals and far-flung international travels—he made more than one hundred international trips—the pontiff tirelessly promoted the idea of human dignity and the imperative of human rights in world affairs. His encyclical *Sollicitudo rei socialis* (1987), issued on the twentieth anniversary of *Populorum progressio*, moved from a description of persistent injustice and suffering in the world to a positive trend in "the full awareness among large numbers of men and women of their own dignity and of that of every human being," and in "the more lively concern that human rights should be respected, and in the more vigorous rejection of their violation" (John Paul II 1987, 26). In 1991, in *Centesimus annus,* he looked back on the wave of democratization that had swept his native Poland and much of the rest of the world over the previous decade, plausibly asserting that "an important, even decisive, contribution was made by *the Church's commitment to defend and promote human rights*" (emphasis in original). Where political and ideological polarization had "obscured the awareness of a human dignity common to all, the Church affirmed clearly and forcefully that every individual—whatever his or her personal convictions—bears the image of God and therefore deserves respect" (John Paul II 1991, 22). During his pontificate, John Paul was widely criticized for not bringing his human dignity agenda into the Church itself, in particular with respect to women's rights. But his emphasis on human dignity and human rights certainly had a significant impact on world affairs.

With the end of the Cold War and the intensification of globalization, the Catholic Church's approach to human dignity and world affairs has paralleled the UN's turn toward a human development agenda and the problems of poverty and social inequality. After declaring the symbolic year 2000 the Church's first Great Jubilee, John Paul closed the event by lamenting that "our world is entering the new millennium burdened by the contradictions of an economic, cultural and technological progress, which offers immense possibilities to a fortunate few, while leaving millions of others not only on the margins of progress but in living conditions far below the minimum demanded by human dignity" (John Paul II 2001, 50). In the decade that followed, through the transition to Benedict XVI (2005–2013), the Vatican aligned itself closely with the Millennium Development Goals and with the idea of global human development, noting parallels with Paul VI's idea of integral human development. In the context of the global financial crisis, Benedict's encyclical *Caritas in veritate* contended, "the risk for our time is that the *de facto* interdependence of people and nations is not matched by ethical interaction of consciences and minds that would give rise to truly human development" (Benedict XVI 2009, 9).

In his pontificate thus far, Pope Francis (2013–) has continued to advocate for human rights and human development by invoking the idea of human dignity and calling for a sweeping reform of the global order. In a June 2013 address to the Food and Agriculture Organization of the UN, for example, he insisted that "the human person and human dignity are not simply catchwords, but pillars for creating shared rules and structures capable of passing beyond purely pragmatic or technical approaches in order to eliminate divisions and to bridge existing differences" (Francis 2013a, 2). The following month, to mobilize support for far-reaching change, he insisted during his pastoral visit to the Italian island of Lampedusa—a major entry point for African migrants to Europe—that Christians and others should develop a greater emotional capacity to identify with the plight of the poor and disenfranchised. "In this globalized world, we have fallen into globalized indifference," he told the crowd. "We have become used to the suffering of others: it doesn't affect me; it doesn't concern me; it's none of my business!" (Francis 2013b).

As the world's most visible religious figure, Pope Francis, like his immediate predecessors, has a significant influence on political controversies surrounding human rights and human development. Although the Roman Catholic Church only fully opened to the wider secular world in the 1960s with Vatican II, its leaders have since skillfully invoked the idea of human dignity—and abhorrence against its violations—to advocate for a broad human rights agenda. The theological foundations of the concept within the tradition have contributed to this success as has its emotional resonance in the wider culture. One should not, of course, overestimate the Church's impact—the politics of human rights remain dominated by states and include a range of other powerful secular players. At the same time, the acceleration of globalization and the growing salience of its religious and cultural dimensions have elevated the voice of the Church and its particular understanding of human dignity and its implications.

Human Dignity, Human Rights, and World Politics: The Interfaith Dimension

The case of the Catholic Church illustrates the political salience of the idea of human dignity when articulated within a particular religious tradition. Of course, attacks on human dignity can resonate politically outside any religious context. But when given a spiritual or transcendent dimension, as the Catholic case suggests, they can exert a particular emotional pull and political weight. To what degree does the same dynamic hold across other traditions? And might convergence around the idea of human dignity across diverse communities—if and where it exists—increase the potential for interfaith dialogue and collaboration to advance a wider interfaith and human rights agenda? The balance of this chapter briefly explores these questions through sketches of two other highly influential world traditions: Islam and Confucianism.

The Case of Islam

It is difficult, if not impossible, to conceive of Islam as a unified actor that brings a particular conception of human dignity to world politics. Like Protestantism, Eastern Orthodoxy, Judaism, Hinduism, and Buddhism, Islam does not have a hierarchical structure and an authoritative leader on the model of the Roman Catholic Church. On the foundation of core beliefs—in the Oneness of God, Muhammad as His Prophet, and the Qur'an as His direct revelation to humankind—Muslims engage in social and political affairs in different ways. The closest thing to a Muslim voice in international affairs is the Organisation of Islamic Cooperation (OIC), a multilateral grouping of more than fifty Muslim-majority countries formed in 1969. Although the OIC does not speak for Islam in any authoritative sense, its declarations often have a religious cast, and its status as an intergovernmental bloc at the UN gives it some clout.

Like Christianity, Islam has considerable scriptural resources for the idea of human dignity and human rights (An-Na'im 2010; Sachedina 2009). In the Qur'an, God breathes his spirit into human beings and calls on them to take possession of the earth and to rule it responsibly: "We have conferred dignity on the children of Adam, and borne them over land and sea, and provided for them sustenance out of the good things of life, and favoured them far above most of Our creation" (Qur'an 17:70).[4] Within Islam, human beings possess the spirit of God; they are rational, moral agents who should love and respect one another, whatever their differences. As the Qur'an puts it in an oft-quoted passage: "We have created you all out of a male and a female, and have made you into nations and tribes, so that you might come to know one another" (Qur'an 49:13).

One of the first modern Muslim statements on human dignity was the Universal Islamic Declaration of Human Rights, which the Islamic Council of Europe endorsed in 1981 out of concern that the emerging international human rights regime was too secular and Western in its thrust. The Preamble references "human rights decreed by the Divine Law" that "aim at conferring dignity and honour on mankind and are designed to eliminate oppression and injustice." Another, more prominent, statement came in 1990, when the OIC (then known as the Organisation of the Islamic Conference) endorsed the Cairo Declaration on Human Rights in Islam, which asserts that "All men are equal in terms of basic human dignity and basic obligations and responsibilities, without any discrimination on the grounds of race, color, language, sex, religious belief, political affiliation, social status or other considerations" (OIC 1990, Art. 1). The Declaration stops short of asserting the right to change one's religion or the full equality of men and women in marriage, two contested issues within Islam. But in its main outline it demonstrates a broad convergence with the theistic grounding of human dignity and human rights in the Catholic and Christian tradition.

The advance of democracy in several Muslim-majority countries since the Islamic Council of Europe's 1981 Declaration, including Turkey, Senegal, and Indonesia, furthered some convergence between human dignity and human rights, as understood in Islam, and more secular understandings of human rights. Issues of religious freedom and women's equality remain contested in these and other countries, but a deep-seated suspicion of human dignity and human rights discourse as part of the historical legacy of Western imperialism has faded somewhat over time. For example, the Preamble to the 2013 Draft Constitution of Tunisia, the most hopeful national case to emerge out of the Arab Spring, referred to its foundation on "the fundamentals and the open and moderate objectives of Islam" as well as "on sublime human values, and on universal human rights that are in harmony with the Tunisian people's cultural specificity" (National Constituent Assembly of Tunisia 2013). And while the OIC has made Islamophobia its overriding contemporary human rights concern, its leaders also emphasize interfaith commonalities, particularly with Christianity and Judaism—fellow Abrahamic traditions. "Many of the underlying principles are common and the ethical foundations overlap," said OIC Secretary-General Ekmeleddin İhsanoğlu at a conference in Vienna in 2012. "They encourage tolerance and protection of human dignity" (İhsanoğlu 2012).

The Case of Confucianism

Confucianism is another influential global tradition, alongside Christianity and Islam, but its impact on the global politics of human rights is more difficult to trace. Confucianism's status as a religious or philosophical tradition—or both—is hotly contested. It has always had a religious element involving ancestor and temple worship, but it is perhaps best understood as a comprehensive personal, social, and political philosophy that endows human existence in the here and now with sacred significance. Confucianism was the official ideology of the Chinese state into the early twentieth century but was subsequently repudiated by generations of nationalist, liberal, and socialist intellectuals and political leaders as a premodern relic. Confucian ideas still have an impact on society and politics in East Asia, particularly in South Korea, Japan, Taiwan, and Singapore, but that influence is broadly cultural rather than religious or political (Bell and Chaibong 2003).

It is as a culture and philosophy that Confucianism is most relevant to contemporary conversations about human dignity in world politics. Most often associated with rightly ordered social and political relationships—and in the popular mind with autocracy—Confucianism also has resources supportive of basic human dignity in terms of reason, moral responsibility, and respect and solidarity with others. For example, Confucius's follower Mencius distinguished between the dignity of the leader and general human dignity, what he termed "natural nobility." The ideal of the gentleman, for whom self-cultivation, benevolence (*ren*), harmony, and service to the wider society are guiding norms, was for him accessible to all in principle. Along these lines, the influential contemporary neo-Confucian thinker Tu Weiming rejects "the accusation that by stressing the importance of the group, Confucian ethics fails to account for the dignity of the individual." Confucianism rightly understood, he argues, accepts "liberty, rationality, due process of law, human rights, and the dignity of the individual" as positive values (Tu 2001, 24, 26).

Whether Confucianism emerges as a global political force and a carrier for ideas of human dignity and human rights will depend in large part on the future of the People's Republic of China (Bell 2008). In an effort to shore up their political legitimacy, Chinese leaders have increasingly taken up Confucian themes over the past decade. For example, in a programmatic speech before the Central Party School in June 2005, then president Hu Jintao cited Confucius to the effect that "Harmony is something to be cherished." As Hu put it, a "harmonious society should feature democracy, the rule of law, equity, justice, sincerity, amity and vitality"—albeit under the leadership of the

Communist Party (Xinhua News Agency 2005). The clearest effort of the Chinese state to draw on the Confucian legacy has been the Confucius Institutes it supports around the world as a vehicle for official cultural diplomacy. Without further political liberalization in China and an official embrace of the humanist dimension of the Confucian tradition, we are unlikely to see a major impact of Confucianism on the global politics of human dignity and human rights.

This very cursory sketch of Islam and Confucianism reveals some of the resources of both traditions when it comes to human dignity and its implications for world politics. It also suggests some convergence with the Catholic view of the human person, not simply or primarily as a rational and autonomous individual but as an inherently social being bound up in relationships of mutual dependence and obligation. For all of Christianity and Islam, as well as for Judaism, this relational conception of the human person has its ground in the loving and just creativity of an all-powerful God. For Confucianism, as for Buddhism and Hinduism, human existence has a sacred character with some ultimate grounding—but without reference to a single all-powerful divinity. These ideas about the dignity of each and every human being as part of creation or a cosmic order, when articulated across traditions in compatible ways, provide one way to cultivate shared moral ground and to increase political consensus around particular human rights agendas (Bloom, Martin, and Proudfoot 1996).

Since the end of the Cold War and with the acceleration of globalization, we have seen a proliferation of efforts to deepen interfaith dialogue around human dignity and human rights in the face of pressing global challenges. Prominent examples include the Declaration Toward a Global Ethic approved by the Parliament of the World's Religions in 1993 and the Universal Declaration of Human Responsibilities put forward by the InterAction Council in 1997 (Parliament of the World's Religions 1993; InterAction Council 1997). As critics have pointed out, these and other declarations tend to elide differences across traditions at a high level of abstraction and have little or no direct political impact (Casanova 1999). For interfaith initiatives to shape politics and policy nationally and internationally, they must be taken up by the leaders of particular religious communities and by political elites responsive to the expectations and—when it comes to human dignity and its violations—the emotions of those communities (Banchoff 2012). With the greater salience of religion in world affairs and the emergence of a more global civil society, we can expect more interreligious and transnational mobilization around global human dignity and human rights agendas in the years ahead.

Conclusion

Over the past half century, the prominence of the idea of human dignity and the emergence of a robust international human rights regime have gone hand in hand. Appeals to human dignity and of the inviolable worth of each and every human person have helped to mobilize national and international co-alitions in support of diverse human rights agendas. Moral outrage in the face of violations of human dignity—the unjust suffering and deprivation of fellow human beings—has advanced the cause of equal human rights of women and children, racial, religious, and ethnic minorities, and other groups over time. Each of these contexts has seen fierce contestation over the precise meaning and implications of human dignity. Most recently, for example, discrimination on the basis of sexual orientation has emerged as a controversial issue within and across countries. Here, as previously, claims about the violation of fundamental human dignity have found emotional resonance and structured human rights debates.

In the context of globalization, religious communities have emerged as key actors in the politics of human dignity and human rights. The idea of human dignity can, of course, be conceptualized and articulated in a secular idiom. But it finds perhaps its most powerful expression in a religious context in which unjust suffering and the violation of human dignity are viewed not only as an ethical affront but as a transgression of divine law or an attack on the cosmic order. Religious communities do not, of course, speak with one voice on the issue of human dignity. For decades, struggles for equal rights and respect regardless of race and gender have divided faith communities internally, and they continue to do so today around questions of sexual orientation and other issues. Religious passions can be mobilized for or against social and political change. Since World War II, however, the mobilization of religious communities against violations of human dignity and in favor of a general widening and deepening of the international human rights regime has been a striking development, unforeseen by the prophets of secularization.

The path of the Roman Catholic Church is the clearest illustration of this trend. With the Second Vatican Council of the 1960s, the Church made the turn from an entrenched opponent of liberal democratic ideas to one of the greatest proponents of human rights on a global scale. The idea of human dignity provided a pivot of continuity. In response to what Pope John XXIII called the "signs of the times," an established theological prism of dignity bestowed by God took on a full social and political dimension in Catholic thought and teaching. In the decades since, successive popes have taken up the idea of human dignity and, through their global diplomacy, emerged as influential proponents of basic economic, social, and political rights. In his first months in office in 2013, Pope Francis made the plight of the world's poor his top priority and expressed his strong support for the UN's global human development agenda.

In the years and decades to come, progress in human rights and human development will depend in no small part on the support of the Catholic Church and other religious communities across multiple traditions. We still live in a world of nation-states in which politics, both domestic and international, center on the clash of material interests. Many have grown inured to violations of human dignity—what Pope Francis calls the "globalization of indifference." In this context, the world's great secular and religious traditions help to keep alive the idea of a common humanity bound by mutual obligation. What religions can add, and interfaith dialogue and collaboration can support, is a spiritual as well as emotional ground for indignation and action—a transcendent, ultimate basis for human fellow feeling and solidarity in practice. Religious communities are not the only players in the politics of human dignity and human rights. But their contributions to date have been critical, as is their potential moving forward.

Notes

1. On the importance of human dignity as a driver of a politics of human rights, see Jeffrey C. Isaac, "A New Guarantee on Earth: Hannah Arendt on Human Dignity and the Politics of Human Rights," *The American Political Science Review* 90, no. 1 (March 1996): 61–73.

2. One exception was Maritain's purported influence on the human dignity language in the 1948 Universal Declaration. See Mary Ann Glendon, *A World Made New: Eleanor Roosevelt and the Universal Declaration of Human Rights* (New York: Random House, 2001).

3. Into the 1970s, many national Church leaders continued to support Catholic dictators in Spain, Portugal, the Philippines, and parts of Latin America. It was only with the wave of democratization in the 1970s and 1980s across those regions and countries, much of it led by progressive clerics and laypersons, that the Church came to be more clearly identified with the human rights and human dignity agenda.

4. All passages from the Qur'an come from Muhammad Asad's translation. See Muhammad Asad, *The Message of the Qur'an*, trans. Muhammad Asad (Gibraltar: Dar al-Andalus, 1980), accessed November 29, 2013. http://www.usc.edu/schools/college/crcc/private/cmje/religious_text/The_Message_of_The_Quran__by_Muhammad_Asad.pdf.

References

Amato, Joseph. 1975. *Mounier and Maritain: A French Catholic Understanding of the Modern World.* Reprint, Washington, DC: Catholic University of America Press, 2010.

An-Na'im, Abdullahi. 2010. *Islam and Human Rights: Selected Essays of Abdullahi An-Na'im*, edited by Mashood A. Baderin. Farnham, UK: Ashgate.

Banchoff, Thomas. 2012. "Interreligious Dialogue and International Relations." In *Rethinking Religion and World Affairs*, edited by Timothy Samuel Shah, Alfred Stepan, and Monica Duffy Toft, 204–14. New York: Oxford University Press.

Banchoff, Thomas, and Robert Wuthnow, eds. 2011. *Religion and the Global Politics of Human Rights*. New York: Oxford University Press.

Bell, Daniel. 2008. *China's New Confucianism: Politics and Everyday Life in a Changing Society*. Princeton, NJ: Princeton University Press.

Bell, Daniel, and Hahm Chaibong, eds. 2003. *Confucianism for the Modern World*. New York: Cambridge University Press.

Benedict XVI. 2009. *Caritas in veritate (Encyclical on Integral Human Development in Charity and Truth)*. June 29. http://www.vatican.va/holy_father/benedict_xvi/encyclicals/documents/hf_ben-xvi_enc_20090629_caritas-in-veritate_en.html.

Bloom, Irene, J. Paul Martin, and Wayne L. Proudfoot, eds. 1996. *Religious Diversity and Human Rights*. New York: Columbia University Press.

Bolívar, Simón. 1826. "Message to the Congress of Bolivia." In *Símon Bolívar: His Basic Thoughts*, edited by Manuel Pérez Vila, 133–52. Caracas: Academia Nacional de la Historia, Comité Venezolano de Ciencias Históricas, 1980.

Casanova, José. 1994. *Public Religions in the Modern World*. Chicago: University of Chicago Press.

———. 1999. "The Sacralization of the *Humanum*: A Theology for a Global Age." *International Journal of Politics, Culture, and Society* 13 (1): 21–40.

Francis. 2013a. "Address of His Holiness Pope Francis to Participants in the 38th Conference of the Food and Agriculture Organization of the United Nations (FAO)" (speech). Vatican City, June 20. http://www.vatican.va/holy_father/francesco/speeches/2013/june/documents/papa-francesco_20130620_38-sessione-fao_en.html.

———. 2013b. "Homily of Holy Father Francis at 'Arena' Sports Camp, Salina Quarter of Lampedusa" (homily). Lampedusa, Italy, July 8. http://www.vatican.va/holy_father/francesco/homilies/2013/documents/papa-francesco_20130708_omelia-lampedusa_en.html.

Huntington, Samuel P. 1991. *The Third Wave: Democratization in the Late Twentieth Century*. The Julian J. Rothbaum Distinguished Lecture Series. Norman: University of Oklahoma Press.

İhsanoğlu, Ekmeleddin. 2012. "Statement H. E. Ekmeleddin İhsanoğlu, Secretary-General of the Organisation of Islamic Cooperation (OIC) at the Symposium on Tolerance Vienna," (speech). Vienna, Austria, November 29. http://www.oicoci.org/topic_detail.asp?t_id=7497.

InterAction Council. 1997. *Universal Declaration of Human Responsibilities*. September 1. http://www.interactioncouncil.org/universal-declaration-human-responsibilities.

Joas, Hans. 2013. *The Sacredness of the Person: A New Genealogy of Human Rights*. Washington, DC: Georgetown University Press.

John Paul II. 1987. *Sollicitudo rei socialis (Encyclical for the Twentieth Anniversary of Populorum Progressio)*. December 30. http://www.vatican.va/holy_father/john_paul_ii/encyclicals/documents/hf_jp-ii_enc_30121987_sollicitudo-rei-socialis_en.html.

———. 1991. *Centesimus annus (Encyclical on the Hundredth Anniversary of Rerum Novarum)*. May 1. http://www.vatican.va/holy_father/john_paul_ii/encyclicals/documents/hf_jp-ii_enc_01051991_centesimus-annus_en.html.

————. 2001. *Novo millennio ineunte (Apostolic Letter at the Close of the Great Jubilee of the Year 2000)*. January 6. http://www.vatican.va/holy_father/john_paul_ii/apost _letters/documents/hf_jp-ii_apl_20010106_novo-millennio-ineunte_en.html.

Kant, Immanuel. 1797. *The Metaphysics of Morals*, edited and translated by Mary Gregor. Cambridge, UK: Cambridge University Press, 1996.

Kateb, George. 2011. *Human Dignity*. Cambridge, MA: Belknap Press of Harvard University Press.

Lauren, Paul Gordon. 2011. *The Evolution of International Human Rights: Visions Seen, Pennsylvania Studies in Human Rights*. 3rd ed. Philadelphia: University of Pennsylvania Press.

Leo XIII. 1891. *Rerum novarum (Encyclical on Capital and Labor)*. May 15. http://www .vatican.va/holy_father/leo_xiii/encyclicals/documents/hf_l-xiii_enc_15051891 _rerum-novarum_en.html.

Maritain, Jacques. 1947. *The Person and the Common Good*, translated by John J. Fitzgerald. New York: Charles Scribner's Sons. Accessed November 29, 2013. http:// www3.nd.edu/Departments/Maritain/etext/CG.HTM.

Marx, Karl, and Friedrich Engels. 1848. *The Communist Manifesto*, edited by Gareth Stedman Jones. London: Penguin Classics, 2002.

National Constituent Assembly of Tunisia. 2013. *Draft Constitution of the Tunisian Republic*, translated by the International Institute for Democracy and Electoral Assistance. April 22. Accessed November 29, 2013. http://www.constitutionnet.org/files /2013_04_23_-_third_draft_english_idea_3.pdf.

O'Malley, John W. 2010. *What Happened at Vatican II*. Cambridge, MA: Belknap Press of Harvard University Press.

Organisation for Economic Co-operation and Development (OECD). 1996. *Shaping the 21st Century: The Contribution of Development Co-operation*. Paris: Organisation for Economic Co-operation and Development.

Organisation of the Islamic Conference (OIC). 1990. *Cairo Declaration on Human Rights in Islam*. August 5. http://www.oic-oci.org/english/article/human.htm.

Paine, Thomas. 1791. *The Rights of Man, Part 1*. In *Paine: Political Writings*, edited by Bruce Kuklick, 57–154. Cambridge, UK: Cambridge University Press, 2000.

Parliament of the World's Religions. 1993. *Declaration toward a Global Ethic*. September 4. http://www.parliamentofreligions.org/_includes/FCKcontent/File/TowardsA GlobalEthic.pdf.

Paul VI. 1965a. *Dignitatis humanae (Declaration on Religious Freedom; On the Right of the Person and of Communities to Social and Civil Freedom in Matters Religious)*. December 7. http://www.vatican.va/archive/hist_councils/ii_vatican_council/documents/vat-ii _decl_19651207_dignitatis-humanae_en.html.

————. 1965b. *Gaudium et spes (Pastoral Constitution on the Church in the Modern World)*. December 7. http://www.vatican.va/archive/hist_councils/ii_vatican_council /documents/vat-ii_cons_19651207_gaudium-et-spes_en.html.

————. 1965c. *Nostra aetate (Declaration on the Relation of the Church to Non-Christian Religions)*. October 28. http://www.vatican.va/archive/hist_councils/ii_vatican _council/documents/vat-ii_decl_19651028_nostra-aetate_en.html.

————. 1965d. "Address by Pope Paul VI to the General Assembly." In *Yearbook of the United Nations: 1965*, 237–42. New York: UN Department of Public Information. http:// www.unmultimedia.org/searchers/yearbook/page.jsp?bookpage=237&volume=1965.

————. 1967. *Populorum progressio (Encyclical on the Development of Peoples)*. March 26. http://www.vatican.va/holy_father/paul_vi/encyclicals/documents/hf_p-vi_enc _26031967_populorum_en.html.

Pius XI. 1931. *Quadragesimo anno (Encyclical on Reconstruction of the Social Order)*. May 15. http://www.vatican.va/holy_father/pius_xi/encyclicals/documents/hf_p-xi_enc _19310515_quadragesimo-anno_en.html.

Pius XII. 1942. "The Internal Order of States and People" (speech). Vatican City, December 24. Accessed November 29, 2013. http://www.ewtn.com/library/papaldoc /p12ch42.htm.

Rosen, Michael. 2012. *Dignity: Its History and Meaning*. Cambridge, MA: Harvard University Press.

Rousseau, Jean-Jacques. 1754. *Discourse on the Origin of Inequality*, translated by Franklin Philip; edited by Patrick Coleman. Oxford, UK: Oxford University Press, 1994.

Sachedina, Abdulaziz. 2009. *Islam and the Challenge of Human Rights*. New York: Oxford University Press.

Simpson, Alfred William Brian. 2004. *Human Rights and the End of Empire: Britain and the Genesis of the European Convention*. Oxford, UK: Oxford University Press.

Smith, Adam. 1759. *The Theory of Moral Sentiments*. New York: Gutenberg Publishers, 2011.

Tu, Weiming. 2001. "The Global Significance of Local Knowledge: A New Perspective on Confucian Humanism." *Sungkyun Journal of East Asian Studies* 1 (1): 22–27. Accessed November 29, 2013. http://sjeas.skku.edu/upload/200605/Tu%20Weiming.pdf.

UN Development Programme. 1990. *Human Development Report 1990*. New York: Oxford University Press. Accessed November 29, 2013. http://hdr.undp.org/en/reports /global/hdr1990/chapters/.

————. 2000. *Human Development Report 2000*. New York: Oxford University Press. Accessed November 29, 2013. http://hdr.undp.org/en/media/HDR_2000_EN.pdf.

UN Educational, Scientific and Cultural Organization (UNESCO). 1945. *Constitution of the United Nations Educational, Scientific and Cultural Organization*. UNESCO. November 16. 4 UNTS 275. http://portal.unesco.org/en/ev.php-URL_ID=15244& URL_DO=DO_TOPIC&URL_SECTION=201.html.

UN General Assembly. 1948. "Universal Declaration of Human Rights." *UN Document A/81*, December 10.

————. 2000. "Resolution 55/2: United Nations Millennium Declaration." *UN Document A/RES/55/2*, September 18.

Waldron, Jeremy. 2012. *Dignity, Rank, and Rights*, edited by Meir Dan-Cohen. New York: Oxford University Press.

Wesley, John. 1757. *The Dignity of Human Nature, Library of Methodist Classics*. Nashville, TN: United Methodist Publishing House.

Witte Jr., John, and Johan D. van der Vyver, eds. 1996. *Religious Human Rights in Global Perspective: Religious Perspectives*. The Hague: Martinus Nijhoff Publishers.

Xinhua News Agency. 2005. "Building Harmonious Society Crucial for Progress: Hu." Xinhua News Agency, June 26. Accessed on November 29, 2013. http://news.xin huanet.com/english/2005-06/26/content_3139097.htm.

CHAPTER 13

Faith-Based Institutions and Human Dignity

A Growing Presence on the Global Stage

NICOLE BIBBINS SEDACA

For decades Mother Teresa epitomized the role of religious actors—faithful people working quietly in the private sphere, serving as missionaries, running relief agencies serving coreligionists, and providing basic services to poor and needy around the world. Today's profile of faith-based actors is much more diverse and complex. Since the 1980s, faith groups have been moving increasingly into the public sphere in an unexpected and unprecedented way, contributing significantly to the advancement of human dignity through both policy and programs.

Although globalization was supposed to have stripped religion from many people's lives, it has in actuality solidified religion as a source of global community, a resource for addressing global challenges, and a key component of international affairs. This enhanced role of religion, along with increased global connectivity, the decline of confidence in states, and the growth of civil society globally, have contributed to faith-based organizations (FBOs) becoming more public and powerful institutions internationally. This more influential position for FBOs has allowed them to contribute to the growing global focus on human dignity, a priority that has been central to most major faith traditions that believe in the inherent value of each person endowed by a higher being.

This chapter examines how FBOs have contributed to—and benefited from—this rise of nonstate actors and the advancement of human dignity as an organizing principle globally, as characterized by Mark P. Lagon and Anthony Clark Arend. First, it looks at how and why faith is playing a more pivotal role in international affairs. Then, it explores the factors that have allowed faith-based actors to capture this more prominent international role, and how this development has impacted the growth of human dignity as an organizing concept for action. Finally, it makes recommendations about key policy issues in light of these developments.

A note before starting: "Faith-based" is an expansive term and can include groups from Catholic Relief Services (CRS) to Hamas and individuals from the Dalai Lama Tenzin Gyatso to Osama bin Laden. Groups and individuals falling into this wide spectrum can come from similar faith backgrounds and yet utilize faith teachings and principles for very different outcomes—some societally beneficial and others highly destructive. Given this book's focus on liberal norms of human dignity, this chapter focuses exclusively on those FBOs and individuals that respect the broader liberal international legal and human rights framework and have contributed to peace and human dignity globally.[1] These liberal organizations are focused on universal or comprehensive human dignity and the inherent value of each individual as opposed to illiberal groups with narrower objectives—political, religious, and social—that represent the interests of only their religious or ethnic group while seeking to disadvantage or eliminate other groups. In addition, this chapter looks specifically at those operating internationally or outside of their country of origin, in light of this book's focus on international norms. Later, the chapter returns briefly to the issue of illiberal international FBOs, as it is important to address the major impact these groups have on both the international landscape as well as on the work of liberal faith-based groups.

Professor Scott Thomas offers a useful definition of faith-based nongovernmental organizations (NGOs) as groups which have a "mission statement [that] explicitly refers to religious faith as a motivation for its work, its personnel are related to some religious hierarchy or theological tradition, and . . . hire all or part of its staff on the basis of a creed or statement of faith" (Thomas 2005, 101). These include organizations which are not affiliated with a specific religion or denomination and those which are an extension of a specific religious body. Likewise of note are those organizations that are single or multifaith consortia made up of FBOs, such as World Conference for Religions of Peace.

Having established that framework, let us turn to the rising role of faith in the international arena.

Growing Religiosity

In his April 2008 speech in Westminster, former British prime minister Tony Blair highlighted key global shifts and the centrality of faith in dealing with them: "Under the momentum of globalisation the world is opening up, and at an astonishing speed. Old boundaries of culture, identity, and even nationhood are falling. The twenty-first century world is becoming ever more interdependent. . . . Faiths can transform and humanize the interpersonal forces of globalization, and shape the values of the changing set of economic and power relationships of the early twenty-first century" (Blair 2008, 1).

Rising global religiosity is a megatrend that defied what many scholars and practitioners have held as sacred since the Second World War: the belief that religion would become obsolete as modernity swept in and the people were exposed to ideas from different parts of the world (Thomas 2005, 29). For decades, scholars and practitioners had upheld the theory of secularization, which posits that with modernization, societies will progress, and religion will lose its voice in the public realms. Now there is a growing recognition among scholars that not only is faith not receding, it is indeed playing a more prominent role in many societies as a driving force in the foreign and domestic policies of many countries and in people's personal experiences, making it a pivotal and influential motivating factor in the lives of the majority of people around the world (Thomas 2005, 26; Abrams 2001, viii; Johnston 1995, 9).

As faith has maintained its centrality in individual lives and communities, globalization has further bolstered the growth of faith globally. Through swift technological developments, significant movements of people, and tremendous connectivity, globalization has created unprecedented opportunity for connection between societies and individuals, which has allowed people to learn about other faiths and for people of faith to become and stay connected with fellow believers around the world in an unprecedented way. Whereas scholars believed that increased exposure to a wider spectrum of information and a plurality of views would weaken faith's impact, today's increased connectivity has allowed people to be part of active global faith communities rather than experiencing their faith only in their local context.

Globalization has also brought significant dislocation, societal upheaval, and the disintegration of conventional community structures and traditions. Again, scholars believed that faith would diminish as such traditional community structures are weakened; the opposite has proven true. People have turned to faith to deal with personal dislocation and to faith-based groups to address the negative factors and affronts to human dignity—poverty, injustice, and suffering—that have come with globalization. Global institutions and response mechanisms, which have relied heavily on states and state-based solutions, have often not adequately addressed these problems or overlooked the importance of faith to aid recipients. Local faith communities as well as international FBOs—alongside secular NGOs—have filled the gap in addressing these issues. For example, a 2007 World Health Organization (WHO) study reported that between 30 percent and 70 percent of the African health infrastructure is currently owned by FBOs (WHO 2007, 1). Globally, one-third of all HIV/AIDS patients are cared for under the auspices of the Catholic Church (Ferris 2005, 316–17).

Global demographic trends further reinforce this rising religiosity, indicating that faith will continue to be relevant for the foreseeable future. Pew Research Center's Forum on Religion and Public Life estimates that in 2010 some 5.8 billion of the world's 6.9 billion people are religiously affiliated adults and children, representing 84 percent of the world population (Pew 2005, 1). Faith is growing in all parts of the world, particularly in the global South where the population size is also increasing. Where faith is receding, as it is in Europe, the population is shrinking as well. In 1900, 32 percent of the world's population was in the North, whereas this number dropped to 18 percent in 2000 and is projected to be as low as 10 percent in 2050 (Thomas 2010, 93). The global percentage of world population that is Christian has remained the same from 1910 to 2010, approximately 32 to 35 percent, but the percentage of those Christians living in Europe or the United States dropped from 93 percent of the global population in 2010 to 63 percent in 2010. Global faith communities are also growing significantly; for example, the world's Muslim population is expected to increase by approximately 35 percent over the next two decades, rising from 2010's level of 1.6 billion to 2.2 billion by 2030 (Pew 2005, 1). Former administrator of the United States Agency for International Development Andrew Natsios's observation that "While most American and European foreign policy elites may hold a secular worldview, much of the rest of the world lives in one of the great religious traditions" highlights the differing lenses of understanding between the West and the remainder of the world (Thomas 2004, 23).

Recognition of Religious Trends

With faith playing a more important role in the international public square and in more individual lives, space has been created for—and claimed by—FBOs to more actively and publicly engage the advocacy and policy processes, partner with states and international organizations, and become implementing arms of secular development organizations and states. Over the last several decades, states and international institutions, such as the UN and World Bank, have recognized the relevant contribution of faith-based activists, the rising role of faith in the public square, and the importance of faith to the clients they are serving and have sought to engage in more dialogue and partnership with the faith-based community. For example, through the Reagan, Clinton, and George W. Bush administrations, the US government increasingly brought FBOs into the policy process, and funding of these organizations increased markedly. The US government's President Emergency Plan for AIDS Relief (PEPFAR) provided 34 percent of its NGO funding through FBOs between 2004 and 2006 (Oomman, Bernstein, and Rosenzweig 2008, 9). Similarly among international organizations, the UN High Commissioner for Refugees (UNHCR), for example, provided $1.09 billion to FBOs between 1994 and 2006 (UNHCR 2007, 11). By 2010, the Global Fund to Fight AIDS, Tuberculosis, and Malaria (Global Fund) utilized forty-four FBOs as principal recipients in twenty-two countries and an additional 566 FBOs as subrecipients. Of the 128 Country Coordinating Mechanisms with active Global Fund grants, ninety-nine (77.3 percent) had at least one faith-based representative (Global Fund 2010, 1–4).

Likewise, the World Bank played a pivotal role in bringing FBOs into the global dialogue on development through its 2000 launch of the World Faiths Development Dialogue, which strengthened the bridge between faith-based and mainstream development institutions. This initiative recognized that FBOs were capable not only of addressing a growing humanitarian need and partnering with donor countries and organizations but also of doing it in a way that recognized the importance of religion in today's calculations. These efforts brought secular and FBOs into greater contact with one another and with the donor community. As faith-based groups have become more integrated into the global community, they have contributed to pushing to the forefront the values and focus on human dignity, which is central to many of these organizations.

> It has been told you, O Man, what is good, And what the Lord requires of you: Only to do justly, and to love mercy, and to walk humbly with your God.
>
> Micah 6:8

Key Factors Contributing to the Growth of FBOs

Rising religiosity is not, however, the only trend which has given faith groups more influence on the global stage. The decline in confidence in the nation-state, the strengthening of global faith identities, and the professionalization and diversification of FBOs have also been instrumental in FBOs taking on a more engaged role.

The global community has been organized almost exclusively around states since the Treaty of Westphalia, but certainly in a more intense way at the end of the Second World War and in the creation of an international architecture based almost exclusively on states. Although other actors, such as multinationals and nonstate actors, have been more active since the 1970s, the international community largely maintained the belief or expectation that states are capable of and interested in protecting the interests of their citizens and providing for their basic needs; this has not proven universally true. Some states—particularly states that resulted from the decolonization process of the 1950s and 1960s—have rarely, if ever, been able to provide for the basic needs of all of their citizens, whereas other states are faltering in service provision in a rapidly changing world where citizen expectations of states are rising. This failure has led to a decline in trust of states and state-based institutions and a demand for nonstate actors to respond. Along with this lack of confidence in state capacity, there has been a growing skepticism in the non–Western world about the motivation of secular Western governments and international organizations, which has left a greater opposition to the public sector and Western government aid as well. These factors have allowed NGOs, including FBOs, to respond, increase capacity, and earn citizen trust. Because they have paid particular attention to local faith traditions as part of their operations, FBOs have also gained access where oversecularization is a particular concern.

In 2009 the *Economist* highlighted this NGO sector growth, noting how this was facilitated by numerous factors, including globalization, economic integration, technological change, democratization in poorer countries, and the end of communism (Economist 2009, 2–3). And the NGO sector has indeed expanded, illustrating a growing acceptance of them. In 1989 there were some 20,000 internationally operating NGOs. By 1999, there were 43,000 and over 56,000 in 2012 (Kaldor, Moorem, and Selchow 2012, 10). NGOs now deliver more aid than the whole UN system (Economist 2009, 4). The shift in service volume from state-based institutions to the NGO sector has expanded NGOs' reach and over time credibility.

FBOs are well positioned at this nexus of religion's growing public face and the increasing confidence in NGOs. Two studies have shown that the level of trust in religious institutions and FBOs is much higher than that in other governmental institutions, police, and even some secular NGOs. A 2009 Latinobarómetro poll showed that although citizen confidence in Latin American governments grew from 24 percent to 45 percent from 1996 to 2009, it still lagged significantly behind the church and religious institutions, which garnered 65–75 percent in this same period (Economist 2009, 56).

Likewise, the World Bank's *Voices of the Poor* study also showed higher marks for faith organizations than government institutions and officials, which received low evaluations for their delivery of services and reliability. Based on the interviews with the poor throughout the world, there was a widely held view that: "[F]ormal institutions are in crisis. While there are pockets of excellence, the poor invariably experience formal institutions as ineffective, inaccessible, and disempowering. The recurrent themes running through the reports are distrust, corruption, humiliation, intimidation, helplessness, hopelessness, and often anger" (Narayan, Chambers, Shah, and Petesch 2000, 222).

The study goes on to state that, "NGOs and religious organizations are more trusted than state institutions . . . [and] receive high praise for being caring and supportive" (Narayan, Patel, Schafft, Rademacher, and Koch-Schulte 2000, 179). These poll results are an indication of not only the low trustworthiness of states but also the high credibility of FBOs, in particular, among the nongovernmental actors.

Professor Thomas further elaborates on this state-confidence deficit, arguing that "The global resurgence of religion can be seen as one of the results of the failure of the secular, modernizing state to produce democracy or development in the developing world" (Thomas 2005, 40–41). Taken together, these factors—increased religiosity, low confidence in states, skepticism about the secular approach of some international organizations, and a growth in the NGO sector as a whole—have paved the way for the growth of the FBO sector.

Another international trend bolstering this growth is the emergence of global identities and connectivity among faith communities. With declining confidence in states, many people have developed a deeper and more profound sense of identification with their faith or tribal affiliation as opposed to their country or a specific territory. Author Olivier Roy outlines how globalization has caused religion, which is now more separated from national and cultural identity, to supersede or even replace these sources of identification. As this happens, the disconnect between citizens and their national identity or country grows, and people identify more closely with those in other parts of the world who share their global identity. This trend is further developed in and by diasporic religious communities, which are connected to their original and new communities, exercising influence on both. FBOs that adhere to the same faith as service recipients in other countries have been able to earn more access or trust. Roy further argues that even when there is a difference in faith, "the fact that they are both 'believers of *a* faith' has given FBOs some resonance in these societies" (Thomas 2010, 98). This phenomenon also underscores the neomedieval concept, as discussed by Lagon and Arend, that states will remain important actors but only alongside a host of other influential players on the international stage.

These global trends have not only created a niche for FBOs but has also allowed them to expand their issue areas, access, reach, and, in some cases, size over the last several decades. Although most faith-based groups have relatively small staffs and budgets, some have grown into multimillion dollar operations with a global reach. For example:

- American Jewish World Service (AJWS) works on four continents to end poverty and promote human rights "inspired by Judaism's commitment to justice" with a 2011 operating budget of over $53 million (AJWS 2011, 1).
- The Aga Khan Development Network, "underpinned by the ethical principles of Islam" supports health, education, and rural development; in 2010 it served in thirty countries with over $625 million (Aga Khan 2013, 1).
- World Vision International, a leading Christian humanitarian organization, had an income of $2.79 billion in 2011 and operated in close to 100 countries (World Vision 2011, 24).

Whereas the size and reach of these particular organizations is not typical, it is indicative of the fact that FBOs today are growing in size and scope.

Expanding beyond their earlier focus on missionary efforts and humanitarian relief, FBOs' reach has expanded significantly to include far more issues. In partnership with secular organizations or in faith-only coalitions, FBOs have been particularly successful in advocacy surrounding poverty alleviation, trafficking in persons, as well as opposition to dictatorial regimes and religious persecution. Likewise although many are programmatically focused, FBOs have also expanded into engagement and partnership with international organizations, global campaigns, and governmental advocacy.

A good example of the impact that faith-based institutions can have is the Jubilee 2000 campaign, an international coalition of both faith-based and secular organizations from over forty countries that mobilized international voices for the cancellation of developing world debt by the year 2000. This alliance argued that the continuation of heavy indebtedness was immoral because it burdened countries that would never be able to escape this liability. The concept of Jubilee derives from the biblical Book of Leviticus and states that, in the jubilee year, those who are enslaved because of their debts should be set free and that lands lost because of debt should be returned to their owners. This effort, since disbanded on an international level and continued on the national level in numerous countries, led to the cancellation of more than $100 billion of debt owed by thirty-five countries.

As FBOs have increased their operational and policy engagement and received greater access to governmental and international organizations' funds, they have also worked to professionalize their operations. There has been a bridging between secular institutions and FBOs as the former seeks to integrate faith into their operations and the latter seeks to operate according to the standards that the secular development institutions have held for decades. In his book, *Sacred Aid: Faith and Humanitarianism*, noted scholar Michael Barnett highlights that as the professional standards of FBOs have increasingly moved closer to those of secular organizations, they have still retained their strong focus on human dignity (Barnett and Stein 2011, 217–18).

> [The righteous are those] who feed the poor, the orphan and the captive for the love of God, saying: "We feed you for the sake of God Alone; we seek from you neither reward nor thanks."
>
> The Quar'an, 76:8–9

Global Networks

Beyond the aforementioned issues—professionalization, the decline of confidence in states, the growth of the NGO sector, and the emergence of global identities—FBOs have also benefited from strong domestic and international networks that provide informational, political, and financial support as well as partnership.

At home, FBOs provide domestic faith communities with real-time information and analysis, raising coreligionists' awareness about global issues where the FBOs operate. This ongoing communication domestically often translates into important political and financial support for FBOs. In the United States, for example, domestic faith communities provided crucial political and financial support for the international work of American FBOs in strong partnership with secular organizations to have a significant policy impact on issues such as human trafficking, Sudan, and religious freedom. Because this support from domestic coreligionists can provide a steady revenue source, it can partially decrease FBOs' reliance on governmental and international organization funding. Naturally, FBOs, like all NGOs, are impacted by international trends as well as the interests and will of large donor countries and international organizations, but this alternative funding source gives some flexibility to pursue policy or project initiatives independent of secular donors (Barnett and Stein 2011, 55). This observation does not minimize FBOs' fundraising challenges or the fact that many continue to take government funding but rather highlights their additional source of nonpublic funding.

Some FBOs have been able to gain access to remote or difficult areas, which benefits not only FBOs' connection with fellow believers at home but also allows FBOs to play a crucial role internationally in providing real-time, grassroots knowledge to policymakers and the international community about crises or unfolding situations. This information also benefits FBOs' analytical capability and delivery strategies as well.

Overseas, FBOs' networks with local faith communities provide FBOs with implementing partners that can reach beneficiary populations effectively and quickly and allow them to capitalize on the contacts and understanding that local groups have. In South Africa, for example, as part of an AIDS Relief consortium and with US government funding, CRS worked closely with the Southern African Catholic Bishops Conference (SACBC) to establish fourteen local churches as care and treatment sites. The project has, in turn, been completely transitioned to the SACBC for full implementation in rural and urban churches (CRS 2013, 1). Secular or governmental groups that do not have an immediate network of implementing partners face the challenge of building these relationships and the knowledge base from the ground up. The faith link between indigenous and international faith-based groups, at times, also minimizes the focus on national differences, thus giving FBOs more open access not always afforded to secular groups, particularly those from the West. This link has given FBOs access to information more easily than many others entering into a country and gives them a more lasting presence in these countries as well.

Receptivity to FBOs on the ground extends to communities of the same faith as well as other faiths. In fact, in some countries FBOs have enjoyed more receptivity from religious communities of different beliefs than have secular organizations because of a higher trust in the motivation of FBOs, even if they are from a different faith. Serge Duss, a well-known humanitarian expert, noted that: "In some non–Christian countries, Christian identification has enhanced our ability to work with local communities and national governments. Unlike Western society, which separates the spiritual from the physical, Islamic societies in particular integrate the spiritual into every aspect of their lives. Both Christians and Muslims believe that there's a witness of faith through charity that is a way of life and expression of obedience to God" (Ferris 2005, 324).

In countries where the population has feared the oversecularization of assistance or the approach of some particular secular actors, FBOs have offered a welcome alternative or even replacement, coming from a more traditionalist approach, which is more palatable to local populations (Pew 2006, 1).

Heal the sick who are there and tell them, "The kingdom of God is near you."

Gospel of Luke 10:9

The Challenges

Although these external and internal factors have combined to pave the way for FBOs to play a greater role on the international stage, the picture of FBOs' engagement is naturally not a perfectly rosy one. The expanding role of FBOs comes with significant challenges and complications.

The receptivity that FBOs enjoy with local populations is not uniform. Although it is impossible to measure the degree and frequency with which faith, in and of itself, is the singular factor that spurs rejection, FBOs do experience opposition from local communities due in part to their faith identity, and at times the skepticism and mistrust FBOs have met because of their faith or national origin directly impact their ability to operate. In the developing world, long histories of colonialism and interventionism have left some populations skeptical of Western Christian FBOs, seeing them as part of a broader effort to expand Western influence or convert locals to Christianity even when Christian FBOs have humanitarian objectives that are similar to secular organizations. Related to this, many countries—particularly those for whom the concept of separating faith and state is unfamiliar—find the notion that foreign governments hire FBOs solely for humanitarian purposes suspect at best. Some populations have viewed Western governments' use of FBOs as a covert means to infiltrate societies to spread Christianity as opposed to provide humanitarian or other services. Likewise, in countries in which Muslim FBOs are active, Western governments and donors have raised concerns about whether these groups have links to Islamic terrorist or other radical organizations (Barnett and Stein 2011, 7). Both of these perceptions have impacted FBOs' ability to operate on the ground.

There are ongoing debates about whether secular governments, international organizations, and financial institutions should fund FBOs or whether this violates the separation between faith and public institutions. One particularly contentious element of this debate has been what the correct balance is between FBOs' exercising their freedom of religion and expression versus broader concerns about nondiscrimination in hiring.[2] Likewise, many in Western donor countries and international organizations have debated the extent to which FBOs should have influence on the policy process. Some have argued that the growing influence of FBOs on the decision-making process of governments is another instance where faith groups overstep boundaries, violating the separation of faith and state (Haynes 2010, 389). Others argue that FBOs, just like any other subset of society, should be able to influence the public policy process. Additionally, some recipient communities are skeptical that FBOs are capable of or committed to providing services without proselytizing, given the strong faith adherence of staff, even when performing nonproselytizing activities. Similarly, some donor organizations and governments remain concerned that FBOs will proselytize with public funds meant for other work (Abrams 2001, 184). Each of these issues adds a challenging layer to FBOs' engagement on policy and programmatic issues.

There continue to be differing views between religious and secular communities around key family issues, such as sexual orientation, women's rights, reproductive rights, and family planning. How the agency and social recognition dimensions of human dignity apply to these specific issues has been at the core of significant substantive clashes between these communities.

These are just a few of the challenges that have emerged with the changing role of FBOs, making clear that this growing role is not without serious, substantive controversy or complications. These important debates, however, also illustrate and reinforce the thesis of this chapter: Faith and FBOs have moved into the public sphere and have become global institutions impacting human dignity. If faith were irrelevant or FBOs largely ineffective, faith and FBOs would be sidelined or absent from the global stage, and these debates would dissipate. Because faith has become more central to the debate on international issues and faith-based actors more vocal on matters of human dignity, FBOs' perspectives on human dignity are germane, whether in congruence or conflict with other voices. Likewise, if the concept of human dignity did not resonate with such a significant portion of the global population, it too would not be gaining traction within the international community.

Illiberal Faith-Based Actors

The factors that created space for liberal FBOs—decline in confidence in states, increasing religiosity, changing identities, and growing connectivity across borders—have also created space for a whole host of illiberal faith-based actors on the international stage. Many of the aforementioned dislocations that have come from globalization are the same ones that drive illiberal groups to fight for increased political influence and expansion of their ideology's prevalence. Some even use language about their fight for "dignity," defined, however, as a virtue extended only to those in their specific religious group and as a justification for the use of violence against those believed to be violating the dignity of their coreligionists. This naturally leads one to ask how the faith that compels some to promote universal human dignity can be the same faith that for others is a source of violence and impetus for the vitiation of the dignity of others.

Monica Duffy Toft, who has done significant research on what contributes to religious groups taking an illiberal orientation, argues that one major factor contributing to this radicalization is the political theology of religious leaders. If religious leaders adopt a political theology—their core doctrine of political authority and justice—that includes liberal ideas, including human rights or religious freedom for all people, followers are unlikely to use violence to advance their objectives. And those leaders who equate religious devotion to violence and eradication of nonbelievers will lead their followers toward destructive behavior. Likewise, Duffy Toft argues that the relationship between the political and religious authorities determines whether a faith-based person or group will choose radicalization or a more peaceful expression of their faith. Those groups that are not afforded religious freedom, are excluded from political processes, or do not have a significant means of political and religious expression will turn to radicalized or violent means of expressing their views (Duffy Toft, Philpott, and Shah 2011, 16). It is when these deeply held religious views are linked with political or social inequalities or imbalances and the inability to rectify them politically (matters of dignity denied) that religious actors use faith teachings to justify the use of violence to restore the sense of justice, which they see as consistent with the will of a higher being. Mark Juergensmeyer also writes that although religion is not completely "innocent" in its links to violence, it does not "ordinarily lead to violence." Rather, he argues religious violence occurs only when there is a "coalescence of a peculiar set of circumstance—political, social, and ideological—when religion becomes fused with violent expressions of social aspirations, personal pride, and movements for political change" (Juergensmeyer 2003, 10).

As one sees throughout the world, illiberal actors significantly impact the international arena, global security and stability, and the realization of universal human dignity. They also significantly impact the work of the liberal FBOs discussed in this chapter. For example, the rise of terrorism and illiberal networks invoking Islam has negatively impacted the perceptions in the global North of those Muslim charitable organizations dedicated to promoting human dignity. Violence perpetrated in the name of any religion has contributed to the polarization between faith communities in some countries, which over the long term inhibits the work of liberal FBOs. Therefore, it is not only important to note the stark differentiation between the impact the liberal and illiberal groups have on promotion of universal human dignity. It is equally significant for scholars and practitioners to continue to look at how the presence and growth of illiberal groups will impact the role of liberal groups promoting human dignity, particularly in light of the efficacy of the latter.

Going Forward: Issues for the International Community

Faith and FBOs are here to stay as global institutions impacting the international landscape. Most major faith traditions and FBOs have had human dignity at the center of their identity and work long before they took a prominent place on the international stage. As faith grows and FBOs gain a greater voice, faith-based groups are contributing to the growing focus on human dignity and raising the concept of human dignity as the unifying principle that will motivate the international community. This raises the question whether the legalistic framework of the human rights regime will be replaced by this more complex understanding of human dignity, recognizing the whole person—physical needs as well as political, social, cultural, and spiritual needs—and the importance of integrating all of these factors into the analysis and programs of the international community. FBOs, many of whom are driven by their spiritual understanding of the inherent value of each person and, in some traditions, that that person is created in the image of God, will be an important part of that debate and will facilitate a pivot to a more comprehensive understanding. They have already had a significant impact, and all indications are that that will continue in the medium to long term.

Returning to Lagon and Arend's original concept, we see that to be meaningful, human dignity must be institutionalized in practice and governance. What will this institutionalization look like within the context of faith groups who are already active in the work of promoting human dignity?

From a scholarly and practical standpoint, there are many issues related to faith and the role of FBOs that must be addressed. Three are listed here:

- Accepting Religion on the International Stage. Although religion is growing and FBOs are increasingly gaining influence, some scholars and practitioners continue to downplay or sideline religion as an element of, and religious actors as important players in, the foreign affairs arena. Will the impact many FBOs are having thus far and the connection that FBOs have with local populations convince policymakers that religion is an essential component of foreign policy, ensuring that it does not remain—as Douglas Johnston calls it—"the missing element of statecraft"? If there is a greater acceptance, the international community will need to consider more intentionally how it engages religion as a dimension of analysis, faith-inspired views of human dignity as an overarching principle, and the FBO community as a partner in implementation.

- New Partnerships and Sharing Best Practices. In light of the trends and successes of FBOs, international organizations and governments will need to consider how FBOs' unique set of competencies should be brought to bear on national and international objectives. It is important to examine whether successful faith-based methodologies or frameworks focused on promoting human dignity are especially applicable or successful in particular country contexts. The mobilization of the unique approach and assets of FBOs will depend on the aforementioned debate about the legality and morality of public funding for FBOs and their integration into the policy process in donor countries, intergovernmental institutions, and hybrid institutions.
- State-Civil Society Division of Labor. As noted earlier, NGOs, including FBOs, fulfill many responsibilities that the international community once assumed would be fulfilled by states. For governments that are not fulfilling their responsibilities fully, this role of NGOs provides an opportunity and a hazard. The opportunity is that governments can partner with NGOs and eventually take on these responsibilities (e.g., poverty alleviation or humanitarian protection). The hazard is that governments will—by choice or capacity—never accept these responsibilities, leaving uncertainty about control, the role of the state, and sovereignty. This poses an important question for those states and intergovernmental organizations as to how to help define or guide that relationship between NGOs and governments, particularly in postconflict or developing countries. How the international community empowers the NGO or narrower FBO community vis-à-vis new or weak governments will prove important to the role of each sector in tangibly advancing people's agency and social recognition.

The past and present standing of FBOs' role is clear—rising and impactful. The future is yet to be written but all indications point to the fact that FBOs will remain pivotal actors on the international stage and will be a key contributor to the growing critical mass in the international community that is committed to making human dignity a central focus of the work of international institutions.

Notes

1. In this chapter the term "liberal" refers to the political philosophy based on the ideals of equality and liberty, as well as pluralism and tolerance. It should be distinguished from the use of the word "liberal" within the context of current US political debates between liberal and conservative political groups.

2. Most FBOs require staff to adhere to specific faith doctrines and have policies that follow their faith tradition, such as the recognition of marriage as a union between one man and one woman or opposition to birth control. Public policy debates have emerged when FBOs that have internal policies that differ from legal rights granted in the wider national context have sought public funding.

References

Abrams, Elliott. 2001. *The Influence of Faith: Religious Groups and U.S. Foreign Policy.* Lanham, Maryland: Rowman & Littlefield.

Aga Khan Development Network. 2013. "Frequently Asked Questions". Accessed August 8, 2013. http://www.akdn.org/faq.asp.

American Jewish World Service (AJWS). 2011. "2011 Annual Report." Accessed August 1, 2013. ajws.org.

Barnett, Michael, and Janice Gross Stein. 2011. *Sacred Aid: Faith and Humanitarianism.* New York: Oxford University Press.

Blair, Tony. 2008. "Faith and Globalisation" (speech). The Cardinal's Lectures 2008. Westminster Cathedral. London, April 3.

Catholic Relief Services. 2013. "HIV Healing Now in Local Church Hands." Accessed August 8, 2013. http://crs.org/south-africa/hiv-care-transition/.

Duffy Toft, Monica, Daniel Philpott, and Timothy Shah. 2011. *God's Century: Resurgent Religion and Global Politics.* New York: W. W. Norton & Company.

Economist. 2009. "A Slow Maturing of Democracy: The Latinobarómetro Poll." *Economist,* December 12. http://www.economist.com/node/15080535.

Ferris, Elizabeth. 2005. "Faith-based and Secular Humanitarian Organizations." International Review of the Red Cross. Accessed June 2005. http://www.icrc.org/eng/assets/files/other/irrc_858_ferris.pdf.

Global Fund. 2010. "Update on the Report on the Involvement of Faith-Based Organizations in the Global Fund." Accessed August 8, 2013. www.theglobalfund.org/documents/civil_society/CivilSociety_InvolvemenOfFaithBaseOrganizationsInTheGlobalFund_Report_en.

Haynes, Jeffrey. 2010. *Routledge Handbook of Religion and Politics.* Oxford: Routledge.

Johnston, Douglas. 1995. *The Missing Dimension of Statecraft.* New York: Oxford University Press.

Juergensmeyer, Mark. 2003. *Terror in the Mind of God: The Global Rise of Religious Violence.* Berkeley: University of California Press.

Kaldor, Mary, Henrietta L. Moorem, and Sabine Selchow. 2012. *Global Civil Society 2012: Ten Years of Critical Reflection.* UK: Palgrave Macmillan.

Narayan, Deepa, Robert Chambers, Meera Kaul Shah, and Patti Petesch. 2000. *Voices of the Poor: Crying Out for Change.* New York: Oxford University Press.

Narayan, Deepa, Raj Patel, Kai Schafft, Anne Rademacher, and Sarah Koch-Schulte. 2000. *Voices of the Poor: Can Anyone Hear Us?* New York: Oxford University Press.

Oomman, Nandini, Michael Bernstein, and Steven Rosenzweig. 2008. "PEPFAR Funding for Fiscal Years 2004 to 2006: The Numbers Behind the Stories." Accessed August 1, 2013. http://www.cgdev.org/files/15799_file_theNumbersBehindTheStories.PDF.

Pew Forum on Religion and Public Life. 2005. "Event: Building a 'Harmonious Society' in China." Accessed August 1, 2013. http://www.pewforum.org/Government/Building-a-Harmonious-Society-in-China.aspx.

———. 2006. "Interview: Katherine Marshall." Accessed August 1, 2013. http://www.pewforum.org/Government/Religion-and-International-Development.aspx.

Thomas, Scott M. 2004. "Faith and Foreign Aid: How the World Bank Got Religion, and Why It Matters." *The Brandywine Review of Faith & International Affairs* 2 (2): 21–29.

———. 2005. *The Global Resurgence of Religion and the Transformation of International Relations: The Struggle for the Soul of the Twenty-First Century.* UK: Palgrave Macmillan.

———. 2010. "A Globalized God: Religion's Growing Influence in International Politics." *Foreign Affairs* 89: 93.

United Nations High Commissioner for Refugees (UNHCR). 2007. "NGO Partnerships in Refugee Protection." Accessed August 1, 2013. http://www.refworld.org/docid/47a7078f0.html.

World Health Organization (WHO). 2007. "Faith-Based Organizations Play a Major Role in HIV/AIDS Care and Treatment in Sub–Saharan Africa." Accessed August 1, 2013. http://www.who.int/mediacentre/news/notes/2007/np05/en/.

World Vision International. 2011. "Annual Report 2011." Accessed August 1, 2013. http://www.wvi.org/publication/world-vision-international-annual-review-2011.

CHAPTER 14

Business, Human Rights, and the Internet

A Framework for Implementation

MICHAEL A. SAMWAY

The primary purpose of this chapter is to offer practical guidance to companies on how to respect human rights. In the context of this book, this chapter is also intended to show the increasing role corporations in the information and communications technology (ICT) sector have in the lives of citizens globally and how this growing influence impacts the traditional balance of power between states and nonstate actors in the international system.

Although focused on ICT companies, many of the recommendations should apply to companies in other industries. The key question in this chapter is the following: How can a company promote and sustain responsible decision making regarding those human rights impacted by the products, services, or corporate actions of the business itself?

Whereas global ICT companies, like other businesses operating in international markets, must grapple with important international labor rights issues having a bearing on human dignity, this chapter is not directly about a company's labor practices, whether related to their own employees or their suppliers' or agents' employees. The human rights in the spotlight here are freedom of expression and privacy. The freedom of expression issues discussed are focused on political speech. The privacy discussion is focused on government demands for user data and not on the related issues of corporate collection of user data for purposes of advancing advertising goals. In this context, the practices by governments or companies, or both, that give rise to challenges around freedom of expression and privacy are online censorship and surveillance.

Although covering some of the conceptual background on the topic of business and human rights, including the UN Framework prepared by the secretary-general's special representative on business and human rights, the emphasis here is squarely on common sense steps a company should take to create, operate, and sustain an internal program focused on protecting human rights that may be implicated by the company's operations. When businesses incorporate these types of steps, they also enlarge recognition of the global voices upon which human dignity rests. And although framed around ICT companies, a number of lessons offered here should apply to global corporations as international institutions more generally.

Technology and Human Rights

America's online innovation epicenter, Silicon Valley, is replete with ICT companies founded by and filled with progressive employees—from engineers to advertising executives—who often reveal an unflinching belief in globalization, in doing right by their company's global customers, and in protecting those customers' internationally recognized rights. The online products and services offered by these international companies, large and small, often have the potential to promote access, openness, learning, and sharing globally. Many employees across companies in the global ICT field are inspired by the potentially transformational impact their companies' products and services might have on people and societies around the world.

Today's ICT company employees, and much of the media and even the US government, often express the belief that online products and services—from search to social media—are basic tools, virtual hammers and nails, essential to building the foundation and structure of democracies globally, in particular in nations with repressive governments. This sentiment is evident even when promotion of democratic values is nowhere to be found in these companies' mission statements or Wall Street securities disclosure language.

Greater access to information and communications tools, especially in authoritarian regimes, has indeed meant citizens are more aware than ever before of their own circumstances relative to the outside world. Those with access to the internet, whether through a personal computer or mobile device, are no longer solely force-fed online or traditional media propaganda by their own governments. They have choices, in this context anyway, like never before (Clinton 2010).

Information available online has been empowering for citizens across the globe. Citizens have used the information and communications products of the internet, including social media tools, to learn, organize, and report. The political, economic and social impact of the internet puts ICT companies at the center of creating, maintaining, and shaping the platform hundreds of millions of people use to improve their lives. ICT companies have become agents of change in today's global system. "Unlike companies that produce sportswear or toothpaste, the value proposition of internet-related companies relates directly to the empowerment of citizens" (MacKinnon 2012, 172).

Though it is not yet clear how large a role these technological tools played and will play in events like the Arab Spring for example, the internet has indisputably allowed citizens to speak out, organize, and communicate with each other and often to the global public on a scale and with a velocity previously unobtainable. Although scholars argue about the impact of the tools themselves as well as the still-pending results of the societal upheavals, the internet has transformed and propelled issue advocacy and awareness. Sometimes this citizen awareness, initiated on the internet, fuels grievances and even violence, as in the case of certain of the global protests against an anti-Islam film trailer distributed online in 2012.

Readily available and inexpensive access to information and communications services online forms one side of the empowerment equation. This information and these tools create power in the hands of the people thanks to the internet, an apparent equalizing force against governments. Advancing the cause of human rights might seem to follow inexorably. That conclusion, however, may be too simplistic and may not capture the often painful interim steps for a repressed citizenry to come to live in a society, as the editors of this book aptly say, in which human dignity is institutionalized in practice and governance.

States use the same online technologies, developed and offered by corporations, to limit information or even manipulate it, and states are becoming more sophisticated in their pursuit of censorship, propaganda, and surveillance. This is the other side of the power equation. Although corporations are one of the multiplicity of actors discussed in this book that threaten to disrupt the traditional balance of power between states and nonstate actors, ICT companies themselves have not yet upset that balance and do not yet maintain shared authority with respect to the rights of global internet users. Similarly, corporations, even in the ICT sector, do not challenge the loyalties of citizens vis-à-vis states. Global internet users are more attached to the platforms of expression and communication—whether those provided by Twitter, Facebook, You-Tube, or Yahoo! Mail—than to the corporations themselves.

The products and services offered by today's largest ICT companies do not, in and of themselves, automatically advance the cause of human rights. Internet scholar Rebecca MacKinnon notes some companies often feel the internet is like "freedom juice" from which all things grow in democratic ways. Advancing human rights requires more than simply pouring well-designed online products into international markets, including into closed regimes, and hoping this fertilizes the seeds and soil of democracy.

In authoritarian regimes today there is a technology and psychological tools arms race between citizens seeking political openings and those in government trying to preserve a closed political system (Morozov 2012). Since corporations are the manufacturers of the technological tools (including software and hardware) in this arms race, companies are often agents for both the people and the state—sometimes at the same time.

Governments like those in China, Cuba, Vietnam, and Iran, among other places, have found an efficient tool for limiting access to information they find threatening and for spreading information glorifying their own authoritarian rule. Those same governments have also found a more nefarious tool— surveillance of their own citizens' electronic correspondence, Web postings (whether photos, whereabouts, or contacts) and general online activities. This surveillance, which includes demands or searches for historical data, is sometimes direct through government system architecture and sometimes conducted by private companies under legal compulsion to assist state-controlled entities.

Many of these governments cloak the motivation for their actions behind national campaigns to restrict online pornography or to intercept electronic messages for national security purposes. These, and other crime-fighting functions, are the rightful responsibilities of all governments when content limitation or data demands and surveillance are conducted for the right reasons and in countries where the rule of law is strong. The challenge for companies in the global market arises when those pursuits mask politically driven censorship and surveillance intended to curtail protected national and international rights to freedom of expression and privacy.

Although the internet—driven principally by the creative and rapid technological developments of corporations—has allowed citizens to challenge state authority, governments use these same high-tech tools to censor and monitor their own citizens. Further, governments—in particular in those countries where the rule of law is weak—use local laws and regulations to compel corporate action that may undermine citizens' human rights.

The first-order responsibility of corporations in this context is to avoid direct violations of human rights or complicity in such abuses. This, in the language of the UN Framework on Business and Human Rights, is the responsibility to respect human rights. Once that primary responsibility is fulfilled, a company may dedicate resources to, and focus on, advancing or promoting human rights—again, to the extent its products or services otherwise have the potential to accomplish that laudable goal. With hope, the internet will eventually prove to be a great liberating force—politically and economically—for citizens around the globe. In the meantime, corporations should put in place internal programs to minimize risks of complicity with those governments that use these same potentially liberating tools of technology as means of oppression.

Corporate Social Responsibility

Until about the 1990s, managing a business within the confines of the law and otherwise remaining good, even active, citizens in local markets by way of charitable events, sponsorships, community involvement, and contributions all made for good business practices and for what was considered good corporate citizenship. Independent of the financial success of the businesses itself, employees and local community members had reason to feel good about those companies that were socially engaged in their communities and were otherwise contributing to admirable local or even national causes. Although some of this corporate involvement was driven by public relations and marketing efforts to enhance the company brand, the employee commitment was genuine, and the positive effect was often tangible and meaningful to local communities.

The most progressive companies tried to address social and environmental challenges through sustainable business practices and recognition of international normative standards in their respective industries. Many companies began to formalize commitments to community engagement and sustainable business practices by forming internal corporate social responsibility teams, commonly referred to as CSR programs. Today, CSR programs abound in business, but the practices encompassed by CSR groups across companies vary greatly (Bader 2008). CSR is viewed by many corporations as an open-ended promise of good corporate actions. It has often meant doing good for local causes, harnessing the products or services of the company itself— whether advertising, clothing and footwear, employee manpower—and generally being a contributor to charitable causes, leveraging the energy and labor of company employees.

Unfortunately, the traditional CSR approach, now widely adopted across business, has not kept pace with the international intersection points of business and human rights, particularly in the technology field. The dramatic changes in the role business plays, across multiple jurisdictions, in the distribution of news and information and in communication make the touch points with human rights issues more common, more complicated, and more closely related to the products and services offered directly by ICT businesses. The change brought about by globalization and the internet in particular demands a new, more focused, model for ensuring companies do not become complicit in government activities inconsistent with citizens' internationally recognized—and often locally and constitutionally guaranteed—rights to freedom of expression and privacy.

Corporate Challenges

The principal challenge in this context for companies in the ICT sector arises where the law, or the day-to-day practice by government entities and officials, in a foreign country in which a company is doing business comes into conflict with internationally recognized human rights enshrined in the Universal Declaration of Human Rights (UDHR) and other international accords, such as the International Covenant on Civil and Political Rights or the International Covenant on Economic, Social, and Cultural Rights.

Companies, once they establish local operations in a certain jurisdiction, are bound as a matter of corporate legal obligation, to follow the law in those places, including the laws involving the regulation of online speech and government access to online records and activities. Failure by a locally incorporated entity to follow the laws of that state might jeopardize the freedom, or even the safety, of the company's employees, potentially substituting one human rights challenge for another. Criminal penalties, including imprisonment, are real risks for locally-based employees who disobey local laws. The decision to open a locally incorporated business, with all it entails from a local legal perspective, is a threshold decision companies should only make after thorough due diligence on the implications for both users and local employees.

In thinking about these challenges while working at Yahoo!, we posed questions on the company's public-facing corporate blog to give others a sense of some of the freedom of expression and privacy challenges confronting the business as it expanded into new, more politically restrictive international markets. These questions included:

How do we deal with obligations to follow laws of nations where the laws themselves or their application may have consequences inconsistent with internationally recognized values and standards? Are partially censored results, with notice to users, better than no results at all in a challenging market? Should we focus our concerns on censorship of political speech? Should companies draw the line on doing business somewhere based on the type of speech a government limits? Would it be a decision based on the quantity or the quality of limitations? And using which standards and measures?

Could Article 19 of the Universal Declaration of Human Rights provide a starting point? Our own First Amendment is quite broad; could that be a global standard? How do companies design product approaches that balance legitimate government rights and requirements for data access with adequate protections for user privacy? Do we agree neither right should be absolute and each should live in balance with the other? Should we design an approach that works in Beijing, Paris, Sao Paulo, Sydney, Toronto, and Washington, D.C. all at once? Is that possible? How far can a company go in challenging local laws and orders? What if it puts locally-based employees at risk? These are just a few of the questions we've been asking ourselves recently.[1]

Companies should anticipate the most likely scenarios involving their own business where local law or practice may come into conflict with international norms and where the company may be compelled by the government to take steps that interfere, indirectly or even directly, with local citizens' rights to freedom of expression and privacy. Companies should develop thoughtful and sustainable ways to address these types of questions, and hundreds more like them, as they relate to their own business decisions. These types of questions merit both thought and action from companies, in an organized and deliberate way, in order for a company to protect human rights implicated by their products and services (Posner 2012).

Background

The UDHR was adopted with near unanimity by the UN General Assembly on December 10, 1948, in the aftermath of World War II and the state-directed genocide of the Holocaust. Although UN member states subsequently adopted covenants including the International Covenant on Civil and Political Rights, the focus for purposes of this chapter is on certain provisions of the UDHR itself. For the discussion on freedom of expression and privacy in the ICT sector, UDHR Articles 19 and 12 apply. Article 19 states: "Everyone has the right to freedom of opinion and expression; this right includes freedom to hold opinions without interference and to seek, receive, and impart information and ideas through any media and regardless of frontiers." Article 12 states: "No one shall be subjected to arbitrary interference with his privacy, family, home, or correspondence, nor to attacks upon his honour and reputation. Everyone has the right to the protection of the law against such interference or attacks" (UN General Assembly 1948).

Why have human rights become an issue for companies? Nobel economics laureate Milton Friedman's theory of corporate responsibility is that a corporation's principal task is to follow the law and maximize value for shareholders. Although he noted that a company may realize long-term benefits from other activities, potentially including social responsibility work, his overall point is clear on the primary responsibilities that should drive corporate decision making (Friedman 1970). This view is often echoed in the corporate community, and the argument most often advanced is that human rights are the responsibilities of governments.

This industry position sidesteps the point that even though governments have assumed primary responsibility in the international system to protect human rights, nonstate actors also have human rights obligations. Whereas the UDHR does not explicitly mention corporations, its preamble refers to individuals "and every organ of society," a term suggesting the obligations enshrined in the document may indeed apply under international law to organs such as corporations in addition to states themselves. The idea that corporations may have responsibilities pursuant to international legal norms or by some accounts even under domestic law (with a number of cases filed in the United States under the Alien Tort Claims Act for example), beyond the treatment of their own employees, with respect to human rights in the communities in which they operate, is a newly evolving field.

Until the 1980s, there was only limited public focus on companies as defenders of human rights. The environmental movement, as applied to business, was brought further into the international community's focus by the chemical plant disaster in Bhopal, India in 1984 with the devastating loss of human life resulting from industrial gas leaks at a corporate pesticide-producing facility. In the 1990s, supply chain and labor rights abuses in the apparel industry became global issues, as newspaper headlines announced stories of sweatshops and child labor. At the same time, the oil, gas, and mining industries came under the spotlight for environmental degradation, labor abuses, and community safety and security concerns. With the growing focus on the sometimes direct role of companies infringing on human rights, company codes of conduct became common by the end of the 1990s.

UN Framework on Business and Human Rights

The Global Compact, a voluntary policy initiative for businesses committed to aligning their operations and strategies with ten universally accepted principles in the areas of human rights, labor, environment, and anticorruption, was established by then UN secretary-general Kofi Annan in 2000. By design, the Global Compact does not monitor its participants' commitments to the elaborated principles even though it does maintain integrity measures that determine ongoing participation in good standing.

In 2005, Secretary-General Annan appointed Harvard University professor John Ruggie as special representative on Business and Human Rights, a role mandated by the UN Commission on Human Rights to advance the discussion on business and human rights. In 2008, Ruggie delivered a framework based on three principles: protect, respect, and remedy. Ruggie's mandate was extended for three years, and in 2011 the UN Human Rights Council endorsed the "Guiding Principles on Business and Human Rights: Implementing the UN 'Protect, Respect and Remedy' Framework" (Ruggie 2011). In short form, the three pillars of the framework are as follows:

> State Duty to Protect. There is a state duty to protect against human rights abuses committed by third parties, including businesses, through policies, regulations, and adjudication. There are significant deficiencies in state regulations in the area of human rights, and one of the largest problems is the gap between the letter of the law and enforcement of those laws in practice.
>
> Corporate Responsibility to Respect. Corporations must act with due diligence to avoid infringing on people's rights. This is not necessarily a legal duty that applies directly to corporations under international law but a "global standard of expected conduct for all business enterprises wherever they operate." This responsibility extends to a company's business partners, agents, suppliers, and other entities in the value chain. This responsibility is interpreted to mean corporations should have a human rights policy and due diligence process.
>
> Access to Effective Remedy. Both states and corporations must support access to effective remedy for victims of corporate-related abuses. States have a responsibility to ensure remedies are available through judicial, administrative, legislative, or other means. Companies must also develop and employ grievance mechanisms that demonstrate a certain set of principles, including dialogue and engagement. In these mechanisms, the company should not sit as the sole adjudicator of the issues.

Recommendations

The practical approach set out in this chapter is based principally on a business and human rights program created at Yahoo! and formally launched in 2008.[2] This section recommends steps essential to building and sustaining a human rights program in the ICT industry. Although each company should tailor its human rights program to meet the needs of its multiple internal and external stakeholders, these steps should form a common thread in any program.

Executive Commitment

A corporate human rights program must have executive level commitment within the company. The board of directors, corporate executive officer, and senior executives must actively support the company's commitment to human rights and understand their own roles and responsibilities in ensuring the company fulfills its commitments in this area. The message, importance, and urgency of human rights in a corporation emanates from the top of the personnel hierarchy, much in the same way business priorities are established for a company and then implemented throughout the corporate ranks. The executive commitment should be communicated directly to employees to have maximum impact. The corporation should also make a public commitment to human rights. In the ICT sector, this is becoming increasingly important since global intersection points with freedom of expression and privacy have become commonplace.

Many socially responsible investment firms (SRIs) and other individual and institutional investors have suggested, often through corporate shareholder resolutions, that company boards of directors form human rights committees responsible for overseeing corporate human rights practices. Corporate legal teams usually respond to these proposals with the argument that given the role of directors versus management teams, the direct responsibility for human rights oversight is more appropriately aligned with executive and operational management than board direction. This mostly persuasive response emphasizes that day-to-day decision making on human rights at the board level confuses the role of a board and its executive management team.

Informing board members in detail of the potential human rights issues associated with the industry and giving in-depth background on a company's responsibilities must be a part of board of director training, whether for new or existing board members. Bringing strategic issues to the board's attention in a timely manner is essential; however, relying on regular board decisions is less effective than positioning that responsibility in the hands of a dedicated team that has executive officer input and support and the ability to act with sufficient speed, understanding, and resources.

Whatever corporate approach taken with respect to senior-level commitment and oversight, a company must have inward and outward facing executive and senior-level commitment to human rights, including from its board of directors. This is particularly true in a global ICT business where the nature of the business itself directly implicates two internationally recognized human rights.

Dedicated and Cross-Functional Teams

A program should be closely connected to the operations teams and integrated into the business decision-making process. The nexus of corporate actions and human rights risks typically arises with legal and regulatory questions in local markets. A company's legal or public policy team, each internally independent of the direct financial pressures that often drive operations or sales teams, is often the most appropriate corporate home for a business and human rights program. A human rights program should not rest under the umbrella of a public relations or marketing function, in part because the internal or external perception, accurate or not, is that those corporate functions have less input and decision-making authority on critical legal, regulatory, and policy decisions. Given the history of CSR, companies should also distinguish the role of a human rights program from traditional corporate giving, philanthropy, and community involvement, which sometimes strike outside observers as attempts to gloss over corporate malfeasance in other areas of the business.

Although companies maintain teams dedicated to priority business areas, human rights challenges have traditionally been viewed as emergency issues, usually requiring impromptu gatherings of knowledgeable employees. Supporting an internal team structure and protocol not only allows for more rapid responses to crises, it allows more advanced planning and thoughtfulness in crisis anticipation, resolution, and avoidance. Maintaining a formal structure, in the form of a dedicated team, also allows a company to sustain its practices beyond the interests, experience, or drive of a single employee or small group of employees.

The employee who leads the human rights program at a company should be senior enough that he or she has decision-making authority and regular access to executive level management, if not already a member of that group. This employee, in addition to providing leadership inside and outside the company must also regularly update and receive feedback from the company's senior executives regarding the company's human rights challenges, responses, and overall strategy. This feedback and strategic input loop lays the groundwork for ongoing executive commitment and involvement in human rights issues.

An effective program also requires centralized senior-level leadership on global strategy, industry initiatives, business decision making, and internal and external stakeholder engagement. In a company's decision-making process—sometimes called its business issues decision tree—the human rights team must have a respected voice in the process early on when business decisions have potential human rights implications and operational choices can be shaped by responsible decision making on human rights issues. Companies can tailor this approach based on their size and resources, and the process might range from a list of employees to consult in certain circumstances to a set of more formal corporate steps (e.g., formal sign-offs) that must be taken before a certain type of decision is made.

A company should form and maintain a business and human rights team with a clear mandate, mission, priorities, budget, and personnel. This includes a core group of employees who work as a dedicated human rights team. Although a human rights program may begin with a single employee (even if that employee has other responsibilities), it should broaden the number of employees with knowledge in the area so one employee's departure does not deplete the institutional memory or capacity of the program. Effective management and sustainability of a business and human rights program requires personal leadership, and it must also count on a group with an overall design and architecture that allows it to survive and thrive through leadership or management changes internally and at the company more generally.

Ideally, once the business and human rights team grows it will span a number of corporate disciplines, bringing cross-functional expertise to the team, including engineering, product, editorial, operations, legal, policy, and so on. One effective approach may be to create virtual team members or members of different departments who are responsible for thinking about and acting on human rights issues in their area of the business and delivering support or feedback internally to the core human rights team.

An argument frequently made by corporations in the ICT sector—where the product reach is wide but the corporations themselves may be small—is that creating a business and human rights program is too expensive. This argument often reflects deeper concerns by companies about a human rights program's necessity or usefulness. The argument made by ICT company executives is that, when boiled to its essence, human rights is not yet a high enough priority to demand greater attention or resources when compared to other business priorities.

Leaving aside the mistaken prioritization point, the ICT industry suffers from a misconception regarding the costs of a human rights program. Most companies already have the core elements of a program's personnel in the form of legal and public policy departments, privacy experts, editorial staff, producers, engineers, and so on. Creating a position and hiring or assigning—internally or externally—someone to direct a human rights program and bring together the expertise in the company is hardly cost prohibitive for ICT companies, even considering travel expenses or fees associated with participating in a multistakeholder initiative. In a start-up or small company, the person directing the program may have other responsibilities on the legal or public policy teams, adding workload of an overlapping nature but not necessarily adding personnel costs. Using virtual teams helps contain costs and also enhances the effectiveness of a program. Furthermore, a small but deeply knowledgeable group of boutique consulting and law firms offers guidance in the area of business and human rights and can be both an excellent starting point as well as an ongoing support mechanism for any company serious about building capacity to make responsible decisions in this area.

Guiding Principles and Operational Guidelines

A company's board and executives should agree on the overarching principles that guide the company with respect to human rights. A company should also publicly announce its commitments to these guiding principles, in most cases the UDHR and related international norms. With ICT companies' global reach, this type of public commitment can have a broader impact than in nearly any other industry. A company should supplement those high-level principles with more tailored and specific commitments. High-level and operational principles in the ICT sector might be contained, for example, in an industry-wide initiative establishing a set of principles and guidelines on freedom of expression and privacy.

A company should also translate those principles into practical steps to be followed by employees, partners, and agents. These operational guidelines may or may not be public in their entirety but should be detailed and should anticipate the intersection points between the company's business and potential human rights issues. Some of the information in the detailed steps may be proprietary, competitive, or involve sensitive information and should be treated accordingly. In some cases, disclosure of detailed corporate policy or practices may be limited by law, including in most national security cases for example. A company should, however, be as transparent as it can be with its users on how company decisions are made with respect to censorship and surveillance demands from governments.

A company should also recognize that detailed guidelines may not address even a majority of situations, and guidelines must provide both flexibility and adaptability to ensure the operational steps allow the company to remain in conformance with the company's guiding principles. Translating principles into practical steps also includes ongoing training for both new hires and veteran employees. Practical steps may include implementing policies directly where a company has operational control of a corporate partner or subsidiary. Where a company does not have the business authority to direct the decision making of a partner or subsidiary, a company should use its best efforts, meaning its influence commensurate with its corporate authority in the relationship, to have the partner implement the policies.

Human Rights Touch-Point Inventory and Clearinghouse

In creating a program, a company should take an inventory of the potential intersection or touch points between its products and services and human rights issues. Company leaders should ask themselves when, where, and why they will encounter human rights challenges. The internal hurdle in creating this inventory is often corporate resistance to what appears to be an internal audit. However, corporations should frame this process as an internal review and assessment and not an exercise to unfairly pry or search for presumed negligent acts by corporate employees. Some form of review will eventually come, whether by lawsuit discovery, public demands, congressional subpoena, external assessment, or media investigations. Beginning with an internally-driven review makes most sense for a company since its own employees not only know where to look for risk areas but can best digest the information in the first instance and translate that into improved policies to protect human rights.

Once a company has created the inventory of human rights touch points, it should create an internal and ongoing clearinghouse so human rights questions and issues are properly routed to the employees charged with decision making or at least with providing substantive input on human rights. The means might be a protocol that employees follow or it may be automated in some ways, with software for example, that alerts certain employees when a particular event occurs. The event might be a government take-down demand regarding content or a law enforcement order compelling data disclosure. The clearinghouse would be part of the operational guidelines and the process by which items surface to the appropriate parties inside and outside the company.

Each of these steps requires constant vigilance and updating. Too often companies rely on important issues escalating by virtue of employees who know the importance of human rights and take the initiative on their own to raise an issue up the corporate ladder. That is a necessary but insufficient approach. With data and events moving rapidly, and employees having a different set of understandings or even values, corporations must have a formal structure and protocols in place. In the ICT industry, with its reach in international markets, employees often face conflicting laws and customs across jurisdictions.

A common misperception by the general public is that an American company must directly apply US law within all its operations and for all its global users, even where the company maintains locally incorporated subsidiaries outside the United States that are entirely staffed by local citizens. Although a US company's foreign subsidiaries may be held legally accountable under certain US laws, such as the Foreign Corrupt Practices Act, locally incorporated companies are required to follow local laws, and US law may not always trump those local regulations. The First Amendment to the US Constitution offers an example of a challenging area for American ICT companies with local operations in other countries. Many other countries, including other democracies, do not guarantee as wide a range of free expression rights to their citizens. A US company doing business in one of those countries must apply local laws even if the law is more restrictive regarding free expression rights.

Human Rights Impact Assessments

Companies must be committed to exploring human rights risks that arise based on corporate products, services, and actions, especially in challenging markets where the rule of law is weak. Companies should conduct extensive research on the human rights landscape in these markets, much as they might do research on a country's tax code or on the backgrounds of the officers of a company they plan to acquire. The idea is not to create from scratch a report that looks like a US Department of State country report or an international nongovernmental organization (NGO) report on human rights. Those reports, prepared by experts, are available to the public. Companies must consult those sources, as well as numerous others, and members of a company's human rights program should also call on individual, academic, NGO, policy, government, and other experts for input and analysis. Forming institutional partnerships and developing relationships of trust in those stakeholder communities allows for confidential consultations and input invaluable to companies in mitigating risk and in creating value.

Using those among many other sources is a starting point for the research or due diligence a company should conduct in the field of human rights as it relates to the ICT sector. From its research, a company should prepare a human rights impact assessment (HRIA). HRIAs are particularly useful when entering new markets or launching new products or services. HRIAs should not be static and should be updated as market circumstances or business plans change. Ultimately, the HRIA informs and guides the evolving corporate strategies to protect ICT company customers' rights to freedom of expression and privacy. As part of a company's executive commitment to human rights, employees should be aware of, and engaged in, the human rights due diligence process. Companies should also publicly commit to this process to demonstrate to the public the company is committed to making responsible decisions where its business may intersect human rights. An HRIA should be in writing and should help form a library of reports inside a company. The detailed report may have significant sensitive and proprietary information and may need to remain confidential in part and redacted if disclosed. The company should also treat the information about local circumstances in a careful manner. For example, publicly criticizing local officials can poison key relationships and undermine business entry into a market. Certain disclosures might present risks of retaliation by state officials against local employees. Local employees should also be made aware of potential risks so they know the parent company's actions may be seen as unfriendly toward the local government and that the repercussions may be felt by the local employees.

One way to route a completed HRIA internally is to send it to corporate executives for review, signature, and assurance they will share the relevant messages or instructions with their own business teams. That may be a message of emphasis and acknowledgement, with the human rights team communicating the detailed operational points to the involved employees and to the executive team members.

An HRIA in the ICT sector should include at least the following topic areas:

The international legal and moral foundations for the rights to freedom of expression and privacy. This section should review the UDHR and covenants, which were later adopted by UN member states, plus the state of customary international law on the subject. The review should also cover the conclusions reached in the UN Framework on Business and Human Rights, including the principles of the state duty to protect, corporate responsibility to respect, and both actors' obligation to provide reasonable avenues for remedy.

The general human rights landscape in the relevant country or region, with a particular focus on rule of law, freedom of expression and privacy. This is the research that gives a company and its employees in-depth background on the issues that relate to the operations or business of the company. Companies perform due diligence on a local market's economy, business conditions, and regulatory climate. Companies must consider the human rights implications in a manner just as in-depth and detailed. Much of this information is already in the public domain and produced by various international human rights organizations, the UN, and national governments themselves.

Local laws regarding free expression and privacy. Companies should have a clear sense of what the law in a local jurisdiction requires of local businesses. This review would include not only the corporate aspects such as registration and filing requirements but also the laws that apply to the area of the business where human rights may be implicated. A company should become familiar with the laws, regulations, court decisions, or administrative practices regarding the protections of free speech and privacy.

Business and product plans for entry into the market. In order to map the company's products and services to the potential risk areas, the team leading the HRIA should outline the projected business plans for the particular market. Support for the HRIA process must come from across disciplines in the business. The operations and strategy teams, for example, must provide input on current plans for product development and distribution in certain markets. This ensures the core team conducting the HRIA knows what the business teams (whether sales, product, engineering, operations, or other) are planning and can develop strategies to limit human rights risks.

The potential to promote human rights. To the extent an ICT company's products have the potential to promote social good and human rights—whether through access to information or communications tools or both—the company should reiterate this objective in the HRIA. It is, after all, part of the decision calculus on entry into a challenging market.

Risk scenarios based on the company's products and operations. In this section, the team leading the HRIA process should explain the possible intersection points between the business and human rights issues. This should be based on experience at the company and also based on what industry counterparts, NGOs, academic experts, media, diplomats, and others might say about likely risk scenarios. One example of a risk area may be where the laws as written provide protections of certain rights, but the laws as enforced in practice do not provide that protection.

Proposed strategies for mitigating those risks and protecting human rights. This section may offer technical detail about system architecture and jurisdictional choices. For example, an ICT company may establish business operations in a local market but limit local employees' editorial decision making, where feasible, in order to limit exposure to content take-down requests by governments. Similarly, a company may limit local employee access to user information. If feasible from a business and engineering perspective, for example, a company may locate computer servers with sensitive information in markets where access can be more effectively limited in a jurisdiction with a stronger rule of law environment. This concluding section of the HRIA should also explain the company's overall commitment to high-level principles and ongoing engagement with internal and external stakeholders.

Internal and External Stakeholder Engagement

The most important stakeholders with respect to freedom of expression and privacy are a company's users—those whose rights are potentially at risk. ICT companies should communicate regularly with their users, and the public more generally, about their beliefs and practices with respect to freedom of expression and privacy. A company must also regularly engage and update its own employees, especially those located in the jurisdictions where human rights challenges may be most present and even more particularly those employees handling the sensitive matters and decision making, around free expression and privacy matters.

ICT companies should also maintain strong relationships with industry peers, human rights groups, academics, lawmakers, and diplomats among other domestic and international actors and institutions. Companies should engage actively in the network of information and thinking on freedom of expression and privacy and in the issues at stake in the ICT industry. Companies should also participate in multistakeholder initiatives with industry peers, NGOs, academics, SRIs, and individual experts. The Global Network Initiative (GNI), founded in 2008, is the principal multistakeholder initiative in the ICT industry and is an example of an emerging hybrid global institution referenced elsewhere in this book.[3] As of this writing, company members include Evoca, Facebook, Google, LinkedIn, Microsoft, Prosera, Websense, and Yahoo!. These companies are among the largest in the industry, with enormous global reach among them. Similarly, the NGOs, SRIs, academics, and individual experts who are GNI members are among the most experienced and knowledgeable in the world. Other ICT companies, large and small, that remain outside GNI risk erosion of user trust and will also miss opportunities for collaboration on issue spotting, public policy advancement, and crisis resolution.

Accountability Framework

Companies working to protect human rights should design and implement an effective accountability framework beginning with an internal human rights system and results assessment. This framework should also include incentives for employee compliance as well as consequences for failure to follow company guidelines. An internal review, which may follow many of the same principles used by existing internal financial or other audit and compliance teams, can combine systems review, data analysis, and in-person assessments to measure and evaluate a company's compliance with its own operational guidelines. The accountability framework should be closely connected to the human rights touch-point inventory, following the nexus between business operations and human rights issues.

An internal assessment is also essential to pave the way for external review and assessment. Public credibility for companies' respect for human rights will also come from submitting to an independent external assessment. Initiatives like GNI should model the way for assessments. GNI's assessment system is designed around third-party review of a member company's process for anticipating and dealing with human rights issues, and the assessment progresses into results analysis—all with a view to assisting companies to strengthen their processes and operational steps to protect freedom of expression and privacy. It is designed to be compatible with a highly competitive industry and as a result does not reveal sensitive corporate data between companies or to the public. Numerous safeguards are in place to ensure confidentiality in key areas. The direct goal of the GNI assessment is to assist the companies in strengthening their internal systems designed to protect human rights.

Another aspect of an accountability framework is for companies, similar to those in multistakeholder initiatives, to create dispute resolution channels for users with legitimate complaints regarding corporate actions impacting human rights. With the global reach of the products and services in the ICT sector, an effective corporate dispute resolution process, or grievance mechanism, must be manageable and scalable—a substantial challenge given the universe of company consumers online.

The Future of Business and Human Rights

Given the nature of the ICT industry and the growing intersection points with human rights challenges around freedom of expression and privacy, the business world is due for a new approach to these issues. Governments, in particular where the rule of law is weak, are using internet technology to infringe on the rights of their own citizens—often rights guaranteed in these same states' constitutions as well as under international law. Unfortunately, governments are manipulating their own regulatory and judicial systems—either in the letter of the law or in practice—and putting ICT companies in positions where they are at risk of complicity in violations of free expression and privacy.

This new corporate model on business and human rights recognizes the growing influence of nonstate actors—in this case corporations—in the lives of citizens globally and the corresponding responsibilities to respect the rights of people whose lives are directly impacted, in good ways and bad, by forces in the ICT sector. The new corporate model requires corporations to focus on building capacity to make responsible decisions, even where these decisions create tension between a company and a government entity.

From a practical perspective, a business and human rights program must have executive support and a dedicated team sufficiently integrated into the business itself, with sufficient resources and a senior voice in operations decision making. The human rights team and the company's employees must also have a road map with detailed directions on how to make decisions on freedom of expression and privacy issues, anticipating different scenarios employees will confront. In creating a decision-making protocol, a company should conduct an internal review of the areas in the business where employees, products, or services may encounter censorship, surveillance requests, or demands by governments.

When considering new products or markets, and in assessing existing ones, companies should conduct HRIAs, using this tool to understand the human rights landscape of a market and developing a strategy to limit the risk to human rights that may arise from company actions in that market. In developing an HRIA, a corporate human rights team should also remain actively engaged with company employees from other departments and with external stakeholders, including users, industry peers, human rights organizations, academic experts, SRIs, and even governments.

Of all the aspects of developing an effective human rights program, companies to date have been most concerned about developing accountability mechanisms, both internal and external. Companies that are not yet members of GNI often mention publicly that the financial costs are too high or that they already have sufficient systems in place to address their users' freedom of expression and privacy concerns. Reading between the lines, however, many companies believe the accountability process is too intrusive and may interfere with their daily operations or, worse, uncover substantial inadequacies in their approach to human rights.

The GNI assessment process was designed with this corporate concern in mind and is a reasonable process in depth, focus, timing, and scale. The assessors are independent and treat findings in confidence, recognizing their review is of an ongoing business in a rapidly evolving and highly competitive multibillion dollar global industry. At the same time, the review is intended to independently, expertly, and credibly assess the systems in place to address human rights issues and also to review the results in a selection of cases. A result of the review should be a detailed description of the strengths and weaknesses in a company's approach to human rights and recommendations for remedying deficiencies and continuing good practices. Corporate accountability is an essential component in protecting freedom of expression and privacy in the ICT sector and corresponds to the role corporations must play today in relation to citizens around the globe.

Today's ICT companies are increasingly confronted with difficult choices on questions of freedom of expression and privacy. Censorship and surveillance are growing practices around the world as governments, in repressive regimes in particular, seek to unfairly restrict access to information and monitor the activities of their citizens. Given the private sector's central role in the infrastructure, management, tools, and content of the internet, governments continue to enlist corporations—through legal compulsion and even extralegal threats—in their broader efforts to restrict political content they find unfavorable and to monitor the activities of citizens who criticize or otherwise oppose those in power.

The internet allows nonstate actors—from individuals to corporations—to challenge the existing international order of state primacy. The information and communications services offered by the ICT industry to citizens across the globe may indeed be tools vital to building more democratic societies, where human dignity is institutionalized in practice and governance. Governments in repressive regimes, however, are using those same tools as wrecking balls against democracy and human dignity, censoring information, expanding propaganda campaigns, and surveilling their own citizens all for unjust purposes. The conflict between the two uses of technology often leaves companies in the middle of the competing forces of citizenry and government. Companies in the ICT sector in particular must adopt a new common sense business and human rights model and build capacity to make responsible decisions when confronted with growing human rights challenges around the world.

Notes

1. I raised these questions in a previously written blog for Yahoo! Inc. The 2007 post can be accessed on the Yahoo! Business and Human Rights Program website: http://yahoo bhrp.tumblr.com/press-archive.

2. More on this can be found in my 2008 blog on the Yahoo! Business and Human Rights Program.

3. The Global Network Initiative, a multistakeholder group of companies, civil society organizations (including human rights and press freedom groups), investors, and academics, was created in 2008 to foster a collaborative approach to protect and advance freedom of expression and privacy in the ICT sector globally. For more information, see http://www .globalnetworkinitiative.org.

References

Bader, Christine. 2008. "Beyond CSR: How Companies Can Respect Human Rights." *Stanford Social Innovation Review* 6 (4).

Clinton, Hillary. 2010. "Remarks on Internet Freedom." The Newseum. Washington, DC, January 21.

Friedman, Milton. 1970. "The Social Responsibility of Business Is to Increase Its Profits." *The New York Times Magazine*, September 13.

MacKinnon, Rebecca. 2012. *Consent of the Networked: The Worldwide Struggle for Internet Freedom*. New York: Basic Books.

Morozov, Evgeny. 2012. *The Net Delusion: The Dark Side of Internet Freedom*. New York: Public Affairs.

Posner, Michael. 2012. "Assistant Secretary Posner's Speech on Internet Freedom" (speech). State of the Net Conference. Washington, DC, January 17.

Ruggie, John. 2011. "Guiding Principles on Business and Human Rights, Implementing the United Nations 'Protest, Respect and Remedy' Framework." *UN Document A/HRC/17/31,* March 21.

UN General Assembly. 1948. *Universal Declaration of Human Rights* (UDHR). December 10.

PART III

INSTITUTIONS AND VALUES: THE FUTURE

CHAPTER 15

Constructing a Dialogue on Dignity

The Path Ahead

MARK P. LAGON AND ANTHONY CLARK AREND

In the introductory chapter of this book we set forth the two goals of our project: First, we sought to explore the extent to which human dignity is already embedded in the practices of international institutions. Second, we sought to develop ways in which human dignity can play more of a role in the work of these institutions. As this book reaches an end, it is clear that there is still much work to be done. On one hand, the book points to areas of future research by others. On the other hand, the conclusions of the authors of this project invite a more thorough discussion in this chapter about how a dialogue on dignity can be constructed. What can be said about these two areas?

Questions for Others

As is the case with any work of this nature, our book raises more questions than it answers and thus invites future research to explore a variety of areas. Although we will not be able to examine these questions in this conclusion, we want to point to two broad questions that merit this exploration:

First, how has the concept of human dignity evolved over time? Even though we developed a particular definition of human dignity that we believe captures the essence of the term today, how has the concept been understood historically? Are there indications in its historical usage that might give us guidance as to how the term's perceived meaning may change in the future?

Second, whereas a number of the chapters in this book explore methods for implementing human dignity in practice, much more research needs to be done about the ways in which human dignity can be realized. In particular, it would be fruitful to explore the effectiveness of international institutions in implementing human dignity. How can such effectiveness be measured? And are there ways in which we can better assess whether certain types of institutions are more conducive to promoting human dignity in specific circumstances? For example, are there circumstances where hybrid institutions are more successful in promoting human dignity than, say, intergovernmental institutions?

It is our hope that future scholars and practitioners of global politics will be able to engage these and other questions that spring from the work in this book. But in this conclusion, we want to propose the next steps in the process to further an intellectual and intercultural dialogue that will enable institutions and partnerships to more conclusively advance dignity in the experienced lives of humankind.

Why: Unity in a Neomedieval World

The premise of this book is that we live in a neomedieval world. Although the international system is populated with nearly 200 states, alongside these states is a wide variety of dissimilar international actors that make claims for political power and vie for the authority and control over and loyalty of individuals. In medieval Europe, despite the many actors and overlapping authorities, there was a vital force that provided unity: Christianity. Prior to the destructive Thirty Years' War, the Christian religion was able to create a common belief system and shared identity for the kingdoms, principalities, and other actors that existed upon the medieval stage.

In the neomedieval world of the twenty-first century, there is no common religion upon which the political order can rely. According to recent estimates (Central Intelligence Agency 2013), approximately 33.39 percent of the world's people are Christian, 22.74 percent Muslim, 13.8 percent Hindu, 6.7 percent Buddhist, 0.35 percent Sikh, 0.22 percent Jewish, 0.11 Baha'i, 10.95 percent other religions, and the remaining percentages nonreligious or atheist. Clearly, the kind of religious unity that existed in the European Middle Ages does not obtain in today's world. But here is where the work of this book provides an alternative. In the diverse and complex neomedieval world, we argue that the concept of human dignity can provide such a unifying force. Just as Christianity could serve as the unifying idea in the past, we believe that human dignity can play that role today.

To be sure, others have asserted both the need and potential for a unifying idea in today's world. As Thomas Banchoff alludes to in chapter 12, just as the Cold War was winding down, theologian Hans Kung championed an effort to advance a postmodern global ethic bridging cultures and faiths—

and even nonbelievers (Kung 1990; Kung and Schmidt, 1993). Recently, Michael Ignatieff also resurfaced the idea of imagining a transcendent "global ethic" (Ignatieff 2012). Why, then, do we put forward human dignity as that unifying idea? As we have argued throughout this book, the concept of human dignity is primordial. It is philosophically prior to the global political system, and yet at the same time, it is the natural end of international society. Moreover, the essence of human dignity is reflected in the sacred texts of the great religions of the world. And, human dignity serves as the underlying justification for international human rights law. The three great human rights instruments—the Universal Declaration of Human Rights, the Covenant on Civil and Political Rights, and the Covenant on Economic, Cultural and Social Rights—all begin with a preamble affirming the "inherent dignity" of "all members of the human family."

But if human dignity is to provide the unifying idea for the twenty-first century, guiding the activities of global institutions, one must ask several questions: First, what would the ideational content of human dignity be in this context? Although we have proceeded from a basic definition of human dignity, how would this concept—as it is envisioned—need to be further developed as the unifying idea of the global system? Second, how would human dignity come to play this unifying role? Third, where would such a dignitarian dialogue take place? In other words, in what fora would this idea develop? Moreover, who would be the agents that would work to promote this idea? Given the multiplicity of actors in the system, which of those actors would most appropriately work to promote human dignity?

It is to these questions we now turn.

What: The Idea Animating a Dialogue

The Idea

The goal of our project is to construct a robust international consensus on human dignity. If this consensus can be achieved and human dignity can be embedded as an element of the social structure of the international system, we believe that international system will be more just and prosperous. In order to create that consensus, we need a better understanding of the content of human dignity. Again, we posit the following working definition: Human dignity is the fundamental agency of human beings to apply their gifts to thrive. As such, it requires social recognition of each person's inherent value and claim to equal access to opportunity. To be meaningful, human dignity must be institutionalized in practice and governance.

Among other influences, this definition draws insights from Plato's and Aristotle's notions of *eudaimonia* (human flourishing), Amartya Sen's and Martha Nussbaum's notions of capabilities-based development, and Francis Fukuyama's interpretation of the Ancients' concept of *thymos* as recognition (Bloom 1991; Aristotle 1999; Sen 1999; Nussbaum 1997; Nussbaum 2001; Fukuyama 1992).

Chapters in this book offer numerous examples of global institutions' efforts to advance both of the pillars of human dignity—agency and recognition. Anoop Singh shows how the International Monetary Fund (IMF) as a traditional intergovernmental organization (IGO) helps build domestic legal institutions yielding agency to individuals to prosper in a predictable and corruption-free economy. Nicole Bibbins Sedaca explores ways that faith-based institutions, in partnership with other actors, can enlarge the agency of marginalized or dispossessed people that they assist through humanitarian, poverty-alleviation, development, and conflict resolution programs. Tod Lindberg enumerates how the International Criminal Court as an IGO offers mechanisms for restitution to survivors of atrocities. He argues that these mechanisms are as important to their recognition as human beings as is prosecution of those who violated them. Benjamin Boudreaux offers recommendations for a hybrid institutional arrangement to deliver social recognition to stateless people.

What exactly is the relationship between human dignity and human rights? As a public health specialist at the Joint UN Programme on HIV/AIDS (UNAIDS), the World Bank, and the International Labour Organization (ILO), Rosalía Rodriguez-García observes in her examination of anti-HIV/AIDS policy in this book that "Rights spring from inherent dignity at the macro level, while at the micro level, especially when human dignity has been suppressed or attacked, the application of human rights would aim at restoring dignity." In short, the relationship between dignity and rights is twofold. First, as noted earlier, human dignity is the premise behind human rights. It is a larger, foundational concept: that all human beings have inherent worth. But second, at the practical level, human dignity is the product of human rights. That is, if human rights are to have meaning beyond norm elaboration in resolutions, treaties, and law and are to be enjoyed in practice, the test of impact is whether they actually yield the agency and social recognition that constitute human dignity.

It is in arguing that human dignity, rather than human rights, should be the idea shaping the mission of the global institutions that the first of two major potential critiques of this book arises. Some might argue that by embracing human dignity one is distancing the work of global institutions from human rights and abandoning hard-fought achievements to embed human rights into international law and institutional practice. Lest we be misunderstood, human rights are indisputably crucial. In his Preface, John J. DeGioia rightly focuses on the Universal Declaration on Human Rights. A project to construct an international system that is dignity centered is an exercise in building upon the concepts of human rights, not jettisoning them. Indeed, human dignity helps transcend the misplaced segregation and prioritization between political-civil and socioeconomic rights respectively. Property and land rights protecting the global poor's means of subsistence, nondiscrimination, and access to antiretroviral drugs for the populations vulnerable to HIV/AIDS, or social protections for human trafficking victims before or after being identified are all cases where political-civil and socioeconomic access to justice is intermingled.[1] Human dignity helps conceptually justify dealing with both types of rights holistically.

Moreover, as Lagon and Kaminski note in chapter 6 on the global architecture on human rights, effective implementation of human rights has fallen far short of the norms promulgated on the national, regional, and global levels as a function of lacking institutional capacity and will. Human dignity offers a philosophical basis for broader consensus for action.

Dimensions of a Dignatarian Dialogue

To build a consensus on human dignity, there must be a philosophical and political dialogue on a global level. There are three necessary dimensions to this dignitarian dialogue.

One dimension relates to first principles. At the outset, open discourse is needed concerning whether there really is a common teleology of human dignity that crosses the divide between cultures, between faiths, and between faith-inspired and secular thought. As noted earlier, the essence of human dignity is reflected in the sacred texts of the great religions all over the world, as Thomas Banchoff notes in chapter 12 in this book. Moreover, Nicole Bibbins Sedaca observed that some societies with a majority population practicing one faith tradition surprisingly often welcome faith-based nongovernmental organizations (NGOs) of another faith that are conducting programmatic work to help the disadvantaged. This observation, although deserving deeper empirical exploration, is encouraging regarding the potential for consensus between faiths and cultures on first principles.

A second dimension deals with operationalizing dignity—on how to better turn norms into action. As just noted, according to Lagon and Kaminski, it appears human rights norms have stalled in their implementation, whether their goal is to shrink atrocities, unfetter political dissent, or economically empower the impoverished. The dialogue must focus on how to build on the achievements of human rights by taking advantage of the power of human dignity as an idea. After all, the aim of dialogue is not dignity asserted, but dignity realized. The emotive and mobilizing power of the dignity concept that Thomas Banchoff emphasizes in chapter 12 has potential to advance the realization of dignity in practice.

Even as a variety of institutions place dignity questions on their agendas, much of the dialogue on operationalizing dignity will take place in the messy, day-to-day world that is global politics. In other words, the dialogue will take place as actors struggle to realize human dignity in practice—when IGOs, NGOs, and states respond to a humanitarian crisis, when groups from the private sector address supply chain issues to prevent human exploitation, and when faith-based organizations assist dispossessed individuals. What is required is that the notion of human dignity figures in these interactions as these diverse groups struggle with real problems in the international system.

The third dimension of dialogue addresses goal prioritization in implementation efforts. In particular, when prioritizing goals in practice, are there any tensions and trade-offs between agency and social recognition as the two major aspects of dignity? Is there a necessary priority of sequencing where recognition must precede agency, or vice versa? Consider, for instance, Mark P. Lagon's chapter 11 in this book on what makes for truly transformative institutional partnerships to combat human trafficking. Victim protection for survivors of human trafficking involves trade-offs pertaining to realization of dignity. Should a humanitarian visa from a national government that regularizes a victim's status as an undocumented migrant or as eligible for state-supported medical and social services be conditioned upon cooperation with law enforcement as a witness against a trafficker? Such conditionality favors social recognition—prosecuting the victim's tormenter—over agency—the victims' freedom to avert deportation or to decide if repatriation is desirable. And even regarding social recognition itself, such conditionality favors one form of recognition—affirming victims' worth by vigorously pursuing prosecution of their trafficker—over another—being treated as inherently worthy of access to state-supported care.[2]

There are numerous other questions of priorities in implementation that a dialogue on dignity could fruitfully address. For example, if human dignity has the potential to bridge the areas of political-civil and the socioeconomic rights and empowerment, what questions of sequencing or balancing still remain? Or for the degrading atrocities, human trafficking, poverty, or pandemic disease addressed by at least six chapters in the book, should remediation for those whose dignity has already been robbed take precedence over prevention of others being robbed of it? Or, although measuring the impact of global institutions' programs based on sound metrics would help show which ones enhance dignity most, what percentage of finite funding should be diverted from directly benefiting beneficiaries into conducting assessments of how much they are benefiting?

In short, a dialogue on dignity must address strategies and tangible priorities for implementation as much as they address first principles.

How: Dialogue by Dialectic and Incorporation

But if our goal is to encourage a dialogue on dignity, what exactly is meant by the term "dialogue" in this context? In the international relations literature on constructivism, there is much discussion of "norm entrepreneurs," a term legal scholar Cass Sunstein helped bring into prominence (Sunstein 1996). A norm entrepreneur is an actor—state, intergovernmental institution, nongovernmental institution, individual, or other participant—who seeks to promote a given norm with a view toward gaining its acceptance and ultimate implementation in the international community. So for example, Canada as a state, its then foreign minister Lloyd Axworthy, and the International Coalition to Ban Landmines might all be understood as entrepreneurs who played a critical role in international efforts to establish a norm against the use of landmines. Their actions led to the development of a norm to ban the use of landmines that was ultimately codified in the Convention on the Prohibition of the Use, Stockpiling, Production, and Transfer of Anti-Personnel Mines and on their Destruction (Dolan and Hunt 1998).

As the chapters in this book demonstrate, there are critical roles to be played by a variety of norm entrepreneurs in advancing the concept of human dignity. Abiodun Williams, for example, explicitly examines the dynamic role of the UN secretary-general as a norm entrepreneur in promoting norms such as the Responsibility to Protect in situations of human rights atrocities. But we want to be clear at the outset that our goal is not simply to gain acceptance of a concept of human dignity that is static and set in stone. Rather our goal is to promote a dialogue on human dignity. What does this mean? Although we believe that our working definition offers the basic contours of human dignity, a true dialogue means mutual exchange and mutual learning.

An example of how this dialogue can work can be illustrated by the development of international human rights law. Following the adoption of the UN Charter, one of the first tasks of the new global organization was to develop an international bill of rights. In the debates that produced the

Universal Declaration of Human Rights and subsequent treaties on human rights, there was a clash of definitions. Western states, led by the United States, emphasized civil and political rights as the true human rights, whereas the Soviet Union and its Allies, focused on economic, social, and cultural rights. As the debate continued in subsequent decades—even while still in a Cold War context of suspicion of Soviet-aligned states conveniently seeking to deprioritize political freedom—it led the United States to a greater appreciation of economic, social, and cultural rights. Indeed, in his Law Day speech of April 30, 1977, US Secretary of State Cyrus Vance was clear in acknowledging the "right to the fulfillment of such vital needs as food, shelter, health care, and education" (Vance 1977). And although it took a bit longer as the Cold War came to an end, the former Eastern-bloc states came to recognize, even if imperfectly, the importance of civil and political rights. This was a dialogue. There were both mutual exchange and mutual learning.

This kind of discourse is what we are proposing for human dignity. As we have posited a working definition of human dignity, we hope that the great diversity of actors in the international arena will engage that definition. And we hope that this discourse will modify, improve, and ultimately construct an even better, more workable definition of human dignity. In a constructive dialectical tension, contending ideas can be accommodated and incorporated.

Where and Who: Venues and Catalytic Actors for Dialogue

But if there is to be a dignitarian dialogue, where is it to take place? Some of the great foundational documents of global politics have been fashioned at a grand international conference—the Paris Peace Conference that produced the League of Nations Covenant or the San Francisco Conference that produced the UN Charter. It might seem that there should be a similar convening to conduct the dialogue on human dignity. But even the San Francisco Conference was preceded by years of negotiations that took place among the Allies during the Second World War. In the current neomedieval system, there can be no literal San Francisco Moment for human dignity. First, it is impossible to bring all the constitutive actors together in one place at one moment in time. Second, a true dialogue on human dignity requires much time and nonadversarial deliberation.

A number of global institutions differing in character could play a particularly valuable role in the three dimensions of building consensus on (1) first principles, (2) operationalizing dignity, and (3) grappling with priorities and trade-offs in implementation. Two types of global institutions in a neomedieval world that would advance this practice and governance are treated in this book. First are the traditional institutions. This category includes states and IGOs, including those discussed in this book, such as the UN, the World Bank, the International Monetary Fund, the International Criminal Court, and a variety of regional organizations. As noted above, some of these institutions—like the UN and regional organizations— can often provide a forum for other actors to engage in a dialogue, but these institutions are also themselves actors and can work in such a way as to promote human dignity.

Second, the book also explores the role of what might be called emerging institutions and partnerships. These include such entities as the Global Fund to Fight AIDS, Malaria, and Tuberculosis (Global Fund), a variety of faith-based institutions, and private sector actors, such as Yahoo! or Google. These actors offer great potential in the human dignity dialogue in part because they can often make things happen more quickly than states or traditional IGOs that have entrenched bureaucracies and structures that can slow down policymaking and agenda-setting. The emergence of such hybrids, partnerships, and nonpublic institutions is not merely a symptom of a more complicated and less accountable landscape of global institutions in a neomedieval world; it offers vital new agents with potential to promote human dignity.

Among these two kinds of global institutions, which ones would be most promising for pursuing the dignitarian dialogue? First, among traditional intergovernmental organizations, universal membership bodies may not be the best place to begin. Just as Lagon and Kaminski focus on regional organizations in their recommendations on the international human rights architecture, so too might these institutions serve the broader dignity project. As Chester Crocker notes in chapter 4, despite the challenges of sovereignty and national security, it is not only regional organizations comprised primarily of democracies—such as the European Union, North Atlantic Treaty Organization, and the Organization of American States—that could prove successful in advancing dignity.

The Arab League, for example, has proven it is a positive voice and force urging action by other actors in recent humanitarian crises in Libya and Syria and elsewhere. It may be counterintuitive that a regional group with nondemocratic governments could advance human dignity, but it is striking how in these cases they adopted such a posture. Perhaps individual Arab states will follow suit and use the Arab League as a forum to address issues such as governance reform, diversifying the bases of their economies and political orders from petroleum, and tapping the squandered social and economic asset of women. Just as governance accountability and dispatching peacekeepers on each other's soil became more palatable topics within the African Union, so too the Arab League shows that promise to engage human dignity.

The Association of Southeast Asian Nations (ASEAN) has an opportunity to evolve from what is called the ASEAN Way—the emphasis on economic coordination and the deference to sovereignty on political matters (Weber 2011, 222). ASEAN avoided candidly confronting the government of Myanmar before its post-2011 reforms, save for circumstances when Myanmar was poised to assume the body's rotating chair. Yet now ASEAN has an opportunity to assist Myanmar's reentry into the regional and world economy and in the process highlight how transparency and free flow of information serve the goals of dignity. Perhaps the occasion of Myanmar's reform might prompt ASEAN to find its voice on dignity too.

Finally, there might be a heightened role for the Organization for Security and Cooperation in Europe (OSCE) on dignity, beyond its current work on election monitoring, conflict resolution, and combating human trafficking. After all, the OSCE springs from the body set up by the Helsinki Final Act of 1975 that provided a framework for the East and West to dialogue on the three baskets of issues—security, economic relations, and human rights. The dialogue on human rights in particular helped create benchmarks for Eastern European populaces to demand basic freedoms from their governments. Moreover, the OSCE offers an asset where the dignitarian dialogue involves bridging the false dichotomy of civil-political and socioeconomic rights, respectively championed by the global North and the global South. The OSCE encompasses the nations of the global North, which would need to engage the global South in discourse about these two realms of rights being inextricably tied together. The global North could caucus within the OSCE in a new role for that body with the purpose of pursuing that North-South dialogue.

Another possible advocate for human dignity is the G–20. Unlike treaty-based or highly formal IGOs, the G–20 offers a more flexible potential for dialoguing on and applying the idea of human dignity. A number of scholars in the wake of the 2008–2009 global financial crisis expressed wildly over-ambitious aims for the G–20 (Alexandroff 2010; Shorr 2012). Hopes for broader economic or even geopolitical roles (where the Security Council deadlocks and cannot plausibly in the foreseeable future be enlarged to incorporate more voices) proved unwarranted. But a body whose twenty members represent over 80 percent share of the world's combined GDP and population and is flexible in character offers an opportunity to go beyond financial policy coordination to facilitate dignity-centered dialogue and policy implementation.

Second, emerging institutions and partnerships could also have a special role to play. As proposed in Anthony Clark Arend's chapter 7 on matters of terrorism, the International Committee of the Red Cross (ICRC) has an opportunity to play a role in advancing dialogue and practice at the nexus of security, counterterrorism, and humanitarian protection of civilians. In particular, the ICRC can seek to draft a new Geneva Convention or related protocol to address the lacunae in the existing agreements in an effort to assure that detainees other than prisoners of war are treated with dignity. It can also play a critical role in educating governments and the global population at large about the importance of affirming human dignity.

There is also an opportunity for emerging partnerships to address the broad nexus of health, development, and human rights. The way has been paved by UNAIDS and the Global Fund in dealing with one pandemic in particular, as discussed in this book by Rosalía Rodriguez-García. Yet a larger dignity-related agenda could be addressed by such partnerships. Mark Dybul, Peter Piot, and Julio Frenk have proposed something akin to a new Bretton Woods agreement on global health. Although according a central role to the World Health Organization as a traditional institution to convene and sustain the effort, they observe that: "Governments, civil society organizations, and the private sector all have a key role to play in designing a new global health architecture and sustainable financing. . . . A focus on the health of a person could provide insights for a post–MDG era that focuses on creating the opportunities needed for every human being to realize his or her full potential" (Dybul, Piot, and Frenk 2012, 18).

This hybrid effort would draw lessons from partnerships more narrowly aimed at combating HIV/AIDS that explicitly sought to advance national ownership of strategies; accountable governance; mobilization of resources from public, private, and philanthropic actors; and a premise of investing in individual people's productive and prosperous futures.

Beyond these two broad types of global institutions, which comprise the focus of most of this book, there are two other special institutions or venues where a dignitarian dialogue can fruitfully take shape.

First, the university is a critical if often overlooked global institution.[3] A liberal education is tremendously pertinent to the exercise of the agency that characterizes human dignity. Moreover, the classic ideals of liberal education embody the values of reason, ethical responsibility, and duties towards others associated with the dignity-centered Universal Declaration on Human Rights and numerous religious and philosophical traditions.

With the advent of globalization, fierce economic competition and cutbacks of public resources have propelled some educational institutions to focus narrowly on business, professions, trades, and technologies. Hence, a liberal education, including in the humanities, is under threat at precisely the time when a complex, integrated neomedieval world demands the kind of broad, holistic knowledge and attention to ethical and cultural dimensions of political, economic, and social issues that demand collective action.

The university can be a crucial vessel in which to achieve the third element of meaningful human dignity posited in this book: that it "be institutionalized in practice and governance." It can nurture the critical thinking, self-reflection, moral reasoning, and engagement with difference needed to set and implement an agenda of realizing human dignity. It can advance a deeper understanding of what connects all human beings in their pluralism: a common longing for agency and recognition as beings acting on reason and conscience. Moreover, the university can become even more of a veritable global institution through student and faculty exchanges, partnerships between far-flung institutions, and creative use of online teaching and inquiry.

As for online inquiry, the second special additional venue for a dignitarian dialogue is the internet and its place in a world with unprecedented connectivity. The electronic medium will allow all actors—including individuals—to discuss, debate, and advance human dignity. It will also provide a virtual forum where the day-to-day challenges to human dignity can be brought to the attention of institutions in ways that were heretofore impossible (Jorgensen, 2013). During the so-called Arab Spring, for example, the use of social media—Twitter in particular—was able to make the world aware of events that would have previously gone unnoticed (Ghonim 2012). It is unlikely that the dignitarian dialogue will culminate in one place, as in San Francisco where the UN Charter was created. Indeed, the answer to the question, "Where will the dialogue unfold?" may not be in particular places or bodies but in cyberspace.

In short, in addition to the traditional IGOs and emerging nonpublic and hybrid institutions examined in chapters 2 through 14, the university and the internet are essential venues for the open and pluralistic dialogue we propose—on basic premises, implementation, and prioritizing tasks to advance the dignity of humankind.

US Role in a Post-Unipolar World

As noted above, both traditional and hybrid global institutions are crucial as the venues for (1) carrying out the dignitarian dialogue and (2) implementing a common vision of human dignity in order to fulfill that element of the definition of being "institutionalized in practice and governance." Yet it will not just happen organically. In socially constructing a consensus on human dignity to be embedded in the international system, the role of the United States as catalyst deserves attention. It is a post-hegemonic world. Acute American unipolarity has passed. Yet the United States has a crucial catalytic role to play, arguably more important than any other single state or even the European Union as an amalgam of states.

On the one hand, the United States must not and cannot be a power attempting to force-feed the idea of human dignity down the throats of the world.[4] That is neither desirable nor feasible. On the other hand, the United States must not act as a timid bystander for fear of tainting a dialogue about human dignity. It can and should back the idea enthusiastically, if not dogmatically, in a dialectical dialogue.

John Ikenberry of Princeton University suggests that the liberal norms and institutions to which the United States applied its hegemony to build in the twentieth century can persist in the twenty-first century now that that hegemony has passed (Ikenberry 2011). Brazil, Russia, India, China, and South Africa—as well as South Korea, Turkey, and Indonesia for that matter—do not seem poised today to act as singular or collective guarantors of liberal norms. Some do not seem even that inclined to share burdens of leadership (Kupchan 2012). One must hence remain skeptical about how Ikenberry's vision will transpire in a neomedieval world without making two revisions. First, the liberal norms the United States helped institutionalize need to be broadened under a human dignity umbrella.[5] Second, vital to that first refinement, the United States will need to play a greater catalytic role than Ikenberry acknowledges.

In the 1990s, President Bill Clinton and Secretary of State Madeleine Albright asserted that the United States is the "indispensable nation" (Albright 1998). Varied observers who identify or even hail the passing of US hegemony reject this characterization—from commentators as different as Chalmers Johnson and Andrew Bacevich (Johnson 2007; Bacevich 2008). Yet in an effort to construct a dignity-centered order, Clinton and Albright were and are still right. With that said, the United States needs to take on a new kind of leadership role. That role is neither boldly gathering a posse as sheriff nor quietly leading from behind. It is not that of a didactic teacher, preacher, or scold on the one hand nor that of a mere exemplar on the other hand—however badly getting its economic and political house in order is desperately needed.

Perhaps the best analogy for the indispensable leadership role of the United States in constructing a dignity-centered international order is that of cultivator. The United States cannot be the overzealous planter of the seeds of a dignitarian dialogue nor overzealous reaper of its fruits—lest it be seen as

seeking zero-sum rather than positive-sum gain. But it can and must cultivate needed dialogue on first principles, on modalities for making dignity
operational, and on priorities of implementation. The dialogue will be a lot
less likely to bear fruit if the United States fails to judiciously but assiduously
cultivate it.

And here lies the second of two major potential critiques of this book
that we anticipate. Some might say that a dialogue about human dignity is a
Trojan Horse for sustaining US power. Put differently, it might just be pouring the old wine of liberal norms into a new bottle labeled "dignity." Dignity
is not a vehicle to perpetuate American exceptionalism—neither in a positive
sense of conferring a special role for the United States to extend freedom, nor
in a negative sense of allowing the United States to escape the scrutiny by the
international system, as Arend's chapter 7 explores in the area of counterterrorism policy. Dignity is not a vehicle for American hegemony redux. It could
not succeed as such, nor should it.

Yet constructing a dialogue and then an order based on the dignity idea
would benefit from and justify self-conscious US efforts as a key catalyst.
Global institutions will be more likely to embrace and indeed apply the idea.
Conversely, this project offers desperately needed cues for what refashioned
global role the United States should play in the twenty-first century, characterized as much or more by diplomatic and intersocietal dialogue on an idea
as by its vast capacity to project military power, extend the reach of globalization, and technologically innovate.

Hope for a Neomedieval World: Kant Reconsidered

To sum up, a neomedieval world is one in which states are no longer the only
participants. In that context, the idea of human dignity offers both the inspiration and an implementation yardstick for global institutions. In particular,
focusing intentionally on the twin pillars of agency and recognition for all
people—equally deserving of justice and opportunity—makes it possible to
operationalize and realize that idea.

Global institutions are essential vehicles for building a consensus about
dignity and then for implementing it. Intergovernmental institutions like the
UN, the International Criminal Court, the World Bank, and the IMF retain
important roles, especially if their work is reoriented to focus even more on
dignity. New partnerships and hybrid institutions add flexible, nimble, and
inclusive means to address dignity on the ground—from the Kiva development partnership using crowdsourcing to direct microloans to deserving en-

trepreneurs that Raj Desai and Homi Kharas explore to the Global Fund that Rosalía Rodriguez-García assesses to those efforts in Brazil described by Lagon to fight forced labor, which take the form of partnerships involving the ILO, the state, NGOs, and even businesses like Ford (Ford Motor Company 2010/2011).

Taken together, these two kinds of global institutions can help make a neomedieval world more peaceful, prosperous, and pluralistic rather than chaotic. Based on a human dignity consensus, a mosaic of global institutions can help tame globalization's hard edges. A dignity-centered mission for global institutions helps offer useful meaning to the expression "global governance," which is, alas, as vaguely defined to date as it is ubiquitously invoked by scholars and policy specialists.

The thinking of Immanuel Kant, refashioned in a few respects, helps define the way forward. First, Kant stressed the basic dignity of every human being—equal in his or her inherent worth. The implication of that emphasis was that human beings must not be treated as mere means; their value entitles them to be treated as ends in themselves. Second, Kant's work focused on institutional arrangements favorable to peace. Those arrangements lay both at the domestic level and at the international level. In his view, liberal institutions were the most promising foundation of durable peace.

Juxtaposing these two legacies of Kantian thought, one can reimagine his vision to apply it to the twenty-first century. His legacy regarding institutional arrangements favorable to peace not only influenced the creation of the League of Nations and the UN as intergovernmental institutions but the idea of a "democratic peace." As no one has explored more subtly than Michael Doyle, Kant posited that institutionalizing democracies will advance the aim of a "perpetual peace" (Doyle 1983; Doyle 1986). The contemporary policy implication is that the international community should actively promote democracy. And even as an organization made up of democracies and nondemocracies as members of equal standing, the UN has embraced that aim from postconflict peace operations to electoral capacity-building to a UN Democracy Fund (whose board Doyle has chaired) (Newman and Rich 2004).

Of course, if democracy is defined to encompass more than just periodic elections and to include access to justice, tolerance, minority rights, and educational opportunity, it would contribute to the establishment of peace and prosperity. We contend, however, that the advancement of human dignity by global institutions is even more critical to the establishment of a peaceful and prosperous world. Reconsidering Kant's two pillars of individual dignity and institutions favorable to harmony of humankind suggests that what is needed even more than a democratic peace is a dignitarian peace.

Building a concept of dignity—which draws, in part, from the thinking of Francis Fukuyama—does not imply a claim of an imminent or inevitable end of history once the idea of dignity takes hold following dialectic struggles between contending ideas. Nor do we claim that a dignitarian peace is perpetual and perfect.

Nonetheless, the best hope for the twenty-first century as an epoch is not solely a great power shaping the order, nor is it a particular religion or democratization as an end in itself or technology and networked connectedness (Slaughter 2009). It is the idea of human dignity. This collaborative book offers not the end but something closer to the beginning of a process of constructing a dignitarian order. That process would first construct and refine consensus on dignity—incorporating insights from challenges raised in an intercultural dialogue, in part within a mosaic of global institutions. Then it would involve constructing new, and redirecting existing, global institutions to make human dignity not merely an aspiration but an enjoyed reality. Global institutions would serve as the primary means to ensure that human beings are treated as more than means, namely as the justly recognized agents of their own prosperity.

Notes

Many thanks go to Mathew R. Caldwell of Georgetown University and Andrew Reddie of the Council on Foreign Relations for their comments and assistance.

1. We thank Dylan Groves who works on a Millennium Challenge Corporation-funded development impact assessment project in Namibia for insights on land rights. On legal empowerment and land rights to combat poverty, see also Irene Khan, *The Unheard Truth: Poverty and Human Rights* (Westford: Courier, 2009), 119, 201–5.

2. The authors want to thank Director of Communications and Policy Outreach for AidData and Georgetown University Master of Science in Foreign Service alumna Samantha Custer for her insights about the tensions between agency and social recognition in implementation and her thoughts on how it applies in the case of human trafficking.

3. Appreciation and credit goes to Thomas Banchoff for raising, and helping to develop these observations about the university as a global institution in our own dialogue among contributors to the book, notably at a conference at Georgetown University School of Foreign Service on March 19, 2013.

4. The uncomfortable allusion to the US response to Guantanamo hunger strikes is intended.

5. Ikenberry and co-author Daniel Deudney emphasize the importance of John Dewey and FDR's New Deal as inspirations for the United States applying its hegemony to institutionalize liberal norms globally after World War II. They argue for engaging rising developing world powers in burden-sharing to sustain liberal norms. Some of their insights about FDR's economic thinking (the fear from fear and from want among his Four Freedoms) are consonant with developing consensus on a widened concept of human dignity that includes

not just political-civil rights but socioeconomic rights. See Daniel Deudney and G. John Ikenberry, "Democratic Internationalism: An American Grand Strategy for a Post-Exceptionalist Era," International Institutions and Global Governance Working Paper, Council on Foreign Relations, November 2012. Accessed October 1, 2013 at http://www.cfr.org/grand-strategy/democratic-internationalism-american-grand-strategy-post-exceptionalist-era/p29417.

References

Albright, Madeleine. 1998. Interview by Matt Lauer on the *Today* show. February 19. Accessed April 23, 2014. http://www.fas.org/news/iraq/1998/02/19/98021907_tpo.html.

Alexandroff, Alan S. 2010. "Challenges in Global Governance: Opportunities for G-x Leadership." The Stanley Foundation. Accessed October 10, 2013. www.stanleyfoundation.org/publications/pab/AlexandroffPAB310.pdf.

Aristotle. 1999. *Nicomachean Ethics*, translated by Terence Irwin. 2nd ed. Indianapolis, IN: Hackett Publishing Company.

Bacevich, Andrew. 2008. *The Limits of Power: The End of American Exceptionalism.* New York: Macmillan.

Bloom, Allan David, trans. 1991. *The Republic of Plato.* New York: Basic Books.

Central Intelligence Agency (CIA). 2013. "World Factbook." Accessed September 9, 2013. https://www.cia.gov/library/publications/the-world-factbook/geos/xx.html.

Dolan, Michael, and Chris Hunt. 1998. "Negotiating in the Ottawa Process: The New Multilateralism." *Canadian Foreign Policy Journal* 5 (3): 25–50.

Doyle, Michael W. 1983. "Kant, Liberal Legacies and Foreign Affairs." *Philosophy and Public Affairs* I and II: 205–35, 323–53.

———. 1986. "Liberalism and World Politics." *American Political Science Review* 80 (4): 1151–69.

Dybul, Mark, Peter Piot, and Julio Frenk. 2012. "Reshaping Global Health." *Policy Review* 173: 3–18.

Ford Motor Company. 2010/2011. "Case Study: Forced Labor in the Pig Iron Supply Chain in Brazil." Ford Motor Company. Accessed September 1, 2013. http://corporate.ford.com/microsites/sustainability-report-2010-11/issues-supply-materials-brazil.

Fukuyama, Francis. 1992. *The End of History and the Last Man.* New York: Free Press.

Ghonim, Wael. 2012. *Revolution 2.0: The Power of the People Is Greater than the People in Power: A Memoir.* New York: Houghton Mifflin Harcourt.

Ignatieff, Michael. 2012. "Reimagining a Global Ethic." *Ethics & International Affairs* 26 (1): 7–19.

Ikenberry, G. John. 2011. "The Future of the Liberal World Order: Internationalism after America." *Foreign Affairs* 90 (3): 56–68.

Johnson, Chalmers. 2007. *Nemesis: The Last Days of the American Republic.* New York: Metropolitan Books.

Jorgensen, Rikke Frank. 2013. *Framing the Net: The Internet and Human Rights.* Northampton, MA: Edward Elgar Publishing.

Kung, Hans. 1990. *Global Responsibility: In Search of a New World Ethic*, translated by John Bowden. London: SCM Press Ltd.

Kung, Hans, and Helmut Schmidt, eds. 1993. *A Global Ethics and Global Responsibilities: Two Declarations*, translated by John Bowden. London: SCM Press Ltd.

Kupchan, Charles A. 2012. *No One's World: The West, the Rising Rest, and the Coming Global Turn*. New York: Oxford University Press.

Newman, Edward, and Roland Rich, eds. 2004. *The United Nations Role in Promoting Democracy: Between Ideals and Reality*. New York: United Nations University Press.

Nussbaum, Martha C. 1997. "Capabilities and Human Rights." *Fordham Law Review* 66 (2): 273–300.

————. 2001. *Women and Human Development*. Cambridge, UK: Cambridge University Press.

Sen, Amartya. 1999. *Development as Freedom*. New York: Knopf Publishing Group.

Shorr, David. 2012. "Making the G–20 a Reservoir of Global Leadership—A Maximalist Argument." The Stanley Foundation. Accessed October 10, 2013. www.stanleyfoundation.org/publications/pab/ShorrPAB411.pdf.

Slaughter, Anne-Marie. 2009. "America's Edge: Power in a Networked Century." *Foreign Affairs* 88 (1): 94–113.

Sunstein, Cass R. 1996. "Social Norms and Social Roles." *Columbia Law Review* 96 (4): 903–68.

Vance, Cyrus. 1977. "Human Rights and Foreign Policy" (address). University of Georgia Law Day Ceremonies on April 30, 1977. Accessed September 18, 2013. http://digitalcommons.law.uga.edu/cgi/viewcontent.cgi?article=1015&context=lectures_pre_arch_lectures_lawday.

Weber, Katja. 2011. "Lessons from the ASEAN Regional Forum: Transcending the Image of Paper Tiger?" In *The Security Governance of Regional Organizations*, edited by Emil J. Kirchner and Roberto Dominguez. New York: Routledge.

CONTRIBUTORS

Anthony Clark Arend

Professor of Government and Foreign Service and director of the Master of Science in Foreign Service at the Walsh School of Foreign Service at Georgetown University. He is author of *Pursuing a Just and Durable Peace: John Foster Dulles and International Organization; Legal Rules and International Society;* co-author of *International Law and the Use of Force: Beyond the UN Charter Paradigm;* editor and contributor of *The United States and the Compulsory Jurisdiction of the International Court of Justice;* co-editor and contributor of *The Falklands War: Lessons for Strategy, Diplomacy, and International Law; International Rules: Approaches from International Law and International Relations.*

Thomas Banchoff

At Georgetown University, he serves as vice president for global engagement; director of the Berkley Center for Religion, Peace, and World Affairs; and professor in the Government Department and the School of Foreign Service. His research centers on religious and ethical issues in world politics. He is the author of *Embryo Politics: Ethics and Policy in Atlantic Democracies; The German Problem Transformed: Institutions, Politics, and Foreign Policy, 1945–1995;* co-author of *Legitimacy and the European Union: The Contested Polity;* editor of *Religious Pluralism, Globalization, and World Politics; Democracy and the New Religious Pluralism;* and co-editor of *Religion and the Global Politics of Human Rights.*

Benjamin Boudreaux
Foreign affairs officer at the Office of the Coordinator for Cyber Issues at the US Department of State, where he is responsible for the Middle East and South Asia portfolio. He holds a Ph.D. in philosophy from the University of California, Berkeley with an area of specialty in political philosophy, and a master of science in Foreign Service from Georgetown University. He formerly worked at the US Institute of Peace.

Chester A. Crocker
James R. Schlesinger Professor of Strategic Studies at the Walsh School of Foreign Service at Georgetown University. He served as assistant secretary for African Affairs at the US Department of State, chairman of the board at the US Institute of Peace and is founding member of the Global Leadership Foundation. He is the author of *High Noon in Southern Africa: Making Peace in a Rough Neighborhood*; co-author of *Rewiring Regional Security in a Fragmented World*; *America's Role in the World: Foreign Policy Choices for the Next Administration*; *Taming Intractable Conflicts: Mediation in the Hardest Cases*; *Turbulent Peace: The Challenges of Managing International Conflict*; *Herding Cats: Multiparty Mediation in a Complex World*; *Managing Global Chaos: Origins of and Responses to International Conflict*; *African Conflict Resolution: The US Role*; co-editor of *Leashing the Dogs of War: Conflict Management in a Divided World*; *Grasping the Nettle: Analyzing Cases of Intractable Conflict*.

John J. DeGioia
President of Georgetown University and member of the faculty of the Department of Philosophy at Georgetown University.

Raj M. Desai
Associate professor of International Development at the Walsh School of Foreign Service and in the Department of Government at Georgetown University. He is a nonresident senior fellow at the Brookings Institution. He formerly served as a private sector development specialist at the World Bank. He is an author of *World Development Report 2005: A Better Investment Climate for Everyone*.

Ryan Kaminski
Leo Nevas human rights fellow with the United Nations Association of the USA. He is a former research associate in the International Institutions and Global Governance Program at the Council on Foreign Relations.

Homi Kharas
Senior fellow and deputy director in the Global Economy and Development program of the Brookings Institution in Washington, DC. He is formerly lead author and executive secretary of the secretariat supporting the High Level Panel advising the UN secretary-general on the post–2015 development agenda. Previously, he spent twenty-six years at the World Bank, serving for seven years as chief economist for the World Bank's East Asia and Pacific region and as director for Poverty Reduction and Economic Management. He is co-author of *After the Spring: Economic Transitions in the Arab World* and *Catalyzing Development: A New Vision for Aid*.

Mark P. Lagon
Chair for global politics and security and professor in the practice of international affairs within the Master of Science in Foreign Service Program at Georgetown University. He served as ambassador-rank director of the Office to Monitor and Combat Trafficking in Persons; deputy assistant secretary of state for International Organization Affairs; and as executive director and CEO of Polaris Project. He is author of *The Reagan Doctrine: Sources of American Conduct in the Cold War's Last Chapter*.

Tod Lindberg
Research fellow at the Hoover Institution and adjunct faculty at Georgetown University. He was previously editor of the journal *Policy Review*. Formerly senior staff member, Genocide Prevention Task Force, US Holocaust Memorial Museum. He is author of *The Political Teaching of Jesus*; co-author of *Means to an End: U.S. Interest in the International Criminal Court;* editor of *Beyond Paradise and Power: Europe, the United States and the Future of a Troubled Partnership*; co-editor of *Bridging the Foreign Policy Divide*.

Rosalía Rodriguez-García
Currently, adviser to the International Labor Organization, UNAIDS, and the World Bank. Formerly the World Bank's team leader of a major research portfolio on community-level effects of HIV/AIDS investments and co-Chair of the UN Cosponsoring Agencies Group of UNAIDS (2012). Previously, senior adviser in the Global Fund to Fight AIDS, Tuberculosis, and Malaria; and professor and chair of International Health at George Washington University, from which she holds a PhD. She is co-author of *Investing in Communities Achieves Results: Findings from an Evaluation of Community Responses to HIV and AIDS;*

Self-Assessment in Managing for Results: Conducting Self-Assessment for Development Practitioners; Microenterprise Development for Better Health Outcomes.

Michael A. Samway
Former vice president and deputy general counsel of Yahoo! Inc. He is founder of Yahoo!'s Business and Human Rights Program and a co-founding board member of the Global Network Initiative.

Nicole Bibbins Sedaca
Director of the Washington, DC Office of Independent Diplomat. She is adjunct faculty at Georgetown University. She serves on the boards of directors for the Institute for Global Engagement and the International Justice Mission. She previously worked for the Department of State and in nongovernmental organizations promoting democracy and human rights.

Anoop Singh
Managing director and head of regulatory strategy and policy, Asia Pacific, with JP Morgan in Hong Kong. He wrote his chapter herein as director of the Asia-Pacific Department of the International Monetary Fund. He previously served as director of the Western Hemisphere Department, and director of Special Operations, at the IMF. He has been adjunct faculty at the Master of Science in Foreign Service Program at Georgetown University. He is co-editor of *Australia Benefiting from Economic Reform; Stabilization and Reform in Latin America; and Macroeconomic Issues Facing ASEAN Countries.*

Nancy E. Soderberg
Senior fellow at the Enough Project. She is former president of Connect US Fund. She served as ambassador-rank alternate representative to the UN and as deputy assistant to the president for national security affairs on the National Security Council. She is author of *The Superpower Myth: The Use and Misuse of American Might;* co-author of *The Prosperity Agenda: What the World Wants from America—and What We Need in Return.*

Abiodun Williams
President of The Hague Institute for Global Justice. From 2008 to 2012, he served at the United States Institute of Peace, first as vice president of the Center for Conflict Analysis and Prevention and later as senior vice president of the Center for Conflict Management. From 2001 to 2007, Dr. Williams was director of Strategic Planning for UN Secretaries-General Ban Ki-Moon and Kofi Annan. He served as associate dean of the Africa Center for Strategic

Studies at the National Defense University in Washington, DC, and held faculty appointments at Georgetown, Rochester, and Tufts universities. He is author of *The Brilliant Art of Peace: Lectures from the Kofi Annan Series*; *Preventing War: The United Nations and Macedonia*; and the editor of *Many Voices: Multilateral Negotiations in the World Arena*.

INDEX